Towards a Standard English

Topics in English Linguistics
12

Editors

Jan Svartvik
Herman Wekker

Mouton de Gruyter
Berlin · New York

Towards a Standard English

1600 — 1800

Edited by

Dieter Stein
Ingrid Tieken-Boon van Ostade

Mouton de Gruyter
Berlin · New York   1994

Mouton de Gruyter (formerly Mouton, The Hague)
is a Division of Walter de Gruyter & Co., Berlin.

∞ Printed on acid-free paper which falls within the guidelines of the
ANSI to ensure permanence and durability.

Library of Congress Cataloging-in-Publication Data

> Towards a standard English, 1600 – 1800 / edited by Dieter Stein, Ingrid
> Tieken-Boon van Ostade.
>   p.   cm. — (Topics in English linguistics : 12)
> Includes bibliographical references (p.) and index.
> ISBN 3-11-013697-X
> 1. English language — Early modern, 1500-1700 — History. 2. English
> language — 18th century — History. 3. English language —
> Standardization. I. Stein, Dieter. II. Tieken-Boon van
> Ostade, Ingrid. III. Series.
> PE1083.T69   1994
> 420′.9′09032 — dc20   93-36930
>   CIP

Die Deutsche Bibliothek — Cataloging-in-Publication Data

> **Towards a standard English** : 1600 – 1800 / ed. by Dieter Stein ; Ingrid Tieken-
> Boon van Ostade. — Berlin ; New York : Mouton de Gruyter, 1994
>   (Topics in English linguistics ; 12)
>   ISBN 3-11-013697-X
> NE: Stein, Dieter [Hrsg.]; GT

© Copyright 1993 by Walter de Gruyter & Co., D-10785 Berlin
All rights reserved, including those of translation into foreign languages. No part of this
book may be reproduced or transmitted in any form or by any means, electronic or
mechanical, including photocopy, recording, or any information storage and retrieval
system, without permission in writing from the publisher.
Typesetting: Lewis & Leins, Berlin.
Printing: Gerike GmbH, Berlin.
Binding: Lüderitz & Bauer, Berlin
Printed in Germany.

Contents

Dieter Stein
Sorting out the variants: Standardization and social factors in the
English language 1600–1800 1

James Milroy
The notion of "standard language" and its applicability to the study
of Early Modern English pronunciation 19

Lawrence Klein
"Politeness" as linguistic ideology in late seventeenth- and early
eighteenth-century England 31

Thomas Frank
Language standardization in eighteenth-century Scotland 51

Carey McIntosh
Prestige norms in stage plays, 1600–1800 63

Roger Lass
Proliferation and option-cutting: The strong verb in the fifteenth
to eighteenth centuries 81

Jenny Cheshire
Standardization and the English irregular verbs 115

Laurel J. Brinton
The differentiation of statives and perfects in Early
Modern English: The development of the conclusive perfect . . . 135

Terttu Nevalainen and Helena Raumolin-Brunberg
Its strength and the beauty *of it:* The standardization of the third
person neuter possessive in Early Modern English 171

Ingrid Tieken-Boon van Ostade
Standard and non-standard pronominal usage in English, with
special reference to the eighteenth century 217

Susan Wright
The critic and the grammarians: Joseph Addison and the
prescriptivists 243

Frances Austin
The effect of exposure to standard English: The language
of William Clift 285

Index 315

Sorting out the variants: Standardization and social factors in the English language 1600–1800

Dieter Stein

Introduction

On 22 May 1990 a workshop with the title *The effects of standardization and literacy on the English language (1600–1800)* was held at the University of Helsinki in conjunction with the Sixth Conference on English Historical Linguistics. The aim of the workshop had been formulated as follows:

> There is a consensus that either nothing much happened in the period under discussion or that there is a big research gap. The most obviously visible process is a sorting out of variants into goodies/nobilitated and baddies/demoted/dialectal variants leading to a difference in prestige between standard and dialectal forms. It is an obvious suggestion to relate this sorting out to selectional processes under the cover term 'standardization'. On the uniformitarian principle, and judging from language change in present-day conditions, this must have been very much a function of the rise of prestige norms. It is clear, however, that the notion of the rise of a standard language is not broad enough to capture all of the processes involved in the rise of these prestige norms, but must encompass the type of society or societal change, with societal, economic, communicational functions to the extent that they will also 'generate' social elites and prestigious norms. So the scope of the papers is wider than the notion of the rise of a standard.

The following remarks will try to make visible some of the issues that surfaced in the discussions at the workshop and to provide a theoretical set of coordinates within which to locate individual studies collected in the present volume.

1. Notions of "standard"

A major theoretical issue lies in the fact that it is not the case that all of the incipient or, to various degrees, embryonic forms of more widely used prestige varieties in the history of English could, by a more strict definition, be called standard languages. There seem to be three uses of the term *standardization*. There is an extended use which would apply to all manner of varieties, the notion of standardization with *standard* as the resulting variety. To this type of variety James Milroy (this volume) assigns the term "supra-local" language norms. These constitute "localized" or "regional" norm standards. Such varieties are instances of language convergence in various degrees and certainly carry prestige, which is largely a function of their use in various combinations of the following situations, such as are listed by Görlach (1988: 133–134):

a) as a written language
b) as a literary language
c) as a religious language
d) as a language of education and science
e) as a language of the law courts, parliament and the court etc.
f) as a lingua franca
g) as a national language
h) as a language of the mass media (newspaper, radio, television etc.).

This first, wide, notion of the term standard seems to be inherent in the majority of work on at least the history of English (Görlach 1988, Trahern 1989).

A second, narrow or restricted, definition of standardization was developed in language planning research in countries with no nationally accepted varieties and with the problem of having a language in addition to a range of dialects. Haugen (1966) describes the following constitutive processes in creating a standard language:

- selection
- codification
- elaboration
- acceptance.

Garvin (1964), based on Garvin and Mathiot (1960), gives the following defining features for a standard language:

1. the intrinsic properties of a standard language;
2. the functions of a standard language within the culture of a speech community;
3. the attitudes of the speech community towards the standard language (Garvin 1964: 522).

These dimensions of a standard language are also the ones given by Bartsch (1987: 243), who discusses standard norms in the comprehensive context of language norms:

1. attitudes attributed to the standard variety, such as *spoken by the educated, good, pure, melodious*, or in the case of Indian English, *speaking like a Brahman*;
2. functional factors such as use in certain situations like education, administration, trade and the homes of the educated elite;
3. linguistic properties, such as non-nativized loan words or certain syntactic constructions like nominalization and complex hypotaxis.

The only significant difference to the list given by Garvin is the reversed order as far as one and three are concerned. The list given by Görlach (above) makes reference to Garvin's number two only.

This second, more technical, approach is clearly more restricted than the first use mentioned of *standard language*. For instance, the tenth-century, relatively unified manuscripts centered around Winchester certainly constituted a local norm with supra-local prestige. The same applies to a much larger extent to the fourteenth-century Chancery standard (Fisher 1977; Richardson 1980). These were certainly standards, but not standard languages in the technical sense of the definitions in the second sense of the term "*standard*". On the other hand, there certainly are local *dialectal* norms, i.e. definitely with the status of a norm (Milroy, this volume) and a few of the features of standard language, in particular some of the attitudinal properties, such as group defining and Garvin's (1964: 522) "*separatist*" attitudinal function, including prestige. But these varieties do not carry a notion of correctness. They did not go through the process of codification or functional elaboration (cf. Haugen cited above).

It is clear that the definitional features given by Garvin (1964) and Bartsch (1987) are intended to cover all standard languages. At the same time, it is also clear that an attempt at such a definition must be, not categorical, but prototypical, so that it can accommodate the specific varietal and historical conditions of each individual case. Even between such closely related languages as English and German there are important differences, e.g., in the degree of liberalness in accepting variants of pronunciation as acceptable within the standard or not. Even within English as a whole the question is whether Scottish or American, not to mention even more complicated cases, are *national* standards in their own rights or not.

To mention one last example: one would assume the existence of a *natural* association between a standard language and the written form of that language. However, it does seem possible (Bartsch 1987: 238) to have cases of standard languages (in the case of Amharic and Somali) with little unification of spelling.

2. Selecting variants

By way of a first approximation to the specifics of the English situation it should be stated that all of the criteria of a narrow definition of a standard language apply to the English situation. With regard to the specifics of the English situation it seems useful to further foreground three criteria, following Milroy (this volume). They point out that a standard in the strict sense

1. is imposed from above;
2. involves legislation;
3. contains an ideology of standardization.

Criterion one looks at standardization as a type of linguistic change (cf. below). Criterion two refers to the metalinguistic activity involved in codification and the subsequent *Sprachkritik* activities including moral judgment on variants and varieties as good or bad. The third criterion refers to Bartsch's (1987) number one and Garvin's (1964) number three and is perhaps the most salient characteristic in the case of English. It is also the one that is sociologically the most consequential in that it both provides the link to present sociological issues in the distribution of varieties and in the evolution of those social consequences (cf. below).

Milroy (this volume) looks at the concept of the standard in terms not only of a property of a variety, but as a process. Any variety may be subject to standardization. The end point of a developmental scale is a fully-fledged standard language with all of the properties cited above present to the fullest possible degree. According to Milroy (this volume), standardization may be present in incipient or partial degrees. Such seems to have been the case with Chancery standard. If we follow the definition of *standard variety* and *standardization* in the strict sense of the term and with the further accentuation by Milroy (this volume) we can formulate the questions which the papers in this volume address as follows:

If standardization operates on varieties and variants, it is clear that part of the formation of a standard variety is a further selection process, after the rough regional variety has been chosen. How does a given variant get selected and become a part of the standard, whilst others are rejected? Why is *spoke* correct and not *spake*? What were the internal developmental paths and factors of this selection process?

If one variant is selected to become the correct form, the other candidate will be demoted and referred to as "dialectal", "vulgar", "incorrect". In English, this seems to be the automatic corollary of promoting one variant to the status of "correct" and an essential component of the ideology of standardization: out of several candidates there can only be one "correct" form. Consequently, an important question to be asked, and addressed by contributions in this volume, has to be: What social processes and mechanisms are involved in the attribution of these attitudinal satellites to varieties and variants?

Given the definitional prolegomena, from when onwards do we have to assume standardization in the fullest sense to have been present in English? There seems to be a consensus of opinion that the process has to be located in the late seventeenth and eighteenth centuries. Consequently, the present volume focuses on those centuries, in contrast to previous volumes on the subject which espouse the wider view of standardization. To focus even more sharply: From when onwards do we have a standard as a transcendental norm, with concomitant codification, legislation and a conscious ideology?

The turning point seems to be the middle of the eighteenth century (Klein this volume; cf. also Berger 1978). While there was a distinct earlier surge of standardizational processes and activities (cf. below), it was not until the second half of the eighteenth century that we have the onset of massive legislation and prescription. To be sure, apart from the massive increase in selectional activities (i.e. choosing one variant rather than another) there had existed part of the ideology of the standard or typical attitudinal features, such as social prestige patterns involving politeness (Klein this volume; McIntosh this volume) with valorization of certain forms over others. But the full appearance of all the attitudinal satellites as the component part of the ideology of standardization does not seem to appear until the second half of the eighteenth century.

Before elaborating on the development of the ideological or attitudinal aspects of standardization it should be pointed out that a constituent part of this ideology is the focus on written language as the paragon of language generally. This is related to the fact that most of the high functions (cf. Görlach's list, section 1.) are carried out in the written medium.

This prestigious image of the written language as the trendsetter for selectional mechanisms is, as Bartsch (1987: section 2.3) points out, a reversal of the ontogenetic and phylogenetic status of written language and syntax: syntax becomes an organizational necessity to regulate expressive traffic above all in the written language, where the absence of nonlinguistic, gestural and situational context information necessitates the support of the conventionalized and socially controlled organization principles (Bartsch 1987: 15) to ensure its functioning. Given this logically and developmentally posterior nature of syntax it is as well to question the wisdom of language theories that focus on syntax in an effort to elucidate language and language development.

Any theory of syntactic development in English is open to the question to what extent the observed developments – and the hypotheses based on them – are the consequence of the data taken from the written standard language and not from spoken and dialectal varieties, which, too, are English. Regularization, that is, selection of one variant in preference to another, sets in first. The regularized spelling and, because of the exposed status of written language, the syntax of the written language become the focus of standardizational attitudes and activities. In turn, written language becomes one of the criteria for selecting as correct variants of the spoken standard language. Because of these differences in the degree of exposure to standardization, the effect of standardization is historically staggered in that phonology is permissive for much longer than semantax (morphosyntax + semantics), which has to meet the scrutiny of the eye. Variant pronunciations were widely recognized until at least the late nineteenth century (McCrum et al. 1986: 21–22). Milroy (this volume) makes the point very decisively that we must assume coexisting prestige norms in pronunciation with no stigmatization at least until that time and that we must not be misled by contemporaneous statements; e.g., Puttenham's, that existing *supra-local* prestige norms were actually standards in any strict sense. Though prestige is certainly a component attitudinal part of a standard, it does not suffice to define it.

The fact that the written language was at the forefront and the early focus of standardization seems to be connected to a particular role of written language in very prestigious functions: the administration of the emerging empire. It is variously acknowledged that the *onset* of standardization is related to an outside trigger of a political or economic event which requires the existence of a standard. In the case of Chancery English it has been hypothesized (Richardson 1980) that Henry V's motivation for having administrative documents written in English was entirely political and opportunistic. Heath (1980: 22) relates the rise of correctness, prescriptivism and the concomitant ideology in the United States of America to the consequences of the Civil War. "The Civil War heightened regional consciousness and rivalry. The educated urban elite wanted to justify their differences from their *country cousins*, who spoke the idiom of the farm [. . .]. Increasingly the educational hierarchy came to associate sameness with national stability." Despite the obvious differences between England and the United States in historical, sociological and intellectual conditions, and the internal evolution of standardization tendencies, as well as the time of the onset of standardizational ideology on a major scale, there is an obvious parallel here in the existence of an external trigger.

Both Klein (this volume) and Milroy and Milroy (1985) identify as the trigger the development of the Empire and the need for a stable, variation-free tool to govern it, in the written medium.

3. Politeness and social dimensions

As was observed above, the massive onset of the process of standardization with all attitudinal trappings seems to be a feature of the second part of the eighteenth century. The socially most effectual aspect of these attitudes is a sort of a three-argument associative chain:

1. in a process of selection, certain variants are not elected as the correct ones;
2. the ones not elected receive a connotation as "vulgar" and "dialectal";
3. the people using these vulgar or dialectal forms are branded as socially and intellectually inferior.

Notice that this associative chain contains three logically and in principle separate phenomena. In the case of English, and British English more than American, and English more than German, these three component parts of standardization go together and are an important temporal demarcation point for the onset of full standardization.

Bartsch (1987: 238–239) defines three ways which are conducive to the rise of a standard language in a natural way:

1. a variety is spoken by a prestige group, where prestige means political or economic power and education.
2. a variety has a history of literature with "great" authors.
3. a variety is spoken in a centrally located area with plenty of group and dialectal contact, as well as immigration, and for which the area in question is a centre of commerce and political power, with the consequence of attracting government and trade.

All three factors were operative, but, for the late eighteenth-century process under discussion, the first factor takes precedence, in particular since it operates in conjunction with factor three. Klein's and McIntosh's papers in this volume make this very clear. A key term is *politeness* and its history (Berger 1978). The term has a history which goes back to the seventeenth century. A first phase in the development of politeness defines a social ideal, the polite urban, metropolitan gentleman, well-versed in the art of "polite" conversation, a man about town. Originating at the court, this ideal was easily detached from the court and made a social ideal for a metropolitan elite, thereby creating a favorable locus in Bartsch's number three sense (above) – the town (Klein, this volume). While this first phase of politeness seems to have centered on pragmatic language behavior, such as not to impose, Klein and McIntosh identify a distinct shift in the concept and social connotations of politeness. The later phase is characterized by what Klein calls "polite prescriptivism", i.e. the "overt statement of rules in support of a single and specific standard" (Devitt 1989: 99, Footnote 3) as a middle class enterprise. Given that certain forms were selected as correct, the use of the correct form was considered polite language use, and the inference was made that whoever used polite language must be a "polite" person. The assumption made was that "the formal aspect of things had serious moral, social and political implications" (Klein his volume). *Ex negativo*, this meant that those who did not use the correct forms were downgraded in terms of social prestige.

The cultural concept of politeness and the change in its content in the second part of the eighteenth century seems to provide the vehicle for the label "incorrect" coming to assume the further attitudinal predicate of socially or intellectually inferior, thereby acquiring the first of the three qualities mentioned by Bartsch (1987), i.e. association of not correct with socially and intellectually inferior. Berger (1978: 71–72) points out that the notion of polite language very early (in the early seventeenth century at the latest) implied a two-way negative cutting-off effect against speakers from other regions and against speakers from other, i.e. non-aristocratic classes. From the social hotbed of the later eighteenth century arose the notion of *correctness* as a linguistic and ideological phenomenon, and the rise of the middle classes provided the societal locus of that notion. Originally one of the groups discriminated against, this class adopted and identified with the linguistic and social behavioral forms of the older aristocracy, and in the process established the use of correctness norms as a linguistic class shibboleth. Having themselves been discriminated against, this class now discriminated against the lower classes (vulgar) and speakers from other regions (dialectal) (Berger 1978: 71–72). Crowley (1989: 133), who gives the most detailed account in the literature of the development of the ideology of standardization, points out explicitly that the branding of a form as dialectal does not necessarily imply that it actually occurs in any specific dialect or that it has a local, genuinely dialectal restriction of occurrence. In that sense, dialectal was synonymous with barbarism.

This period seems to carry all the prerequisites for the rise of a language internal purism as a mechanism of defence against outside groups such as described by Jernudd (1989: 3):

> It is in periods of transition such as the period of early modernization in Turkey that puristic responses are especially likely to arise. A clearly defined dominance by a High Language of the Great Tradition, god-given, is eroded by a mobilization of colloquial language and borrowing of foreign usages into the language, to accompany deliberate modernization or contact-induced socio-economic and/or political change. A period of generally agreed standards for the language of literature and public usage would follow the mobilization/change period as societies claim success of standardization and national consolidation. Later yet, a period of accommodations of marginal groups of people into broader society (i.e., of the so-called minorities, rural "deviant" dialect speakers, immigrant laborers, refugees) may again upset "standards". In the former period of transition into modernization, some people may feel empowered by knowledge bestowed by a Past to protect the community and language from the New and Foreign as well as to protect their own positions; in the latter period of accommodation of marginal groups and "democratization", some seek privilege in their construction of a different Future while others brace to resist further erosion of communal values and standards of language. In either case, purism may provide the appropriate political gestures of expression and evaluative constraints on language correction. Purism may constitute the ideology that provides a source for adjustment strategies to resist or replace exogenous language norms with the indigenously self-asserting in periods of communal or national resistance and self-empowerment, or to uphold norms felt to be threatened by erosion within the society.

Consequently, we do not find explicit comments on and a branding of forms as vulgarisms, "low" and dialectal, documenting the effects of this ideology, until the later eighteenth century. Whatever explicit comment is made in earlier periods comes from a vantage point of older, more aristocracy-orientated bases of a politeness ideal. We must bear in mind that the rise of the middle classes and the rise of a notion of correctness with a collateral demotion of incorrect speech variants as part of an ideology of the standard are features of the later eighteenth century. There is, therefore, an intimate connection between sociological developments, including class demarcational needs, political and governmental developments and the development of standardization in the late eighteenth century, such as defined by Milroy (this volume). The tremendous social attraction of this "new look of English" is illustrated in Austin's paper, who traces the way in which the transition within the lifetime of a single person and within the same family from a dialectal to a metropolitan area effects a very distinct linguistic accommodation process. The nation-wide social appeal of this social connotation of the standard is also documented by Frank's study of language-correctional activities in the context of the eighteenth-century Scottish Enlightenment in Edinburgh.

4. Cutting out variation

Just as in choosing, on the macro-level of language planning, one variety in preference to another, establishing speech variants as correct involves a selection process as a logically and temporally posterior process of ratification by codification and evaluation in an ideology of standardization. Selection concerns the linguistic substance of standardization. Consequently, most of the papers in the present volume deal with classic cases of the selection process, such as the ones discussed by Tieken, and Nevalainen and Raumolin-Brunberg.

In a detailed statistical analysis, the use of *its* as third person neuter possessive (instead of *his*) is shown to have established itself in a rather sudden development just before 1700. Tieken looks at a classic battlefield of eighteenth-century normative grammarians, namely choices in questions of pronominal usage. One of the key issues is the relationship between the codifiers of the time, the grammarians, and the actual usage of the time. Another famous classic case of selection between variants, strong verb forms, is treated in two papers here, Lass and Cheshire. It seems important to point out that selecting forms as correct is largely not due to the issue of politeness. The role of politeness is to confer on the use of the correct form a social evaluative dimension with an effect on the social and intellectual value of the user (or non-user) of correct (= polite) language. Politeness does not make or provide criteria for choices between variant forms. Instead it endows the correct use by the metropolitan, middle-class professional elite with a filtering social/qualitative evaluation, with the described effects for non-correct use and users.

What emerges clearly from not only the papers in this volume is that the selection process, as the initial stage of standardization, takes place appreciably (a century) earlier, long before an ideology of standardization as described above is developed on a major scale. A key issue in the selection process are the trendsetters (Bartsch 1987: 226; Ray 1963; 61). Looking at a range of classic grammatical variables, Wright (this volume) identifies Addison as an early figure with trendsetting force, not least because of his healthy middle-of-the-road position in terms of modernity and conservatism. The hypothesis on the earliest models of a written standard would then be an element of what Bartsch (1987: 238) mentions as the second (among three, cf. section 1) factor in defining a standard, that is, a literary canon and "great" authors. Crowley (1989) points to the intimate relationship between establishing a canon of "good" authors and the evaluation of the New English Dictionary as the codification of "good" words and meanings.

Cheshire's paper on strong verbs raises a topic that is highly relevant for any history of English. To what extent is the history of English a history of the standard language only, and to what extent do the forms not nobilitated as correct continue to exist as part of English and provide a continuity of the English language from a pre-standard period (cf. Milroy, this volume). In particular, the paper suggests that the effect of standardization is the suppression of natural tendencies. The paper also raises the question to what extent standardization is a force external to language (cf. Gerritsen-Stein 1992). The very fact of a sorting-out of variants in itself, that is, a specialization of forms for certain meanings, may, as a one-form, one-meaning tendency, well constitute a force internal to language, indeed a natural force. It seems, however, that the range of linguistic specialization and sorting-out processes occurring at roughly the same time as the selection part of standardization is in fact externally conditioned, although certainly not going against the structural grain of the language at that point. The very fact that at roughly the same time a number of such sorting-out processes were observed makes it highly unlike that in each case a structural necessity has to be there as a trigger.

The fact that these changes such as described by Nevalainen and Raumolin-Brunberg happened very rapidly could well be taken as first rate evidence that they were externally caused, although the authors of the contribution give priority to an "internal" explanation. The parallelness of the changes makes an external cause, in our view, a reasonable assumption. An obvious explanatory candidate for an external explanation would be the tendency to minimize variation, a tendency in keeping with the spirit of the times in the age of reason. Numerous grammatical variables fall under this heading, such as *shall/will,* the relativizers, the move towards establishing direct forms for the present and past participles, the tendency to avoid constructions with split constituents and so on. The development in the area of strong verbs described by Lass in this volume seems to fall within the same bracket: The effect of writing in making visible paradigm structures and their asymmetries before the eye. Nevalainen and Raumolin-Brunberg's paper describes in great detail the micro-structure of this process of straightening out the paradigm.

To cite a last example of this type of clearing-up of variation, the developmental process which resulted in the present use of periphrastic *do* in the English standard language (not in the dialects!) has to be analysed in two basic stages, with entirely different forces at work in each of the stages. The first stage, described in Stein (1990), leads to a situation around 1700 in which the modern uses were current but with plenty of *exceptions* still evident, such as *do*-less negatives and questions, or non-stressed *do's* in declarative sentences. The process described (within the period 1500–1700) as the first stage is mostly due to internal forces of linguistic change. The remaining area of variability can be interpreted as the upper flattening-out area of the S-curve of linguistic change in which the speed of change has lost its impetus and a residual area is not (yet) reached by the innovation. It is the stage, described in detail by Tieken (1987), that is defined by the operation of rational, external, forces which put an end to what variation was still left in the language. This part of the development of *do* is due to standardization.

The question to be raised here is whether there are linguistic properties inherent in standardization or, more precisely, what are the functions of the standard that make the expression of certain meanings in certain forms more desirable than others, as described by Bartsch (cf. section 1).

The tendency to create order in grammar means primarily a sorting-out of forms and meanings in such a way that one form should only signify one cognitive meaning. This is one of the points made by Brinton (this volume). She cites an abundance of further evidence, such as the sorting-out of *have/be* with intransitives (Rydén and Brorström 1987), to show that the period under investigation was characterized by a massive cleaning-up of the huge amount of variation that had existed in Early Modern English.

All of these developments taken together make it seem utterly unlikely that syntactic or structural factors should have been at work. Rather, the conclusion seems inevitable that it was indeed the effect of standardization as an external force that was at work. Devitt (1989: 1–2) argues quite correctly that the linguistic process of the reduction of variation may operate at any period in any history of a language, and that, furthermore, a number of them may operate to effect what she calls the purely linguistic aspect of standardization, without the social consequences of the introduction of a notion of correctness and the concomitant ideology of standardization. As I have argued above, these social attitudinal predicates operate as a logically and temporally posterior process after prior selection processes, which took place from the seventeenth century on. However, compared to the case of Scottish

English described by Devitt (1989), there is in the present case a distinct quantitative and qualitative difference (cf. section 5). In the seventeenth and eighteenth centuries there are such a large number of selection processes that make the assumption of an external force imperative. In this respect, there is similarity to the case described by Devitt (1989).

5. Written language and standardization

There is, however, a significant difference that is also brought out by Brinton's paper. The difference concerns the types of meaning involved and the rise of the written medium, and seems to account for why there should have been such syntactic sorting-out processes.

Brinton makes the point that what we observe in the early selection processes (seventeenth century) amounts to a sorting out of meanings, in particular epistemic meanings. The evidence presented and discussed by her can only be interpreted in such a way that epistemic meanings, and their clear and unequivocal, that is, non-polysemous, expression must have become very important. To these developments can be added the acquisition of unequivocal epistemic meanings of *do*, with the other non-epistemic meanings of *do* continuing to exist in the non-standard varieties (Stein 1990: section 13.4). This centering on epistemic meanings is part of what Bartsch (1987: 243) calls the linguistic properties of standard languages (cf. section 1).

Taken together, these linguistic characteristics of standard languages point to the connection between medium and function: they are geared to the requirements of written transactional language, suitable for "communicating information-bearing messages" (Milroy, this volume), that is, a decontextualized, autonomous language. It is part and parcel of what has been called an "essayist literacy" (Besnier 1988: 732), part of which has been de-oralization, that is, the banning of all elements reminiscent of oral language. The intimate relationship between written language standardization and prescriptivism is also pointed out by Chafe (1984): "To a large extent, prescriptivism itself arose from the fact that written language is visual rather than auditory, and thus has tended to be more permanent than spoken language. The fact that it can be leisurely examined has made it highly subject to reification, to treatment as an object of critical comparison and analysis." This point is also elaborated by Joseph (1987: section 2.2) and Tieken (1990) with respect to the role of eighteenth-century grammarians.

This medium-based and functional characteristic of the written standard provides a clue as to why the selection processes of the seventeenth and eighteenth centuries started to develop in the first place: the development of rational(istic) and scientific prose and the relevant stylistic ideal. A written variety of a language sorted out and selected the expressive means – unequivocal expression of epistemic meanings in appropriate syntactic shape – for its purpose and in its medium. It is this variety which came to be associated with the notion of *the English language*, with the known consequences for the explanation of historical facts about English.

This is also a point highlighted by Lass, who follows the historical development of strong verbs and who looks at how the grammarians' account of strong verb variation tallies with linguistic reality as represented in the Helsinki Corpus of English Texts. The interesting conclusion is that the grammarians provide much more evidence of variation than the written materials of the Helsinki corpus. This further evidence that the selecting and unifying effects of written language was very early (i.e. in the seventeenth century) much stronger than anything at least the earlier still more descriptive-orientated grammarians effected. It could well be argued that inherent in the written printed language of the time there was a codifying effect *per se*, coupled with an increasing view, based on the prestigious function of this authoritative medium, of written language as the best language, long before (with e.g. Johnson and Lowth) a prescriptivism based on codification proper set in; followed by the rise of the social evaluational attitudes discussed in section 4, without which any account of the rise of the English standard as an abstract norm would be incomplete.

While Devitt (1989: 3) is pessimistic about finding out about the "causes" of linguistic change in general and of the linguistic aspects of standardization in particular it would not seem unreasonable to look for an explanation for the linguistic focusing processes in the nature of the medium: the linguistic properties discussed in this section, including the semantics of the form, point to the functional uses of the written medium as the cause of this conspiracy of local developments.

A further effect of this paragon effect was the equation of language with the letter, of standard English with English, and of the history of English, as repeatedly pointed out by Lass (this volume and elsewhere) and Milroy (this volume, also quoting Lass), as a history of English as a "single-minded-march", with the incumbent consequences for theories about the history of English (cf. section 2).

References

Adamson, Sylvia – Vivien Law – Nigel Vincent – Susan Wright (eds.)
    1990 *Papers from the 5th International conference on English historical linguistics.* Amsterdam, Philadelphia: Benjamins.
Ammon, Ulrich – Klaus J. Mattheier – Peter H. Nelde (eds.)
    1988 *Sociolinguistica. Internationales Jahrbuch für Europäische Soziolinguistik* 2. Tübingen: Niemeyer.
Bartsch, Renate
    1987 *Sprachnormen: Theorie und Praxis.* Tübingen: Niemeyer.
Berger, Dieter A.
    1978 *Die Konversationskunst in England, 1660–1740.* München: Wilhelm Fink.
Besnier, Niko
    1988 "The linguistic relationships of spoken and written nukulaelae registers", *Language* 64;4: 707–736.
Chafe, Wallace
    1984 "Speaking, writing and prescriptivism", in: Deborah Schiffrin (ed.), 95–103.
Crowley, Tony
    1989 *The politics of discourse: The standard language question in British cultural debates.* Basingstoke: Macmillan.
Devitt, Amy J.
    1989 *Standardizing written English: Diffusion in the case of Scotland 1520–1559.* Cambridge: Cambridge University Press.
Fisher, John
    1977 "Chancery and the emergence of standard written English in the fifteenth century", *Speculum* 52: 870–899.
Garvin, Paul L.
    1964 "The standard language problem: Concepts and methods", in: Dell Hymes (ed.), 521–526.
Garvin, Paul L. – Madeleine Mathiot
    1960 "The urbanization of the Guarani language: A problem in language and culture", in: Anthony F. C. Wallace (ed.), 783–790.
Gerritsen, Marinel – Dieter Stein
    1992 *Internal and external factors in syntactic change.* Berlin, New York: Walter de Gruyter.
Görlach, Manfred
    1988 "Sprachliche Standardisierungsprozesse im englischsprachigen Bereich", in: Ulrich Ammon – Klaus J. Mattheier – Peter H. Nelde (eds.), 131–185.
Haugen, Einar
    1966 "Dialect, language, nation", *American Anthropologist* 68: 922–935.

Heath, Shirley Brice
    1980 "Standard English: Biography of a symbol", in: Timothy Shopen – Joseph M. Williams (eds.), 3–32.
Hymes, Dell (ed.)
    1964 *Language in culture and society: A reader in linguistics and anthropology.* New York: Harper & Row.
Jernudd, Björn H. (ed.)
    1989 *The politics of language purism.* (Contributions to the sociology of language 54) Berlin: Walter de Gruyter.
Joseph, John Earl
    1987 *Eloquence and power. The rise of language standards and standard languages* (Open Linguistics Series). London: Frances Pinter.
Leonard, Sterling A.
    1929 *The doctrine of correctness in English usage, 1700–1800.* Madison: University of Wisconsin.
McCrum, Robert – William Cran – Robert McNeil
    1989 *The story of English.* London, Boston: Faber & Faber (BBC Books).
Milroy, James – Lesley Milroy
    1985 *Authority in language. Investigating language prescription and standardization.* London: Routledge & Kegan Paul.
Ray, Punya Sloka
    1963 *Language standardization: Studies in prescriptive linguistics,* (Janua Linguarum. Series minor 29).
Richardson, Malcolm
    1980 "Henry V, the English Chancery and Chancery English", *Speculum* 55: 726–750.
Rydén, Mats – Sverker Brorström
    1987 *The be/have variation with intransitives in English. With special reference to the late modern period.* Stockholm: Almqvist & Wiksell.
Schiffrin, Deborah (ed.)
    1984 *Meaning, form, and use in context: Linguistic applications.* Washington: Georgetown University Press.
Shaklee, Margaret
    1980 "The rise of standard English", in: Timothy Shopen – Joseph M. Williams (eds.), 33–62.
Shopen, Timothy – Joseph M. Williams (eds.)
    1980 *Standards and dialects in English.* Cambridge, MA: Winthrop.
Stein, Dieter
    1990 *The semantics of syntactic change. Aspects of the evolution of "do" in English.* Berlin/New York: Mouton.
Sundby, Bertil – Anne K. Bjorge – Kari E. Haugland
    1991 *A dictionary of English normative grammar 1700–1800.* (Amsterdam studies in the theory of linguistic science, series 3:63.) Amsterdam: Benjamins.

Tieken-Boon van Ostade, Ingrid
    1987 *The auxiliary "do" in eighteenth-century English. A sociohistorical-linguistic approach.* Dordrecht: Foris.
    1990 "Exemplification in eighteenth-century English grammars", in: Silvia Adamson – Vivien Law – Nigel Vincent – Susan Wright (eds.), 421–496.
Trahern, Joseph B. (ed.)
    1989 *Standardizing English: Essays in the history of language change, in honor of John Hurt Fisher.* Knoxville: University of Tennessee Press.
Wallace, Anthony F.C. (ed.)
    1961 *Culture and personality.* New York: Random House.

The notion of "standard language" and its applicability to the study of Early Modern English pronunciation

James Milroy

Standardization is a process that is constantly in progress in any language that undergoes it. It isn't something that affects a language at a given time (e.g., in the eighteenth century) and then ceases to operate: a standardized form of language is never universally established in populations and is therefore always in a state of being promoted and maintained. The kind of language that this process affects is usually, but not always, a widely used one, like English or French, but certainly a language in which there is a self-conscious sense of nationhood or common identity: a small-scale example of this is Icelandic. Presumably, there are many languages in the world that we cannot reasonably describe as standard languages, and there are many historical states in which standardization is either absent or in a very early stage of implementation. From the point of view of the observer of linguistic change, standardization (to the extent that it is successful) manifests itself as the extreme case of the development of non-localized norms of usage, and in sociolinguistic interpretations of language variation the whole concept is quite difficult.

The immediate reason for this is that we frequently find that a speech community will gradually agree on some common norms of usage that are functional outside the close community (they are supra-local or exocentric), but that these norms are quite different from those of the national "standard". This applies especially, but not exclusively, to phonetic/phonological norms, which vary much more than other linguistic norms (as my concern in this paper is to consider phonological history, this is the most relevant issue here). However, because there can be very marked differences between locally agreed norms and standard norms, sociolinguists will often resort to the concept of "localized" or "regional" *standard* languages. I think that the choice of this term is unfortunate, because standardization has many properties besides its supra-local character, and these properties can hardly be said to apply to these so-called localized standards. It is better to think of the process of standardization as having been facilitated in the history of English by the prior development of these agreed norms in certain dialect areas. In other words, standardization is superimposed upon suitable pre-existing convergent states of language.

Whereas the natural tendency of dialects and languages is to diverge from one another, standardization is one of those processes that promotes *convergence*. However, this applies equally to the development of non-standard consensus on supra-local norms of language – they too promote convergence. Standardization differs from these more regionalized processes in the fact that it is explicitly imposed from above and carries with it a conscious ideology. Furthermore, standardizing norms of language are subject to legislation. Sometimes this is overt (as in the case of the Académie Française), and sometimes covert: in the latter case the legislation appears as codification in dictionaries, and in manuals of grammar, pronunciation and elocution. It is this covert legislation that applies to English. As it consciously promotes uniformity of structure and openly suppresses variation and change, there is an apparent paradox in the idea that a so-called standard language (if such a thing is ever fully established) can undergo internally-induced change of structure, and this becomes even more awkward when we recall that the chief manifestation of the standard is the written language: changes in phonetics and in many structural parts of language (phonology, morphology and some aspects of syntax) do not originate in writing, but in face-to-face interaction between live speakers. These structural changes are negotiated in speaker-encounters.

There is another important difference between the superimposed norms of the standard and the consensus norms of regional speech-communities, and this is one of the issues that we wished to explore in our research projects in Belfast. All varieties of language are maintained – to the extent that they are reasonably stable – by normative pressures of some kind, but whereas standardization promotes uniformity, the norms existing in real speech communities are *variable* norms. A stable speech community is not one in which everyone speaks in the same way on every occasion, but one in which there is general agreement on the nature and functions of variation. Thus, in New York City, Labov (1966: 7) found – for five variables, for a number of contextual styles, and for an ordered series of socio-economic class groupings – that the variation (e.g., in short /a/) tended in the same direction "in almost every case". Similarly, we discovered stable sex/style/network variation for many variables in Belfast, especially in the relatively socially stable East Belfast community (Milroy – Milroy 1978). Thus, variation is functional in the speech community in so far as the choice of variant X as against variant

Y will depend on speaker-perceptions of the situation: for example, variant X might be most likely to occur when the conversation is casual, when the speaker is male, and/or when there are close ties between the participants (or a combination of these factors and probably other factors, such as topic), and variant Y will occur when a converse set of conditions apply. It is orderly variation that is normal and stable in the community, and uniformity would actually be dysfunctional – as Weinreich, Labov and Herzog (1968) have pointed out. The difference between this situation and the standard is that standardized norms are – overwhelmingly – uniform.

All this, if it is correct, implies that people don't actually speak standard languages: they speak vernaculars (in the sense that we defined these in the Belfast work: see, for example, L. Milroy 1987: 24), and they observe patterns of variation appropriate to these vernaculars. At certain times and places, and in certain styles (especially formal and public styles) these vernaculars may approximate quite closely to the (fundamentally literary) norm of the standard, and at other times and places and in other styles they may diverge – sometimes quite radically – from the standard. In present-day English, however, and in many other languages, there is a general consciousness of correctness in language, largely as a consequence of the spread of literacy, and this amounts to a consciousness of "the standard ideology". The effect of this appears to vary in degree for different language communities: the situation differs between French and German, and these in turn differ from English. In Britain the situation is that only a very small proportion of speakers habitually use an accent (RP = received pronunciation) that is close to the uniform standard (as described by, e.g., Gimson 1970): the vast majority range on a continuum rather like a Creole continuum and are able to move up and down this continuum, which at its extreme end can be so divergent from the standard that the variety used is almost like a different language.

It follows from these arguments that we are not entitled as observers to superimpose the norm of the standard as a primary methodological tool on our descriptions of phonological variation in real speech communities, or to use the standard ideology directly to interpret our findings. The problem may be illustrated by means of a simple example. Inner-city Belfast speakers seem generally to be only passively aware of what the phonological norms of the standard actually are – and then only to a limited extent (O'Kane 1977) – and these seem to have no effect whatever on their actual usage (i.e., on their "vernacular"). Yet, if we had approached our analysis with the norm of the standard in mind, we could easily have been misled. For example, inner-city Belfast English has a long, back variant of /a/ before voiceless fricatives (as in *grass, path*), and this is virtually identical to RP. It is only when we discover that the general phonological distribution of back /a/ is different from RP, and that the vowel system as a whole is organized in a totally different way, that we realize that this is an independent development. Furthermore, the middle class pattern shows a development away from back /a/ towards the front vowel, which means that pronunciations similar to RP are dispreferred in favour of short, front vowels in, e.g., *grass, path*. Thus, RP has no direct effect on the convergence pattern displayed by Belfast middle class speakers (J. Milroy 1982): they move in the opposite direction. Therefore, if we start with the standard norm and then attempt to measure a non-standard variety against it, we can falsify the situation totally: in this instance the falsification would be that hundreds of thousands of speakers who are not remotely interested in RP have "borrowed" back [a] from RP. It would also appear from such an analysis that working-class people are converging towards RP and middle-class people diverging from it, when in fact there is no evidence to suggest that the usage of these speakers is influenced by RP in any way at all.

If it is dangerous to apply this kind of analysis to present-day states of language, it must be at least equally dangerous to do this in dealing with past states. Indeed, the limitations of historical data-bases would seem to make it considerably more dangerous, as the historical investigator does not have "experimental" control over the data. However, this standard-based reasoning has quite frequently been used in diachronic description, and it has affected the conceptualization of language history that we inherit from older generations of scholars. It arises of course from acceptance of the standard ideology (and the doctrine of uniformity that is associated with this) on the part of many of these scholars. To H.C. Wyld, it was common sense that, as RP seemed to be the most important accent of Modern English, he should devote his career to describing its history. But only in certain areas of historical linguistic research is it appropriate to use standardization and "the standard language" as a basis of argument, and phonology is not one of these areas. It is justified to use the standard language as our reference point if our primary interest is in those developments that themselves largely depend on the standard ideology: for example, elaboration of vocabulary and certain developments in clausal syntax, because literacy – and hence standardization – are plainly involved in these, and their role can be investigated. But it is a different story when we focus on phonological change. In this respect, the logical conclusion arising from my arguments in this paper is that the history of English phonology is not a history of the standard at all, but a history of vernaculars. Thus, the most general consequence of concentrating on standard English here is that a multidimensional history of phonology is made to appear as unidimensional – it becomes what Roger Lass (1976: xi) has called "a single-minded march" towards RP and standard English.

This unidimensionality is imposed on history by a backward projection of present-day standard phonology (of the Oxford Common Room and the Officer's mess, as Wyld put it) on to the past, and it can be seen as an attempt to historicize the standard language – to create a past for it and determine a *canon*, in which canonical forms are argued for and unorthodox forms rejected. This in itself can be regarded as part of the process of "legitimization" of the standard language. The method used can be demonstrated by referring to the influential work of E.J. Dobson on Early Modern English pronunciation. As this work is so close to being encyclopaedic, I don't think it can be ignored.

Despite his adversarial attitude to Wyld on other matters (such as the use of "occasional spellings"), Dobson (1955, 1968) continues the tradition of his predecessor in focusing very closely on the history of the entity known as Early Modern Standard English. References to this are common; on one page (1968, II, 548), for example, there are two:

> ME *a* had become [æ] in ... less careful Standard English in the late sixteenth century ...
> In the sixteenth and seventeenth centuries there were two pronunciations of ME *a* in use in Standard English.

These comments do not seem to be based on the notion of standardization as a *process*, but seem to assume that a standard language is a coherent entity – a *variety*, like any other variety. But they do make sociolinguistic assumptions: they seem to assume the early development of a socially elite variety, and it's clear in the first quotation that "carefulness" is also involved. But, although these concepts (standardness, eliteness, carefulness) are of different orders, Dobson does not apparently see any reason to keep them separate.

What is more interesting here, however, is the method of reasoning by which Dobson reaches his conclusions on how Early Modern English pronunciation is to be codified and legitimized as part of the canon. Essentially, any evidence which can be characterized as "vulgar" or "dialectal" is simply rejected. For example, he notes that one source (Pery) "shows the vulgar raising of ME *a* to [e]". This, according to Dobson, is not surprising because Pery's speech "was clearly Cockney ... The evidence of such a writer does not relate to educated StE" (1968, II, 551). On the same page, evidence from the Paston Letters is rejected as "dialectal", and the *Diary of Henry Machyn* is rejected on the grounds that Machyn was a Yorkshireman. Dobson seems to be quite sure of this – but Machyn was almost certainly a Londoner, and his *Diary* is one of the most valuable primary sources for the study of Early Modern English London pronunciation. But as he was not an *upper-class* Londoner, we can guess that his testimony would have been rejected in any case.

Perhaps the most startling piece of reasoning occurs in Dobson's long argument against accepting early "occasional spelling" evidence for raising of [a, æ] to [e]. It goes as follows:

> The most important objection, and it alone is a decisive one, must be that no Englishman could conceivably use *e* as a means of representing [æ]. It may seem natural to a foreign scholar [presumably Zachrisson: JM] to suppose that the sound [æ] ... might be spelt *e*; but it is little short of incredible that native English-speaking scholars should have accepted this view. No English-speaking child learning to spell ... would write *ket* for [kæt]; the distinction between [æ] and [e] is an absolute one for him (since otherwise he could not distinguish, for example, *man* from *men*) ... (1968, II, 549)

But – obviously – this is not decisive, as no evidence is given to prove the negative – that English speakers do not confuse [e] with [a, æ]. In fact native speakers do overlap here; they do have differential phonological rules controlling the distribution of /a/ and /e/, and they do make spelling mistakes involving *a* and *e* (see, e.g., J. Milroy 1981, 1984). Furthermore, it is likely that the distribution of these sounds in Early Modern English was quite different from the RP distribution today, and that the doctrine of (retrospective) phonemic purity (as displayed in the remark about *man* and *men*) is therefore inappropriate. Moreover, it is also certain that English-speaking scholars do not have reliable retrospective intuitions about Early Modern English pronunciation any more than foreign scholars do. So the argument is pure nonsense.

However, it is of great interest, because it demonstrates a familiar mode of argumentation that has been more widely used in historical descriptions and which can be found in many places (for example, in the rejection of certain Middle English spellings as evidence for pronunciation on the grounds that the scribes involved were "Anglo-Norman": J. Milroy 1983). The reasoning is not aimed at supporting a positive argument: it is negative – it is aimed at rejecting the arguments of other scholars and at excluding evidence that cannot easily be accommodated into a unilinear historical canon. The underlying idea is – simply – that some forms are "genuine" and some are not. Ultimately, it does not matter very much what arguments are used to reject evidence: the point is that all possible post hoc arguments must be marshalled to defend one's position against other scholars – the more arguments that can be used, the better. In this case the immediate position defended is that orthoepic evidence is better than other evidence, but the underlying assumption (which is more relevant here) is that it is possible to write a continuous unilinear history of "standard" English pronunciation.

Of course, it may be true that the structural history of English since 1600 has been more convergent than its previous history (even though dialects of British English are still grossly divergent from one another). Yet, it is noticeable that this convergent conceptualization of linguistic history conflicts in one important respect from the ideas that underlie orthodox nineteenth-century historical/comparative linguistics. For ancient language states, the Indo-European family tree provides a model of *divergence*, not of convergence. As we come closer to the present, we find that in the study of medieval English, divergence is still tolerated by commentators (partly because the states attested in writing are unquestionably divergent states), but there are also attempts to launder the Middle English data retrospectively in such a way as to focus on those features that lead to modern standard English and ignore or reject those features that can be labelled as "errors" or "corruptions". This is how the "canonical" forms of the history of English begin to be established. If we put all these things together, however, the model of language history that emerges can be compared to a funnel (the kind that is used for pouring liquids): at about the year 1600 the pyramidal base of the funnel suddenly narrows and then proceeds in a straight and narrow line to the present day. But as there is no such thing as a uniform language or dialect, and as sound-change does not proceed in straight lines, this cannot possibly be a correct conceptualization of phonological history.

But what, you may well ask, does all this have to do with the Early Modern standard English situation? It is clear that some of the processes associated with standardization were well under way around 1600 (elaboration of function, use of a supra-regional writing system), but it looks as if some of them were still at the stage of being localized developments associated with the establishment of consensus on local norms, and this applies particularly to pronunciation. In this dimension, I don't think we can speak of Early Modern "standard" English. Perhaps I can make this clear by distinguishing between the (admittedly unsatisfactory) notion of *prestige* and the notion of *standard language*.

Standardization is not primarily about prestige: it comes about for functional reasons and its effect is to make a language serviceable for communicating decontextualized information-bearing messages over long distances and periods of time. It is imposed through its use in administrative functions by those who have political power. Once it spreads into other functions, it acquires prestige – in the sense that those who wish to advance in life consider it to be in their interests to use standard-like forms. Prestige, however, is a different concept altogether, as it can be subjectively attached by speakers to forms and varieties which are very distant from, and in conflict with, the codified norms of the standard. In recent years, Arab linguists (Abd-el Jawad 1987; Alahdal 1989) have found it difficult to reconcile the concepts of "standard" and "prestige", because rural norms that are identical to standard Arabic are shown to be dispreferred in favour of urban "non-standard" forms. Our own work, and that of Peter Trudgill (1986), has tended towards very similar conclusions. In this context, the well-known late sixteenth-century comments about "the best English" being spoken in the London area should be understood for what they are, and not necessarily as a sign of "standardized" pronunciation. They arise from a consciousness of the development of a stable (but variable) urban vernacular norm in London, knowledge that its norms differ from those of other varieties, and a belief in the superiority of London norms over those of other regions. What we are dealing with here is sociolinguistic: the development of supra-local regional and social attitudes to language. What we are not dealing with is a fully-fledged "standard" pronunciation that can then be most usefully described in terms of a unilinear history since that time. If we think in this way, we may well be tempted to dismiss or devalue evidence that is of the utmost importance for our understanding of language history.

If, however, we take the view that the history of Early Modern English is multidimensional (because vernacular norms are variable, and not uniform, states), and reject the notion of "standardized" phonology from our basic analysis, we can make greater progress. I can refer here only selectively to a few relevant studies. Houston (1985) and Labov (1989) have investigated the participial (ing) variable and shown that there has been variation in this for centuries; similarly, I have argued (contrary to traditional views) that variation in initial (h) has been a relatively stable variable since the thirteenth century (J. Milroy 1983), and Romaine (1984) has done the same for final dental stop deletion (of the type *han'* for *hand*). Therefore, it's likely that Kökeritz is right to emphasize the tolerance of variability in Early Modern "standard" English (but recall that tolerance of variability is not a characteristic of "standard" languages). As for the "enfants terribles", such as the reported merger of MEAT/MATE, it would seem that we can accept the possibility that merger could have taken place in some varieties and styles, but not in others, and that apparent reversal of merger depends on the availability in the speech community of varieties with merger, varieties with approximation, and varieties with the alternative MEAT/MEET merger. As long as the varieties co-exist, it is possible to reverse a merger in one of them, because the social history of a language must be multidimensional.

In order to understand the history of so-called standard English pronunciation, therefore, we need to assume – paradoxically – that there is no such thing as standard English. Standardization is not about varieties of language, but about processes. Therefore, it must be treated as a process with an underlying socio-political motivation, which attempts to promote uniformity and suppress variability. If we take this point of view, it seems that we will gain a better understanding of the history of what is usually called standard English, because we will be able to separate out those issues which primarily involve the development of standard norms from those which do not. The history of pronunciation is one of those issues that do not primarily involve standardization, because it is primarily about the history of speech in face-to-face interaction and because standardization has always had less effect on pronunciation than on other linguistic levels. The history of standard pronunciation is not, therefore, something that we can usefully chart in a unilinear temporal continuum, as though co-existing varieties had no role except to "feed" the standard "variety" from time to time. This is an over-simplification – and a distortion – of language history. The role of standardization in the history of English is not simple, but complicated, and to explain its relevance to phonological history is a complex and challenging task.

References

Abd-el-Jawad, Hassan R.
    1987   Cross-dialectal variation in Arabic: Competing prestigious forms, *Language in Society* 16: 359–368.

Alahdal, Hassan
    1959   *Standard and prestige: A sociolinguistic study of Makkan Arabic*. [Unpublished Ph.D. thesis, University of Reading.]

Blake, Norman F. – Charles Jones
    1984   *English historical linguistics: Studies in development*. Sheffield: University of Sheffield.

Davenport, M. – Erik Hansen – Hans Frede Nielsen
    1983   *Current topics in English historical linguistics*. Odense: Odense University Press.

Dobson, Eric J.
    1955   "Early Modern Standard English", *Transactions of the Philological Society* 53: 25–54.

1968 *English pronunciation, 1500–1700*. (2nd edition.) 2 vols. Oxford: Clarendon press.

Gimson, Alfred C.
1970 *Introduction to the pronunciation of English*. (2nd edition.) London: Edward Arnold.

Houston, Anne
1985 *Continuity and change in English morphology: the variable (ING)*. [Unpublished Ph.D. dissertation, University of Pennsylvania.]

Labov, William
1966 *The social stratification of English in New York City*. Washington DC: Center for Applied Linguistics.
1989 "The child as linguistic historian", *Language variation and change* 1: 85–97.

Lass, Roger
1976 *English phonology and phonological theory*. Cambridge: Cambridge University Press.

Lehmann, Winfred P. – Yakov Malkiel
1968 *Directions for historical linguistics*. Austin: University of Texas Press.

Milroy, James
1981 *Regional accents of English: Belfast*. Belfast: Blackstaff Press.
1982 "Probing under the tip of the iceberg: Phonological 'normalisation' and the shape of speech communities", in: Suzanne Romaine (ed.), 35–47.
1983 "On the sociolinguistic history of /h/-dropping in English", in: M. Davenport – E. Hansen – H. F. Nielsen (eds.), 37–53
1984 "Present day evidence for historical change", in: Norman F. Blake and Charles Jones (eds.), 173–191.

Milroy, James – Lesley Milroy
1978 "Belfast: Change and variation in an urban vernacular", in: Peter Trudgill (ed.), 19–36.

Milroy, Lesley
1987 *Language and social networks*. (2nd edition.) Oxford: Basil Blackwell.

O'Kane, Domini
1987 "Overt and covert prestige in Belfast vernacular speakers: The results of self-report tests", *Belfast Working Papers in Language and Linguistics* 2: 54–77.

Romaine, Suzanne (ed.)
1982 *Sociolinguistic variation in speech communities*. London: Edward Arnold.

Romaine, Suzanne
1984 "The sociolinguistic history of final t/d deletion", *Folia Linguistica Historica* 5: 221–255.

Trudgill, Peter
1986 *Dialects in Contact*. Oxford: Basil Blackwell.

Trudgill, Peter (ed.)
    1978 *Sociolinguistic patterns in British English*. London: Edward Arnold.
Weinreich, Uriel – William Labov – M. Herzog
    1968 "Empirical foundations for a theory of language change", in: W. Lehmann – Y. Malkiel (eds.), 97–195.

"Politeness" as linguistic ideology in late seventeenth- and eighteenth-century England

Lawrence Klein

It is well known that the pace of comment on the English language quickened in the eighteenth century. Moreover, the nature of that comment changed in that the eighteenth century saw a new emphasis on setting a "standard" and defining "correctness". Though the printing of language-related texts increased most rapidly after mid-century, the new concern with "correctness" was evident in the early eighteenth and even in the later seventeenth century.[1]

Throughout the eighteenth century, these initiatives in linguistic prescription were linked to ideals of "politeness". The most frequently cited early eighteenth-century example of the new prescriptivism is Swift's *Proposal for Correcting, Improving and Ascertaining the English Tongue* of 1712. Writing in the name of "all the Learned and Polite Persons of the Nation", Swift explained how the natural impoliteness of the English language had been aggravated by historical factors that kept English speakers from "Patterns of Politeness" (Swift 1712: 8, 19, 25). Swift's remedy for linguistic impoliteness was an academy. However, even earlier, Defoe had proposed an academy "to encourage Polite Learning" and "to polish and refine the *English* tongue" (Defoe 1697: 233).

Indeed, for the whole century and in many less luminous instances, language was assessed according to the practice of its most "polished Speakers" (Rice 1765: 308, 313n; Kenrick 1784: Advertisement) and with respect to its "Purity and Politeness of Expression" (Philip Withers, *Aristarchus*, cited in Leonard 1929: 169). Writing in the same year as Swift, the anonymous author of *Bellum Grammaticale* (1712: 4) offered a proleptic summary of the century when he inferred from the quantity of linguistic comment that the age was "weary, or asham'd of that general Barbarism, which has spread through our Writers in all the politer Arts; and that we may hope, if Emperics do not intrude with their empty Pretences, in a few years to see our Nation as *polite*, as *brave*". Much later in the century, Thomas Sheridan (1798: 353–354) deployed the identical idiom, writing that "... a neglect of their speech, is not only a characteristical mark of barbarism in all nations, but the sure means of continuing them in that state; as on the contrary, the regulation and refinement of language is a necessary step towards introducing politeness".

What did "politeness" really mean when it was applied to language? Since "politeness" was a verbal fixture in the eighteenth century, it was often used vacuously, adding little to the general notions of "refinement" and "correctness". However, at least in the early part of the eighteenth century, "politeness" had a more specific set of resonances, which it is the central object of this paper to expose. Indeed, the paper suggests that, by the later part of the century, the term had lost these specific resonances. In other words, mapping the contours of early eighteenth-century "politeness" makes visible an important rift in linguistic thinking in the mid-eighteenth century. The focus, then, of this investigation of the linguistic relevance of "politeness" is the early eighteenth century and, to an extent, the later seventeenth. Although the idiom of "politeness" was cultivated in important ways by writers of the Restoration decades, it was crystallized during the reign of Queen Anne in the treatises of the third Earl of Shaftesbury (1714) and in the great Whig periodicals of Addison and Steele.

That the classic formulators of "politeness" embedded discussions of language in wide-ranging writings of moralist and cultural commentary is significant since it suggests that a full history of linguistic thinking cannot be reconstructed on the basis of a narrow selection of works in the rhetorical or grammatical tradition. To gather the meanings of "politeness", we have to look beyond specific genres of linguistic discourse to a wide variety of texts. By the early eighteenth century, "politeness" was central to a number of important areas of discussion; it ranged in use over the domains of social behavior, formal and informal expression, and the condition of society and culture at large.[2] One pays a price for broadening the bibliography in this way since the more strictly linguistic genres tended to be most precise in referring to actual linguistic usages. However, the gain is a better understanding of the larger normative framework in which linguistic evaluation proceeded. Large normative frameworks for linguistic practice are increasingly interesting to sociolinguists just as large normative frameworks for linguistic inquiry are increasingly interesting to archaeologists and other investigators of knowledge.[3]

"Politeness" was exactly such a normative framework since, in broad terms, it was a tool for the reconstruction of culture. The language and suppositions of "politeness" were first established in Continental courtesy literature of the sixteenth and seventeenth centuries. However, in early eighteenth-century England, the courtly assumptions of this literature were abandoned in favor of a more inclusive and more wide-ranging ideal. At its most elaborate, "politeness" could be used to evoke a vision of social life and culture, appropriate to modern times. This vision, linking moral improvement and cultural refinement, was epitomized in urbane and gentlemanly conversation. The main body of this paper investigates three elements of this vision, with their opposites, as key components of the meaning of "politeness": conversibility and unsociability, gentlemanliness and pedantry, urbanity and provinciality.

"Politeness" was, in general, a condition of refined social interaction, but social "politeness" was paradigmatically conversational. When writers defined "politeness" as a dextrous management of words and actions in company (Boyer 1702: 50, 106), words had pride of place. According to one guide, "... nothing is more important in the commerce of life, than to please in Conversation ... " (Vaumorière 1691: 5). According to another, "whoever will live in Society must make himself Sociable; and the only way to learn to be Sociable, is to be often in Society. Conversation is the great Book of the World ... " (*Management of the Tongue*, 1706: 2–3). Thus, "politeness" was, among other things a theory of conversational manners. In courtesy literature, conversational values and banes proliferated. Ortigue de Vaumorière's *Art of Pleasing in Conversation* examined "what may render a man troublesome" in order that a recognition might emerge of "how to make a Spirit of gayety and politeness reign in Conversation". Thus, conversational "politeness" pursued verbal agreeableness, which was captured in a characteristic vocabulary: "easie", "remote from affectation", "never tiresom", "soft", "polisht", "natural" (1691: 7, 17). Another text defined fully realized conversation in terms of the free, the sweet, the agreeable, the amusing and the open-hearted, open-minded and open-ended; it juxtaposed to these forms of constraint, dryness, closure and studied bookishness (*Management of the Tongue*, 9–10).

Behind such criteria were certain general principles. As the "art of pleasing", "politeness" involved the submission of the self to the disciplines of social interaction. These disciplines had been worked out in numerous Continental courtesy books and translated into English (Brauer 1959, Magendie 1925, Mason 1935). The social disciplines aimed to enhance social interaction, making it more pleasurable and agreeable and sometimes also more useful and instructive. Such social disciplines demanded the ability to locate oneself in a complex social situation, recognizing one's own desires and interests while comprehending the legitimate desires and interests of others. Contemporary exhortations to modesty, discretion, decorum, propriety and politeness were demands that the moral agent recognize the social context of his or her actions.

Thus, the art of conversation was the technique for negotiating between the poles of self and other, and conversation itself was a dialectic of self-presentation and self-effacement, of confidence and modesty, of egoism and solicitousness. Paradoxically, self-love achieved its own goals through satisfying the self-love of others. "The more you'll give to other Men occasion to please in Conversation, the more you'll please them. By such an obliging Behavior, we find that we never come out of a Conversation better pleased, than when we can flatter our selves that others are pleased with us" (*Management of the Tongue*, 3–5). The point at which one was doing most for others was the point at which one was doing most for oneself.

The pursuit of sociability implied various specific prescriptions: one did one's best to give others a favorable platform; one did not correct all errors that slipped into conversation; one did not ask questions that conversants could not answer. As for his or her own contributions, the conversationalist, while recognizing that silence often had its uses, avoided taciturnity, which amounted to self-withdrawal and extreme unsociability. However, the conversationalist also eschewed the other extreme, an unsociable excess of sociability and self-projection. Good conversationalists skirted the pitfalls of the ego: they avoided conceit, pride and vanity; they were never too full of themselves, never too talkative, never too eager and never too solicitous of their own singularity in conversation.

Though its original subject matter was social interaction, "politeness" came to sanction an exemplary role for conversation in written discourse: a "polite" text was specifically conversational. As early as Dryden, one finds conversation identified as a key component of literary refinement. In terms broadly relevant to literary language, Dryden declared that the superiority of the plays of his own era to "the dramatic poetry of the last age" (1912: 105–107) was a matter of their greater refinement. This refinement could be referred to general conditions: "the language, wit, and conversation of our age are improved and refined above the last" (1912: 105–107). Instances gleaned from Jacobean plays showed that the language of the present "is become more courtly, and our thoughts are better dressed" (1912: 105–107). As for former wit, it "was not that of gentlemen; there was ever somewhat that was ill-bred and clownish in it, and which confessed the conversation of the authors" (1912: 105–107). Language (implicitly) and wit (explicitly) were both traced back "to the last and greatest advantage of our writing, which proceeds from *conversation*" (1912: 105–107). The superiority of conversation in the present age, the growth of gallantry, the expansion of conversational freedom, and the greater accessibility of writers to conversation at the highest social levels had nourished the soul of comedies: "discourse and raillery" (Dryden 1912: 105–107).

Dryden was sketching and condoning a process of conversationalization that was restyled in Shaftesbury and his contemporaries as literary "politeness". Literary "politeness" was a diffuse entity since it served as an umbrella for a range of stylistic and critical campaigns. In part, it seems to have corresponded to a recognized event in the history of English prose, the trend to what has been called "speech-based prose".[4] However, my concern here is not with objective stylistic functions of "politeness" but rather with traits of metalinguistic discourse.

Shaftesbury advocated "politeness" as a reform of modern discourse, which he thought paralyzed between the vacuity of most ordinary conversations and the inaccessibility of most learned writings. He endorsed educated conversation as a paradigm for both modern sociability and modern inquiry. This conversational model underwrote his most typical and influential proclamations, such as the contention that "*Wit* will mend upon our hands, and *Humor* will refine it-self; if we take care not to tamper with it, and bring it under Constraint, by severe Usage and rigorous Prescriptions. All Politeness is owing to Liberty. We polish one another, and rub off our Corners and rough Sides by a sort of *amicable Collision*" (Shaftesbury 1714: I, 64).

Shaftesbury's conversational commitments shaped his own writing in the influential *Characteristicks of Men, Manners, Times, Opinions*. It might be shown how he adopted a variety of voices throughout *Characteristicks* and set them in discussion with one another, how he deployed such conversational genres as dialogue and epistle, and how his own style, for all its elegance, aspired to be conversational. It is enough to cite his own self-characterization as a conversational writer. At different points, he embraced the "extemporary air" in writing, the pleasures of "variation, interruption, and digression", the virtues of the spontaneous and random over the planned and formal, the "familiar style", and "the way of chat" (Shaftesbury 1714: III, 1–6, 21–22, 82, 96–97).

The conversational ideal operated to validate certain genres and stylistic modes. For instance, Shaftesbury assigned centrality to the genre of the letter. Since the letter, he thought, was a continuation of conversation at one remove from conversation itself, it was the literary form best able to carry the particular burdens of conversation, namely, the apt amalgamation of seriousness with informality (Shaftesbury 1714: III, 19–20). This endorsement of the epistolary genre was widely shared in the eighteenth century (D.A. 1683: 64; Walsh 1692: preface; *Tatler* #30) and an obvious foundation of many characteristic literary practices during the era (Anderson et al. 1966; Redford 1986).

"Politeness" endorsed the conversational idiom, but it also pegged conversation at the social level of the gentleman. The prestige of "politeness" corresponded to the rise of the gentlemanly as a cultural standard.

This phenomenon makes sense against the shifting socio-political landscape of the later seventeenth and early eighteenth centuries. The period saw a decisive end to monarchal threats to the powers and interests of the landed elite. Famous constitutional developments (1688 and all that) contributed to this, but so did the personalities, aspirations and limitations of the various post-1688 monarchs. Moreover, general economic conditions were highly beneficial to leading elements of the landed elite (Plumb 1967; Cannon 1984: 126–147; Clark 1985: 93–118; Holmes 1981). It therefore makes sense that a related phenomenon of this period was the seizing of the cultural initiative from the Crown by the gentlemanly elite.

In these cultural politics, "politeness" played an important role. While the social disciplines of "politeness" had been forged in the setting of royal courts, it was not hard to detach them from specifically courtly arrangements. Even in the golden age of the French Court, "politeness" flourished outside the Court in salons, which enjoyed an ambiguous relationship with the royal court, sometimes a complementary locale, sometimes an alternative locale. In England, the royal court had rarely aspired to, and never achieved, the particular constellation of elements in a Medicean or Bourbon court. That sort of courtly ideal became obsolete after 1688, when "politeness" came into its own in England. "Politeness" was no longer a discipline for courtiers primarily, but one relevant to the elite generally.

The question is: Just what were the boundaries of the elite? We might say that to be a gentleman meant living off one's accumulated wealth (usually land but not excluding stocks and the public funds), but, increasingly in the eighteenth century, commercial and professional people, who worked for a living, aspired to gentility. Thus, while "politeness" could serve as a cultural apology for aristocratic hegemony, "politeness" was also an appealing ideal for many individuals of the middling sort. In fact, "politeness" was marketed in a wide range of periodicals, pamphlets and books to an audience much wider than the gentry. Thus, the identity of the "polite" cannot be confined to patricians. This was not a society in which social boundaries were being tended, or could be, with maximal tidiness, especially when we think of those segments of the population whose paths intersected in the urban and commercial zone. As contemporaries recognized and historians have reiterated, English society was a finely calibrated gradient of conditions, without crude and easily legible gaps. Moreover, prosperity, social and geographic mobility and consumerism meant that it was common for people to experience changes of condition during their lives, often for the better (Porter 1982: 63–67; Earle 1989: 5–9, 31, 69, 73, 76, 85, 218; Rogers 1979; Staves 1988; McKendrick 1985). Hence people were in a position to redefine their own horizons and identities by looking farther along the social incline. Prosperity allowed the commercial community to engage in the pursuits of gentility.[5] Nonetheless, it was under the closely related rubrics of "gentility" and "politeness" rather than any autonomous bourgeois norm that the middling sought self-improvement.[6] Therefore, it has to be remembered that crucial ambiguities surrounded the use of "politeness" in apposition with the gentlemanly.

Notwithstanding the ambiguity of its precise reference, however, "politeness" was used, from the later seventeenth century, to discriminate an elite – "the Politer Part of Great Britain", "the elegant and knowing Part of Mankind" (*Spectator* nos. 13, 218) – from the rest of the population in England and did circumscribe a territory of elite activities, interests and manifestations. It was in the first instance a means of social classification, demarcating the upper stratum. The "polite People", the "polite Men", were "the Quality", "the better sort", gentlemen and ladies (*Tatler* nos. 38, 39).

However, aside from status, what constituted the politeness of the "polite"? While writers had haggled for several centuries about the precise weighting of genealogical, economic, political, juridical, moral and cultural elements in the gentlemanly make-up, "politeness" foregrounded the moral, social and cultural qualifications for gentility.

To begin with, the "polite" gentleman was conversible in the sense already explored. His physical and mental refinement made him agreeable in company. As Matthew Prior once wrote: "Beyond the fix'd and settl'd Rules/Of Vice and Virtue in the Schools:/Beyond the Letter of the Law,/Which keeps our Men and Maids in Awe;/The better Sort should set before 'em/A Grace, a Manner, a Decorum ... " ("Paulo Purganti and His Wife" in Prior 1709: 116). This sort of stylishness made gentlemen pleasant in company and, indeed, could only be cultivated in company as well. In a statement with great resonance in eighteenth-century England, Saint-Evremond (1692: 296) wrote that "Study makes a greater Difference between a Scholar and an ignorant Man, than there is between an Ignorant Man and a Brute: but the air of the World yet makes a greater distinction still, between a Polite and a learned Person. Knowledge begins the Gentleman, and the Correspondence of the World compleats him."[7] "Politeness" aligned conversibility with gentlemanliness under the rubric of worldliness.

As Saint-Evremond indicated, learning was a component of polite gentlemanliness. While intellectual and cultural achievements had long been in the repertoire of the English gentlemen as he was confected in courtesy books, "politeness" discriminated among kinds of intellectual and cultural achievement. "Politeness" demarcated the literary and artistic region of intellectual and creative endeavor: the "polite arts" were the fine arts; "polite writing" was poetry, history, criticism and miscellaneous "belles lettres" (Klein 1984–1985: 200–202). It was these that the "polite" gentleman was expected to embrace. However, the gentleman was never to sacrifice his agreeableness to learning: if learning was to be "polite", it had itself to submit to the disciplines of good company. One way for the gentleman to preserve his "politeness" was for him to approach learning as an amateur and generalist. Specialization, which, in any case, smacked of trade, was an enemy of sociability. This generalist ethic was captured by Pascal when he remarked: "We should not be able to say of a man, 'He is a mathematician', or a 'preacher', or 'eloquent'; but that he is a 'gentleman'."[8]

It is perhaps then not surprising that the "polite" writers expressed a powerful animus against matters that did not conform. From the "polite" perspective, most learning, scholarship and philosophy (natural or "school" philosophy) appeared unsociable and hermetic as well as crooked, ill-formed and charmless. "Politeness" derogated these endeavors by a battery of aspersion, at the front of which stood "pedantry". In the early eighteenth century, "pedantry" – not "vulgarity" – was the real opposite of gentlemanly "politeness". The horror of "pedantry" haunted accounts of gentlemanly conversation, which eschewed the studied and the bookish in favor of the worldly. The survival of the polite ideal of conversation demanded an ordinary language appropriate to non-specialists: one had to avoid technical subjects and technical language; similarly, the polite speaker was to avoid jargon, neologism and arcana of any sort.

The argument between the gentleman and the pedant, under the auspices of "politeness", stamped discussion of the varieties of verbal and artistic expression. If "politeness" endorsed conversibility in texts, it also struck a social register in which the gentlemanly asserted itself. "Politeness" was aggressive gentlemanliness, self-confident, appropriating. The spread of "politeness" from discourse to discourse reflected the appropriation of the world of social, intellectual and literary creation by gentlemen.

Gentlemanliness became an underlying figure in critical diction. For one thing, the social personality of the writer was said to contribute to the character of the writing: "polite writing" came from the pen of gentlemen. Thus, according to the earl of Roscommon (1685: 5), "... none have been with Admiration, read/But who (beside their Learning) were Well-bred." John Hughes (1735: 247–248) made the same connection between breeding and writing, unpacking its anti-pedantic implications:

> When, by the Help of Study, a sufficient Stock of solid Learning, is acquired the next Business is to consider how to make use of it to the best Advantage. There is nothing more necessary to this than Good Sense and Polite Learning ... So that if there was nothing else to recommend Polite Learning yet methinks this were enough that it files off the Rust of the Academy, and is the same of the Mind, as Dancing to the Body, a Means of giving it a free Air and genteel Motion. In a Word, it adds the Gentleman to the Scholar, and when these two meet they challenge all Mens Respect and Love.

However, this passage also suggests that "polite writing" not only was the product of "polite gentlemen" but also shared the traits of "polite gentlemen". Thus, "politeness" bestowed gentlemanly attributes on literary expression: "polite" writing was free from pedantic stiffness and uncleanliness; it enjoyed "a free Air and genteel Motion"; it gained the love of others. A text such as Hughes's exploited an ambiguity in the notion of "polite writing": the same vocabulary came to characterize the "polite" writer and his product.

The vocabulary of "politeness" proliferated in critical discourse of this period. Perhaps the most remarkable example of a language of social behavior infesting a literary discourse was *A Dissertation on Reading the Classics* (1713), prepared for the young Lord Roos by Henry Felton, tutor in the household of the Duke of Rutland. Felton wrote that, aside from its foundation in basic linguistic knowledge and in classical learning, a just and beautiful style derived particularly from breeding and conversation. Addressing the young Lord Roos, he wrote:

> Persons of Your Lordship's Quality have so fine a Turn, so genteel an Air from their Breeding, and courtly Conversation in every Thing they write or speak, that it giveth an inimitable Grace to the Words and Compositions; and I never knew a nobleman equal in Learning to other Men, but he was superior to them in Delicacy and Civility of his Style (67).

The "politeness" of the writer as a social personality left its stamp on the writing, and the writing in turn assumed the characteristics of gentlemanly "politeness": "Grace", "Delicacy", and "Civility". Such a passage evinced the thorough fusion of the vocabularies of gentlemanly behavior and literary style.

Felton went on to categorize ancient and modern authors by their breeding and concomitant quality as writers. As Horace and Virgil fell short of Ovid in "Courtliness of Expression", so Dryden and Oldham lacked the "distinguishing Character of Affability, Courtesy and fine Breeding" of Rochester, Dorset, Buckingham and other noble writers of the Restoration era. Though Dryden was "the greatest Master of Poetry the last Age could Boast", there was still something "like a Scholar" in him which deprived him of "that Easiness and Familiarity, that Air of Freedom and Unconstraint, that gentle and accomplished Manner of Expression", marking the truly polite writer (Felton 1713: 70–76). Fifty years later, Archibald Campbell (1767: xviii–xx) used the same polarity between the gentle author (whose birth assured "elegance and purity of style") and the *roturier* author (whose status as a trader induced affectation and pedantry) to launch his attack on Samuel Johnson.

"Politeness" evoked the figure of the conversible gentleman but that was not all. This conversible gentleman was firmly situated in a metropolitan environment: he was urbane.

Here again there is a relevant historical context, namely, the development of English cities. The phenomenon was not just the growth or expansion of English cities, but a particular form of growth, the creation of neighborhoods with a distinct character for gentlemen and ladies. The new and distinctive building which proceeded in seventeenth-century London – the appearance of the West End – was only an anticipation of what went on in massive dimensions in the eighteenth century. Similarly, what went on in London was only the most thorough instance of changes that marked all English cities and many towns. These changes were central in fabricating a new relation between the English elite and the urban environment. The very rubric, "the Town", involving a semantic reinvestment of an old word, was an innovation in the discourse of urbanness, supplementing the more traditional label, "the City". The new neighborhoods were suitable for the extended visits to Town of the landed elite, though the neighborhoods perhaps more frequently served other forms of gentle population: cadets of the landed elite; landed households taking a turn at belt-tightening (since life in Town was cheaper than in the Country); professionals and civil servants and others whose cultural and social identification was with the landed elite, even if these "urban" or "pseudo-gentry" were technically not among the number of that elite (Brett-James 1935; Stone 1980; Summerson 1946; Borsay 1989). In addition, a wide range of middling sorts, resident in the City or the suburbs, might take advantage of the "polite" facilities offered in "the Town".

The novelty of this form of urbanness witnessed an altered pattern of gentle life in the eighteenth century, and it was the language of "politeness" through which this sort of urbanism could be represented and characterized. The "politeness of the Town" became a platitude. Though an eighteenth-century re-edition of John Stow's *Survey of London* (1733) found instances of "polite" architecture in the City as well as the West End (I, 9), the West End was the generally accepted "polite end" of London (Rudé 1971: 209).

This elite urban world was given monumental verbal existence, for the first time, in Richard Steele's *Tatler*. The novelty of the *Tatler* rested in the specific sort of London that it presupposed, a London revealed through the experience of the work's narrative focus, Isaac Bickerstaffe, Esquire. Bickerstaffe was a gentleman, the heir of a stock of English virtue and wisdom, amassed in the traditional English environment of the landed elite. However, his chief aim was bringing this heritage to bear on an urban environment, a gentleman's London. He visited all corners of London but recurred to the West End, the site in which *The Tatler* erected its particular social world. Though this urban environment was necessarily socially mixed, Bickerstaffe was principally an observer of "the polite and the busy". This social world was an eminently sociable world, in which conversation was an exemplary scene of social performance and a constitutive practice for a series of interlocking social environments (drawing rooms, coffee-houses, taverns, assemblies, theaters, and other places of public resort, such as parks and gardens). *The Tatler* embraced the metropolis, which became in its pages the site where the ethical opportunities of English gentlemen and ladies were being lost and gained. In number after number, the *Tatler* pursued the role of "a Sort of Puritan in the polite World", making it his "Endeavor to distinguish between Realities and Appearances, and to separate true Merit from the Pretense to it", all in the service of "the perfection of good breeding and good sense" (*Tatler* nos. 29, 165, 12).

When Bickerstaffe retired, the Spectator took over the task of perfecting "good breeding and good sense". Spectatorial politeness was also situated in Town as the famous pronouncement in the tenth number indicated: "It was said of *Socrates*, that he brought Philosophy down from Heaven, to inhabit among Men; and I shall be ambitious to have it said of me, that I have brought Philosophy out of Closets and Libraries, Schools and Colleges, to dwell in Clubs and Assemblies, at Tea-Tables and in Coffeehouses." This passage indicated a turn away from the learned culture of the country gentleman (from whose "Closets and Libraries" philosophy was to be removed) and from educational institutions, principally universities (from which philosophy was also to be dislodged) and towards the Town, the very site of club and assembly, tea-table and coffeehouse.

"Politeness" was thus aggressively involved in advancing the claims of the metropolis as against alternative cultural resources that might arise in non-urban institutions and places. Just as the strand of gentlemanliness in "politeness" magnified the grotesqueness of pedantry, so this sort of metropolitanism transformed the legitimate cultures of British regions and the manifold expressions of the English Country into provincialism. Although the language of London had long before established itself as the model of propriety among linguistic commentators, the normative influence of "politeness" validated an energetic dismissal of dialectal competitors. Hugh Jones (1724: 11) listed five English dialects, denominating one "the *Proper*, or *London Language*", and besmirching the others in these terms:

> For want of better Knowledge, and more Care, almost every Country in *England* has gotten a distinct Dialect, or several peculiar Words, and odious Tones, perfectly ridiculous to Persons unaccustomed to hear such Jargon: thus as the Speech of a *Yorkshire* and *Somersetshire* downright *Countryman* would be almost unintelligible to each other; so would it be good Diversion to a polite *Londoner* to hear a Dialogue between them.[9]

The horror of the provincial must have had an effect, if we are to judge by at least one interesting example.[10] When James Boswell first came to London, he was in rebellion against Scotland, against his father, and against the legal study that his father had foisted on him. He characterized his early stay as an exercize in self-fashioning:

> Since I came up, I have begun to acquire a composed genteel character very different from a rattling uncultivated one which for some time past I have been fond of. I have discovered that we may be in some degree whatever character we choose. Besides, practice forms a man to anything. I was now happy to find myself cool, easy, and serene. (Pottle 1950: 47)

Here was a provincial eagerly shedding bumpkinism and embracing politeness. His journal witnessed his daily efforts. He surrounded himself with people whom he described as "polite" and sought to emulate. After participating in a long conversation about the differences between "a rude and a polished state of society" (an instance of the general interest among the cultivated in cultural and historical politeness), he assessed his personal progress from "rude" to "polished", remarking, "I kept up a *retenue* and spoke only when I was sure that I was right." (Pottle 1950: 48)

Moreover, throughout the journal, he was constantly admitting that he derived his notions from the very periodicals which at the beginning of the century crystallized ideas of politeness. One of his most revealing remarks reflected on a carriage ride to Haymarket: "As we drove along and spoke good English [a particular anxiety to a would-be "polite" of Scottish origin], I was full of rich imagination of London, ideas suggested by the Spectator and such as I could not explain to most people, but which I strongly feel and am ravished with" (Pottle 1950: 130). The era when any one was in danger of being ravished by Addison was, no doubt, soon to end. However, Boswell still fell within the epoch of "polite" cultural ideals, during which language use, and much else, was to be submitted to the standards of the conversible, the gentlemanly and the metropolitan.

The prestige of "politeness" in the earlier eighteenth century has a number of significances for our understanding of linguistic issues in the period.

The most obvious is that it encouraged the idea that language did have a standard. In advocating the virtues of conversibility, gentlemanliness and urbanity, "politeness" set standards for all manner of human domains, including the various forms of cultural expression. "Politeness" assumed that the formal aspect of things had serious moral, social and political implications. Thus, cultural expressions needed to be assessed and, then, tended in the light of their moral, social and political characteristics. In fact, cultural expressions could be placed on a continuum, ranging from barbarity to politeness. Since language was itself a prime cultural expression, it is not surprising that, in this mental world, writers began to see specific issues of linguistic usage, such as the choice of relative pronouns or the ease of contraction, as morally, socially, or politically charged.

To this extent, this examination of "politeness" tends to confirm the view that eighteenth-century linguistic thought was, in powerful and novel ways, oriented toward standardization. However, in other ways, this examination unsettles some commonly received opinions.

Aside from the general encouragement "politeness" gave to an ideology of standardization, "politeness" was most immediately relevant to linguistic thinking because it dictated a pragmatics of linguistic usage. While "politeness" may have encouraged the search for correctness in vocabulary and grammar, it most directly addressed the question of the conditions for effective language use: it sought not so much lexical or grammatical correctness as pragmatic correctness, founded on the conditions of gentlemanly and urbane conversation.

Shaftesbury's writings epitomize the features of "politeness" that this paper has investigated, and his concerns were more typical of the early eighteenth century than the complaint on verbal peccadilloes in Swift's *Proposal*. According to John Earl Joseph (1967: 3–4), Shaftesbury was the first writer to use the word "standard" with reference to language, but he commented little on lexical choice or grammatical appropriateness (though he did discuss style). However, his writings comment extensively on the conditions of discourse, projecting a vision of a polite culture on the model of gentlemanly conversation.

To generalize, the linguistic thinking of the early eighteenth century was heavily oriented toward pragmatic concerns rather than lexical and grammatical ones, which only rose to the top of the agenda later in the century when grammatical prescriptivism really took off.[11] Thus, it is important to avoid ascribing to the era of Shaftesbury a characterization based on the era of Lowth.

There is another respect in which it is important to distinguish the earlier eighteenth century from the later. On the basis of the efforts of the later eighteenth-century grammarians to submit language use to a "transcendantal" standard, the linguistic writing of the century is usually characterized as rationalizing, classicizing and authoritarian.[12] Although, in his classic survey, S.A. Leonard recognized the wide diversity of standards which the eighteenth-century doctrine of "correctness" harnessed, his account is typical in emphasizing the weak appeal of custom and usage as appropriate canons in comparison with the power of rationalist or classicist models.[13]

However, "politeness" was precisely a standard of usage since it assessed language according to a social standard. In the "polite" idiom, the standard for language was appropriateness to a certain social practice, the urbane conversation of gentlemen and ladies. This sense of appropriateness led to an endorsement of comprehensibility and accessibility. This was an immanent standard arising within linguistic practice, not a transcendent standard generated in the logical or historical imagination and brought to bear on practice. Within the "polite" idiom, it was hard to imagine the chasm between standard and practice expressed in Lowth's famous assertion that "the English Language as it is spoken by the politest part of the nation, and as it stands in the writings of our most approved authors, often offends against every part of Grammar" (1762: vii).

In this stance, Lowth saw himself as an ally of Swift. Indeed, Lowth's generation turned elements of Swift's *Proposal* into a full-blown and multifaceted campaign, the effectiveness of which relied on the prescriptivists' assumption in their writings of the authority of experts.[14] In doing so, they violated the canons of "politeness", even as they continued to deploy the vocabulary of "politeness" in their standards for language. For "politeness" valorized the generalist and amateur as against the specialist and expert. As we have seen, it defined good language use as that of ladies and gentlemen and distinguished the "polite" from the language of scholars and pedants. "Politeness" was invented, in part, to confront an academicism, which the later eighteenth-century linguistic writers sought to revive. Of course, while some of the prescriptivists were teachers, many were not. Nonetheless, they cloaked themselves with the authority of expertise and of a proto-professional ethic of inquiry. Writings after 1750 should probably be seen as operating in a new atmosphere, responding to a new set of anxieties arising out of Britain's changing internal social and political situation and the larger national and imperial situation. All that needs to be stressed here is that, in the concluding decades of the eighteenth century and the early ones of the nineteenth, this new identity of the linguistic inquirer made war and ultimately defeated the woolly but amiable amateurism embodied in the language of "politeness".

Notes

1. Some general accounts of these developments are Leith (1983), Leonard (1929), and Strang (1970). At a higher level of abstraction is Haugen (1972).
2. Klein (1984–1985). Susan Wright's paper in this volume is also concerned with the contribution of this broader literature to the development of language and linguistic thought in the eighteenth century. The popularity of the idiom of "politeness" can be related to a number of historical developments, which I will point out below. One implicit argument here is that not only does an understanding of "politeness" help us understand the development of linguistic thinking in the eighteenth century but also that the conditions that promoted "politeness" were important matrixes for changes in linguistic practice and usage.
3. For the sociolinguistic viewpoint, see James Milroy's contribution to this volume. For the archaeological standpoint, Cohen (1977). Another important historical perspective is Barrell (1983).
4. Gordon (1966: 120–143), where the period 1660–1760 is identified as one in which dominated "a prose style close to the movement of speech, and ... the speech of gentlemen at that" (133). The "tendency both in poetry and in prose ... towards the conversational norm" is also discussed in Williamson (1951: 336–352).
5. On the propensity of the socially insecure to seek guidance about specifically linguistic matters, see Tieken-Boon van Ostade (1987 and 1990). In Frances Austin's contribution to this volume, William Clift provides an example of an individual whose social mobility encouraged an interest in conforming to linguistic prescriptions.
6. I am describing the early eighteenth-century situation here. By the later eighteenth century, polite prescriptivism had become a more confidently middle-class enterprise – in the manner suggested by Carey McIntosh's contribution to this volume. The sociology underlying the developments described here was characteristic of the 1660–1760 period, precisely bracketed by the two periods examined in McIntosh's paper.
7. This passage is from "Of Study and Conversation", which is not recognized as a genuine Saint-Evremond text by René Ternois in the standard edition. The passage is a clear echo of a passage by Gracian (which appears in translation in

The Courtiers Manual Oracle 1685: 84). The passage reappears in Boyer (1702: 225).
8. Pascal, Blaise, *Pensées* (1904): I, 35.
9. Among those who associated the metropolitan, the correct and the polite were: Price (1665: A3v); Jones (1701: 1); Rice (1765: 3, 3n, 308, 313n); Kenrick (1784: Advertisement and 1). On the earlier history, see Strang (1970).
10. See Thomas Frank's contribution to this volume.
11. The 1750–1775 period *is* used to launch periods in Strang (1970) and Burchfield (1985).
12. " 'Transcendental' standard" is the expression of Warburg (1962: 315–316). This view is available in: Milroy and Milroy (1985: 33–34); Nist (1966: 272–276); Bourcier (1981: 204–207); Bambas (1980; 162); and Baugh (1957: 306–355). An important exception is Barrell (1983).
13. Leonard (1929: 13–14 and Chapter 7, 137–163, titled "The Appeal to Usage and Its Practical Repudiation").
14. For the evolution of authoritative claims, see Susan Wright's paper in this volume.

References

A., D.
    1683 *The whole art of converse*. London.
Anderson, Howard – Philip B. Daghlian – Irvin Ehrenpreis (eds.)
    1966 *The familiar letter in the eighteenth century*. Lawrence: University of Kansas Press.
Bambas, Rudolph C.
    1980 *The English language*. Norman: University of Oklahoma Press.
Barrell, John
    1983 *English literature in history 1730–80*. New York: St. Martin's Press.
Baugh, Albert C.
    1957 *A history of the English language*. New York: Appleton-Century-Crofts.
Bellum Grammaticale
    1712 London.
Bond, Donald F. (ed.)
    1965 *The Spectator*. 5 vols. Oxford: Clarendon Press.
    1987 *The Tatler*. 3 vols. Oxford: Clarendon Press.
Borsay, Peter
    1989 *The English urban renaissance*. Oxford: Clarendon Press.
Boswell, James
    See   Pottle, Frederick A. (ed.).

Bourcier, Georges
    1981   *An introduction to the history of the English language.* (trans. Cecily Clark.) Cheltenham: Stanley Thornes.
Boyer, Abel
    1702   *The English Theophrastus.* London.
Brauer, George C.
    1959   *The education of a gentleman: Theories of gentlemanly education in England. 1660–1775.* New York: Bookman Associates.
Brett-James, Norman G.
    1935   *The growth of Stuart London.* (London & Middlesex Archaeological Society.) London: George Allen & Unwin.
Burchfield, Robert
    1985   *The English language.* Oxford: Oxford University Press.
Campbell, Archibald
    1767   *Lexiphanes.* London.
Cannon, John
    1984   *Aristocratic century.* Cambridge: Cambridge University Press.
Cannon, John (ed.)
    1981   *The Whig ascendancy.* New York: St. Martin's Press.
Clark, J. C. D.
    1985   *English society 1688–1832.* Cambridge: Cambridge University Press.
Cohen, Murray
    1977   *Sensible words: Linguistic practice in England 1640–1785.* Baltimore and London: The Johns Hopkins University Press.
Courtiers manual oracle, The
    1685   London.
Defoe, Daniel
    1697   *An essay upon projects.* London.
Dryden, John
    1912   *Dramatic essays by John Dryden.* London and New York: J.M. Dent & Sons, Ltd. and E.P. Dutton & Co.
Earle, Peter
    1989   *The making of the English middle class.* London: Methuen.
Felton, Henry
    1713   *A dissertation on reading the classics and forming a just style.* London.
Gordon, Ian
    1966   *The movement of English prose.* London: Longmans Green and Co., Ltd.
Haugen, E.
    1972   "Dialect, language, nation", in: J. B. Pride – Janet Holmes (eds.), 97–111.
Holmes, Geoffrey
    1981   "The achievement of stability: The social context of politics from the 1680s to the age of Walpole", in: John Cannon (ed.), 1–22.

Hughes, John
    1735   *Poems on several occasions. With some select essays in prose.* London.
Jones, Hugh
    1724   *An accidence to the English tongue.* London.
Jones, John
    1701   *Practical phonography.* London.
Joseph, John Earl
    1967   *Eloquence and power.* London: Frances Pinter.
Kenrick, William
    1784   *A rhetorical grammar of the English language.* London.
Klein, Lawrence
    1984–85   "The third Earl of Shaftesbury and the progress of politeness", *Eighteenth-Century Studies* 18: 186–214.
Leith, Dick
    1983   *A social history of English.* London: Routledge & Kegan Paul.
Leonard, Sterling A.
    1929   *The doctrine of correctness in English usage, 1700–1800.* (University of Wisconsin Studies in Language and Literature 15.) Madison: University of Wisconsin Press.
Lowth, Robert
    1762   *A short introduction to English grammar.* London.
Magendie, Maurice
    1925   *La politesse mondaine et les théories de l'honnêteté en France au XVIIe siècle de 1600 à 1660.* Paris: F. Alcan.
Malament, Barbara C. (ed.)
    1980   *After the reformation: Essays in honor of J. H. Hexter.* Philadelphia: University of Pennsylvania.
The management of the tongue
    1706   London.
Mason, J. E.
    1935   *Gentlefolk in the making: Studies in the history of English courtesy literature.* Philadelphia: University of Pennsylvania Press.
McKendrick, Neil – John Brewer – J. H. Plumb
    1985   *The birth of a consumer society.* Bloomington: Indiana University Press.
Milroy, James – Leslie Milroy
    1985   *Authority in language.* London: Routledge & Kegan Paul.
Nist, John
    1966   *A structural history of English.* New York: St. Martin's Press.
Pascal, Blaise
    1904   *Pensées.* Paris: Librairie Hachette.
Plumb, J. H.
    1967   *The growth of political stability in England, 1675–1725.* London: Macmillan.

Porter, Roy
    1982 *English society in the eighteenth century.* Harmondsworth: Penguin.
Pottle, Frederick A. (ed.)
    1950 *Boswell's London Journal, 1762–1763.* New York: McGraw-Hill.
Price, Owen
    1665 *The vocal organ.* Oxford.
Pride, J. B. – Janet Holmes (eds.)
    1972 *Sociolinguistics.* Harmondsworth: Penguin.
Prior, Matthew
    1709 *Poems on several occasions.* London.
Quirk, Randolph
    1962 *The use of English.* London: Longmans.
Redford, Bruce
    1986 *The converse of the pen: Acts of intimacy in the eighteenth-century familiar letter.* Chicago and London: The University of Chicago Press.
Rice, John
    1765 *An introduction to the art of reading with energy and propriety.* London.
Rogers, Nicholas
    1979 "Money, land and lineage: The big bourgeoisie of Hanoverian London", *Social History* 4: 437–454.
Roscommon, Wentworth Dillon, earl of
    1685 *An essay on translated verse.* (2nd edition.) London.
Rudé, George
    1971 *Hanoverian London, 1714–1808.* Berkeley and Los Angeles: University of California Press.
Saint-Evremond, Charles de Marguetel de Saint-Denis, seigneur de
    1692 *Miscellaneous essays.* London.
Shaftesbury, Anthony Ashley Cooper, the third earl of
    1714 *Characteristicks of men, manners, times, opinions.* (2nd edition.) 3 vols. London.
Sheridan, Thomas
    1798 *A course of lectures on elocution.* London.
Spectator
    See   Bond, Donald F. (ed.).
Staves, Susan
    1988 "Pope's refinement", *The eighteenth century* 29: 145–163.
Stone, Lawrence
    1980 "The residential development of the West End of London in the seventeenth century", in: Barbara C. Malament (ed.), 167–212.
Stow, John
    1733 *A survey of the cities of London and Westminster.* London.
Strang, Barbara M. H.
    1970 *A history of English.* London: Methuen.

Summerson, John
    1946 *Georgian London*. New York: Charles Scribner & Sons.
Swift, Jonathan
    1712 *Proposal for correcting, improving and ascertaining the English tongue*. London.
Tatler
    See   Bond, Donald F. (ed.).
Tieken-Boon van Ostade, Ingrid
    1987 *The auxiliary do in eighteenth-century English*. Dordrecht and Providence: Foris.
    1990 "Betsy Sheridan: Fettered by grammatical rules?", *Leuvense Bijdragen/ Leuven Contributions in Linguistics and Philology* 79: 79–90.
Vaumorière, Pierre d'Ortigue, sieur de
    1691 *The art of pleasing in conversation*. London.
Walsh, William
    1692 *Letters and poems*. London.
Warburg, Jeremy
    1962 "Notions of correctness", in: Randolph Quirk, 313–328.
Williamson, George
    1951 *The Senecan amble*. London: Faber and Faber.

Language standardization in eighteenth-century Scotland*

Thomas Frank

1. Introduction

The case of eighteenth-century Scotland, i.e., the speech of the urban middle classes of Scotland particularly during the second half of the century, can be looked upon as emblematic of a conscious attempt on the part of a community to bring its speech in line with that of a particular locality of the same linguistic area, namely the capital. This type of speech was held to be superior, "more polite", to use the contemporary terminology (see also Klein this volume; Wright this volume), than the local speech forms still widely used in the developing and emerging urban centres of Scotland, such as Edinburgh and Glasgow, and to some extent also Aberdeen. This is clearly not the place to trace the intricate history of the English language north of the border: we shall here be concerned with some, perhaps rather marginal aspects of its development during the eighteenth century. Nevertheless, these developments are of interest precisely because the rather restricted, but highly influential minority concerned made considerable efforts to adopt new speech models which would make its members indistinguishable from polite London and Court society of the time. To what extent these attempts were successful is of course another matter.

2. An age of renewal

Before pursuing these matters further it is probably appropriate to offer a brief sketch of the social-historical-cultural situation of eighteenth-century

---

* This may well be the last paper Thomas Frank wrote before his death during the summer following the Workshop. In editing the text of the paper, we are grateful to Peter Davidson for his comments and valuable suggestions.

Scotland. The seventeenth century in that country had been a particularly turbulent period of bitter internal religious and political strife. Though since 1603 England and Scotland were ruled by the same (Scottish) sovereign, the relations between the two countries were far from idyllic. The almost complete union of 1701 between the two countries – almost complete, because Scotland retained, among other things, its own church and a system of law – sought to iron out these differences, but there were large sections of Scottish society that did not accept the Union and wished to preserve a more marked separate Scottish identity in the political as well as in the cultural field. The concrete expression of this was of course Jacobitism, that is to say the political movement that worked for a Stuart restoration. The 1745 Jacobite rebellion was mainly an affair of the Highland clans and it is probably fair to say that it enjoyed only limited support in Edinburgh, where for a brief period Prince Charles Edward set up his court.

What is certainly true is that the so-called Scottish Enlightenment, which is associated particularly with Edinburgh but also with Glasgow and Aberdeen, was not firmly established until after the Scots had in the main abandoned the Jacobite cause, willingly or under coercion in the aftermath of the failure of the 1745 rebellion. Even so it must be said that some of the most significant achievements of the age, like David Hume's *A Treatise of Human Nature*, predate the rebellion. Be that as it may, it was only during the second half of the century that Edinburgh began to be hailed as the "Athens of the North", or, in the words of Tobias Smollett, as "a hotbed of genius". In this climate of intellectual renaissance the universities and the Church, as represented by the "moderates" within it, took a leading part. Many of the outstanding Scottish academics of the time, with the notable exception of Adam Smith, were also churchmen. The other profession that contributed significantly to this movement was the Law, though it should be pointed out that the second half of the eighteenth century was also a great age of Scottish science and engineering. Who can forget the magnificent contribution to British architecture of the Adam brothers, especially Robert, and what is probably still the most lasting attempt at urban renewal in Britain, that is, the Edinburgh New Town, which began to take shape towards the end of the century?

I have briefly listed these great achievements because they demonstrate that Scotland, and in particular Edinburgh, was no longer a remote corner of the British Empire, good for a sneering joke à la Samuel Johnson about the barbarous customs (and speech) of its inhabitants. In many ways Edinburgh was now at the centre of European culture, as witnessed by the enthusiastic welcome accorded to Hume during his stay in Paris in the years 1763–1766. Scotland had been firmly put on the European cultural map.

The exponents of this great cultural renaissance were moderate in matters concerning both the Kirk and politics. They supported the Hanoverian dynasty and all that this implied for British society; whereas in religion they did their best to tone down the asperities of the eighteenth-century heirs of the sternly Calvinist Covenanters. Progress was certainly welcomed in all fields, provided it was orderly and did not call into question the established social order: the eighteenth century in Scotland was an Age of Renewal, certainly not an Age of Revolution. In the light of all this, therefore, it is difficult to understand why many Scots tended to be ashamed of the language they spoke, and indeed of their origins, such as Boswell on his first meeting with Dr Johnson; nor, why they did their best to ape their southern cousins in accent as well as syntax.

3. A language contact situation

However, let us first return to the linguistic situation in Scotland. Most recent authors (McLure 1979; McArthur 1979; Aitken 1979; Aitken 1984a and Aitken 1984b) reject the idea of a neat diglossia situation for Scots, i.e., Lowland Scots – some form of Scotticised English. Instead, they prefer to think of the linguistic situation in present-day Scotland as representing a cline all the way from distinctly rural Scots (now very much in decline), via forms of standard English with an occasional sprinkling of typically Scottish lexis or syntax but with distinctly Scottish phonological features, all the way down to what is known as Scottish Standard English (SSE), and to forms of speech that are barely distinguishable from southern British received pronunciation. To this continuum, Aitken (1984a) adds a further refinement which he calls "educated Scottish Standard English". Scottish speakers therefore can draw on a wide range of styles, and Aitken (1979) talks of "style drifters", that is, speakers whose use of a particular variety of the language is fluctuating and essentially unpredictable, alongside more traditional "style switchers". All the authors cited here agree that modern Scots in any of the forms hypothesized is not a direct descendant of Middle Scots, which from the sixteenth century onwards was subject to the considerable anglicizing influences active during this period of great upheaval in Scottish history. These tendencies, which are attributed to literary and religious factors, led to a considerably diminished language loyalty, that is to older forms of Scots, so that the seventeenth century saw the rise of a mixed dialect (Aitken 1984b). McArthur (1979) discusses the question of what counts as the "same" and what counts as "different" language as being to a large extent dependent on political and historical factors, and a similar point is made by Aitken (1984b): had older Scots preserved its autonomy from southern English we would today have a situation similar to that of Swedish-Danish or Catalan-Castilian.

Be that as it may, there certainly seems to have been a language or rather dialect contact situation in the sixteenth and seventeenth centuries, with a strong substratum (on the concept of substratum within the framework of recent theories of language contact, see Thomason – Kaufman 1988) of original Scottish phonological features, but with an essentially southern grammar as well as, to a considerable extent, lexis. In fact Aitken (1979) points out that the internal history of Scots, that is, Scots syntax, is very similar to that of southern British, giving as examples the development of *do*-support and of the progressive form even though the use of this latter construction in Scotland is not entirely identical with that of southern British Standard (I would hazard the guess that a sentence like *the school is still being built* does not come naturally to a Scottish speaker, but I may well be wrong in this). On the other hand certain divergent features within the verb phrase (such as the presence of two modals in the same verb phrase, as in *the manager will can tell you*, cf. Brown – Millar 1980) indicate that the convergence in the history of syntax between Scots and southern British is by no means complete. We shall have more to say on lexis and phraseology when we come to examine James Beattie's pamphlet on Scotticisms (see section 5 below).

What is certain is that practically all Scotsmen preserved a distinctive Scottish pronunciation, although as we shall argue below members of the upper classes began to look upon this as a distinct disability and as a sign of inferiority. For this reason they made conscious efforts to "correct" their pronunciation and bring it in line with a form of speech closer to the London standard. Indeed, it would be difficult to conceive how the majority of the Scots in the eighteenth century could use anything but a Scottish accent – which I think it is fair to assume must have been pretty similar to present-day Scottish Standard English; probably, however, there was greater variety of local speech forms than today. Before the days of the mass media it would have been difficult for most Scots actually to hear an English "voice". Communications between Scotland and London were slow and at times hazardous, and though there were a number of Scotsmen, like Boswell or Lord Monboddo, who made a regular habit of visiting London, most members even of the Scottish Enlightenment remained firmly rooted in their home ground, especially since, as we have seen, the reset of the world began to take notice of Scotland and its culture. David Hume, who is said never to have "lost" his Scottish form of speech throughout his life, writes in a letter to Gilbert Elliot of Minto on 2 July 1757:

> Is it not strange that, at a time when we have lost our Princes, our Parliaments, our independent Government, even the Presence of our Chief Nobility, are unhappy, in our Accent & Pronunciation, speak a very corrupt Dialect of the Tongue which we make use of; is it not strange, I say, that, in these Circumstances, we shou'd really be the People most distinguish'd for Literature in Europe? (Greig 1932: 255)

It would obviously be senseless to rebut in any way Hume's contention that Scots was a "corrupt Dialect"; what is important is that it was perceived to be such and that therefore the Scottish upper classes, and especially the Edinburgh *literati*, made frantic efforts to rid themselves of the taint of provincialism.

McElroy (1969) records a number of episodes that purport to show that it was not merely a question of a reputedly harsh Scottish accent, but that there were cases of downright failure to communicate between Scots and Englishmen, though it is to be doubted that this was the main motivation for the fashion for acquiring a "polite" accent that swept Edinburgh society during the early sixties. In the summer of 1761 Thomas Sheridan visited Edinburgh and set out to teach the Scots "correct" English. Sheridan was of course a well-known teacher of elocution, though it is difficult to know at this stage whether his speech preserved traces of his Irish origin. His lectures were an enormous success and were attended by more than 300 gentlemen, "the most eminent in the country". In August 1761 the Select Society, an intellectual society gathering together the crème de la crème of the Edinburgh *intelligentsia*, set up a "Select Society for Promoting the Reading and Speaking of the English Language in Scotland", stating in an advertisement in the *Scots Magazine* that the Scots were acutely aware in their intercourse with the English of the "disadvantage under which they labour, from their imperfect knowledge of the English tongue, and the impropriety with which they speak it". They proposed to set up a school and engage teachers to instruct both adults and children in the correct use of the language. Among the directors of the Society were some of the most eminent Scotsmen of the time, but nothing came of these early enthusiasms, and the Society achieved no tangible results: by 1764 it had petered out.

What is interesting about this episode is the motivation behind it, the frantic desire of the Edinburgh establishment, in spite of its awareness of the superiority of Scotland in many fields over the English, to ape fashionable London society in its forms of speech, convinced as it was that this was the only valid kind of English. Even in the eyes of the anglicized Edinburgh *literati* Scotland continued to be a nation separate from the English (if anything they looked upon themselves as North Britons), with its own proud traditions, history and institutions (like the Kirk), and with the unquestionable intellectual eminence it had achieved vis-à-vis the rest of Europe. Yet none of this justified a distinctly *Scottish* form of speech: Scots was a mere dialect and a pretty rough one at that, unworthy of being spoken by men of culture. When some years later Burns began to publish his poems in Scots, this was considered to be fine in so far as he was just a simple ploughman, and he was soon turned into one of the myths of Scottishness, together with a phoney tartan and bagpipe culture – phoney, of course, because they are expressions of the culture of the Highlands and have nothing to do with Lowland Scots, the language in which Burns wrote. All this has to do with a view of a "romantic" Scotland that developed as the influence of the Scottish Enlightenment gradually began to wane. However, fascinating though all this is, it is a subject well beyond our brief in the present paper, so that it is time to return to more strictly linguistic matters.

4. Scotticisms as sociolinguistic markers

It is perhaps worth pointing out that most sociolinguistic varieties are characterized by a limited number of typical features which have a very strong indexical value. Even the presence of only two or three such features is enough to "classify" a speaker in a sociolinguistic sense. For example, the consistent use of forms like *he ain't, you was* or *they gone* is enough to identify the speaker concerned as "uneducated, non-standard", whether or not these features are accompanied by a particular type of pronunciation, as in fact they usually are. The same applies undoubtedly to "Scotticisms". Obviously, the greater the number of such features in the speech of a particular individual, the more specifically Scots his or her speech will be along a cline that goes all the way from traditional rural Scots to "educated Scottish Standard English". Even so, a sprinkling of them is usually sufficient to identify the speaker as a Scot. These remarks should be borne in mind when considering to what degree dialect levelling or standardization, in this case anglicization, has taken place.

5. Beattie's list of Scotticisms

In 1779 James Beattie published, anonymously, *A list of Two Hundred Scotticisms*. This was reissued in Edinburgh (the original edition appeared in Aberdeen) in 1787 in a greatly enlarged and more systematic form under the title of *Scoticisms [sic], Arranged in Alphabetical Order, Designed to Correct Improprieties of Speech and Writing*; in 1797 another edition was published, likewise in Edinburgh. The 1797 edition is preceded by a lecture on elocution by Hugh Blair, in which the author recommends such things as clear and careful enunciation, and correct voice modulation. On the face of it, the lecture seems to be directed mainly at preachers, advocates and such others as have occasion to speak in public. From our point of view, what is more interesting is the list of Scotticisms drawn up by Beattie, their nature and classification, and it is to these that the remainder of this article will be devoted.

The words and expressions stigmatized as Scotticisms can roughly be divided into the following categories:

a. lexical items considered as Scots for which other (English) lexical items are suggested. English in this context is to be understood as a form typical of the southern standard;
b. lexical items with the same meaning which exist in variant forms in Scots and in English;
c. lexical items which are used ("misused") in a different sense in Scots and in English;
d. variants in grammatical usage.

According to David Daiches (in a public lecture; I have not come across this or a similar statement in any of his published writings) most of these Scotticisms have become part of the standard language. While "most" is obviously an exaggeration, this is certainly true of a number of the items and expressions listed by Beattie. What is perhaps chiefly remarkable about his long list is that none of his Scotticisms are of the "wee bairn" type. Many of them represent either more latinate forms than the standard ones, or a meaning closer to the Latin than is current in English. In other cases the Scotticisms are simply technical terms in Scottish jurisprudence, which, as is well known, is in many ways closer to Roman Law than to English Common Law. In all these cases we are dealing with a learned and not with a popular form of Scots. In other cases the forms cited are part of the general non-standard language of the period and are in no sense peculiarly Scots, as Beattie himself recognizes. Perhaps the most typically Scots items are the grammatical variants (uses of adverbs and conjunctions, verb forms and phraseology in general). Let us now look at some of the items in Beattie's list following the classification suggested above. (The equals sign, =, means "glossed as".)

a. *anent* = 'concerning': this is widely recognized as being a typical Scottish usage.
corn the horses = 'feed ... '.
to ken = 'to know': this is clearly a generally northern rather than a peculiarly Scottish form.
   Among typically learned forms we find:

to abort = 'to miscarry',
to adduce evidence = 'to bring ... ',
to detract used like Latin *detrahere* = 'to subtract from',
dure = 'hard, difficult',
to evite = 'to shun, to avoid',
to incarcerate = 'to imprison'.

Somewhat curiously, *to liberate* is given as a Scotticism for 'to set at liberty'.
   Other clearly latinate forms include: *to subsist* in the sense of 'to support', e.g., *her son subsists her*, and *vocable* = 'word, term'.
   Among the terms that have become part of the standard language (though it is not certain whether they ever really were Scotticisms in the true sense) we find *to militate against, to narrate, onerous* and *to succumb*.

b. Among variant Scottish forms of the same word we might mention: *baxter, brewster, dyster, webster* for *baker, brewer, dyer, weaver*. Note that at least two of these have become common surnames.
   Among the many other items listed I choose the following:

dubiety = 'doubt',
debitor = 'debtor',
timeous = 'timely',
wrongeous = 'wrongful'.

Of particular interest is the backformation *greed* (< OE *grædig*), the gloss being 'greediness'. The *Oxford English Dictionary* confirms that the original backformation was of Scottish origin and the *Scottish National Dictionary* gives it as part of general English (i.e., a standard form) from the nineteenth century onwards.
   The verb *roves* in *he roves in a fever* is given as 'roam, wander'. The Oxford English Dictionary gives this as Scottish dialect (first quotation 1720),

as does the *Scottish National Dictionary*. It would appear to derive from a rare Old Norse form *räfa* meaning 'to wander' and has nothing to do with *to rave*, which derives from Old French and first appears in Chaucer.

c. This group comprises a large number of items and is something of a hotchpotch of variant expressions ("misuses") in eighteenth-century Scots. The impression is that in many cases there is a good deal of pedantry about the so-called Scots expressions or words stigmatized. Thus, for example, *altogether about fifty pound* is glossed as 'in all', since *altogether* is given as 'completely', and *funeral* is preferred to *burial*, which is said to indicate *the act of burying*. Whereas *dull*, meaning 'deaf', *coarse* applied to the weather and *foot of the table* (to which is preferred the non-metaphorical *lower end*) may be peculiarly Scottish usages, it is difficult to understand the author's objection to *close* rather than *shut the door*. *Mind* in the sense of 'remember' will generally be recognized as typically Scots and so will *water* in the sense of 'river' (the Water of Dee). One would probably hesitate to classify *roar* = 'cry' of a baby or *stay* = 'live, lodge' as distinctly Scots, and in some cases the purportedly Scots expression is simply an older usage which Standard English has largely abandoned, as for example *meat* for *food* in general. My impression is that where Beattie is not giving way to personal idiosyncracies, he is out to make the language of the readers of his booklet more genteel and polite according to what he feels are the accepted canons of his age, and that genuine Scotticisms really have very little to do with this.

d. The last of the categories distinguished above, however, does seem to me to register genuine Scottish variants, chiefly in the use of adverbs and conjunctions. Some examples are:

> *as* = 'than': *more as that, I would rather go as stay*,
> *out* = 'off': *cut out your hair*,
> *that* = 'as, because': *I am the more impatient of pain, that I have long enjoyed good health*,
> *without* = 'unless': *I will not go without I am paid*.

The use of *whenever* in the sense of 'when, as soon as' (*I rose whenever I heard the clock strike eight*) will I think be generally recognized as a peculiarly Scottish expression.

As regards verbs we may note for certain strong verb forms which still had variant forms during the earlier part of the eighteenth century (see Lass this volume) that some of these have since become decidedly non-standard, such as *drunk* and *run* as past tense forms (see Cheshire this volume) or *broke* as a past participle. Beattie decidedly prefers the verbal forms that have since become standard. He recognizes that forms like *seed* and *you was* are really what he calls "vulgar English" and are common in England as well as in Scotland. From this we may deduce that part of the purpose of the pamphlet was to eliminate not only genuine Scots forms, of which, as I think I have shown, there are not really a great many, but also to impose certain standard usages preferred by polite London society. In this his strictures are not very different from those of normative grammarians like Lowth (1762 and Leonard 1929). In other cases some older English verbal constructions like *I would have you to know* are condemned as incorrect, and not unexpectedly the author animadverts on the absence of *shall* in Scots, or, as he puts it, "the Scots are more apt to misapply *will* than *shall*, especially in the first persons singular and plural." [Beattie 1797]

An insight that I have certainly found borne out by my reading of eighteenth-century Scottish writers is the concordance of impersonal *one* with the possessive *his*. One example is from Blair: "*when one arrives at the end of such a puzzled sentence, he is surprised*"; other examples might be cited from William Leechman, Professor of Divinity at the University of Glasgow, and other Scottish writers. Though the *Oxford English Dictionary* says that "*his, him, himself* were formerly usual, and are still sometimes used" with *one* (s.v. *one*) there is no indication that this does appear to be a genuine Scottish usage at least in the eighteenth century. Whether or not the analogous present-day American usage is due to Scottish influence is of course difficult to say.

6. Conclusion

To conclude our observations on Beattie's pamphlet: it is certainly true that its contents form part of the general tendency to bring Scottish writing in line with standard southern usage, to make it more polite and genteel. The question is, however, to what extent his long list of Scotticisms can all be regarded as genuine examples of Scottish speech. If anything, they represent certain traces of earlier Scottish forms in educated Scottish writing, and are thus a testimony to the desire of members of the Scottish Enlightenment proudly to preserve their separate identity in everything but their speech, in which they cravenly sought to imitate their "betters" south of the border.

References

Aitken, Adam J.
    1979   "Scottish speech: A historical view with special reference to the standard English of Scotland", in: A. J. Aitken – Tom McArthur (eds.), 85–118.
    1984a   "Scottish accents and dialects", in: Peter Trudgill (ed.), 94–114.
    1984b   "Scots and English in Scotland", in: Peter Trudgill (ed.), 517–532.

Aitken, Adam – Tom McArthur (eds.)
    1979   *Languages of Scotland*. Edinburgh: Chambers.

Beattie, James
    1779   *A list of two hundred Scotticisms*. Aberdeen.
    [1787, 1797]   [Reprinted as: *Scoticisms, arranged in alphabetical order, designed to correct improprieties of speech and writing*. Edinburgh.]

Brown, E. Keith – Martin Millar
    1980   "Auxiliary verbs in Edinburgh speech", *Transactions of the Philological Society*, 81–133.

Greig, J.Y.T. (ed.)
    1932   *Letters of David Hume*. 2 Vols. Oxford: Clarendon Press.

Hume, David
    See Greig, J.Y.T. (ed.).

Leonard, Sterling A.
    1929   *The doctrine of correctness in English usage 1700–1800*. Madison: University of Wisconsin.

Lowth, Robert
    1762   *A short introduction to English grammar*. London.
    [1967]   [Reprinted in: Alston, R.C. (ed.), *English Linguistics 1500–1800* 18. Menston: Scholar Press.]

McArthur, Tom
    1979   "The status of English in and furth of Scotland", in: A. J. Aitken – Tom McArthur (eds.), 50–67.

McElroy, Davis
    1969   Scotland's age of improvement. [Unpublished Ph.D. dissertation, University of Edinburgh.]

McLure, Derrick
    1979   "Scots: its range and uses", in: A.J. Aitken – Tom McArthur (eds.), 26–48.

The Oxford English Dictionary
    1989   Prepared by J.A. Simpson and E.S.C. Weiner. Oxford: Clarendon Press.

The Scottish National Dictionary
    1930–1976   Edited by William Grant – David D. Murison. 10 vols. Edinburgh: The Scottish National Dictionary Association.

Thomason, Sarah Grey – Terrence Kaufman
    1988   *Language contact. Creolization and genetic linguistics.* Berkeley: University of California Press.
Trudgill, Peter (ed.)
    1984   *Language in the British isles.* Cambridge: Cambridge University Press.

Prestige norms in stage plays, 1600–1800

Carey McIntosh

An analysis of thirty-seven plays published in the periods 1600–1630 and 1770–1800 uncovers five groups of speakers for whom there is a strong correlation between language and social class. Certainly one and possibly three of these groups illustrate a change in (or displacement of) prestige norms during these two centuries.

The groups discussed here are not defined primarily in socio-economic terms. Although Britain had begun to develop a wage economy in 1600, neither income nor education played as dominant a role in the determination of social class as they do now – the world in which these stage plays were performed was still feudal in many respects, and people were differentiated as much by "station" as by wealth. Richard H. Tawney puts it nicely for the earlier period:

> The England of Shakespeare and Bacon was still largely medieval in its economic organization and social outlook, more interested in maintaining customary standards of consumption than in accumulating capital for future production, with an aristocracy contemptuous of the economic virtues, a peasantry farming for subsistence amid the organized confusion of the open-field village, and a small, if growing, body of jealously conservative craftsmen (1926).

Let me sketch out the makeup of these five groups:

1. Characters representing the lowest strata of society, both in 1600 and in 1800, are uneducated rustics and working-class townsfolk; they speak more or less the same informal, colloquial, sometimes dialectal English in the eighteenth century as they did in the seventeenth, an English studded with proverbs, catchphrases, slang, vulgar (not fashionable) swearwords, and physical (not abstract) nouns.
2. In 1600 the highest social ranks – kings and heroes – speak in poetry or in poetic prose, stately and complex, given to complex metaphor and hyperbole.
3. By 1800 a new cultural elite has emerged, "truly polite" not heroic. Their language, usually prose not poetry, is courtly-genteel and periphrastic,

abstract not concrete; it tends to long sentences (often periodic), balanced structures, antithesis.
4. Country squires of the late eighteenth century are neither truly polite nor truly rustic; their speech is self-consciously non-urban and informal, sometimes archaic.
5. The main purpose of the fifth group, "language fops" (e.g., Osric in *Hamlet*), is to satirize linguistic affectation or ignorance; they embody, therefore, what authors and audiences considered to be violations of the rules that ought to govern relations between language and social class.

Texts of plays have special assets as a corpus for sociolinguistic research, but they have also liabilities. The language that the dramatis personae speak has been tidied up and edited for publication in print. It is subject at all times to literary conventions and constraints. No matter how keen a playwright's ear for the way other people talk, his or her own idiolect is sure to influence the final shape of locutions ascribed to stage characters. However, variation owing solely to the personal styles of authors may be canceled out in a broad sample, and the language of successful plays must always include utterances that a great many people, audiences as well as authors, feel are appropriate for those speakers. Plays have also the advantage that they depend on and therefore preserve the interactional dimensions of language; dramatic dialogue responds to strategies of interpersonal relations of many kinds (Brown – Gilman 1989).

My corpus is small; even so, what it yields as data is too voluminous to permit anything but select quotation here. As in all inductive procedures, the sampling will certainly influence the results. I settled on thirty-seven plays by eighteen authors, all well known in their time and popular. I chose more comedies than tragedies because the settings of tragedies were often self-consciously remote from Jacobean or Georgian England. It is not easy to say why some plays in my sample fail to register the sociolinguistic differences I am interested in here. Personal style, the dynamics of actual performance, and the tides of taste must have played a role. For example, Ben Jonson's gritty brilliance illuminates almost every speech in *Epicoene* (1610) and *Bartholomew Fair* (1614); his noblemen and common thieves sometimes sound very similar. At the same time, they sound different from the noblemen and thieves of other writers of the period (see Barish 1960). In the 1780s and 1790s, the vogue for "refinement" and the increasing popularity of "sentimental" drama seem to have drastically reduced the number of lower-class characters permitted on stage.

The five sociolinguistic groupings that I discern in my sample are not consistent – it is not the case, for example, that every working-class speaker in all these plays uses "lower-class" language as I describe it. The categories that these five groups represent must be defined as we define so many categories for daily rough-and-tumble use, on the basis of "new, variable, contradictory, and endemically insufficient data" (Schauber – Spolsky 1986: 7). Other groupings are of course possible: some that represent a profession (lawyer), or a social-ethical category (rake, virtuous wife), or a region (Welshman). The five groups identified above, however, are the only ones I encountered where broad correlations between language and social class are clear.

The distinctive style of rustics, menial servants, shopkeepers, uneducated artisans, laborers, and tramps does not change significantly from 1600 to 1800 (though, of course, it evolves as the language itself evolves). Some of these people speak what seems to have been intended as a version of a regional dialect; some use archaisms which may have been regional at an earlier date. Their conversation is generally informal, "incorrect", unpolished, unbookish, and obviously colloquial (Salmon 1967). Some of them are identified as lower-class by their names: Sisly Milk-pail, Roger Brickbat, Doiley, Coachman, Carter. They and their language are "literary" in the sense that as character types they have held an established position in stage comedies almost since the first comedy was staged. Nevertheless, their speech, lack of education, and social class are their only consistent traits: in all other respects they vary as much and as unpredictably as people can – some are urban, some rural; some are smart, some dumb; some good, some bad; most are poor but some are rich.

Major features of lower-class language in these plays include:

(1) Dialectal variants on Standard English:
"Chill not let go, zir, without vurther cagion ... And chud ha' bin zwagger'd out of my life, 'twould not ha' bin zo long as 'tis by a vortnight ... keep out, che vor' ye, or Ice try ... " (Shakespeare 1607)
"I loves to hear him sing, bekeays he never gives us nothing that's low ... bauld as a lion ... no pleace of mine ... for sartain" (Goldsmith 1773)
"I can't say as how I know she" (Cowley 1782) (See Tieken, this volume)
"A well enough, when a's pleased – tho' I canno' say as I do like him much, for a measter" (Holcroft 1787).
My sample from the early period does not include dialectal variants other than this well-known one from *Lear*. Perhaps the popularity of stage Irishmen and other comic provincials in the 1770s explains the comparative commonness of these non-standard forms in the late eighteenth century.

(2) Slang: *pishery-pashery, blubbered, you that speake bandog and bedlam* (Dekker 1600); *you were not resolv'd to play the jacks, if any of them all blow wind in the tail on him, I'll be hanged* (Beaumont – Fletcher 1613); *smoke* ('discover'), *cull* ('victim'), *I fancy he'll stand it, Crow, and advance the crop for the younker* (the three preceding locutions are explicitly presented as thieves' cant, in Kelly 1775); *stands gaping like mum-chance, don't think to come over me with your flim-flams* (Cowley 1782).

(3) Proverbs and catch-phrases: *past the cure of bay salt and gross pepper* (Beaumont – Fletcher 1609); *Let him stay at home and sing for his supper, I'll be hanged for a halfpenny, and if there be any tricks abrewing – let 'em brew and bake too, husband, a God's name* (Beaumont – Fletcher 1613); *much noise to little purpose, There have worse faces looked out of black bags, man* (Ford – Rowley – Dekker 1621); *I may be allowed to rear a chicken of my own hatching, fit only to bribe electors in a borough* (Cumberland 1771); *you must mind your P's and Q's with him, I can tell you* (Cowley 1779); *secret as a coach-horse, I thought you wa'n't rich enough to be so nice!* (Sheridan 1775); *I wasn't born in a Wood to be scar'd by an Owl* (Cowley 1782).

(4) Interjections: *by my stirrop, Mary gup, mary foh* (Dekker 1600); *Beshrew me, I'm a thief if, by Gad* (Beaumont – Fletcher 1613); *O gemini! O lud! Odd's life! Odd rabbit it! by the Mass! Oons!* (Sheridan 1775); *Indeed and indeed, mercy on me* (Cumberland 1783); *Ecod, Lack-a-daisy* (Goldsmith 1773); *for the matter-o'that, elseways, hang it, ifags!* (Cowley 1782).

(5) Low, physical, vulgar words: *If you had but look'd big, and spit at him, as you'ld thrust a cork into a hogshead, wether tods, prig* (Shakespeare 1611); *bread, beer, and beef, yeoman's fare; we have no kickshaws: full dishes, whole bellyfulls* (Ford – Rowley – Dekker 1621); *mealy mouth, firking* ('frisking'), *sowce wife, that gapes to be fed with cheese curdes, cramme thy slops with French crownes* (Dekker 1600); *netting-box, all in a breath* (Cumberland 1783); *sweetheart, gaping, suitoring, flim-flams* (Cowley 1782). Notice how few examples of "vulgar" words I found in the later period: presumably the general trend toward refinement made these words unacceptable on stage; thus, *blanket, knife*, and *dun* were considered too "low" for tragedy by Samuel Johnson in 1752.

(6) Archaisms are often a sign of lower-class status in the late eighteenth century, and they are often also solecisms, words or expressions that had been condemned by the prescriptive grammarians (e.g., Lowth 1762, Campbell 1776: see Platt 1926, and McIntosh 1986: ch. 1): *Sure, you ben't sending them to your father's as an inn, be you?* (Goldsmith 1773); *a mort of fine things, I knows the Groom* (Cowley 1782); *we are not at home to nobody, nor no pleasure whatsoever, What! shall I go for to give the labour of thirty*

years to a young Jackanapes? (Cowley 1779). Such expressions continued to be used by middle- and upper-class writers less in touch with literary and social doctrines of correctness and politeness than Goldsmith or Cowley (see Matthews 1937).

Pompous, conservative, huff-and-puff country squires are so common in eighteenth-century drama that it is tempting to dismiss them merely as a literary type; but a large number of the gentry at this period were in fact provincial, ignorant, and conservative: the Stones call them "parish gentry", to distinguish them from the wealthier elite who, having traveled frequently to London and the Continent, were cosmopolitan and educated enough to qualify for ambassadorial and cabinet status (Stone – Stone 1984). Their speech is informal, eccentric, and old-fashioned, like their politics: *lack-aday, old fogrums, all their brains a gadding* (Cumberland 1783); *all agog, the wench, what the devil, popping about, hang the signing and sealing, and yet I can't say that neither* (Cowley 1782); *add twenty to twenty and make money of that, many a long year* (Goldsmith 1773).

Language fops are characters who use what they take to be fashionable locutions in imitation of speakers from a higher social class. In Shakespeare's time they are mainly courtiers; in the late eighteenth century they are middle-class social climbers. Thus the language of Osric in *Hamlet* and Archidamus in *The Winter's Tale* abounds in coinages, periphrasis, self-conscious and improbable metaphor, hyperbole: *of very soft society, the card or calendar of gentry, carriages ... responsive to the hilts*; *that your senses (unintelligent of our insufficiency) may, though they cannot praise us, as little accuse us, royally attorney'd* (Shakespeare 1603, 1611).

By 1750 the court had lost social prestige and ceased to be of much concern to playwrights, while an increasingly wealthy and numerous middle class was pushing into prominence and clamoring for attention. The famous Mrs Malaprop, who runs amok through the lexicon in Sheridan's *The Rivals* (1775), hasn't the ghost of a connection with the court; she is the sister of a country squire; she is a snob with a passion for pseudo-erudite words. She aspires to be *the very Pine-apple* [i.e., 'pinnacle'] *of politeness*. What touches her vanity most is *an aspersion upon my parts of speech* [punning on the older meaning of *parts*, 'abilities']. She prides herself on *the use of my oracular* ['vernacular'] *tongue, and a nice derangement* ['arrangement'] *of epitaphs!* ['epithets'?!] It is noteworthy that Shakespeare assigned malapropisms only to lower-class characters, such as the irrepressible, slatternly tavernkeeper Mrs Quickly, not to middle-class types; for him, malapropisms count more as comic blunders or as pedantry than as social climbing (Schlauch 1965).

Quite often in 1615, royalty, upper aristocracy, and heroes speak the same. The one consistent correlation between high social class and language in this period derives more from political than from social values. We are assured that in the early seventeenth century a certain "divinity [did] hedge a king" (see Tillyard 1943). In John Ford's history play of 1634, *Perkin Warbeck*, the only credentials an imposter to the throne thinks fit to present are his royal, superlatively dignified way of talking, and the King of Scotland is won over to him by style alone, by the imposter's "royal" manner of speech: "He must be more than subject who can utter / The language of a king" (Ford 1634).

In the "high" style appropriate to Renaissance kings and heroes "eloquence was supplied by rhetoric and richness by lexical invention" (Blake 1983: 18). "Latinate vocabulary is used for the high style and it would be inappropriate for it to occur in low style scenes" (1983: 43). Other features of the most prestigious language in 1600 include the "royal *we*," stately iambic rhythms (perhaps influenced by Marlowe's "mighty line" [Waith 1962]), long, complicated sentences, and patterns of metaphor associated with ambition, pride, the four elements (especially earth, personified and identified with England), eagles, lions, gold, jewels, the blood (and health generally) of a nation, astronomical bodies. "This very ground thou goest on," says Philaster, true heir to the throne, "shall gape and swallow / Thee and thy nation like a hungry grave" (Beaumont – Fletcher 1609). The words and looks of a king, says another heir to the throne, "Are like the flashes and the bolts of Jove; / His deeds inimitable, like the sea" (Chapman 1607).

Since royal/heroic language is an emblem as much of political as of social status, it is a public medium; in private its speakers often lapse into less strenuous styles. Erich Auerbach has shown how effective these lapses may be in service of realism, literary realism grounded in the ordinary physical circumstances of everyday life. So Shakespeare's Prince Henry, who will shortly be Henry V of England, confesses ruefully (and playfully) that he is "exceeding weary" and would welcome "small beer" as eagerly as would the humblest of soldiers (Auerbach 1946). Literary tides were running in another direction, however, pulled by "decorum" and the "separation of styles" that required kings and heroes to speak always and only like kings and heroes, farmers like farmers, and so on. Decorum is intimately entwined with genre. It decrees that the dignity of tragic actions must not be diluted by vulgar characters or speech. We can be confident that authors and audiences were more sensitive to relations between a character's social class and the way he or she spoke on stage after c. 1650 because of the literary-critical doctrines of decorum that England was assimilating from France and Italy (Rapin 1674; Kranidas 1965). In England before 1650, comparatively few playwrights (see

Jonson 1620) paid real attention to this implication of the general principle of decorum.

Yet another literary value that complicates the relationship of language to social class is "wit". At least from the end of the sixteenth century till the rise of sentimentalism in the eighteenth, it was fashionable to be witty; and though fashions in wit were various (Euphuistic wit gave way to Metaphysical, which in turn gave way to the libertine wit of the Restoration), all of them encouraged bold experiments in language, unconventional metaphors, neologisms, paradox, pun, and what Auerbach would call "creatural" allusions to human physicality. Accordingly, a witty nobleman or hero of 1600 can sometimes be as scurrilous and vulgar as a plowman or a common criminal.

For example, a certain courtier speaks dignified blank verse to his friend the duke in Scene 1 of *The honest whore*, but as soon as the duke has departed from the stage he descends to slangy, cynical prose: " 'Sblood, the jest were now, if having ta'en some knocks o' th' pate already, he should get loose again, and, like a mad ox, toss my new black cloaks into the kennel" (Dekker 1604). The hero of another comedy, though not a courtier, is manifestly more genteel and better educated than his companions; but since he is also a wit (and his name is Witt-good) his usual speech is a ranting, vivid, violent jargon full of colloquialisms and verbal extravagances:

> He is either swallowed in the quick-sands of Law-quillits ['quibbles'], or splits upon the Piles of a Praemunire; yet these old Foxe-braind – and oxe-browde Uncles, have still defences for their Avarice. ... Let mee see, Horses now, a bottes on em; Stay, I have acquaintance with a madde Hoste, never yet Bawde to thee, I have rinzde the whoresons gums in Mull-sack many a time and often ... (Middleton 1608)

Hamlet himself, though far more subtle and thoughtful than Witt-good, expresses his "wit", his mind, with a grim, introspective suppleness of language that ignores the separation of styles.

The royal/heroic mode of speaking is almost extinct in 1785: not quite; it lingers on in poetic drama, but it is derivative, pallid, and anachronistic. Poetic drama of the late eighteenth century is ordinarily set in the romantic past, in 'days of old', and its heroes are (for example) a fifteenth-century king or a fourteenth-century Earl of Northumberland. One late eighteenth-century tragic character borrows clumsily from Shakespeare to proclaim that "a monarch, tow'ring in royal strength, like Jove's proud eagle, should boast such bold and lofty flights of spirit – that while he soars, the o'er strained strings of vision shall crack with gazing" (Colman 1790; compare *Macbeth*, II, iv).

"Truly Polite" prose of the late eighteenth century does not take the place of the royal/heroic mode, but it shoulders it out of the way, overshadows it in importance. It owes its vitality as much to the contrast it makes with vulgar or rustic speech, as to its identification with a particular social class. We may speculate that as literary culture evolved, as the genres of stage plays changed (see Hume 1981), audiences lost interest in that contrast, and playwrights stopped cultivating this particular form of linguistic gentility. That is, when melodrama comes into prominence in the 1790s, pathos upstages tragedy and comedy alike; characters in these later plays speak almost all the same.

The metamorphosis of Kate Hardcastle in *She stoops to conquer* (Goldsmith 1773) may serve as a paradigm of the contrast between lower-class language and "Truly Polite", since Kate's disguise as a servant girl includes her manner of talking, and since her gradual shedding of that disguise and her resumption of an upper-class role is engineered not only as a change of attitudes but of language also. (The same process occurs in Hannah Cowley's *The belle's stratagem* of 1782, an obvious and highly competent imitation of Goldsmith's masterpiece.) Kate wishes to be mistaken for a bar-maid in Act III, though not for a vulgar slut of bar-maid; her language is simple and unrefined:

> O la, Sir, you'll make one ashamed. . . .
> No, Sir, we have been out of that these ten days. . . . Nectar! nectar! That's a liquor there's no call for in these parts. French, I suppose. We keep no French wines here, Sir.
> You did not treat [her] . . . in this obstropalous manner, I'll warrant me . . .

In Act IV, Kate wishes to be mistaken for a poor but honest relation of the Hardcastles, and her speech is noticeably more polished than in Act III: "I hope, Sir, I have done nothing to disoblige you. I should be sorry to affront any gentleman who has been so polite, and said so many civil things to me." By Act V, the hero is in love with her and she can resume the speech proper to her rank in society; and as spokesperson for the most sophisticated gentility in the play, her language is super-polite, almost courtly:

> I must remain contented with the slight approbation of imputed merit; I must have only the mockery of your addresses, while all your serious aims are fixed on fortune.
> Do you think I would take the mean advantage of a transient passion, to load you with confusion? Do you think I could ever relish that happiness which was acquired by lessening yours?

Kate's manner of talking here associates her with the other wellborn young lovers in the play, Marlowe, Hastings, and Miss Neville. These four are more cosmopolitan and refined than anyone else on stage. I take them as a model of gentility, not only for this drama but for the period.

The "Truly Polite" language that identifies very refined characters in late eighteenth-century drama has the following characteristics:

(1) Courtly-genteel: it inherits some of the verbal mannerisms of courtly negotiations between a (feudal) lord and his vassal; the courtier's *duty* and *obligation* are to acquire *merit* by doing *services* to his lord, in return for which he receives *honor* and *favors* (see McIntosh 1986: ch. 2). Note Kate's reference to "merit" above, echoed by Marlowe twice later in the scene. Hastings claims that "our passions were first founded in duty". Kate tells her father that "your kindness is such, that my duty as yet has been an inclination".

(2) Balance and antitheses: Note the self-conscious antitheses of Kate's language above. When she is giving Marlowe a lesson in courtship and elegant compliment in Act II, she tells him that "An observer, like you, upon life, were, I fear, disagreeably employed, since you must have had much more to censure than to approve" – and Marlowe stammers out another antithesis in reply: "The folly of most people is rather an object of mirth than uneasiness." Similarly, in Cumberland (1771): "By Heav'n my soul is conquer'd with your virtues more than my eyes are ravish'd with your beauty."

(3) Compliments. An ability to pay compliments, that is, to praise someone in what seem to us extravagant terms, was part of the standard equipment of politeness in the eighteenth century. Courtesy books taught this skill (and courtly-genteel terminology as well, e.g. *Cupids Schoole: Wherein young-men and maids may learne divers sorts of new, witty, and amorous com-plements* (1632). In 1752 Jean-Jacques Rousseau refused a pension so as not to have to go to court and stumble over a compliment to the king (*Confessions* 1781: 354). Thus Charlotte in *The West Indian*: "O Charles, Charles, rich in every merit and accomplishment, whom may you not aspire to? And why think you so unworthily of our sex, as to conclude there is not one to be found with sense to discern your virtue, and generosity to reward it?" (Cumberland 1771). And thus Jack Absolute in *The rivals* (Sheridan 1775): "Sir, your kindness overpowers me – such generosity makes the gratitude of reason more lively than the sensations even of filial affection."

(4) Obvious rhetoric. The politest prose of this period is rhetorical in an obvious way: it uses rhetorical questions, exclamations, and imperatives far more often than ordinary conversation does. Repeated words, especially at the beginnings and ends of successive clauses (anaphora, epistrophe, anadiplosis),

are also common. "Oh, may this soft, this sensitive alarm be happy, be auspicious! Doubt not, deliberate not, delay not" (Cumberland 1771).

(5) A nominalized syntax: ample use of the verbs *to be* and *to have*; the passive voice; deverbal nouns rather than finite verbs; "light" verbs plus deverbal nouns rather than finite verbs ("make an attempt" rather than "try"); impersonal constructions (see McIntosh 1992: 720–735).

(6) Polysyllabic and "literary" vocabulary. Thus Kate Hardcastle in her genteel role: *approbation, imputed, transient. Levity, sensibility, ardour* (Holcroft 1787); *intimidate, bosom, atonement, perilous* (Colman 1790).

(7) Numerous abstractions and comparatively few concrete, humble, physical nouns. "The peculiarity of your father's temper, joined to my want of fortune, made it necessary for me to keep our engagements inviolably secret; there is no merit, therefore, either in my prudence, or in my labouring assiduously to cultivate the good opinion of the General" (Kelly 1775).

(8) Elegant interjections (*O ye Heavens!*) instead of ordinary swear-words.

The data of language change presented above is perhaps more usefully considered in terms of style than in terms of global language change. Traugott and Romaine (1985) suggest that in order to link style with social class one must ask, "What prestige norms apply in a given community at a particular time, and how do they change?" Thus, the shift from royal/heroic verse in 1600 to "Truly Polite" prose in 1800 is not primarily a matter of syntactic evolution, though English syntax did in fact evolve during those 200 years; rather, it is the displacement of one "high" style by another, a change in prestige norms.

Research on the gradual move from "oral" to "literate" cultures seems relevant to the appearance of "Truly Polite" language in the 1780s. Among the characteristics of oral culture listed in Ong (1982) are a number of values or traits that the exceedingly genteel heroes and heroines of Goldsmith's and Cumberland's plays shun and avoid: they would rather be "analytic" than "aggregative," "objectively distanced" than "empathetic and participatory", "abstract" than "situational" or "close to the human life world".

Biber (1988) and Biber and Finegan (1989) derive three "dimensions" of prose, empirically, from statistical analysis of co-occurring linguistic features, all three "associated with" 'literate' and 'oral' differences in English: informational vs. involved production; elaborated vs. situation-dependent reference; and abstract vs. nonabstract. It seems likely that "Truly Polite" language is located at the extreme "literate" end of all three of Biber's and Finegan's dimensions. Long words, high type/token rations, WH-relative clauses on object and subject positions, pied-piping constructions, nominalizations, and passives all co-occur at the "literate" end of these dimensions; and contractions, discourse particles, final prepositions, *that*-deletion, and "general emphatics" co-occur at the "oral" end. On the other hand, several features associated with "oral" language seem to crop up in "Truly Polite" prose as well: *be* as main verb, general hedges, possibility modals.

Theories of politeness with one foot in sociology or anthropology and the other in linguistics may also help explain these new developments in the late eighteenth century. Grimshaw (1980) approaches politeness as a form of manipulative behavior – which certainly applies to the compliments that appear so frequently in "Truly Polite" language. Brown and Levinson (1978) define the politeness of a speech in terms of social distance between speaker and hearer, power of hearer over speaker, and severity of the threat to hearer's "face" posed by the speech itself. Several of the strategies they list for increasing politeness are built into "Truly Polite" language: the use of in-group identity markers (courtly-genteel jargon); deference and "humiliatives"; use of elaborate language where plain talk would convey the same operational meaning; impersonalization (passive voice, indefinite, and impersonal constructions); nominalizations.

If oral/literacy research and politeness theory are a helpful context for some of the distinctive locutions that belong to "Truly Polite" speech in late eighteenth-century drama, an understanding of how and why literacy and politeness were more likely to exert strong pressures on prestige norms in language at the end of these two centuries than at the beginning depends on a wider perspective. Social history of the sort practiced by Stone and Stone (1979, 1984) is enlightening in this connection: it explores critical changes in interpersonal relations between 1600 and 1800 from "distance, deference and patriarchy" to "affective individualism"; it describes historical changes in the aristocracy from a landed elite educated chiefly in horsemanship and war to a more open and urban and literate coterie of wealthy and cosmopolitan gentlefolk, changes that closely parallel the shift from royal/heroic to "Truly Polite" language. The "polite society" ("beau monde") that played such a central role in eighteenth-century culture was something new in northern Europe (Girouard 1985); and the "Truly Polite" speech it favored seems in harmony with a "trend toward greater privacy, exclusion, and separation of the classes" (Fabricant 1987).

We cannot assume that ideals of politeness have an impact on ordinary language or literary language in every culture at every period in history, but English-speaking people in the seventeenth and eighteenth centuries were unusually interested in politeness, as Lawrence Klein's essay in this volume shows. Courtesy books dating from the sixteenth to the late eighteenth centuries, cited by Norbert Elias (1939), suggest that ordinary social behavior was being "refined" in the most basic and fundamental ways during this period. In 1600 spitting and farting and eating with one's fingers and nakedness in bed and uninhibited outbursts of rage or joy were pretty much accepted as part of everyday life; by 1800 they had been proscribed, curbed, and outlawed. The "emotional control" suggested by the very syntax of "Truly Polite" language was not crucial in late medieval social relations (Elias 1939: 201). By contrast, "the essential basis of what is required and what is forbidden in civilized society" was established by 1800 (1939: 104–105). A vogue of "polite conversation" in the eighteenth century must have had some effect on locutions favored by those who pretended to upper-class status (Berger 1978). The word "vulgar" itself did not come to mean 'ill-bred, lacking in refinement' until the mid or late seventeenth century (*OED*, s.v. 13).

Economic and intellectual histories must also be taken into account, since they deal with the conditions that permit literacy to have an effect on large numbers of people and make politeness a popular ideal. During the eighteenth century printed English texts proliferated as never before, via the first daily newspaper (1730), the first monthly magazine (1731), the first circulating subscription library (1725), the first substantial number of people making a living as professional writers (e.g., Defoe, Eliza Heywood), the first modern novel (1740), the first copyright laws (1709, 1733). More people could read these printed texts because there were more schools (founded by "infant societies", corresponding societies, mechanics' institutes, as Sunday schools, factory schools, private schools: see Levine 1986). Perhaps secular and rationalist tendencies in the Enlightenment encouraged literacy. The *philosophes* wrote dictionaries and encyclopedias, and they put into print a great many technologies (belonging to craftsmen and the guilds) that had never been written down before (d'Alembert 1751). Courtesy books (including some of the most popular essay-journals, e.g., *The Spectator* [1710] and novels, e.g., *Pamela* [1740] were best-sellers, displacing religious tracts that had been best-sellers in the mid-seventeenth century. The flood of prescriptive grammars between 1750–1800 taught people to avoid vulgarisms, solecisms, and archaisms; they made explicit the connection between fastidious speech and gentility.

It is possible to argue that politeness and literacy were stronger forces for language change during the period 1600–1800 than standardization. Leonard has shown how far from uniform the standards of standardization really were (1929). James Milroy points out (in this volume) that standardization is never complete or fully established. "People don't actually speak standard languages; they speak vernaculars ... , and they observe patterns of variation appropriate to these vernaculars." If, according to Milroy, "standardization is not primarily about prestige", then probably changes in prestige norms are not primarily about standardization. "Truly Polite" speech norms did not last long; they were too courtly, they smelled too strongly of wigs and minuets and the *ancien regime* for nineteenth-century writers. If during the eighteenth century they overlapped with norms of standardization, if standardization became an aspect of politeness, the net effect of these two "social" factors for language change (Stein 1990) is something to be reckoned with.

List of plays examined

a. The period 1600–1630

1600 Thomas Dekker, *The shoemakers' holiday*, ed. Davies [1968].
1603 William Shakespeare, *Hamlet*, ed. Evans [1974].
1604 Thomas Dekker, *The honest whore*, ed. Baskervill et al. [1934].
1607 Thomas Heywood, *A woman killed with kindness*, ed. Baskervill et al. [1934].
1607 George Chapman, *Bussy D'Amboise*, ed. Baskerville et al. [1934].
1607 William Shakespeare, *King Lear*, ed. Evans [1974].
1608 Thomas Middleton, *A trick to catch the old one*. [Facsimile reprint, 1970] Menston: The Scolar Press.
1608 William Shakespeare, *Coriolanus*, ed. Evans [1974].
1609 Francis Beaumont – Thomas Fletcher, *Philaster, or love lies a-bleeding*, ed. Ashe [1974].
1610 Ben Jonson, *Epicoene, or the silent woman*, ed. Beaurline [1967].
1611 William Shakespeare, *The winter's tale*, ed. Evans [1974].
1612 George Chapman, *The widow's tears*, ed. Yamada [1975].
1613 Francis Beaumont, *The famous history of the knight of the burning pestle*, ed. Doebler [1967]. (Probably acted in 1607; printed 1613.)
1614 Ben Jonson, *Bartholomew Fair*, ed. Hussey [1964].
1619 Francis Beaumont – John Fletcher, *A king and no king*, ed. Bowers [1970].
1621 John Ford – William Rowley – Thomas Dekker, *The witch of Edmonton*, ed. Baskervill [1934].
1625 Philip Massinger, *A new way to pay old debts*, ed. Baskervill [1934].
1632 Philip Massinger, *The city madam*, ed. Hoy [1964].
1634 John Ford, *Perkin Warbeck*, ed. Anderson [1963]

b. The period 1770–1800

1771 Richard Cumberland, *The West Indian*, ed. Borkat [1982].
1773 Oliver Goldsmith, *She stoops to conquer*, ed. Quintana [1952].
1775 Richard Brinsley Sheridan, *The rivals*, ed. Price [1973].

1775 Hugh Kelly, *The school for wives*, ed. Carver [1980].
1777 Richard Brinsley Sheridan, *School for scandal*, ed. Price [1973].
1778 Hannah More, *Percy, The Works of Hanna More*, 1853. London: Bohn.
1779 Hannah Cowley, *Who's the dupe?*, ed. Link [1979].
1782 Hannah Cowley, *The belle's strategem*, ed. Link [1979].
1783 Richard Cumberland, *The mysterious husband*, ed. Borkat [1982].
1786 Hannah Cowley, *A school for greybeards*, ed. Link [1979].
1787 Thomas Holcroft, *Seduction*, ed. Rosenblum [1980].
1788 George Colman, *Ways and means, or, a trip to Dover*, ed. Tasch [1981].
1788 Elizabeth Inchbald, *Such things are*, ed. Manvell [1987].
1790 George Colman, *The battle of Hexham*, ed. Tasch [1981].
1791 George Colman, *The surrender of Calais*, ed. Tasch [1981].
1792 Thomas Holcroft, *The road to ruin*, ed. Rosenblum [1980].
1793 Elizabeth Inchbald, *Everyone has his fault*, ed. Manvell [1987].
1795 Richard Cumberland, *The wheel of fortune*, ed. Borkat [1982].

References

Anon.
    1632   *Cupids schoole: Wherein youngmen and maids may learne divers sorts of new, witty, and amorous complements*. London: E. Purslow for F. Grove.
Auerbach, Erich
    1946   *Mimesis: The representation of reality in western literature*. Bern: A. Francke
    [1957]   [Translated by W. Trask. Garden City, N.Y.: Doubleday Anchor, 1957]
Barish, Jonas A.
    1960   *Ben Jonson and the language of prose comedy*. Cambridge, MA: Harvard University Press.
Berger, Dieter A.
    1978   *Die Konversationskunst in England, 1660–1740*. München: Wilhelm Fink.
Biber, Douglas
    1988   *Variation across speech and writing*. Cambridge: Cambridge University Press.
Biber, Douglas – Edward Finegan
    1989   "Drift and the evolution of English style: A history of three genres", *Language* 65: 487–517.
Blake, Norman Francis
    1983   *Shakespeare's language: An introduction*. New York: St. Martin's.
Blank, Claudia (ed.)
    1992   *Language and civilization: in honour of Otto Hietsch*. Frankfurt: Peter Lang.

Brown, Penelope – Stephen Levinson
  1978   "Universals in language usage: Politeness phenomena", in: Esther N. Goody (ed.), 56–324.
Brown, Roger – Albert Gilman
  1989   "Politeness theory and Shakespeare's four major tragedies", *Language in Society* 18: 159–212.
Campbell, George
  1776   *The philosophy of rhetoric*. London: W. Strahan.
  [1963] [Reprinted Carbondale, IL: : Southern Illinois University Press.]
d'Alembert, Jean Le Rond
  1751   Preliminary discourse to the encyclopedia of Diderot.
  [1963] [Translated by Richard Schwab. Indianapolis: Bobbs-Merrill, 1963.]
Dil, Anwar (ed.)
  1981   *Language as social resource*. Stanford, CA: Stanford University Press.
Elias, Norbert
  1939   *The history of manners: The civilizing process*.
  [1978] [Translated Edmund Jephcott. New York: Pantheon, 1978.]
Fabricant, Carole
  1987   "The literature of domestic tourism and the public consumption of private property", in: Felicity Nussbaum – Laura Brown (eds.), 254–275.
Girouard, Mark
  1985   *Cities and people: A social and architectural history*. New Haven: Yale University Press.
Goody, Esther N. (ed.)
  1978   *Questions and politeness*. Cambridge: Cambridge University Press.
Grimshaw, Allen
  1980   "Selection and labelling of instrumentalities of verbal manipulation", in: Anwar Dil (ed.), 234–264.
Hume, Robert D.
  1981   "The multifarious forms of eighteenth-century comedy", in: George Winchester Stone (ed.), *The stage and the page: London's "whole show" in the eighteenth-century theatre*. Berkeley: University of California Press, 3–32.
  [1983] [Reprinted in: Robert D. Hume, *The rakish stage*. Carbondale, IL: Southern Illinois University Press, 214–244.]
Johnson, Samuel
  1750–52 *The Rambler*. London: Cave.
  [1969] [Reprinted New Haven: Yale University Press.]
Jonson, Ben
  1620   *Timber, or Discoveries*.
  [1908] [Reprinted in: J. E. Spingarn (ed.), *Critical essays of the seventeenth century*. London: Oxford University Press, 1908, 17–64.]

Kranidas, Thomas
    1965   *The fierce equation: A study of Milton's decorum*. The Hague: Mouton.
Leonard, Sterling Andrus
    1929   *The doctrine of correctness in English usage 1700–1800*. Madison: University of Wisconsin Press.
Levine, Kenneth
    1986   *The social context of literacy*. London: Routledge & Kegan Paul.
Lowth, Robert
    1762   *A short introduction to English grammar*. London: A. Millar, R. & J. Dodsley.
    [1967] [Reprinted. Menston: Scolar Press.]
Matthews, William
    1937   "Polite speech in the eighteenth century", *English* 1: 493–511.
McIntosh, Carey
    1986   *Common and courtly language: The stylistics of social class in 18th-century British literature*. Philadelphia: University of Pennsylvania Press.
    1992   "The gentrification of English prose, 1700–1800", in: Claudia Blank (ed.), 720–735.
Nussbaum, Felicity – Laura Brown (eds.)
    1987   *The new eighteenth century: Theory, politics, English literature*. New York: Methuen.
Ong, Walter
    1982   *Orality and literacy: The technologizing of the word*. New York: Methuen.
Oxford English Dictionary, The
    1989   Prepared by J.A. Simpson – E.S.C. Weiner, Oxford: Clarendon Press.
Platt, Joan
    1926   "The development of English colloquial idiom during the eighteenth century", *Review of English Studies* 2: 70–81, 189–196.
Rapin, René
    1674   *Reflections on Aristotle's treatise of poesie*.
    [n.d.]   [Wing R270: Ann Arbor, MI: University Microfilms, n.d.]
Rousseau, Jean-Jacques
    1781   *Confessions*.
    [1954] [Translated J.M. Cohen. Harmondsworth: Penguin, 1954.]
Salmon, Vivian
    1967   "Elizabethan colloquial language in the Falstaff plays", *Leeds Studies in English* 1: 37–70.
Schauber, Ellen – Ellen Spolsky
    1986   *The bounds of interpretation: Linguistic theory and literary text*. Stanford, CA: Stanford University Press.

Schlauch, Margaret
    1965   "The social background of Shakespeare's malapropisms", in: Stanislaw Helsztynski (ed.), *Poland's homage to Shakespeare.* Warsawa, 203–231.
    [1987]   [Reprinted in: Vivian Salmon – Edwina Burness (eds.), *A reader in the language of Shakespearean drama.* Amsterdam: John Benjamins, 1987, 71–99.]

Stein, Dieter
    1990   *The semantics of syntactic change.* New York: Mouton de Gruyter.

Stone, Lawrence
    1979   *The family, sex and marriage in England, 1500–1800.* New York: Harper & Row.

Stone, Lawrence – Jeanne C. Fawtier Stone
    1984   *An open elite? England 1540–1800.* Oxford: Clarendon Press.

Tawney, Richard Henry
    1926   *Religion and the rise of capitalism.*
    [1962]   [Reprinted Gloucester, MA: P. Smith, 1962.]

Tillyard, E. M. W.
    1943   *The Elizabethan world picture.* London: Chatto & Windus.

Traugott, Elizabeth Closs – Suzanne Romaine
    1985   "Some questions for the definition of 'style' in socio-historical linguistics", *Folia Linguistica Historica* 6: 7–39.

Waith, Eugene M.
    1962   *The herculean hero: In Marlowe, Chapman, Shakespeare and Dryden.* New York: Columbia University Press.

Editions of plays examined

Anderson, Donald K. (ed.)
    1963   John Ford, *Perkin Warbeck*, Lincoln, NE: University of Nebraska Press.

Ashe, Dora Jean (ed.)
    1974   Francis Beaumont – John Fletcher, *Philaster, or love lies a-bleeding.* Lincoln, NE: University of Nebraska Press.

Baskervill, Charles Read – Virgil B. Heltzel – Arthur H. Nethercott (eds.)
    1934   *Elizabethan and Stuart plays.* New York: Henry Holt.

Beaurline, Lester A. (ed.)
    1967   Ben Jonson, *Epicoene, or the silent woman.* London: Edward Arnold.

Borkat, Roberta F. S. (ed.)
    1982   *The plays of Richard Cumberland.* New York: Garland.

Bowers, Fredson (ed.)
    1970   *The dramatic works in the Beaumont and Fletcher canon.* Cambridge: Cambridge University Press.

Carver, Larry (ed.)
    1980   *The plays of Hugh Kelly*. New York: Garland.

Davies, Paul C. (ed.)
    1968   Thomas Dekker, *The shoemakers' holiday*. Berkeley: University of California Press.

Doebler, John (ed.)
    1967   Francis Beaumont, *The famous history of the knight of the burning pestle*. Lincoln, NE: University of Nebraska Press.

Evans, Gwynne Blakemore (ed.)
    1974   *The Riverside Shakespeare*. Boston: Houghton Mifflin.

Hoy, Cyrus (ed.)
    1964   Philip Massinger, *The city madam*. Lincoln, NE: University of Nebraska Press.

Hussey, Maurice (ed.)
    1964   Ben Jonson, *Bartholomew Fair*. London: Ernest Benn.

Link, Frederick M. (ed.)
    1979   *The plays of Hannah Cowley*. New York: Garland.

Manvell, Roger (ed.)
    1987   Elizabeth Inchbald, *Selected comedies*. New York: University Press of America.

Hanna More, the Works of, 1853. London: Bohn.

Price, Cecil (ed.)
    1973   *The dramatic works of Richard Brinsley Sheridan*. Oxford: Clarendon Press.

Quintana, Ricardo (ed.)
    1952   *Eighteenth-century plays*. New York: Random House.

Rosenblum, Joseph (ed.)
    1980   *The plays of Thomas Holcroft*. New York: Garland.

Tasch, Peter A. (ed.)
    1981   *The plays of George Colman the Younger*. New York: Garland.

Yamada, Akihiro (ed.)
    1975   George Chapman, *The widow's tears*. London: Methuen.

Proliferation and option-cutting: The strong verb in the fifteenth to eighteenth centuries

Roger Lass

1. Preliminaries

This is a very provisional and – for me – hesitant paper. It is as much concerned with problems of interpretation as interpretations, and as much with the meta-question of how you can tell which is which, perhaps, as anything else. In another way, it is partly a study in English morphology during the period of initial standardization (or "standardization"), and partly a study in the use of a text-corpus for investigating this sort of phenomenon. I am not clear to what extent it is any or all of these things, and this itself may be of interest. I am, however, convinced that on the face of it one is likely to get better results from a carefully planned and exquisitely organized source like the Helsinki Corpus, which is largely my base here, than by simply relying, as previous historians have often done, on what texts one happens to have read. Even if one has read like Wyld or Jespersen (which, of course, I haven't), a reliable corpus might still tell some rather different and probably better stories.

The term "standardization" is widely used, and everybody I suppose agrees that from around the late fourteenth century on, gathering momentum into the eighteenth and early nineteenth centuries, whatever "standardization" was had begun to happen to English, and was more or less completed by around 1800 or so. But the nature of the process is somewhat obscure, and there are some very interesting indeterminacies that ought to affect our judgement of what is actually happening at any given time. We also agree – more or less – on what a "standard language" is, from both functional and formal points of view; but the process by which such an entity (or to be more realistic, usually a cluster of related entities) arises is not all that well defined, and the study of a great number of texts can lead to some confusion. (This on the general principle, known to but repressed by most historians, that the more information you have, the muddier the situation is; this is the ignorance-is-bliss factor, and we all teeter on the edge of the real-language abyss when we try to write history.)

The process of standardization can be visualized, loosely, as approximation to a set of functional and formal criteria. The functional criterion is often called "elaboration" (Haugen 1966 [1972] and a later tradition, e.g., Hudson 1980: 32–33). This involves the adaptation of whatever has been chosen as a base for the standard to increasing numbers of contexts and uses, until there exists a "single, widely accepted norm ... felt to be appropriate with only minor modifications or variations for all purposes for which the language is used" (Ferguson 1962, quoted in Haugen [1972]: 107). This process had been going on in most regional varieties of English since the Old English period, and will not concern us here (though it does of course pick up steam in the sixteenth century, in the debates on the vernacular, etc.); my interest here is in the formal side of the process, what Haugen calls "codification", and others "regulation", a term I am adopting here in this article. In English this is clearly a later development, and in some ways a much more complex one.

If we begin with the assumption that possession of a written form is a *sine qua non* for a proper standard, since otherwise it cannot "establish models in time and space" (Haugen [1972]: 105), there are two subsequent stages in the evolutionary story:

i. *Selection*. Choice of some (dia)lectal type is the basis of the nascent standard: normally a socio-regional complex such as the upper-class speech of a capital, etc.
ii. *Regulation*. Development of an "authorised" form with minimal variation, which eventually becomes a supraregional norm, even if it retains its primary regional character. Thus in phonology, Received Pronunciation (RP) is a supraregional (set of) norm(s) in England, even though it is recognizably southeastern in type; a northern speaker adopting RP not only makes a sociolinguistic move, he moves south across a major isogloss-bundle.

The notion of codification, while intuitively transparent, is hard to define in detail; Hudson (1980: 33) for instance thinks that in order for it to occur, "some agency such as an academy must have written dictionaries and grammar books to 'fix' the variety, so that everyone agrees on what is correct", but this is in fact not usually the case. It is often only after the emergence of what is generally perceived to be a standard that the written codification in this strong sense occurs – if at all. English is a case in point, since the normative grammatical tradition (outside of certain aspects of phonology) emerges only a good two centuries after the clear perception of standardization. (In extreme cases, like Dutch, people may perceive themselves to be speaking a standard, but be unable to agree on what it is: it is quite possible to have a "perceived standard" at the same time as extensive variation and partisan debate.)

There is no doubt that by the mid sixteenth century there existed in England at least a "typological" conception of a standard variety, "the best", usable for all public and learned purposes; and that this, if not "codified", was certainly "selected", on both a regional and a social basis. Perhaps the most familiar early delineation is Puttenham's circumscription of 1589: "the vsuall speach of the Court, and that of London, and the shires lying about London within lx. myles and not much aboue"(Puttenham 1589: iii). Twenty years earlier, in a less well-known passage, John Hart (1570: iiib) had remarked on people of "farre West, or North Countryes, which vse differing English termes from those of the court, and London, where the flower of the English tongue is vsed"; and a year earlier (1569: 20b–21a) Hart says that even though nobody would blame a native of Newcastle or Bodmin for writing his own dialect in a book printed there, or a letter – "yea, though he wrate so to London" – this would not do in a book printed in the Metropolis. London speech, that "the learned sort ... do vse, is that speach which euery reasonable English man, will the nearest he can, frame his tongue therevnto". Comments of this sort increase in the seventeenth century: see Dobson (1955 [1969]: 421) for more examples.

It is worth noting that "the best" English at this early stage is usually explicitly defined not only socially but regionally: with London at the centre, Puttenham's circle passes through Oxford, Cambridge, and Canterbury. Later on the regional identification may become implicit (or the dialect becomes supraregional): a century after Hart John Wallis can talk simply of "puram et genuinam linguae Anglicanae pronunciationem", which is distinct from "singulas vero locorum dialectos" (1653: 73).

Obviously complete regulation was never achieved on any linguistic level in English. But the period 1500–1700, in which the standard really begins to emerge, shows some very clear developments of the regulating type – as well as others. One is the elimination of coexisting variants; or, to be more accurate, a tendency in linguistic behavior for certain variants to be eliminated, and a parallel (but not identical) concern in metalinguistic discourse with variation as an issue. I have chosen one story out of many – the clean-up of the strong verb – to illustrate both the process and the problems.

However, before I get to the meat of the discussion, there is a methodological problem to address: when we look at, for example, a large text-corpus and see "evidence of standardization", what in fact are we seeing? From a diachronic viewpoint, there are actually two (often confused, always eminently confusable) appearances that can be conflated under the same heading:

a. Change in "phenotypic provenance": texts gradually cease to appear to come from particular (types of) dialects from particular places. Thus as we go from later Middle English to early Early Modern English, it gets harder to tell where a writer of high-style matter comes from. Chaucer's and Gower's south-easternness is pretty much as apparent as Rolle's northernness, and there are traces of Kentish origin in Wyatt (Kökeritz 1965); but after about 1550 it becomes very hard to tell where most writers come from (whatever their speech might have been like, which we usually don't know). Or, conversely, anybody can see where a text *looks* as if it comes from, but this may reflect neither the provenance of the text nor its writer.
b. Change in Actual Lects. Rather than being a "corpus-effect", there is in a given writer's output a decrease in variation, a gradual dissociation of private and public styles, with regionalisms being purged from the latter, variation decreasing, removal of native forms and constructions and substitution of (quasi-)standard ones.

Type (a) is a corpus artefact, and is macrolinguistic: it may reflect adoption of a new style/lect for a particular purpose, and may not in fact represent "linguistic change" *sensu stricto* at all. Type (b) is intralectal, and is a matter of the "structural history" of a language variety. In all fairness, it is very rare indeed that we have the kind of materials we need to identify Type (b) in our period; there must be such a thing, and indeed "standardization of a language" must in essence mean this rather than Type (a). Unfortunately, we rarely see it, and we talk of "the language" and sequences of texts as if they were the same thing.

This problem is built into the Helsinki Corpus, in fact into any sample that attempts to provide materials for a chronological (or any other kind of) "history of English". The reasons are obvious: we have to take our texts – especially in the early periods – where we find them, and the apparent "chronological sequences" in our standard text collections are not, of course, straight-line series, but geographical hodge-podges, constrained by the places texts at particular points happen to come from. For instance, except for the *Ormulum* and the *Peterborough Chronicle*, the corpus of "early Middle English" is terribly skewed toward the South and West. A "chronological sequence" PC-Orm-Katherine Group is also a geographical sequence: East-Midland – North-East-Midland – West-Midland.

There are other corpus problems as well: a form which at one stage may reflect only a "chronolect" may come, through differential regional changes, to be a regional marker; and this status may later reverse. So a preterite singular form of a class I strong verb spelled with nuclear <a> (*draf, wrat(e)*) in the twelfth – thirteenth centuries is a chronological phenomenon: Old English /ɑ:/ has not yet rounded, and we would expect such a form in any dialect. In later Middle English it would, after the rounding, be a marker of northern provenance; but in Early Modern English, because of dialect borrowing attendant on various demographic shifts, a form with (historically northern) /a:/ or some later development, spelled <a>, would have no regional indexicalness at all. Thus <a>in the pret sg of *drive* in early texts is simply a mark of age; but in the Helsinki Early Modern English materials, *drave/draue* stands to (expected southern) *drove* in the ratio of 4:3, in texts of London provenance and clearly "standard" style and genre.

The upshot is that apparent "standardization" in a corpus is not a clear-cut or simple thing, and it may not always be really clear what exactly we are observing. I will not "solve" any of these difficulties, but merely suggest that we keep them in mind while listening to the story that we can extract.

2. The strong verb: Origins and early history

The Germanic strong verb is usually thought of as an "Indo-European inheritance"; the weak verb is the real Germanic invention. This is not quite true: while the strong verb vocalic alternations do show remnants of Indo-European verbal ablaut (hence "Ablautsreihen" for strong verb classes), they do not do so in a way that has genuine Indo-European parallels.

The strong verb as such is a Germanic construction, built out of the debris of the late proto-Indo-European aspect system (or more precisely, cf. Dolgopolski 1989, the late Western Indo-European one). When Germanic developed a tense- rather than aspect-based verb, it deployed the old ablaut grades in a quite new way: in general, the old *e*-grade present remained as present, the *o*-grade perfect became the preterite 1, 3 sg and the zero-grade (in heavy stems) or the lengthened *e*-grade (in light stems) aorist became the preterite 2 sg and plural.[1] To illustrate for classes I–IV, see Table 1 below.[2]

These three categories continue the verbal ablaut proper; the past participle is quite different, a thematic verbal noun in */-nó-/, with zero-grade of the root due to suffix accent: so -*bunden* < */βundð-a-na-z/ < */bhṇd-o-nó-s/, etc.[3]

These and later developments lead to a complex and fairly regular set of paradigms, with as many as five root vocalisms in a single verb: so class III

Table 1.

Class		Pres	Pret₁ Perf	Pret₂ Aorist
I	IE	-eiC-	-oiC-	-iC-
	Gmc	-i:C-	-aiC-	-iC-
	OE	-i:C-	-a:C-	-iC-
	e.g.	wrītan	wrāt	writon
II	IE	-euC-	-ouC-	-uC-
	Gmc	-euC-	-auC-	-uC-
	OE	-eoC-	-æaC-	-uC-
	e.g.	flēogan	flēag	flugon
III	IE	-eRC-	-oRC-	-R̥C-
	Gmc	-eRC-	-aRC-	-uRC-
	OE	-eRC-	-æRC-	-uRC-
	e.g.	helpan	healp	hulpon
			(< */xalpi/)	
IV	IE	-eR-	-oR-	-e:R-
	Gmc	-eR-	-aR-	-æ:R-
	OE	-eR-	-æR-	-æ:R-
	e.g.	beran	bær	bǣron

helpan, present 2 sg *hilpst*, pret₁ *healp*, pret₂ *hulpon*, past participle (pp) *holpen*, etc.[4] Some of the Old English complexity was undone by phonological mergers in late Old English (e.g., loss of breaking, low-vowel mergers); some was lost morphologically (e.g., levelling of the infinitive and present 1 sg vocalism to the 2, 3 present). By earliest Middle English, with various other changes operating as well, the vocalic patterns had, in terms of paradigm-complexity, stabilized into three main types:

Table 2.

	Pres	Pret₁	Pret₂	PP
4-Grade	helpen	halp	hulpen	holpen
3-Grade	wrīten	wrāt		writen
2-Grade	tāken		tōk(en)	tāken

This is the input to the later Middle English development, whose output is the basis for the Early Modern English changes, and the present-day system.

3. Paradigm restructuring: General features

From this point on I will use as convenient period labels the useful and reasonable divisions chosen for the Helsinki Corpus. For Middle English (ME) and "Early British" (EB) the periods are:

Middle English	ME 1:	1150–1250
	ME 2:	1250–1350
	ME 3:	1350–1420
	ME 4:	1420–1500
Early Modern English	EB 1:	1500–1570
	EB 2:	1570–1640
	EB 3:	1640–1710

Interpreted with proper latitude, this periodization captures divisions between significant phases in the development of the language: e.g., no plural marking of verbs after ME4 (and very little during it), etc. Since the Corpus does not run into the period after 1710, and has certain lacunae in what it does contain, I will be using other kinds of information as well in the discussion that follows.

Throughout early Middle English (ME1), the expected inventory of paradigm types remains more or less according to the model (Table 2), though there are a few adumbrations of later changes. In Old English there had already been a certain amount of analogical transfer of forms from one paradigm (class) to another, but nothing really destructive: in late Old English and early Middle English the strong verb system overall can be (etymologically) recognized for most verbs as a legitimate descendant of a conservatively reconstructed West Germanic archetype.

But during ME2 and beyond, a fairly extensive restructuring begins, triggered by two general reorganizations in English morphosyntax:

i. A typological trend to an "invariant-base" morphology, disfavoring multiple stem-allomorphy (Kastovsky 1989a, b).
ii. Erosion of number as a concordial category of the verb, and stabilization of tense as the main (or only) inflection (Lass forthcoming).

Tendency (i) helped to isolate the strong verb as even more of a minority type than before (if a very salient one, even a target for minor analogical shifts from the weak paradigm); (ii) led to the scrapping of the $pret_1/pret_2$ vocalic opposition, leaving in many cases a "surplus" or "junk" (Lass 1990) vowel grade that could be redeployed. In both cases, intraparadigmatic ties between grades were loosened, and the strong verb became subject to major internal restructuring.

Not that the (ultimate) simplification was – in implementation – itself particularly simple. The deterioration of the relatively cohesive set of Old English class-archetypes served at first as a trigger for "proliferation" of new forms and paradigm types: different modes of reduction in grade-numbers for instance led to competing paradigms, and – in particular – analogical levelling across class boundaries created new "unhistorical" forms.

We might visualize the Middle English and post-Middle English history of strong verbs somewhat animistically, as an attempt to answer the following questions:

- How many grades should a strong verb have?
- Which should be kept, which scrapped?
- Should the past participle end in *-(e)n* or not?
- Should the pret/pp contrast be maximized or minimized?
- Should a verb be strong at all?

These might be regarded, simplistically but not uninformatively, as a checklist for regulation in a complex and variable morphological system. The process showed itself in the following major tendencies:

(a) *Grade-reduction by intraparadigmatic levelling.* The loss of the $pret_1$/$pret_2$ distinction not surprisingly goes hand in hand with the loss of suffixal *-en* as a plural marker: both begin in the North, but percolate down through the country quite rapidly, and are complete early in ME4. In principle, the $pret_1$/$pret_2$ opposition could be levelled under either vocalism, or under that of pp (where this is not the same as $pret_2$, as in class III (non-nasal)–V). Only the first and last of these were really common, though all occurred.

Levelling under $pret_1$ (Wyld's "Northern Preterite", 1927: 268) starts in the North c. 1300 (e.g., *Cursor Mundi* with both sg/pl *dranc, rade*, etc., S *drank* ~ *dronk/drunken, rood/riden*). Levelling under the pp vowel (Wyld's "Western Preterite") begins later in the West, and moves eastward; this begins to appear as a minority variant in the fourteenth century, and stabilizes for many verbs only in the period EB3 and later. Typical surviving Western preterites are *bore* for BEAR (first Corpus attestation ME4), *got* as pret of GET (EB1). This type has become quite general in class III /-Nd-/ verbs (*found* < *fund-, bound* < *bund-*), and in some /-Ng-/ ones (*flung*) or old /-NN-/ (*spun*); but it was once commoner, and until the nineteenth century alternated with the original /a/>/æ/ type (*flang, span*). More on this in section 5. There is also some extension of $pret_2$ (where different from pp) to the whole finite past; Chaucer for instance has both *bar* < *bær* and *beer* /bɛːr/ from the grade of *bǣron*.

(b) *Hybridization (inter-class transfer)*. This was not uncommon in Old English, but increases considerably in later periods, even into EB2/3. One of the most frequent transfers is of the class IV pp vowel to pret and pp of class V verbs: e.g., pret sg *broke* (rare) in Corpus EB1, pp *broken* as early as ME2 (see Campbell 1959: section 743 for Old English examples as early as *Beowulf*).

(c) *Transfer to weak conjugation*. This was common throughout Middle English, with a climax in the fourteenth and fifteenth centuries. The earliest of the Corpus examples (and there are not many: see section 5) is in ME1: *ʒettede* ~ *ʒette* for pret of *get* (*Juliana*).

Two other tendencies worth noting also have their parts to play in both the simplification and proliferation that serve as the basis for later codification:

(d) *Loss of participle suffix*. This shows up as early as ME1 in some verbs, with -(*e*)*n* lost in *bigunne*. In general this is commoner in nasal-stem verbs than others: for obstruent-finals the suffix-less forms are later (*drive* pp as early as *Bevis*, ME2, *broke* only ME4). As is clear from the examples, in verbs like DRIVE, loss of -(*e*)*n* ending can produce homophony between pp and pret (cf. Modern English *slide/slid/slid*); in verbs like BREAK, BEGIN other changes are necessary to produce this, Western Preterite in BEGIN, transfer from class IV in BREAK.

(e) *Preterite-to-pp shift*. In late Middle English (rarely), but increasing in Modern English, the final result of this "desystematization" emerges: transfer of preterite vocalism to the past participle, e.g., *I have sang, I have wrote*. This could coexist as an option with both western preterite (*I sung*) and the historical continuation (*I sang*), which gives us the following possibilities for a three-grade strong verb by the late ME4-early EB1 period (not the same for all individual verbs, of course):

Table 3. SING

pret	pp
sang	sung (historical)
sung	sung ("Western" type)
sang	sang (pret-shift)
sung	sang ("crossover")

All of these types are represented *somewhere* in post-ME English; the "crossover" type for instance is common in parts of the southern United States, as is the simple pret-shift. The Corpus data is for the most part insufficient to discern what patterns occur in a given writer: most often we have either the preterite or the past participle from a given source for one verb, rarely both. However, examples of the basic shift itself are common, as we will see – though not as common as the writings of grammarians in the seventeenth and eighteenth centuries suggest they ought to be.

This sketch then suggests that as early as ME1 the strong verb begins to "decompose": general paradigm structure becomes less orderly, as a first stage in ultimate simplification. The variant-inventory and number of (potential) paradigm-types however increases as well as decreasing: innovation in this system could be either reductive or proliferative.

Given the modern paradigms, the scenario overall seems to have been of this sort:

Table 4.

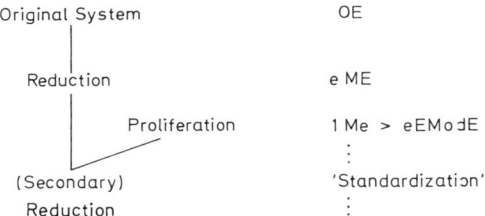

Given the general idea of "codification" (regulation) of a standard, one would expect the momentum of variant-reduction to increase more or less *pari passu* with (a) the explicitness of perception that a standard does indeed exist, and (b) the development of metalinguistic discussion, in particular the increase in normatively oriented grammatical description. This is not quite what happens, though in outline something rather like it does. It might be interesting to look at the story in more detail.

4. Some case histories

The scenario as in Table 4 is what emerges from a reading of the standard historical treatments (Wyld, Jespersen, etc.), and from examination of a number of individual texts in detail (see Lass 1990 for discussion and general history); it is also what emerges from the Helsinki Corpus materials, but in a rather strange and indirect way, which is worth exploring. The content of the previous section is just a skeleton, with not much in the way of exemplifying verbs or numbers attached; as an alternative strategy I want to look at the histories, both in terms of forms and coexistence/variation, of a few characteristic verbs, as they emerge from the Corpus materials.[5]

I give below outline histories of a number of typical strong verbs, with graphs showing fluctuation in numbers of attested forms per paradigm, and for each one some notes on the content of the inventory at a given period. As we will see, the inventory may remain stable in size from one period to another, but show change in content; this is especially important when innovations show up late, or when (as is not uncommon) the preterite inventory loses a form while the participle gains one. This looks like stasis, but qualitatively it is activity.

So let us begin by looking at the number of forms attested per verb at the various Corpus sampling-points; this will show e.g. whether proliferation/reduction in preterite and past participle run parallel or not, and when – for each category – the maximum proliferation and reduction occur. As we will see, the results are not the same for all verbs (there is an element of *chaque mot a son histoire* here, as in many messy categories), but some interesting generalizations do appear.

In Table 5 below we see the pattern for BEAR:

Table 5. Corpus forms of BEAR

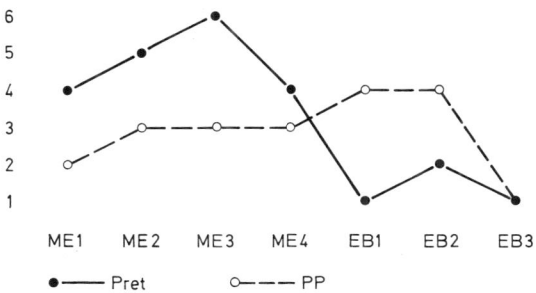

In ME1, aside from expected *bar* < *bær*, we also find some "Western" *ber(e)* for pret$_1$ and an innovative *baren* pret$_2$. If this is the ancestor of later pret *bare*, it has a long vowel (i.e., is not an extension of pret$_1$ vocalism, which is unlikely in non-N texts of this period anyhow); it may be a Middle English /aː/ < Old English /æː/, i.e., "Ostsächsisch *ā*" (Jordan 1934: section 50). In the past participle, suffixless forms already appear. In ME2 we get the first pret$_2$ *bore(n)* types, with transfer from pp; also syncopated past participles of the type *born(e)*. Pret$_1$ *bor(e)* does not appear until ME4, where it is rare; pret$_2$ here is only *bar(e)*, and there is only one weak form, *berryde*. There is no change in EB1/2, except for one odd weak pp *bornte* in EB1; otherwise the usual pret is *bare*, and the commonest pp *born(e)*. By EB3 *bore* has replaced *bare*, and the pp is only *born(e)*. This is a pretty clear instance of the early proliferation/late codification (regulation) pattern we expect; but note the innovative bursts at EB1 (pp) and EB2 (pret). We will see more of these below. Note also the "crossover" in pret/pp at EB1, which is also repeated for other verbs (six out of ten in this mini-sample).

Table 6. Corpus forms of BEGIN

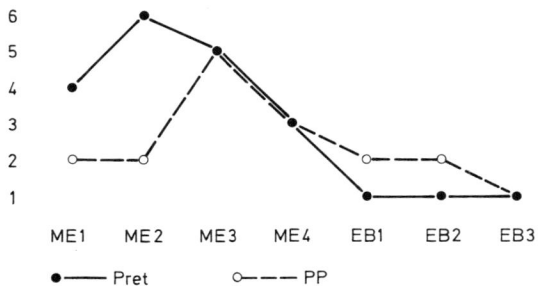

Verbs of this type are problematic, since <-oN-> spellings (*bigon, bigonnen*) are difficult to interpret. In a western text, <bigon> could be (phonologically) a continuation of Old English pret$_1$ *bigann/-gonn*, with West Saxon pre-nasal raising and rounding. On the other hand, given the convention of writing <o> for <u> in minim environments, it could be a "Western Preterite" shift to /u/ in pret$_1$. I have made the general distinction that if a text shows <o> in both pret$_2$/pp, this is probably to be taken as meaning /u/; a shift of pret$_1$ vocalism into pp in ME1/2/3 is unlikely. Besides, many western texts in fact do show <a> in pret$_1$ (e.g., Robert of Gloucester); in such a case <o> certainly means /u/. The main developments here involve movements of pp vocalism into pret, and loss of suffixal *-(e)n*.

In ME1, both expected *brac* and innovative (pp or pret$_2$-derived) *brec* occur for pret$_1$; pret$_2$ has *breke/breken*, and pp *brocen(e)/breken/broeken*. In ME2, pret$_1$ shows mainly low vowels, but *braak* suggests length, which is innovative. There is also one pret$_1$ *breke*. Pret2 shows all possible vocalisms (*breken, brake, broken*), and both suffixed and endingless forms; pp is only

Table 7. Corpus forms of BREAK

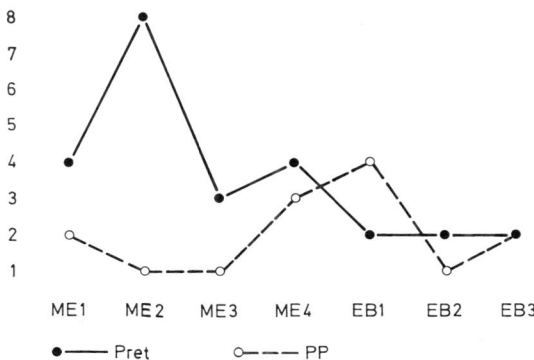

broken, as in ME3 as well. In ME3, the only pret is *brak*, while pret$_2$ shows (historical) *breke(n)*; pp has only /o/-vocalism, and a suffix (*broken, -yn*). At ME4 there is still one occurrence of pp *breken* (presumably its earlier absence is a Corpus artefact), and the first occurrences of endingless pp *broke*, as well as a pret *broke* (Capgrave), which being endingless suggests that pret$_1$ would be *broke* as well. In EB1 the pret is both *brake* (presumably continuing the Middle English *braak* type) and *broke*, while pp shows *broke(n)* as well as weak *braked* (Madox, diary). Madox also has *brake* ~ *broke* pret, not atypical for this period. In EB2 only *broken* pp occurs, but *broke* returns (having, of course, never really gone) at EB3, and *broke/brake* still coexist.

Table 8. Corpus forms of GET

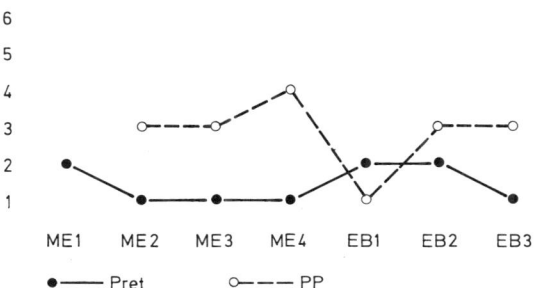

ME1 here shows a common problem in a corpus like this: lack of a particular form. But this is not a problem in context, as ME1 is not in any case a period where great activity is expected. This verb, like GIVE below, adds an extra variable: palatal (<3 ~ y>) vs. velar (<g>) initials. Thus ME1 has only <3>

94 Roger Lass

forms (and only weak ones at that, but this does not imply absence of strong ones); ME2 has only <g>, and this holds for the rest of the Corpus, here because of the low or back vowels in forms like *gat*, *got/ten*), etc. (Actually "because of" is not quite right: note in Table 9 that <y> appears before back vowels in some forms of GIVE. Up to ME4 the only strong pret is of the *gat* type; the historical pp *geten* appears in ME2, the class IV type *goten* (~ *get(en)*) in ME4. For the preterite, *got* appears first in EB2, with both *gotten*, *getten* for the past participle; EB3 has preterite *got* only, pp *got*, *gotten* (but without the semantic distinction that holds in modern varieties with both).

This verb shows particularly clearly the potential complication produced by differential activity in different parts of the paradigm, as does GIVE below: pret and pp do not evolve in parallel, with respect to simplification.

Table 9. Corpus forms of GIVE

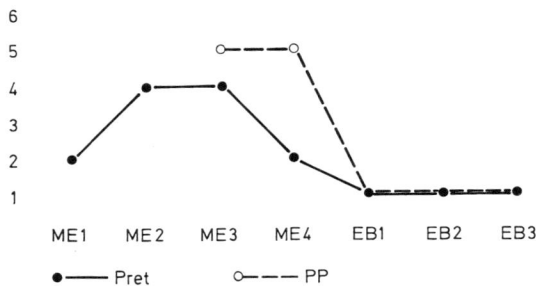

Here the maximal proliferation in both pret/pp occurs at ME3 – rather late, but in keeping with textual evidence outside the Corpus as well. The past participle forms here are historical *yeven*, *given*, analogically devoiced *yeffen*, and innovative *yove*, *yoven*. Regulation is early here: from EB1 on only *gave* (ultimately <g(e)af* with analogical voicing and lengthening), *given* occur.

In Table 10 the Corpus material is helpful only from ME3, where we find both weak *helped* and transferred *holp* (from pp) in pret, along with original type *halp* < *healp*, and pp *holp(e)* ~ *holpen*. In ME4 the only pret is weak *helped*, pp *helped*, *holpen*; in EB1 pret is again only *helped*, but *helped*, *holpen/holp* appear for pp. EB3 has no pret forms (one imagines *helped* only), and pp only *helped*. This is a rather low-profile verb, but its patterning is still similar to that of the others.

Table 10. Corpus forms of HELP

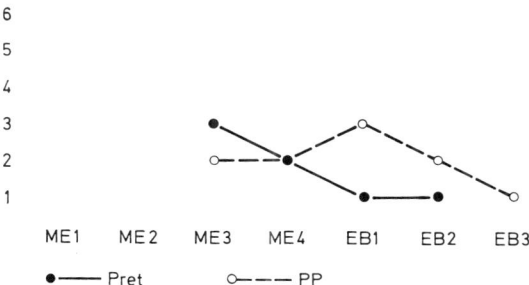

In ME2/3, the usual paradigm is *ran/ron* (= *ran*) for pret, *run* pp (though later occurrences of *runnen*, etc. tell us that this was current earlier). In ME4, *rone* is pret along with *ronnyn ronne* pp. In EB1 a new form is added: *ran* pp (Leland); in EB2 *ran/run* pret, only *run* pp, as in EB3.

Table 11. Corpus forms of RUN

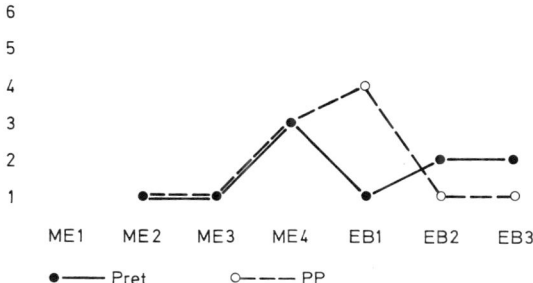

Neither ME1 nor ME2 have any past participle forms for SPEAK; the pret$_1$ in ME1 is *spac* < *spæc*, while ME2 has *spak*, and innovative *spaak* (assuming that <aa> represents a long vowel, which must have appeared at some point anyhow to account for later *spake*); pret$_2$ here has *spaken* with presumably the same vocalism, and transferred *spoken*. ME3 has *spak/spaak* pret$_1$, pret$_2$ *spoken/spak/spaken*. The pp here is only *spoken*. ME4 retains the two pret types *spak/spake* (at least some of these must = *spaak* /spa:k/); pp now shows both *spoken* and endingless *spoke*, though the *spoke* type has not penetrated into pret sg (it did appear in pret$_2$ earlier). In EB1 pret sg *spoke* appears for the first time, along with *spake*; pp is *spoken/spoke*. The same situation holds for EB2, though here we get some evidence for variation in a single lect: Hooker has *spoke spoken* pp, and both *spake/spoke* pret appear in some diary samples (Madox, Hoby). EB3 has more or less the same picture, but there is one occurrence of pp *spake*.

Table 12. Corpus forms of SPEAK

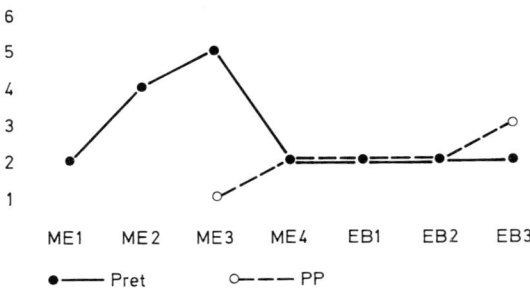

The Corpus data here (as elsewhere) gives us some evidence as well for the quantitative distribution of new vs. old types. If we look at the innovative pret *spoke* in EB1–3, for instance, we find it developing as follows: EB1 2.4% of all pret, EB2 6.5%, EB3 46.3%. It is clear that even by the turn of seventeenth century there is still a good deal of regulation to be done.

Table 13. Corpus forms of TAKE

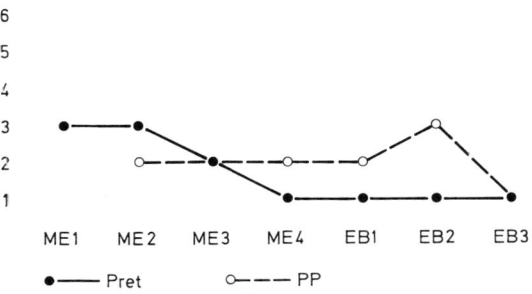

ME1 shows only pret forms; these include $pret_1$ *toc*, $pret_2$ *token* with expected vocalism ($pret_{1/2}$ are the same in class VI, but already weak *takede*. ME2 adds analogical $pret_2$ *taken* (transfer of pp), along with *token*; pp has the expected vocalism, but there is suffix-loss: *take taken*. From ME4 on all pret are of the *took* type, but at EB2 a shifted pp *took* occurs (Gifford; Middleton ~ *taken*).

Table 14. Corpus forms of WRITE

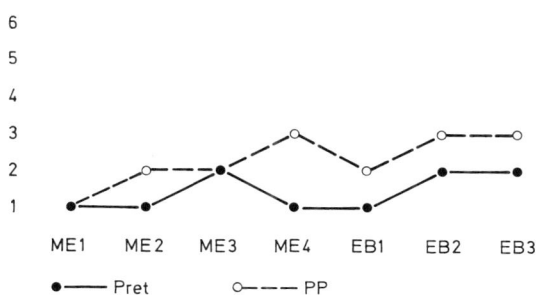

ME1 has pret *wrat*, pp *writen*; ME2 has $pret_1$ *wrot*, no $pret_2$, but pp *writen write*, though on the basis of ME3 $pret_2$ *writen* we would assume this form even if it were not attested outside the Corpus. ME3 pp is still *writen write*. By ME4, pp *wrote* first appears, and the others remain; EB1 is the same, though pp *wrote* does not occur. In EB2 pret is *writ* ~ *wrote*, and pp *writ*, *writen*, *wrote*, as at EB3.

Table 15. Average forms/verb, ME1–EB3

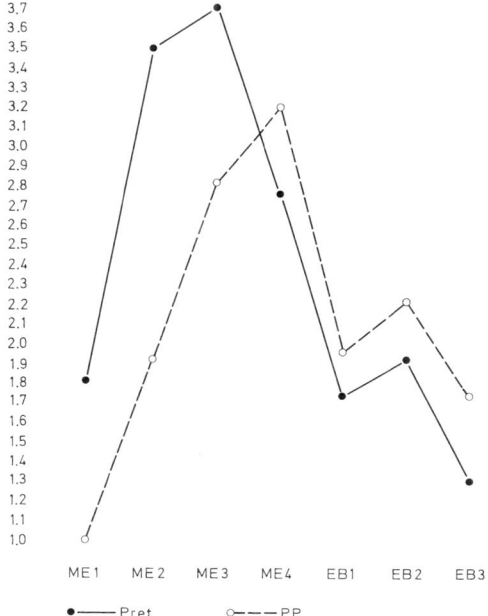

What kind of overall picture do these figures give us? Are there any general trends that can be extracted from the individual graphs for particular verbs? If we take an average of the forms per verb in each period (with silent reservations for Corpus gaps, etc.), an interesting pattern emerges, as we can see in Table 15. A graph like this can't of course be interpreted literally: an "average" past participle with 2.8 forms makes about as much sense (positively and negatively) as an "average" nuclear family with 2.4 children. But the numbers, if not taken seriously as numbers *per se*, but rather as indices of trends and general period-characters, are a useful heuristic for producing a visual model of a historical scenario. They indicate the nature of a pair of epigenetic trajectories.

5. Double standards? Grammarians and the Corpus

One of the earliest writers to comment explicitly on the strong verb as a category, and to give a detailed account of formal variation, is John Wallis. In his *Grammatica linguae Anglicanae* (1653), he has a chapter "De Verbis Anomalis"; these he identifies correctly as a special native type, "quae ab antiqua lingua teutonica ... originem ducunt" (115).

He notes first that in general the use of *-en* to mark pp is variable (118–119):

> Scilicet tam *written, bitten, eaten, hidden, chidden, shotten, rotten, chosen, broken*, etc. quam *writ, bit, eat, beat, hid, chid, shot, rot, chose, broke* etc. in Participio Passivo ... promiscue efferuntur.

The important point is that he notes the variation, but does not evaluate it; his choice of a term for the variation, *promiscue*, carries in Latin no overtones of disapproval,[6] but has the senses "without distinction", "in general practice", "commonly". Thus for Wallis, who is at times quite normative on other matters,[7] this variation (and the more extensive kind discussed below) is simply a fact about normal educated usage.

The extent of variation throughout the system is immense, and not only in the past participle. So in a section on "special anomalies" (119–120) Wallis discusses the group *win, spin, begin, swim, strike, stick, sing, sting, fling, ring, wring, spring, swing, drink, sink, shrink, stink, hang, come, run, find, bínd, grínd, wínd*. For these, "tam in Praeterito Imperfecto [= pret] quam in Participio Passivo", we find *wònne*,[8] *spun, begun, swum, struck, stuck, sung, stung, flung, rung, wrung, sprung, swung, drunk, sunk, shrunk, stunk, hung, còme, run, found, bound, ground, wound*. I.e. the "Western Preterite" (original past participle vocalism in pret/pp), except for *strike*, which is a transfer from class I. However, he notes, "et eorum pleraque formantur etiam in Praeterito Imperfecto per *a*, ut *wan, began, sang, rang, sprang, drank, came, ran*. Others too, "sed rarius". In addition, some have *en* in pp (*stricken/strucken, drunken, bounden*); but in most ("fere in omnibus" – though he doesn't list the exceptions, unfortunately), a "regular form" ("forma analogia", i.e. weak) occurs as well: *spinned, swimmed*. The only possible (implicit) judgement we can extract from this is one of "normalcy" or judged frequency: the list-order *swum, swam, swimmed* may indicate such a judgement. (On the other hand, it might just as well indicate the salience of "anomaly" in the face of the general expectation of "analogy".)

Potentially, then, Wallis would allow for a verb like SPIN the following inventory of forms:

Table 16. SPIN

pret	pp
spun	spun
span	spunnen
spinned	spinned

Note that for the class II nasal type he doesn't appear to allow the pret → pp shifted variety (no pp **span*): but see below. This is rather a richer collection than the Corpus materials show for just about any verb in either pret or pp (the only thing like it at all is GET pp) in EB2/3.

Pret → pp shift however does appear in another group (120–121): e.g. *take, shake, drive, write, get* have pret/pp *took, shook, drove, wrote, got* (there are others like this as well). But for the class I verbs "utrobisque dicimus etiam" *writ, driv* (pret). There are also verbs with <o> and <a> alternants in pret: *bore/bare, spoke/spake, got/gat* (as indeed in the Corpus) – "et fortasse quaedam alia, sed rarius". This group may also have *-en* in pp: *taken, shaken, broken, born, driven, written, gotten*. The order of listing, again, may suggest that Wallis takes the non-suffixed forms as normal. If so, this presents quite a different picture from what the Corpus gives for any point in Early British: in EB2, the only place where *took* pp occurs, it accounts for just under 2%

of the total (2 out of 102). There are also weak forms, e.g. "regular" *bared, choosed, seethed* (in the latter case ~ *sod/sod(den)*).

Wallis' "normalcy judgements" (if indeed that is what they are, which seems likely) appear curiously at odds with the quantitative picture exhibited by the Corpus materials. Overall, suffixless, pret-shifted and weak past participles for instance are rare, and do not seem – for any of the verbs I've looked at – anywhere near as frequent as Wallis' judgements (and those of many later writers) suggest they ought to be.

If, for instance, we take the past participle forms of seven verbs for the whole Early Modern Period, we find the following percentages of the various types (rounded off to one decimal place):

Table 17. Strong past participle types in the Helsinki Corpus: % of total occurrences, EB1-3

	-en	-∅	Pret-shift	Weak	Other
BREAK	77.4	21.0	–	1.6	–
EAT	90.0	10.0	–	–	–
GET	76.7	23.0	–	–	1.3
GIVE	100.0	–	–	–	–
SPEAK	83.5	15.3	1.2	–	–
TAKE	97.1	2.1	0.8	–	–
WRITE	74.2	21.6	4.2	–	–
Type Average	85.5	13.1	0.9	0.2	0.2

There is no "period-effect" in this data – i.e., statistical masking of forms common at one period by overwhelming preponderance of other types at other periods. I have, therefore, felt safe in averaging over EB1–3 for exposition, since the overall profiles are not that different from one to another, except for the rise of pret-shift in EB2–3. However, what is notable is the extremely low frequency of weak forms (only one verb in this group shows any), and the relative rarity of suffixless and pret-shifted forms. In short, the apparent fluidity suggested by Wallis' description is not borne out even in the data from the "pre-normative", "pre-codified" EB1 period. I will return to this problem, which may cast an interesting light on both what the language was doing and grammarians' attitudes, after looking at some other sources.

If the disparity were merely a peculiarity of Wallis, it would not be worth mentioning except as a curiosity; but a quite similar picture emerges three decades later in Christopher Cooper's *Grammatica linguae Anglicanae*

(1685).⁹ Cooper is more precise about the variety he is describing than Wallis: "educatus fui meridianâ regiona, quâ partem vitæ occupatæ plurimam, primis in annis, scholæ præfui grammaticæ, ubi etiam purissima & emendata loquendi consuetudo norma est" (Cooper 1685: b4r). Whatever the precise sense of "purissima & emendata", the concept is clear; but as Cooper tells us there is a problem in teaching this variety; there are no really accepted ("received") grammars that set things out in the necessary detail, so it has been difficult up to now to teach it adequately (Cooper: b4v): "Hæc sola linguam nostram in acquirendo difficultatis est ratio, quod nulla grammatica generaliter in usum sit recepta, & nemo ad hunc finem dictionarium accomodavit." What is needed is for the language to be codified – its rules laid down in writing – both in order to overcome this, and to prevent its "decay" (Cooper: b4v and following unnumbered folio): "lingua quæ ab ore dictata, sine regulis scriptis (quæ summo probatæ judicio optimè disponi possunt) & sine fundamenti ratione acquiritur, fluctuare et citò evanescere certum est."

It is against the background of these two types of concerns – what in the period are typically called "ascertaining" and "fixing" the language – that Cooper's reports are to be seen. He is a bit less clear in some respects than Wallis, but his framework is the same: there are two main classes of verbs, "regular" and "anomalous" (1685: 154), and only (a) those regular (= weak) verbs with morphophonemic peculiarities, and (b) the genuine strong verbs, are discussed in detail.

It's of some interest to see how Cooper parcels out (our) strong verbs into different classes. His "conjugatio primo" (1685: 154) consists of verbs in which "tempus præteritum deducitur à præsenti annectendo *ed*", and where preterite and past participle are formally the same. This includes fully regular items like *prepare/prepared*, and those that show suffix change, mainly vowel deletion and assimilation (*gird/girt*). There are also subclasses where "vocalis longa mutatur in brevem" (*bereav/bereft*, but note also *réap/reapt, reach/reacht*); where past is marked by devoicing (*send/sent*); where the vowel is shortened but there is no final devoicing (*bleed/bled*). Some verbs in this set also have alternative pasts: *swéat* (presumably /swe:t/) past *sweat* /swɛt/ ∼ *sweated*. There are also some "invariabilita", like *cast, spread*.

But this group includes another class (1685: 156–157): some verbs he says, "quæ exeunt in *ed*, alteram habent terminationem magis usitatam". One subset is historically weak velar or palatal-finals: *beseech-ed/besought, work't/wrought, teach-ed/taught, catch't/caught*. The other is made of strong verbs proper, mainly from historical class III. Here we find not only strong variants, but typically more than one; and the types are now familiar. So *shine-'d/shon; sting-ed/stung/stang; spin-ed/spun/span; shrink-ed/shrunk/shrank; win-*

ed/wun/wan; *wring-ed/wrung/wrang*. Only one has no <a> = /æ/ variant: *stick*, past *stuck*. For this group then, Cooper's judgement seems to be that they are "basically" weak, but may have one or more strong alternants; he also clearly prefers the "Western" <u> types (a preference Wallis did not express): *stand*, *span*, *shrank*, etc. "præteritum sine signis denotant, at melius forsitan prorsus relegentur" (1685: 156–157).

On further reading, it looks as if the "first conjugation" is not only preferentially weak, but also does not have the other prime strong verb marker: participial *-en*. His "conjugatio secunda" (1685: 157) "exit in *-en*"; but this is an even untidier group than the first. Some "sunt anamola [sic] & redundantia". I find it hard to see why this conjugation is so much more excessive or "superfluous"[10] than the first, though Cooper's fastidiousness is itself of interest. It is however important to note that even though he is apparently unhappy with these verbs, he does not proscribe any of the "excess" forms.

Among the paradigms he gives are the following (in this discussion he considers only the past participle, as the preterite can be deduced from a past participle form either by dropping the suffix or just taking it as it is):

Table 18.

present	pp
beget	begot-ten, begat
bid	bid-den, bade
bind	bound-en
chide	chid-en, chode
drîve	driv-en, drov-n, drove
slide	slid-en
rîse	ris-en, rose
speak	spoke-n, spake
strive	striven, strove, strave

This class also contains mixed weak/strong paradigms (159), e.g. *hew/hew'd* ∼ *hew'n*, *lade/lode* ∼ *laded* ∼ *loaded* ∼ *loaden*.

A final group includes verbs with neither *-en* ending nor weak forms: these may have one or more pasts, e.g. *come* with only *came*, *fling* only *flung*, *find* only *found*, *grind* only *ground*; but *swim* with *swum/swam*, *ring* with *rung/rang*, *stink* with *stunk/stank*, *spring* with *sprung/sprang*. He also makes a curious distinction between *wring* "obtorqueo" which is conjugation 1 with primary weak *wringed*, and *wring* "torqueo" which only has *wrung*, *wrang*. The only normative comment is on *strike*, which has *struck*, but "malè *stroke*".

The point of all this – as was evident in Wallis as well – is that the "standardizing" or "language-planning" concerns of these writers do not lend, as might be expected, to under-reporting the amount of actual variation. On the contrary, with respect to the Corpus and much other textual data of the period, what we find looks very like *over*-reporting. The general tone adopted by Wallis and Cooper does not suggest hyper-permissiveness; and they are both too good at their descriptive tasks in various ways, and too intelligent and observant, to allow us to take all this "redundantia" as fantasy. There is something here to be explained, which I will return to in a rather speculative way later on, after we have looked at a few more grammarians of the period.

The "over-reporting" (with respect to text-occurrences) is in fact quite persistent. Sixty years after Cooper, John Kirkby (*A new English grammar, or guide to the English tongue*, 1746) gives, without comment on preference, the paradigms for some of the strong verbs, rearranged alphabetically (Table 19). These verbs are described (1746: 89–94) simply as "out of the common Rule" (i.e. not weak), and are presented in a list in no discernible order. Where alternate forms are given, there is no explicit indication of preference, judgement of frequency, etc. – unless the order of listing is an implicit ranking (certainly the totally consistent <u>-form, <a>-form order for preterite of class III may be such a comment). Kirkby does, however, as the data suggests, show a slight aversion to pret-shifted past participles, at least for class III. He notes (1746: 94) that whenever the preterite of a verb has nuclear <a>, it cannot also serve as past participle, except for *clad* < *cloath* (which he does not recognize as weak, but presumably associates with the *seethe/sod(den)* type), "and perhaps sometimes *drank*". This suggests that the pret-shifted type so common in earlier descriptions is on the way out; but in fact it survives as a standard possibility (for some users) well into the nineteenth century, and is noted by later eighteenth-century normative writers (see below on Lowth).

Curiously, at least at first, there are writers considerably earlier than Kirkby who teach a much more restricted (and in many ways more "modern") strong verb system. What seems to be the case is that Kirkby in a way represents an older, more "descriptive" tradition of grammatical writing; from the late seventeenth century on this is joined by another stream, the more characteristically late-Enlightenment "ascertain-and-fix" tradition. What has been felicitously called the "ideology of standardization" Milroy – Milroy 1985) begins to show up with some clarity at this point. The basic components of this stance, as manifested in the earlier commentators (most classically, perhaps, and certainly best known in Swift 1712) are (a) what the Milroys (1985: 17)

Table 19.

	pret.	pp
BEAR	bore, bare	bore, born
BEGIN	begun, began	begun
CHOOSE	chose, chused	chose, chosen
CLING	clung, clinged	clung, clinged
DRIVE	drove, drave	drove, driven
FLING	flung	flung
FORSAKE	forsook	forsook, forsaken
GET	got	got, gotten
RING	rung, rang	rang
RISE	rose	rose, risen
SHAKE	shook	shook, shaken
SHRINK	shrunk, shrank, shrinked	shrunk, shrinked
SING	sung, sang	sung
SINK	sunk, sank	sunk
SLING	slung	slung
SMITE	smote, smit	smote, smite /smɪt/, smitten
SPIN	spun, span, spinned	spun, spinned
SPRING	sprung, sprang	sprung
STINK	stunk, stank	stunk
SWING	swung, swang	swung
SWIM	swum, swam, swimmed	swum, swimmed
TAKE	took	took, taken
THRIVE	thrive /θrɪv/, thrived	throve, thriven
WIN	won, wan	won
WRITE	wrote, writ	wrote, writ, written

call "suppression of optional variability", and (b) the buttressing of restrictive/normative attitudes and pronouncements with logical or (more rarely in the early days) etymological or historical argument. One more modern component of the ideology – confusion of writing and speech, and elevation of written language to the position of sole permissible type – does not appear until rather late. Indeed, I will suggest later that the disparity of Corpus data and early (contemporary) grammatical description is due precisely to lack of this conflation.

A good example of early ideological standardization is to be found in James Greenwood (*An essay towards a practical English grammar*, 1711). While listing a number of alternant pret and pp for some strong verbs, Greenwood does classify a good number of forms as "not proper or usual" (1711: 138–141). As a general rule, we might justifiably take Wallis' "rarius" as meaning simply uncommon; but when frequency judgements are paired with comments on "propriety", we have good grounds for suspecting that the forms in question are commoner than the writers says – else he'd not have to remark on their propriety.

In Table 20 below, Greenwood's "not proper or usual" forms are marked with a following asterisk; virtually all of them are older (historical) forms, e.g., descendants of Old English /-a-/ pret$_1$ for class III nasal stems, or strong forms of verbs that early developed weak alternants. Like Wallis and Cooper (and we'll see, later writers as well at least up to the 1760s), Greenwood shows a preference for the "Western" preterite (1711: 139–140):

Table 20.

	pret.	pp
BEAR	bore, bare*	born
BREAK	broke, breake*	broken
DRINK	drunk, drank*	drunk
GET	got	gotten
HELP	helped, helpt	holpen*
RIDE	rid, rode	ridden
SHRINK	shrank	shrunk
SING	sung, sang*	sung
SINK	sank	sunk
SPEAK	spoke, spake*	spoken
STINK	stunk, stank*	stunk
SWIM	swum, swam*	swum
SWING	swung, swang*	swung
THRIVE	throve, thrived*	thriven
WIN	won, wan*	won
WRITE	writ, wrote	written

Greenwood is not slavishly following older sources (a common vice in the period); they report more forms than he allows. Nor is he describing a general current state of affairs, since Kirkby three decades later is still reporting forms of a type current in the 1650s. We see here the beginnings of a programme of reduction, an active purging of the kind of "redundantia" that displeased Cooper. It is also notable that the class III nasal stems are a particularly problematic group; we will see that they remain so for at least another half-century.

Perhaps the most magisterial "ascertainer" of the eighteenth century was Dr Johnson (even though of course he knew perfectly well that the task was Sisyphean). In the grammar prefaced to his *Dictionary* (1755), he has some useful (and in one instance puzzling) comments on the strong verbs. He furnishes no large-scale lists, but he does comment on two issues: the possibility of pret-shifted vs. historical past participles, and class III nasal stems. On participles, he has this to say: "Many words have two or more participles, as not only *written, bitten, eaten, beaten, hidden, chidden, shotten, chosen, broken*; but likewise *writ, bit, eat, beat, hid, chid, shot, chose, broke*, are promiscuously used in the participle ... " (sig. b 2v). We also have *sown, shewn, hewn, loaden/laden* as well as *sow'd, shew'd, loaded/laded*.

It is interesting that Johnson uses the English word based on the Latin term that Wallis used in precisely this connection (see the beginning of this section); in fact this passage may be an echo (conscious or unconscious) of Wallis (1653: 118), since the examples are the same: where Wallis has "promiscue efferuntur", Johnson says "are promiscuously used". But the term seems to have potentially pejorative overtones for Johnson: his definition (1755, s.v.) is "with confused mixture; indiscriminately".

There is however a way out of this "confusion":

> Concerning these double participles it is difficult to give any rule; but he shall seldom err who remembers, that when a verb has a participle distinct from its preterite, as *write, wrote, written*, that distinct participle is more proper and elegant, as *The book is written* is better than *The book is wrote*, though *wrote* may be used in poetry.

To these words he added in a later edition: "... at least if we allow any authority to poets, who, in the exultation of genius, think themselves perhaps entitled to trample on grammarians." There is an amusing anachronism here: many of the poets traditionally cited in the later eighteenth century as using pret-shifted past participles (especially by Johnson's contemporary Lowth, for instance) were in fact contemporaries of grammarians who had no problems with them, and even at times recommended them (e.g., Milton and Wallis, Dryden and Cooper).

Johnson's comment on the class III verbs is especially interesting, because it not only conflicts with later historical development, but also with the prescriptions of other grammarians of the time. His view of these verbs does however accord with earlier ones, e.g. that of Greenwood. For *win, spin, begin, swing, sing, fling, drink, come* he gives <u> forms as normal in both pret and pp. However, he adds, "most of them are also formed in the preterite by *a*, as *begun, rang, sang* ... and some others; but most of these are now obsolete". There must be something to this assertion, since it runs directly counter to his "logical" desire for pret/pp distinctness; nevertheless it is the pattern adopted a littler over a decade later by the enormously influential Robert Lowth, and for most of these verbs the historical pattern is what has now finally become standard (except for *fling, spin, swing* and a few others).

Lowth's *A short introduction to English grammar* (1762) has a fairly detailed section on irregular verbs of all kinds (1762: 64–90). For many of them he allows only one preterite and/or past participle form, but for others he gives a pair, normally in the form "X, or Y"; in Table 21 below all pairs separated by a comma are given by Lowth in this form:

Table 21.

	pret.	pp
BEAR	bare, bore	born
BREAK	brake, broke	broken
BEGIN	began	begun
CLING	clang, clung	clung
GET	gat, got	gotten
HELP	helped	helped, holpen
DRINK	drank	drunk, drunken
RING	rang, rung	rung
SHRINK	shrank, shrunk	shrunk
SINK	sank, sunk	sunk
SING	sang, sung	sung
STING	stung	stung
STINK	stank, stunk	stunk
SWIM	swam, swum	swum
WIN	won	won
WRITE	wrote	written

Lowth's comments on forms and their uses mostly take the shape of footnotes to particular verbs, often with no remarks, but a set of citations of "improper" forms from a range of earlier writers, including Shakespeare, Milton, Burnet, Dryden, Pope and Addison. He notes for some alternants that they belong to a particular register (note 13): "The antient Irregular form *holpe* is still used in conversation"; in other cases he attributes a kind of universal or panchronic validity to (what he claims are) contemporary usages, e.g. (note 15) that "*Rise*, with *i* short, hath been improperly used as the Past Time of this verb", citing Burnet "the earth, which *rise* ... out of chaos"; for *write* (note 17) he observes pret *writ* and pp *writ* in some writers, "but, I think, improperly". He has a long list of pret-shifted past participles from a great range of writers, including *chose, spoke, rode, drank*, which he does not comment on, but clearly dislikes.

Let us assume as a working hypothesis the warrantability of these two assertions:

i. The Helsinki Corpus materials – at least in type – reflect a true picture of "the state of the language" in the text-varieties and at the times chosen for inclusion.
ii. The reports of variant forms and the "normality" judgements in Wallis, Cooper and Kirkby (at least) represent an equally true picture of "the state of the language" – if not quantifiable in the same way.

If these are both true, then the mismatch between Corpus and grammarians needs explanation. In particular, why should grammarians – even if they are not "ascertain-and-fix" fanatics – provide *so* much more evidence of variation than a well-chosen corpus of texts contemporary with them? Why should weak forms and pret-shifts be so much rarer in the Corpus than the judgement of some verbs sharp and sophisticated observers predict?

The answer in a way is so obvious as to be anticlimactic; though it needs stating, and on the basis of the kind of comparison I have been making here, it can be stated with greater certainty than if we had relied purely on intuitive or impressionistic grounds. Very simply, there are two issues involved:

a. The seventeenth-century grammarians and the more "enlightened" eighteenth-century ones ("enlightened" in the anachronistic sense of "less normative") did not have any particularly strong prejudice in favor of written over spoken language. Their "sources" for intuitive judgement, therefore, were more or less indifferently both. Hence the range of behaviors that could count as "English" (in the "best" sense) for them was wider than it was for say Johnson or Lowth.
b. "Silent" or inexplicit regulation of the written standard language (at least in its more public guises) was considerably further advanced in the mid-seventeenth century than was regulation in educated colloquial speech – even that of users of the more regulated written variety. (Note that even Lowth observes this in his reference to pret *holpe*.)

The most sensible conclusion to be drawn from the disparity in variation is that Wallis, Cooper and Kirkby are reporting on a more diverse set of registers and channels than the Corpus, Greenwood, Johnson and Lowth. We thought we were looking at "the evolution of the southern standard", but in fact we have quite likely been looking at two parallel evolutions, or let us say the out-of-phase developments of two parallel standard varieties. The earlier writers and Kirkby are either not aware of this or not troubled by it, and are (consciously or not) working at pushing a monolithic version of "the language", in a form based on the more highly regulated written standard. I suggest that the careful and detailed study of contemporary grammarians of all kinds of ideological persuasions – along with the study of corpora – might be the best way into a more highly differentiated and truer picture of all the things going on at one time in the complex evolution of a standard that is – at all periods in its history – both a written and a spoken medium.

Notes

* I am grateful to the folks at Porthania for allowing me a hectic ten days at Makkaratalo with the Helsinki Corpus; and for patience, helpfulness and not laughing out loud while I learned how to use it. Especially to Matti Rissanen for inviting me in the first place, and to Merja Kytö for kindness, tea, aid above and beyond any possible call of duty, and saintly forbearance with my endless questions – as well as a flood of ideas I've not yet digested.
1. For details and remarks on some of the oversimplifications here, see Lass (1992).
2. The terms $pret_1$, $pret_2$ as in Lass & Anderson (1975). Class V (*brecan*) is the same as IV except that the root ends in an obstruent; class VI (*faran*) is complicated by a historical laryngeal in the root that confuses original ablaut grades; and "class VII" is not a proper ablauting class at all, but a mixture of old reduplicating perfects and other rubbish.
3. Many verbs (e.g. *helpan*, pp *-holpen*, *beran*, pp *-boren*) have Old English /o/ in pp rather than expected /u/, due to lowering before the old thematic vowel */ɑ/ < */o/; this is blocked by following /-NC/, and does not affect the second element of a diphthong. Class V does not show the expected zero-grade, but usually an analogical vocalism based on the present: *brecen* < *brecan*, not expected **burcen* (where /ur/ is the expected reflex of Indo-European */r̥/: see Lass 1986).
4. The /-i-/ in *hilpst* reflects an early precursor of *i*-umlaut: original */xelp-i-s-/ – cf. German *helfen/hilfst*, etc.
5. To avoid having this (preliminary) study run on forever, I worked primarily with a sample of 15 verbs, where the Corpus materials were more or less adequate. The group discussed in detail has the best attestation; others have gaps, but still contribute to the discussion and general picture in an interesting way. The verbs examined are: BEAR, BEGIN, BREAK, DRINK, DRIVE, EAT, GET, GIVE, HELP, RIDE, RUN, SING, SPEAK, TAKE, WRITE. Some potentially interesting verbs (FLING, SWIM) were omitted because the Corpus sample is too small to be of use. (For readers unfamiliar with the Helsinki Corpus, there is much useful information in Kytö – Rissanen 1988 and Nevalainen 1983; see also Nevalainen – Raumolin-Brunberg 1989.)

6. It appears to be the conventional term for describing common or general usage: cf. Seneca *Contr.*. 9.2.23 "deinde in usu uerbum esse coepit et *promiscue* pro discipulo 'auditor' "; or Gellius 10.21.2 "cum et M. Cato et Sallustius ... uerbo isto [sc. 'nouissimus'] *promiscue* usitati sunt". I owe these examples to Kate Coleman.
7. E.g. he describes the use of /ɜ/ rather than [u] in *come, done, some* as characteristic of the "negligentius pronuntiantes" (7).
8. In Wallis' notation, <ò> means an <o> pronounced like short <u>.
9. Cooper was familiar with Wallis (whom he calls "acutissimus": 1685: a4v), but while taking over some of his descriptive apparatus is not a slavish follower. Indeed, he avoids much of Wallis' latinizing terminology, and does not hesitate to stigmatize forms that Wallis found perfectly acceptable. Thus the (Kentish) plurals *meece, leece* which Wallis simply notes as alternants of *mice, lice* (1653: 78) are not mentioned in the discussion of noun plurals, but are reserved for condemnation under the heading *De barbara dialecto* (1685: 79).
10. On the sense of *redundantia* cf. Lewis and Short 1879: s.v. *redendantia, redundatio, redundo, redundam* (etymologically sharing the sense 'overflow' < *re-d-und-*, cf. *unda* 'wave', Old English ȳð < */unð/). As late as the mid-eighteenth century the same or related senses held for E *redundant*: so Johnson (1755: s.v.) has "superabundant; exhuberant; superfluous". The term is potentially pejorative (see Johnson's sense 2 in reference to prolixity of literary style). But neither the English nor the Latin probably were in the eighteenth century.

References

Bessinger, Jess B. – Robert P. Creed (eds.)
    1965   *Franciplegius. Medieval and linguistic studies in honor of Francis Peabody Magoun, Jr.* New York: New York University Press.

Blake, Norman F. (ed.)
    1992   *The Cambridge history of the English language.* Vol. 2, *1066–1476.* Cambridge: Cambridge University Press.

Campbell, Alistair
    1959   *Old English grammar.* Oxford: Clarendon Press.

Cooper, Christopher
    1685   *Grammatica linguae Anglicanae.* London.

Dobson, Eric J.
    1955   "Early Modern standard English", *Transactions of the Philological Society*: 25–54.
    [1969]   [Reprinted in: Roger Lass, *Approaches to English historical linguistics.* New York: Holt, Rinehart & Winston, 419–439.]

Dolgopolski, Aron
 1989 "Cultural contacts of Proto-Indo-European and Proto-Indo-Iranian with neighbouring languages", *Folia Linguistica Historica* 8: 3–36.

Ferguson, Charles A.
 1962 "The language factor in national development", *Anthropological Linguistics* 4: 23–37.

Fries, Udo – M. Heusser (eds.)
 1989 *Meaning and beyond: Ernst Leisi zum 70. Geburtstag.* Tübingen: Narr.

Greenwood, James
 1711 *An essay towards a practical English grammar*, London.

Hart, John
 1569 *An orthographie, conteyning the due order and reason, howe to write or paint thimage of mannes voice, most like to the life or nature.* London.
 [1969] [Facsimile edition. Menston: Scolar Press.]
 1570 *A methode of comfortable beginning for all vnlearned, whereby they may bee taught to read English, in a very short time, with pleasure.* London: Henrie Denham.
 [1955] [Reprinted in: B. Danielsson, *John Hart's works on English orthographie and pronunciation (1551, 1569, 1570). Part I.* Stockholm: Almqvist & Wiksell.]

Haugen, Einar
 1966 "Dialect, language, nation", *American Anthropologist* 68: 922–935.
 [1972] [Reprinted in: J.B. Pride – Janet Holmes (eds.), *Sociolinguistics. Selected readings.* Harmondsworth: Penguin, 97–111.]

Hudson, Richard A.
 1980 *Sociolinguistics.* Cambridge: Cambridge University Press.

Jacobson, Sven (ed.)
 1983 *Papers from the second Scandinavian symposium on syntactic variation.* Stockholm: Almqvist & Wiksell.

Johnson, Samuel
 1755 *A dictionary of the English language.* 2 vols. London.
 [1968] [Reprinted in facsimile. Hildesheim: Georg Olms Verlagsbuchhandlung.]

Jordan, Richard
 1934 *Handbuch der mittelenglischen Grammatik: Lautlehre.* 2nd ed. Heidelberg: Carl Winter's Universitätsbuchhandlung.

Kastovsky, Dieter
 1989a "Typological changes in the history of English word-formation", in: H.J. Müllenbrock – R. Nod-Wieman (eds.), 281–293.
 1989b "Typological changes in the history of English morphology", in Udo Fries – M. Heusser (eds.), 159–178.

Kirkby, John
 1746 *A new English grammar, or guide to the English tongue, with notes.* London.

Kökeritz, Helge
  1965 "Dialectal traits in Sir Thomas Wyatt's poetry", in: J.B. Bessinger – R.P. Creed (eds.), 294–303.
Kytö, Merja – Matti Rissanen
  1988 "The Helsinki corpus of English texts: Classifying and coding the diachronic part", in: Merja Kytö – Ossi Ihalainen – Matti Rissanen (eds.), 169–179.
Kytö, Merja – Ossi Ihalainen – Matti Rissanen (eds.)
  1988 *Corpus linguistics, hard and soft. Proceedings of the eighth international conference of English language research of computerised corpora.* Amsterdam: Rodopi.
Lass, Roger
  1969 *Approaches to English historical linguistics.* New York: Holt, Rinehart & Winston.
  1990 "How to do things with junk: Exaptation in language evolution", *Journal of Linguistics* 1: 79–103.
  1992 "Phonology and morphology", in: Norman F. Blake (ed.).
  Forthcoming "Phonology and morphology", in: Roger Lass (ed.).
Lass, Roger (ed.)
  Forthcoming *The Cambridge history of the English language.* Vol. 3, *1476–1776.* Cambridge: Cambridge University Press.
Lass, Roger – John M. Anderson
  1975 *Old English phonology.* Cambridge: Cambridge University Press.
Lewis, Charlton T. – Charles Short
  1879 *A Latin dictionary.* Oxford: Clarendon Press.
Lowth, Robert
  1762 *A short introduction to English grammar.* London.
  [1967] [Reprinted in facsimile by R.C. Alston (ed.), *English Linguistics 1500–1800.* Menston: Scolar Press.]
Milroy, James – Lesley Milroy
  1985 *Authority in language. Investigating language prescription and standardization.* London: Routledge & Kegan Paul.
Müllenbrock, Heinz-Joachim F. – Renate Nod-Wieman (eds.)
  1989 *Anglistentag 1988 Göttingen: Vorträge.* Tübingen: Niemeyer.
Nevalainen, Terttu
  1983 "A corpus of colloquial Early Modern English for a lexical-syntactic study", in Sven Jacobson (ed.), 109–123.
Nevalainen, Terttu – Helena Raumolin-Brunberg
  1989 "A corpus of Early Modern standard English in a socio-historical perspective". *Neuphilologische Mitteilungen* 90: 67–110.
Puttenham, George
  1589 *The arte of English poesie.* London.

Swift, Jonathan
    1712   *A proposal for correcting, improving and ascertaining the English tongue.* London.

Wallis, John
    1653   *Grammatica linguae Anglicanae. Cui praefigitur, de loquela; sive de sonorum omnium loquelarium formatione: tractatus grammatico-physicus.* London.

Wyld, Henry C.
    1927   *A history of modern colloquial English.* Oxford: Blackwell.

Standardization and the English irregular verbs

Jenny Cheshire

1. Introduction

Present-day standard English has relatively little inflectional morphology, and those inflections that do exist tend to be invariant forms. This lack of morphological variation is not surprising, for the process of standardization openly suppresses variation and change, as Milroy points out in his contribution to this volume. Thus the present tense indicative *-s* suffix occurs invariably with third person singular verb forms in written English and in the spoken English of "educated" native speakers, though it occurs variably in some of the nonstandard varieties of the language, such as the English spoken in East Anglia. Nevertheless, a small amount of variation still exists in one area of standard English verbal morphology: the preterite and past participle forms of certain irregular verbs. There is a small set of verbs, including "burn", "spoil" and "learn", whose preterites and past participles have both *-t* suffixes and *-ed* suffixes (as in *burnt/burned*; *spoilt/spoiled*; *learnt/learned*); there is a further set of verbs whose past participle forms may have an *-ed* or zero inflection (these include "quit", "wed" and "sweat"). A few other verbs with variable preterite and past participle forms are listed by Quirk et al. (1985: 105–120).

The variation that survives in standard English verbal morphology is so unusual that it invites investigation; and this paper takes up the invitation. It compares the preterite and past participles that occur in present-day standard English with those that occur in present-day nonstandard varieties. It is important to remember that there is more to "English" than the standard: Strang (1970:148), for instance, writes of a "confused picture" in the form of preterites and past participles during the seventeenth and eighteenth centuries, remarking: "this area of the grammar shows very clearly, by the amount of divided usage, what is meant by saying that the language after 1770 is a regulated language compared with what went before". However, usage continues to be divided in the nonstandard varieties, and the majority of present-day native speakers of English still cannot be said to speak a regulated language. For example, in Reading, Berkshire, there are at least five preterite forms for the verb "see": *saw* (as in standard English), *see, seen, seed* and *sawed* (Cheshire 1982). Furthermore, although we cannot assume that the patterns of variation that can be seen today are identical to those that existed at earlier stages of English, it is nevertheless true that nonstandard Englishes are, by definition, spoken varieties which have been less directly affected by the processes of standardization and literacy. By comparing the preterite and past participle forms that exist in present-day standard and nonstandard English, therefore, it is possible to identify some of the effects of standardization and literacy on the verbal morphology of English.

There is, of course, a very wide range of variable verb forms in the nonstandard English that is spoken throughout the world. Whilst acknowledging the magnitude of the variation that exists, it is nevertheless possible to single out three general tendencies which appear to reflect processes of linguistic change that have significantly affected the verbal morphology of present-day English. Although these processes are still in evidence in many of the nonstandard varieties, they seem to have been brought to a stop in standard English during the codification of the language that took place between 1600 and 1800.

2. The productive weak verb pattern

Generally speaking, English strong verbs can be said to change the root vowel of the stem in their preterites and, usually, in their past participles (for example, *sing–sang–sung*), whereas the weak verbs have the *-ed* suffix added to the verb stem to form their preterite and past participle forms (as in *walk–walked*). The strong verb pattern is historically older than the weak verb pattern. The origin of the newer weak pattern is not known, but it occurs in all the Germanic languages (Baugh and Cable 1978: 51, 61) and it has been extremely productive throughout the history of English. During the Old English period the majority of verbs already formed their preterites and past participles on the weak pattern, and during the Middle English period many verbs that were historically strong came to adopt weak forms. The greatest number of transfers to the weak class occurred during the fourteenth and fifteenth centuries (see Lass, this volume); after this, wholesale transfer gradually slowed down, though variation between the weak and strong forms of individual verbs continued. Baugh and Cable (1978:164) report that there were only about a dozen new weak formations during the fifteenth century, and that since then there have been only about as many more. Nevertheless the weak pattern has continued to be the favourite one for English, used for borrowings (such as *judge* from French *juger*) as well as for verbs derived from nouns or adjectives (for example, *explete, bin, humidify*). According to Strang (1970: 147), there are only about 60 strong verbs in modern English, whereas there were 360 in Old English.

Strang, of course, was referring to those verbs that are strong in the modern standard. In modern nonstandard English the number is greater, for many of the verbs that are strong in standard English exist in weak forms in the nonstandard varieties. Sometimes, though not always, weak forms co-occur with the strong forms. Some attested examples from the British Isles are: *catched, drawed, fighted, gived, holded, knowed, runned, seed, telled, waked* (Cheshire 1982; Edwards –Trudgill – Weltens 1984; Shorrocks 1980). Most of these weak forms also occur in the USA (Feagin 1979; Wolfram –Christian 1976). Similar forms are found in Australia: Eisikovits (1987: 11) gives the following preterites and past participles from her corpus of inner city Sydney English: *breaked, catched, costed, fighted, hitted, goed, lied, seed, spreaded, teared, winded*. Most of these weak forms are known to have been in use in England since the sixteenth century and, as Lass (this volume) points out, the work of eighteenth-century descriptive grammarians suggests that several were still used in educated spoken English as late as the eighteenth century. Thus although the transfer of strong verbs to the weak class is usually considered to have virtually stopped by the end of the fifteenth century, it would be more accurate to say that strong and weak forms of the same verb co-existed for a further three centuries but that present-day standard English now contains only the strong forms of about sixty of these verbs. A few verbs still have variable strong and weak forms in present-day standard English: "awake", for example, has the preterite forms *awaked* and *awoke* (and the past participles *awaken* and *awoken*), similarly, "weave" has the two preterite forms *weaved* and *wove*. Sometimes there is a distinction in function between the weak and strong variants of a single verb: thus "shone" distinguishes in its preterite forms between causative and intransitive functions, as in *I shined my shoes / the sun shone all day*. In standard English, however, this kind of variation is relatively rare. Transfer of the strong verbs to the productive weak verb pattern has virtually stopped in the standard language, then, but it has continued in nonstandard English.

Why should standard and nonstandard varieties of English have diverged in this way? Given that those eighteenth-century writers who were preoccupied with "ascertaining" and fixing the language had uniformity and analogy as their professed aim, we might expect their work to have helped the development of a uniform, simplified verbal system, with the result that all verbs would have transferred to the productive weak pattern in standard English. Two interconnected factors, however, can be suggested for the differences that exist today, both deriving from social changes that were taking place during the period 1600–1800. First, we can assume a sociolinguistic motivation for the elimination of certain strong verb forms in cultivated speech. Between 1600 and 1800 a gradual distinction emerged between public and private styles of writing, with regionalisms purged from the public styles (see Lass, this volume). As a number of the papers in this volume show, a class of urban society was developing which was preoccupied with demonstrating its refinement and politeness. Linguistic behaviour played a large part in the demonstration of politeness, and given what we know today about sociolinguistic differentiation there is little doubt that members of this class would have exploited linguistic variation as a way of distancing themselves linguistically from those sections of society that they considered to be less refined than themselves. As we have seen, there was a great deal of variation in the form of strong verbs at that time, so that these would have been prime linguistic candidates for the marking of a social distinction. It seems likely that purists who wanted to appear cultivated and refined would have tended to avoid using new linguistic forms, in much the some way that some present-day speakers of English, for example, refuse to use the relatively new derived adverb *hopefully*. Defoe (1697 [1969]: 93) mentions a dislike of new forms in his proposal for the establishment of a society which would "encourage Polite learning and polish and refine the English Tongue", writing that the work of the society should include purging the English tongue of "all those innovations in speech ... which some Dogmatic Writers have the Confidence to foster upon their Native Language". We can assume that amongst the newer linguistic forms to be avoided were the weak forms of many verbs that historically were strong.

Furthermore, since the productivity of the weak verb pattern was well established by then, we can assume that overgeneralization of the *-ed* preterite formation to produce preterites such as *gived* and *comed* was a developmental feature of children's English, as it is today. People who were anxious to appear refined and cultivated would presumably have wanted to mark their linguistic distance from the immature speech of children.

All this seems intuitively obvious, given what we know about sociolinguistic differentiation in present-day English, but it would have to remain at the level of informed speculation unless there were some evidence of sociolinguistically conditioned variation in the use of verb forms during the period 1600–1800. There is, however, some evidence of both stylistic and social variation. Lass, in his analysis of preterite and past participle forms in the Helsinki Corpus of written English (this volume) found a preference for strong variants in the written English of the period, with only one verb – "break" – occurring in a weak form. Several of the lexical verbs in the Helsinki Corpus (including "win", "sing", "choose", "thrive") are thought to have had both weak and strong forms in the spoken English of the time; it seems, therefore, that strong forms had become the preferred forms for written English. Furthermore, the influence of written English on the speech of the educated, cultivated sections of society seems already to have been underway for, as Lass points out, grammarians of the period who described "cultivated" speech tended to list the weak forms after the alternating strong forms, suggesting that these were the less frequent variants.

Other sections of society, who were less concerned about appearing to be cultivated, presumably had fewer qualms about using the newer weak forms. This is indicated by Philip Withers, a grammarian who tended to describe usage rather than to prescribe it. Leonard (1929: 63) notes that in 1788 Withers wrote, in *Aristarchus*, about an eighteenth-century social difference between alternating weak and strong preterite forms of "catch", with well-bred people in London preferring the strong form *caught*. By the mid-nineteenth century the weak form *seed* was used by Mrs Gaskell to indicate a character from a lower social class, suggesting that by then social differentiation in the use of irregular preterites had become well established (Blake 1981: 153).

One reason, then, for the persistence of strong verb forms in standard English is that they became used for the marking of social differentiation. This sociolinguistic motivation, however, does not explain why some verbs rather than others have survived in a strong form: why, for example, does present-day standard English have the strong preterite forms *saw*, *sung*, and *chose*, but the weak preterites *knitted*, *sewed* and *kneaded*? After all, strong forms for "knit", "sew" and "knead" persist in some of the nonstandard varieties of English (Edwards – Trudgill – Weltens 1984: 19). Here a second, psycholinguistic motivation can be suggested for the retention of certain strong forms. The sixty or so strong forms that survive in modern standard English are amongst the most frequently used verbs in the language (Strang 1970: 147). Because these strong verbs occur so frequently in everyday conversation, it is thought that children acquiring English learn the preterite forms by rote, so that they are then accessed as separate lexical entities. By contrast, the weak verb pattern is thought to act as a morpho-phonological rule for speakers of English, operating on verb stems to produce their preterite and past participle forms (see Kuczaj 1977 for discussion). The rule is an efficient and economical way of maintaining a formal marking of "pastness" for the very large number of weak lexical verbs that exist in English, avoiding the necessity of storing their preterites and past participles as separate lexical items.

The frequency of occurrence of the strong verbs in everyday speech would have made them prime candidates for use as social markers. If strong forms are stored and accessed as separate items, they would have been securely embedded in the mental lexicons of speakers of English, and resistant to the spread of the morpho-phonological rule that produces weak preterite forms. Gradually, as strong forms were used more often in written English and in the spoken English of those who wanted to appear cultivated, the strong forms of these verbs became "fixed" as standard. In nonstandard English, on the other hand, where strong forms continue to co-occur with weak forms, speakers have two possibilities: they may access the strong form as a lexical item, or they may apply the morpho-phonological rule to the verb stem and produce the weak form.

Again, some evidence exists which can lift this proposed explanation somewhat above the level of informed speculation. Although the transfer of historically strong verbs to the weak class has continued in nonstandard varieties of English, there are also several verbs that have weak forms in the standard but strong forms in some of the traditional nonstandard varieties. Here, then, it is the nonstandard varieties that are the more conservative. Shorrocks (1980) gives *sew*, *snew*, *tret* and *bet* as preterite forms of "sow", "snow", "treat" and "beat" in the Farnworth area of what was formerly Lancashire. Strong preterite forms of "climb", "knead", "knit", and "scrape" occur in some other British English dialects (Edwards – Trudgill – Weltens 1984: 19). *Clim* occurs as a preterite of "climb" in Anniston, Alabama (Feagin 1979) and *het* and *drug* as the preterites of "heat" and "drag" in Appalachian English (Wolfram – Christian 1976). These varieties of English are all spoken in rural areas, and it is not unreasonable to assume that the lexical verbs in question would have been used more frequently by people living and working in the country, than by those members of urban society who were concerned with developing cultivated, polite society. Perhaps these lexical verbs were less salient, because less frequent, for urban, literate speakers, and they did not, therefore, develop into social markers; perhaps, also, people who were anxious to appear cultivated could demonstrate their preference for "civilised" pursuits and their lack of familiarity with more down-to-earth activities by using different forms for verbs that referred to homely pursuits. This would have applied to "knit", "knead", "beat" and several of the other verbs that transferred to the weak pattern in nonstandard traditional varieties.

The sociolinguistic and psycholinguistic motivations that have been suggested here would, presumably, have acted in conjunction with each other.

In other words, the strong forms of certain verbs that occurred frequently in everyday speech came to be used to mark social distinctions, their frequency making them salient and therefore particularly appropriate as social markers. Their frequency would have allowed them to be acquired, stored and accessed as separate lexical items, thereby freeing them from the application of the -*ed* rule. Other verbs which were not used as social markers, on the other hand, would have been stored in their stem form and would have been subject to the application of the morpho-phonological rule producing weak preterite and past participle forms.

3. A past tense schema

Although the weak verb pattern has undoubtedly been the most productive process in the development of English verbs, there is also a moderately productive strong verb pattern. The pattern is best described not by a simple rule, like the weak formation, but as a general schema – the phonetic shape /ʌ/ followed by a nasal and/or a velar consonant (see Bybee – Moder 1983; Bybee – Slobin 1982). Preterites with this phonetic shape can be considered to form a natural morphological class, whose prototypical member contains the /ʌ/ vowel followed by a velar nasal: hence *strung* or *sung* represent the prototype. Other preterites share at least one attribute with the prototype, so that their final consonant may be a nasal consonant, as in *run* or *spun*; a velar consonant, as in *dug*; or both a nasal and a velar consonant, as in *slunk* (see further, on natural categories, Lakoff 1987; and on prototypes Rosch – Mervis, 1975; Rosch 1978).

Bybee – Moder (1983) discuss the persistence of this pattern in the evolution of preterite and past participle forms in English. They present two related classes of verbs, set out in Table 1 overleaf.

Class 1 verbs in Table 1 have distinct forms for preterites and past participles in modern standard English, whereas class 2 verbs have a single form, and one which conforms to the past tense schema (a phonetic shape /ʌ/ followed by a nasal and/or a velar consonant). Bybee – Moder point out that there has been a historical trend for members of class 1 to lose their separate forms, and to become members of class 2, with a preterite form that has the vowel /ʌ/.[1] This is well documented in Lass' paper in this volume: every one of the verbs listed in Bybee and Moder's class 1 (original class III nasal stems) appears to have had a preterite form in /u/ in spoken English in the seventeenth century, as well as an etymological /a/ form and often a weak form

Table 1. English strong verbs with preterite or past participle in /ʌ/

Final	Class 1			Final	Class 2	
/m/	swim	swam	swum	/n/	spin	spun
	come	came	come		win	won
/n/	begin	began	begun	/ŋ/	cling	clung
	run	ran	run		fling	flung*
/ŋ/	ring	rang	rung		sting	stung*
	sing	sang	sung		string	strung*
	spring	sprang	sprung		swing	swung
/ŋk/	drink	drank	drunk		wring	wrung
	shrink	shrank	shrunk		hang	hung*
	sink	sank	sunk		bring	brung**
	stink	stank	stunk	/ŋk/	slink	slunk
				/k/	stick	stuck*
					strike	struck*
					sneak	snuck**
					shake	shuck**
				/g/	dig	dug*
					drag	drug**

* = verbs not in this strong class in Old English
** = dialect forms not in this strong class in Old English
(from Bybee – Moder 1983: 252)

too. The /u/ form appears to have been the more frequent variant in speech; James Greenwood, for example, in his chapter on irregular verbs, listed the <a> variants for "drink", "sing", "stink", "swim", "swing" and "win" with an asterisk signifying "not proper or usual" (Greenwood 1711 [1968]: 138). Dr. Samuel Johnson (1785) also noted variation between forms such as *sung* and *sang*, again finding that most of the <a> forms were "now obsolete". Despite Greenwood's and Johnson's observations, however, it is the <a> forms that have become standard for "drink", "sing", "stink", "swim", "swing" and "win" as well as for the other verbs listed in Bybee and Moder's class 1. It seems that this is one case where prescriptive grammarians have had a lasting effect on usage (see also Ekwall 1975: section I, 225; Hogg 1988: 38). Lass (this volume) gives some indications of their preference for forms in *a*: for example, the influential Bishop Lowth prescribed only *a* forms for "begin" and "drink" and, where he allowed a pair of variant forms, such as *rang* and *rung* for the preterite of "ring", he listed the *a* form first. Not all verbs, however, were affected by the efforts of the prescriptivists: the verbs in class 2 in Table 1 all have /ʌ/ forms as preterites and past participles, and class 2 includes several verbs for which the /ʌ/ form is unexpected: "dig", "fling", "hang", "sling", "stick", "sting", "strike" and "string".

A psycholinguistic explanation has been suggested to account for the development of preterite forms with an unexpected /ʌ/. Hogg (1988: 38) notes that unetymological preterite and past participle forms in /u/ (later /ʌ/) became increasingly common between the sixteenth century and the end of the eighteenth century, and concludes that for some verbs the only explanation seems to be that /u/ (> /ʌ/) was becoming seen as a marker (or "ideaphone") of "pastness". This is precisely the point that is made by Bybee and Moder, though for them the phonetic shape that is associated with "pastness" is longer, and more general, as we have seen: the sequence /ʌ/ followed by a nasal and/or by /k/ or /g/.

If this were the case, we would expect nonstandard varieties of English to contain a greater number of preterite and past participle forms that conform to the past tense schema, since these varieties would have been less affected by prescriptive ideas about usage. Bybee and Moder give a few examples of nonstandard forms that conform to the schema, as shown in Table 1 (preterite and past participle forms for "bring", "sneak", "shake" and "drag"), but many more can be added if we include forms that have been attested in sociolinguistic variationist studies, as Table 2 shows.

Table 2. Nonstandard preterite forms in /ʌ/ + nasal and/or velar consonant

/ʌ/ + nasal	(for example, *begun, come, done, run, rung, sung*)
/ʌ/ + nasal + /k/ or /g/	(for example, *drunk, sunk, stunk*)
/ʌ/ + /k/ or /g/	(for example, *drug, tuck*)

Sources: Cheshire (1982); Edwards – Trudgill – Weltens (1984); Feagin (1979); Eisikovits (1987); Wolfram – Christian (1976); Wolfram – Fasold (1974)

As mentioned in section 2, many of the irregular verbs that have survived in a strong form in present-day English had alternating weak forms during the period 1600–1800. Two interrelated reasons were suggested for the survival of strong forms: their frequency of occurrence (and the implications of this for language processing), and their development as social markers. A further reason can now be suggested to account for the survival of certain strong forms. The weak pattern, it seems, is not the only productive pattern to have affected the development of English verbs: an additional productive pattern is the past tense schema /ʌ/ followed by a velar nasal. This phonetic shape constitutes a natural morphological class, which includes many nonstandard preterite and past participle forms, as well as some standard forms. The implications for language production are not yet entirely clear, but we can now modify the suggestion in the previous section that the strong verbs are simply learnt by rote and accessed as separate lexical items. Some of the strong past tense forms are presumably grouped together in the mental lexicons of speakers, organized according to a schema that relates their phonological form to their morphological function of signalling "past tense". The mental process that is involved seems to be a product-oriented process, for it is the preterite forms of this group of strong verbs that seem to have significance for speakers of English, rather than their base forms. Bybee and Moder (1983) suggest that children tend to form product-oriented schemas when they are acquiring language, and that these are precursors to source-oriented rules, such as those that may add an -ed suffix to the regular, weak verbs. For some classes of verbs, such as the verbs of class 1 and 2 in Table 2, source-oriented rules presumably cannot be formed, and so the product-oriented schema remains as a generalization according to which this part of the mental lexicon is organized (Bybee – Slobin 1982: 288).

This pattern, which has been quite productive in the development of English verb forms, has been brought to a stop in standard English, but has been freer to continue in nonstandard, spoken English. Interestingly, there is evidence that the schema is still productive for educated speakers of English today, even if many of the verb forms that they actually use do not conform to it. Bybee – Slobin (1982) and Bybee – Moder (1983) report a series of experiments in which the participants were asked, amongst other things, to provide as quickly as possible the preterite form for a large number of verbs, both weak and strong. A statistically significant proportion of the participants gave a preterite form in /ʌ/ for class 1 verbs reflecting, Bybee and Moder claim, "a clear historical trend toward substituting the past participle form in /ʌ/ for the past form in /æ/" (1983: 254). Additionally, in these conditions of experimental stress, several participants produced a preterite form in /ʌ/ for verbs that ordinarily have a different vowel in the preterite form. For example, some participants produced /ʌt/ instead of /ɛt/, for the past tense of "eat", and *clunk* instead of *clank*, for the past tense of "clink" (Bybee – Slobin 1982: 280). Some of the forms that were produced were dialect forms, such as *brung* – though not, apparently, dialect forms that were normally used by these participants. Other forms were clearly spontaneous innovations. Thus there is evidence not only for the historical productivity of this past tense pattern, but for its continuing psychological "reality" for present-day speakers of English.

4. Preterite and past participle forms

A further difference between standard and nonstandard English is that the preterite and past participles of some verbs are distinct in standard English but identical in nonstandard English. Thus, where standard English has *I forgot it* and *I've forgotten it*, many of the nonstandard varieties have *I forgot it* and *I've forgot it*. In working-class adolescents' speech in Reading, Berkshire, the following verbs occurred with identical preterite and past participle forms (that is, without *-en* forms): "take", "forget", "run", "break", "throw", "beat", "see" (Cheshire 1982: 47). Similar examples for these and other verbs are given for the nonstandard English that is spoken in parts of the USA, by Wolfram and Fasold (1974), Wolfram and Christian 1976), Feagin (1979); and in Australia, by Eisikovits (1987).

The use of a single form for strong preterites and past participles in nonstandard English can be seen as analogy with the favourite weak verb pattern, where the *-ed* suffix occurs with both preterite and past participle forms. It is a move in the direction of greater transparency, reducing distinctions that are redundant (Milroy – Milroy 1985: 83). The tendency to use a single form for preterites and past participles has a long history: Shakespeare, for example, used the past participles *rode* and *chose* where present-day standard English has *ridden* and *chosen* (Milroy – Milroy 1985: 84). There is general agreement that eighteenth-century prescriptive grammarians stood in the way of the "normal" process of simplification that was taking place with the strong verbs (Leonard 1929: 76; Hogg 1988: 38; Milroy – Milroy 1985: 84). The prestige of Latin lingered on and English, with its relative lack of inflections, was seen as a greatly inferior language. This led prescriptivists to insist on the retention of suffixed participles as a way of marking formally the distinction between preterites and past participles. Priestley's view was typical of the time: "As the paucity of inflections is the greatest defect in our language, we ought to take advantage of every variety that the practice of good authors will warrant, and therefore, if possible, make a participle different from the preterite of a verb; as, a book is *written*, not *wrote*; the ships are *taken*, not *took*" (Priestley 1761 [1968]: 16–17).

This view was endorsed by Dr. Johnson, who wrote in the grammar section of his Dictionary: "he shall seldom err who remembers, that when a verb has a particle distinct from its preterite, as *write*, *wrote*, *written*, that distinct part is more proper and elegant, as *the book is written* is better than *the book is wrote*" (Johnson 1755 [1785]). The idea was reinforced, no doubt, by Lowth: "our ears have grown familiar with *I have writ*, *I have drank*, *I have bore* etc. which are altogether ... barbarous" (Lowth 1762 [1967]: 90).[2]

It is clear from comments such as these that considerable variation existed in the form of past participles. Lass (this volume) shows that eighteenth-century descriptive grammarians gave alternating past participle forms for several of the strong verbs: Kirkby (1746 [1971]: 89–94), for example, lists 95 out of some 160 irregular verbs with two or more participles. Withers (1788: 209) comments explicitly on variation between the past participles *went* and *gone*: "should have GONE is more usual, but not more proper, than should have WENT" (quoted by Leonard 1929: 162). Baker's prescriptions for the past participle forms of certain strong verbs in his *Reflections on the English language* show that there was variation between the forms *worn* and *wore*, and *torn* and *tore*, and that although he preferred *fallen* as the past participle of "fall", *fell* was also in use: "This word is used by almost all incorrect speakers, and even by many writers instead of *Fallen* ... This is not good English. The proper word (as here hinted) is *fallen*." (1770 [1968]: 59).

Variation between a past participle form in *-en* and a regular *-ed* form continues for some verbs in present-day standard English (see Quirk et al. 1985: 111–112, who include "mow", "hew" and "swell") and for a greater number of verbs in nonstandard English. Although there are indications of a trend towards morphological simplification in nonstandard English, with a single form used for both preterites and past participles, it is important not to forget that the simplified *-ed* forms often alternate with older *-en* forms, and that this variation has a long history. Furthermore, one recent analysis has shown that variation in the form of the past participle has a grammatical function. Eisikovits (1987) found that working-class adolescents in Sydney commonly used nonstandard suffixless participles in perfective constructions, whereas they typically used standard *-en* forms in passive constructions. For example, the verb "break" occurred in five perfective constructions (such as – to give a hypothetical example – *you've broke that cup*) and in eleven passive constructions (such as *the cup got broken*). All the passive constructions contained the standard participle form (*broken*), whereas all the perfective constructions contained the nonstandard form (*broke*). This pattern of variation was repeated for ten of the eleven lexical verbs that occurred frequently enough in the corpus to undergo this type of analysis. Eisikovits concludes that a separation of meanings of the past participle is taking place, and that this is reflected in the choice of form that is used: the more stative, adjectival sense of the past participle in passive constructions tends to favour the *-en* participle form, whereas the more active, dynamic sense of the participle in perfective constructions tends to favour the nonstandard form, which is identical to the preterite form.[3]

Other analyses of nonstandard verb forms in present-day English have not considered this factor as a constraint on variation, so it is impossible to say whether the distinction between form and function is widespread. However, although Eisikovits suggests that the distinction is a recent phenomenon, there are indications that it is in fact a long-standing tendency in English. The strong participle of a verb sometimes continued in use long after the preterite form had become weak, and even when the participle had become established as a weak form in standard English the *-en* form sometimes persisted as an adjectival form. Baugh and Cable (1978: 164) provide the examples *cloven, graven, hewn, laden, molten, mown, misshapen, shaven, sodden* and *swollen*, commenting: "for some reason the past participle of strong verbs seems to have been more tenacious then the past tense" (see also Pyles 1964: 198–203).[4] Eisikovits' analysis suggests a specific reason for the tenacity of strong past participles: the variable participle forms that were used in earlier stages of English may have allowed a functional distinction to be made, between participles with a stative, adjectival sense and participles with a dynamic sense. This should, of course, be an empirical question which subsequent research on earlier texts will be able to address – though it is possible that the tendency would have been more marked in spoken English than in the written texts that have to be used as sources of data.

Quirk (1970) suggests that a similar aspectual distinction is marked by the variant *t/–ed* forms of certain preterites and past participles for speakers of present-day standard English, but that the distinction exists in a "dormant" form, in much the same way that the productive strong verb schema appears to exist as a latent psychological reality for some speakers (see section 3). Quirk carried out tests with British and American educated speakers of English, to determine their reactions to the variable preterite and past participle forms of the small class of verbs that variably have a *-t* suffix or an *-ed* suffix (the class includes "burn", "spill", "smell", "dream", "spoil": see Quirk et al. 1985: 105–106). It is commonly assumed that speakers of American English use *-ed* forms more frequently for both preterites and past participles, whereas British speakers use *-t* forms more frequently (Quirk 1970: 304). However, in the tests both British and American speakers showed a statistically significant preference for preterites with the *-ed* suffix and past participles with the *-t* suffix. A further battery of tests revealed a tendency, particularly strong amongst British speakers, for the variation between *-t* and *-ed* forms to be perceived as a marker of an aspectual distinction, with *-t* suffixes corresponding to effective or punctual aspect and *-ed* suffixes to durative aspect. As an example, we can consider the following sentences containing the verb "spill", which were among those used in Quirk's tests:

When I shouted, he spilt his coffee (punctual)
The water spilled out all day until the ceiling gave way (durative).

The tests revealed, however, that the perception of *-t* and *-ed* as markers of an aspectual distinction was less strong than their perception as markers of preterite and past participle forms. Quirk suggests an historical explanation for this. The *-t* inflection in preterite and past participles appears to have originated in the past participle, so that the aspectual distinction between *-t* and *-ed* forms of the preterite can be seen as resulting from extrapolation from the past participle. In those uses of the preterite which are closest to the "perfectivity" of the perfect, "*-t* forms seem more natural to a speaker of English even if he is not in the habit of making such a distinction, or even of making much active use of *-t* forms at all" (1970: 310). Thus the aspectual distinction can be considered to have psychological reality for speakers of English; in Quirk's words, it is in "suspended animation" (1970: 304), like the psycholinguistic schema for strong verbs that was discussed in section 3.

Thus in both standard and nonstandard English there appears to be a relic of an aspectual distinction in the variable forms of some irregular preterites and past participles, between punctual, dynamic processes and stative, adjectival senses. For some speakers of nonstandard Sydney English, at least, the distinction occurs in usage, in the form of the past participles. For educated speakers of British and American English, it seems, the distinction lies in the form of those preterites and past participles that have variant forms in *-t* and *-ed*, and the distinction is a potential one, rather then one that occurs in usage.

It is worth stressing that the formal marking of dynamic processes is a longstanding characteristic of English. In Old English the mutative verbs formed their perfects with "be" rather than "have", and this distinction continued to be made during the Middle English period (Traugott 1972: 144–145). Traugott points out that in Shakespeare's time *he is come* was more frequent than *he has come*, and that "be" perfects with *come* continued in regular use until the nineteenth century. Johnson (1755, [1785]) considered them "more proper" for "intransitive verbs", citing as examples the "mutatives" *I am risen, I was walked out*. It seems that as the marking of mutative verbs with "be" perfects declined, so forms of the past participle developed for certain verbs which enabled the aspectual distinction to be maintained (see Comrie (1976: 49) for discussion of the link between mutative verbs and dynamic states). For the most part, however, this distinction con only be observed in the present-day nonstandard varieties of English.

To what extent can literacy and standardization account for the difference that now exists between nonstandard and standard English? It seems clear that new *-ed* forms of the past participle developed for some verbs during the Middle English period, as a result of a natural tendency towards simplification. As we have seen, there is evidence to suggest that the resulting variation was used to mark an aspectual distinction between stative, adjectival senses of the past participle and dynamic senses. This distinction may then have been extended to preterite forms. Many of the new forms resulted in there being a common form for the preterite and participle forms of the verb, and we can assume that these would have co-existed with the older strong forms, which formally distinguished the preterites and past participles. If we look at the writings of the grammarians who were trying to ascertain the language during the eighteenth century, we find that their preoccupation appears to have been with marking a formal distinction between preterites and past participles, which in most cases meant insisting on the *-ed* form of past participles. None of the eighteenth-century grammars that I have examined note the marking of a distinction between dynamic and stative senses of the past participles, though it is noteworthy that Baker, in his *Reflections on the English language*, prescribes a single form for a past participle and always illustrates the use of this form with both an adjectival, stative construction and a dynamic, verbal construction. For example, for *worn* and *torn* he writes: "These words are better with the auxiliaries then *Wore* or *Tore*. These cloaths are but little worn – He has worn this Suit for some Time – He has torn the writings – The writings are torn" (1770 [1968]: 60). Baker's distaste for *fell* as a past participle was mentioned earlier; as an illustration of incorrect English he gives "The Horse has fell – The Horse is fell" (1770 [1968]: 60). On the whole, however, the main concern of the prescriptivists appears to have been to maintain the *-en* participles as a way of preserving morphological inflections in the English verb, and to eliminate the *-ed* participles. Leonard's survey of eighteenth-century grammars convinced him that although their efforts often produced simply a "clutter of prescriptions", in the case of the strong verbs "they either helped unnecessary forms to prevail in the language or at least failed to assist in the movement towards simplification" (1929: 77). Eisikovits' work on nonstandard English and Quirk's work on standard English suggests that they may also have failed to assist in a tendency towards isomorphism in the past participles, where one linguistic form would correspond to one function.

5. Conclusion

This paper has identified three processes that have affected the form of preterites and past participles in English. First, the productive weak verb pattern has involved a transfer of certain strong verbs to the weak class, sometimes resulting in the co-existence of both strong and weak variants of a single verb. Second, the rather less productive past tense schema in /ʌ/ followed by a velar nasal has effected a change of some verbs to this phonetic shape. Finally, past participles became marked for aspectual function. In each case, these processes can be seen more clearly by analyzing preterite and past participle forms in both standard and nonstandard varieties of English. These processes have been suppressed in standard English, which owes its preterite and past participle verb forms partly to the desire of cultivated polite society to differentiate itself linguistically from less cultivated sections of society, and partly to the work of prescriptive grammarians. The processes survive, to a limited extent, in the variation that persists in the verbal morphology of standard English and in the behaviour of educated speakers of English in experimental tests. They survive to a greater extent in some of the nonstandard varieties of present-day English. It is important, therefore, to include nonstandard English in the study of the English language, since it then becomes possible to observe more clearly those linguistic changes that have been brought to a stop by the processes of standardization and literacy.

Notes

This is a much revised and reworked version of a paper which is to appear in Blank, Claudia (ed.) *Language and civilisation* (Frankfurt: Lang). A preliminary version of the present paper was presented in 1990 at the Helsinki Workshop on Sociohistorical Linguistics. I would like to record my appreciation of the comments which I received at the Workshop, and to give special thanks to Laurel Brinton and Roger Lass for sharing some of their expertise with me. I am also grateful for comments received from Detlef Stark, and from the editors of this volume. The paper is much improved as a result of all this help, but the remaining defects naturally have to remain my own responsibility.

1. Bybee and Slobin (1982) further point out that many educated speakers of American English do not use the past tense forms *sprang*, *shrank* and *stank*, preferring forms with /ʌ/. To this we can add my own observation that many educated speakers of southern British English prefer the preterite form *rung* to *rang* in phrases such as *she rung me to invite me to the party*.

2. Leonard (1929: 63) shows that there was some disagreement about the preferred participle of certain verbs with, for example, Lowth commending Dr. Middleton for "restoring the true participle *sitten*" but Campbell ridiculing the preference for *sitten* (whilst himself using *slidden*).
3. Eisikovits' analysis also found that the nonstandard forms of past participles were more likely to occur in the past perfective than in the present perfective, and that the presence of a preceding modal influenced the use of the nonstandard form (Eisikovits 1987: 22–23).
4. There are also some adjectival forms in *-t* that coexist with verbal participles in *-ed*, such as *wrought/worked* (*the gate is made of wrought iron / she worked hard all day*) or *molten/melted* (*the hill is covered in molten lava / the ice has melted*).

References

Baker, Robert
    1770   *Reflections on the English language*. London.
    [1968] [Reprinted in: Robin C. Alston (ed.), *English linguistics, 1500–1800* No. 87. Menston: Scolar Press.]
Baugh, Albert C. – Thomas Cable
    1978   *A history of the English language*. (3rd edition.) London: Routledge.
Blake, Norman F.
    1981   *Nonstandard language in English literature*. London: Deutsch.
Bybee, Joan L. – Carol L. Moder
    1983   "Morphological classes as natural categories", *Language* 59: 251–270.
Bybee, Joan L. – Dan L. Slobin
    1982   "Rules and schemas in the development and use of the English past tense", *Language* 58: 265–289.
Cheshire, Jenny
    1982   *Variation in an English dialect: A sociolinguistic study*. Cambridge: Cambridge University Press.
Comrie, Bernard
    1976   *Aspect*. Cambridge: Cambridge University Press.
Defoe, Daniel
    1697   *An essay upon projects*. London.
    [1969] [Reprinted in facsimile. Menston: Scolar Press.]
Edwards, Viv – Peter Trudgill - Bert Weltens
    1984   *The grammar of English dialect: A survey of research*. London: Economic and Social Research Council.
Eisikovits, Edina
    1987   "Variations in the lexical verb in inner-Sydney English", *Australian Journal of Linguistics* 7: 1–24.

Ekwall, Eilert
  1975 *A history of modern English sounds and morphology.* Translated by E. Ward. Oxford: Blackwell.
Feagin, Crawford
  1979 *Variation and change in Alabama English: A sociolinguistic study of the white community.* Washington: Georgetown University Press.
Greenwood, James
  1711 *An essay towards a practical English grammar.* London.
  [1968] [Reprinted in: Robin C. Alston (ed.), *English Linguistics, 1500–1800* No. 128. Menston: Scolar Press.]
Hogg, Richard
  1988 "Snuck: The development of irregular preterite forms", in: Graham Nixon – John Honey (eds.), 31–40.
Johnson, Dr. Samuel
  1755 *A dictionary of the English language.* London.
  1785 *A dictionary of the English language.* (6th edition.) London.
Kirkby, John
  1746 *A new English grammar, or guide to the English tongue, with notes.*
  [1971] [Reprinted in: Robin C. Alston (ed.), *English Linguistics, 1500–1800* No. 297. Menston: Scolar Press.]
Kuczaj, Stan A.
  1977 "The acquisition of regular and irregular past tense forms", *Journal of verbal learning and verbal behaviour* 16: 589–600.
Lakoff, George
  1987 *Women, fire and dangerous things.* Chicago: University of Chicago Press.
Leonard, Sterling A.
  1929 *The doctrine of correctness in English Usage, 1700–1800.* Madison: University of Wisconsin.
Lowth, Robert
  1762 *A short introduction to English grammar.* London.
  [1967] [Reprinted in: Robin C. Alston (ed.), *English Linguistics, 1500–1800* No. 210. Menston: Scolar Press.]
Milroy, James – Lesley Milroy
  1985 *Authority in language: Investigating language prescription and standardization.* London: Routledge.
Nixon, Graham – John Honey (eds.)
  1988 *An historic tongue: Studies in English linguistics in memory of Barbara Strang.* London: Routledge.
Priestley, Joseph
  1761 *The rudiments of English grammar.* London.
  [1968] [Reprinted in: Robin C. Alston (ed.), *English Linguistics, 1500–1800* No. 210. Menston: Scolar Press.]

Pyles, Thomas
    1964   *The origins and development of the English language*. New York: Harcourt, Brace and Wold.
Quirk, Randolph
    1970   "Aspect and variant inflection in English verbs", *Language* 46: 301–311.
Quirk, Randolph – Sidney Greenbaum – Geoffrey Leech – Jan Svartvik
    1985   *A comprehensive grammar of English*. Harlow: Longman.
Rosch, Eleanor
    1978   "Principles of categorization", in Eleanor Rosch – Barbara B. Lloyd (eds.), 27–48.
Rosch, Eleanor – Barbara B. Lloyd (eds.)
    1978   *Cognition and categorization*. Hillsdale, N. J.: Erlbaum.
Rosch, Eleanor – Carolyn B. Mervis
    1975   "Family resemblances: Studies in the internal structure of categories", *Cognitive Psychology* 7: 573–605.
Shorrocks, Graham
    1980   *A grammar of the dialect of Farnworth and district (Greater Manchester County, formerly Lancashire)*. [Unpublished Ph.D. thesis, University of Sheffield].
Strang, Barbara M.H.
    1970   *A history of English*. London: Methuen.
Traugott, Elizabeth C.
    1972   *A history of English syntax*. New York: Holt, Rinehart and Winston.
Withers, Philip
    1788   *Aristarchus*. London.
Wolfram, Walt – Donna Christian
    1976   *Appalachian speech*. Washington D.C.: Center for Applied Linguistics.
Wolfram, Walt – Ralph Fasold
    1974   *The study of social dialects in American English*. Englewood Cliffs, N.J.: Prentice Hall.

The differentiation of statives and perfects in early modern English: The development of the conclusive perfect

Laurel J. Brinton

1. Introduction

In *Aspects of the Theory of Syntax*, Chomsky points to the threefold ambiguity of the sentence *I had a book stolen*, explaining the different meanings as follows:

(i) "I had a book stolen from my car when I stupidly left the window open," that is, "someone stole a book from my car"; (ii) "I had a book stolen from the library by a professional thief who I hired to do the job," that is, "I had someone steal a book"; (iii) "I almost had a book stolen, but they caught me leaving the library with it," that is "I had almost succeeded in stealing a book" (Chomsky 1965: 22).

While the passive and causative interpretations of the first two readings are quite obvious, the third reading is "a little idiosyncratic and idiomatic" (Palmer 1987: 168)[1] because the *have* + object + past participle construction seems to imply complete success, unless that success is explicitly qualified as partial or temporary by a word or clause such as *almost* in the following examples:

(1) a. *The way he kept on, he* had *me almost* convinced *Hickok and Smith were innocent* (1965, T. Capote, *In Cold Blood* [New York: Random House] p. 213; cited by Visser 1973: 2387)
   b. *She* had *her face almost* buried (Caldwell, *Georgia Boy*, "The Day We Rang the Bell"; cited by Yamakawa 1958: 170–171).

Without such explicit qualifiers, these constructions appear to have the meaning of 'success' or 'accomplishment of a state', as, for example, the states of having one's mind made up, having a problem worked out, or having a person figured out or cornered in the following:

(2) a. *I* have *my mind* made up (c. 1930, Aldington, *All Men Are Enemies* [Albatross], p. 177; cited by Visser 1973: 2191)
 b. *Then when we* have *that* worked out, *we can probably knock out most and concentrate on what remains* (1947, E. Linsky, *The Kiss of Death* [Penguin], p. 83; cited by Visser 1973: 2191)
 c. *From the very first day you came to work on this ward, I* had *you all* figured out (1959, D. Telfer, *The Caretakers* [Signet Bks.], p. 188; cited by Visser 1973: 2387)
 d. *Christopher* had *her* cornered, *and she knew it* (1965, Iris Murdoch, *The Red and the Green* [London], p. 80; cited by Visser 1973: 2191).

The name of "split perfect" or "conclusive perfect" (Kirchner 1941; 1952) has been given to constructions such as those in (2) with *have* + object + past participle. Historians of the language see the conclusive perfect as preserving the pattern of the perfect found in Old and Middle English and as retaining the stative (possessive or resultative semantics) of the original form. However, this paper argues that the conclusive perfect is not a remnant of the old pattern, but an innovation in the modern period, modeled on earlier *have* + object + past participle constructions expressing indirect causation, indirect passive, and experiential passive. Moreover, its development is part of a more general differentiation of perfect and stative constructions which takes place as part of the process of language standardization during the seventeenth and eighteenth centuries. In this realignment, several previously undifferentiated patterns become distinguished: the sequences *have* + past participle + (object) becomes exclusively perfect in meaning, while the sequences *have* + object + past participle and *be* + past participle become exclusively stative (or passive) in meaning.

2. The conclusive perfect in Modern English

The existence of the conclusive perfect in Modern English is noted in most traditional grammars (e.g., Poutsma 1926: 214; Curme 1931; 358; 1935: 320–321; Kruisinga 1931: 388–389; Jespersen 1940: 16; Zandvoort 1966: 52), and it is accorded fuller treatment in Kirchner (1941: 144–150; 1952: 401–409), Yamakawa (1958: 165–174), and Visser (1973: 2189–91, 2387). Although the construction is said to be particularly common in Hiberno-English and American English (Kirchner 1952: 403; Yamakawa 1958: 168; Visser 1973: 2190; 2387; Harris 1984; 1985), it is also found in British English (see the examples in Kirchner 1952: 408; Yamakawa 1958: 170–172; Visser 1973: 2191, 2387). Almost all scholars see the conclusive perfect as being a remnant of the older form of the perfect, with postposition of the participle and stative/resultative interpretation (Curme 1935: 320; Jespersen 1940: 16; Kirchner 1941: 143, 145; 1952: 402–403; Visser 1973; 2190, 2387; Harris 1982: 6, 18–21; 1984: 320, 322),[2] though Kirchner (1952: 403–405) introduces an element of doubt by suggesting that while the conclusive perfect retains the form of the original construction, it may not continue its meaning and function unchanged.

The conclusive perfect is distinguished from the regular perfect not only by word order, but also by a number of behavioral properties:

(a) in the conclusive perfect, but not in the regular perfect, stress may fall on the participle (*I have the letter wrítten*, but not **I have wrítten the letter*) (Curme 1931: 358; 1935: 220);

(b) the conclusive perfect permits *all* before the participle (*I have my work all completed*, but not **I have all completed my work*) (McCoard 1978: 218–222, 250);

(c) the conclusive perfect may appear in imperatives (*Have your work done by the time I return*, but not **Have done your work by the time I return*) (McCoard 1978: 218–222, 250);

(d) *have got* may substitute for *have* in the conclusive perfect (*I've got my work done*, but not **I've got done my work*) (McCoard 1978: 218–222, 250);

(e) the scope of the negative in the conclusive perfect may be either the entire construction or the participle alone (*I haven't my work completed* or *I have lots of papers not written*) (Harris 1982: 17; 1984: 312);

(f) indefinite past time adverbials (such as *recently, once,* or *often*) may occur with the regular perfect but not with the conclusive perfect (*I have recently done my work*, but not **I have my work recently done*) ((McCoard 1978: 218–222, 250; Harris 1982: 16; 1984: 312; 1985: 44–45), or they may have a different meaning with the conclusive perfect (*He has never arranged anything* vs. *He never has anything arranged*) (Harris 1985: 45); and

(g) *have* has a weak form and auxiliary properties in the regular perfect but not in the conclusive perfect (*I've completed my work*, but not *?I've my work completed; Have you completed your work?*, but not *?Have you your work completed?*) (Palmer 1987: 168).

While several scholars feel that the conclusive perfect and the regular perfect are roughly equivalent in meaning (e.g., Jespersen 1940: 16; Yamakawa 1958: 169; Ando 1976: 654), the majority believe that there is a "real" (Kruisinga 1931: 389) or "considerable" (Poutsma 1926: 214) difference in meaning between the two forms. As Kruisinga puts it, "the [conclusive perfect] expresses a state as the result of an action, the [perfect] expresses an action considered the source of a state" (1931: 389). In other words, the conclusive perfect focuses on the present state resulting from a prior action, expressing stative/resultative meaning (see also Curme 1931: 358; 1935: 320–321; Jespersen 1940: 16; Kirchner 1941: 150; 1952: 406; Visser 1973: 2190; Harris 1982: 16; 1984: 312; 1985: 42–43). A somewhat different view of the conclusive perfect is that of Ikegami (1986; cf. Chomsky 1965: 22), who attributes the meaning of 'successful accomplishment' to this construction. Several scholars also point to the possessive semantics of *have* in the conclusive perfect as well as to the adjectival nature of the postposed participle, and its relative prominence (Poutsma 1926: 532; Yamakawa 1958: 171; Harris 1985: 42), which may lead to "a kind of emotional interest taken in the result reached ... tinged with a feeling of possessorship" (Visser 1973: 2190) or a "decidedly intensifying force" with the centre of interest "on the object of 'have'" (Kirchner 1941: 150).

It is precisely because the conclusive perfect emphasizes the resultant state that not every perfect has a corresponding conclusive perfect. The conclusive perfect seems to be restricted to dynamic verbs (Harris 1982: 16; 1984: 312–313; 1985: 43), specifically those denoting durative activities (Milroy – Milroy 1985: 88; Harris 1985: 44) which "leave behind them identifiable, literal states of some permanence, and durability" (McCoard 1978: 226; Carey 1990: 373–374). Thus, one can say *Mary has John persuaded* but not **Mary has John relied on; John has the book read* but not **John has the book seen;* and *I have the record cleaned* but not **I have the record played*.

3. The development of the perfect in English

The accepted view of both the meaning and the source of the conclusive perfect is consistent with traditional accounts of the development of the perfect in English, which see the perfect periphrasis originating in Old English in a stative construction consisting of full verb *have* or *be* and a past participle functioning adjectivally (see, inter alia, Curme 1931: 358–360; 1935: 320–321; Jespersen 1932: 29–31; Fridén 1948: 38–41; Yamakawa 1958: 166–167; Traugott 1972: 91–94, 144–145; Visser 1973: 2189–2192; Harris 1984: 321; Mitchell 1985: 280–305). While *be* occurs with mutative intransitive verbs, *have* occurs with transitive verbs, with verbs taking genitive, dative, or prepositional objects, and with non–mutative intransitive verbs. *Have* retains its full meaning 'hold, possess'. The participle is an object complement, generally following the object and inflected to agree with it. The construction expresses possession and is purely stative. Reanalysis of this stative construction as a perfect periphrasis, which occurs during the Middle English period, follows from a number of syntactic and semantic changes: (a) loss of the case ending on the participle, (b) transposition of the participle and object, (c) change in the status of *have* from full verb to auxiliary, (d) bleaching of the possessive semantics of *have* to a general relational meaning, and (e) change in the meaning of the construction from possession to resultant state to completed action. Thus, received opinion would have it that in the course of development from the stative *I have the house built*, meaning 'I possess or have the house in a built state', to the perfect *I have built the house*, the concrete meaning of the verb fades from 'possess' to a broad relational meaning, and the focus of the expression shifts from possession of the (built) house, to its finished state, and finally to the act of its construction.

Although the traditional account is repeated without question by most commentators, it is problematical in a number of ways. Even in Old English *have* + past participle constructions with possessive meaning (with the object in the possession of the subject) are extremely rare.[3] Either the nature of the object or the meaning of the verbal may prevent a possessive reading, as in the following, frequently cited example, where, according to Kirchner (1958: 405n.), "kaum von einem eigentlichen 'Besitz' die Rede sein kann":

(3) *Ac hie hæfdon ða hiora stemn gesetenne, 7 hiora mete genotudne* (ChronA [Plummer] 894.27)
'But they had finished their tour of duty and used up their food' = 'they possessed their tour of duty in a finished state and their food in a used up state'.

The presence of actional adverbs, agent phrases, or accompanying preterite verb forms may also militate against a purely stative reading of such constructions (see McCoard 1978: 226–228). In fact, Kirchner (1958: 404–405) thinks that "bereits in der ae. Fügung der Gruppencharakter der Formel im Vordergrund stand, und 'have' weniger 'Besitz' bezeichnete, als ein lediglich 'stützendes' den Hauptbegriff einführendes Formelverb darstellte".

Furthermore, *have* + past participle constructions in Old English do not seem to be exclusively stative rather than perfect in interpretation either; both meanings are possible. The formal evidence used for the stative reading, namely the inflection of the participle along with its position following the object (as in 3), is not reliable. The majority of participles in these constructions are, in fact, uninflected (Harrison 1887; Mitchell 1985: 283–284,

292), and though postposition of the participle is common, position does not correlate with the absence or presence of inflections. In other words, the order of object and past participle is not distinctive in Old English (Carey 1990: 373).[4] The interpretation of *have* + past participle constructions as either stative or perfect seems to depend almost entirely upon contextual clues. As Visser admits (1973: 2189), "For a long time after the Old English period, however, this difference in word-order was without discriminative force ... and the interpretation of constructions with mid-position of the object exclusively depended on situation and/or context." This equivocality seems to hold throughout the Middle English period, as the following examples taken almost at random from the *Middle English Dictionary* (s.v. haven, def. 12a) show:

(4) a. *The hye god* ... hadde *Adam* maked (1395, Chaucer, *CT. Mch.* E1325)
    b. *If we* haue *eny synnes* done (1475, Pecock, *Donet* 140/4).

Although both examples show the participle in postposition, (4a) is probably stative and (4b) perfect in meaning.

In the early modern period, however, the situation changes quite rapidly. During the sixteenth century, the order of the perfect construction seems to become fixed with the object in end position. Though Visser (1973: 2189) finds "numerous instances" of the pattern with mid-position of the object in Thomas More's works, most of these may be given a stative interpretation, as in the following:

(5) a. *our own workes: of which if we* haue *any* done *well, he [sc. the devil] casteth them into our mindes with ouer great liking* (*Last Things* 70 A13)
    b. *What ... griefe was it to his hart ... that he* had *no child of his own body* begotten (*Dialogue of Comfort* 1159 F15).

By the seventeenth century, instances of perfects with mid-position of the object are extremely rare. Milton's prose reveals no examples of this construction (Stern – Kollmeier 1985, s.v.v. *has, hast, had, have*), nor does Dryden's (see Söderlind 1958: 214–216). The Helsinki Corpus of English Texts likewise provides no examples of perfects with postposed participles in the Early Modern period (1500–1710).[5]

4. *Have* + object + past participle constructions in the history of English

With the fixing of the order *have* + past participle + object as the distinctive and exclusive order of the perfect in Early Modern English, the variant order *have* + object + past participle is initially quite rare in the written language, but becomes increasingly more common as the modern period progresses. It is not the case, however, that the conclusive perfect simply continues the meaning of the older *have* + object + past participle sequence found in Old and Middle English, since, as we have seen, this older order is not distinctively stative/resultative in interpretation. Rather, the conclusive perfect acquires an exclusively stative/resultative meaning for the first time in the modern period. As McCoard (1978: 22) observes, "we cannot simply use word order to distinguish the 'old' perfect from the 'new' perfect; the modern distinction in word order was not there originally". Such a development is possible only after the order *have* + object + past participle is freed of its former perfect meaning and can become a distinctive syntactic/semantic construction separate from the perfect. Since the sequence *have* + object + past participle is thus imbued with new significance, it must be viewed as an innovation rather than as a remnant in Modern English.

Furthermore, the development of the conclusive perfect appears to be part of a much larger differentiation of stative and perfect constructions which occurs in seventeenth and eighteenth century English, consisting of the fixing of the patterns *have* + objet + past participle and *be* + past participle with stative/resultative (or passive) meaning and of the pattern *have* + past participle (+ object) with perfect meaning. The conclusive perfect is one of several constructions – and probably the last – in which the order of *have* + object + past participle becomes fixed in the modern period:[6]

(6)   a. indirect causative: *I* had *my suitcase* put *in the corner of a third class carriage and took a seat in the dining-car* (1947, Waugh, *Brideshead Revisited* [Albatross], p. 60; cited by Visser 1973: 2388),

       b. indirect passive: *I* had *twenty boxes of the very best* given *to me once when I was up at Bangalore* (1929, Priestley, *The Good Companions*, p. 205; cited by Visser 1973: 2147,

       c. passive of experience: *Others in gentler ages had* had *their lives* changed *by such a revelation* (Waugh, *The Loved One*; cited by Yamakawa 1958: 190).

These constructions may be glossed as follows: (6a) 'I caused my suitcase to be put in the corner'; (6b) 'I was given twenty boxes of the very best'; and (6c) 'Others had experienced a change in their lives'. While the semantic relationship of these constructions with one another and with the conclusive perfect may not be intuitively obvious, it will be argued below (section 6) that they have a common stative/resultative (or passive) meaning and are all subject oriented.[7] All three constructions pre-date the conclusive perfect, but with undifferentiated order – *have* + object + past participle or *have* + past participle + object. In the modern period the former pattern becomes fixed, thus providing a model for the development of the conclusive perfect.

4.1. Indirect causative

The existence of the causative *have* construction is noted in most grammars of Modern English (see, for example, Poutsma 1905: 574; Curme 1931: 126; 1935: 220; Kruisinga 1931: 388; Jespersen 1940: 21–22; Scheurweghs 1959: 168; Zandvoort 1966: 51; Quirk – Greenbaum – Leech – Svartvik 1985: 1207–1208, 1412n.; Palmer 1987: 168, 195) and discussed in greater detail in Kirchner (1952: 393–394), Yamakawa (1958: 179–180), and Visser (1973: 2387–2388). This construction has the meaning 'to cause something to be done' or 'to cause someone to do something'; it may serve as a means of avoiding the passive infinitive after a causative verb, as in *I caused my suitcase to be put in the corner* (Jespersen 1940: 22). The grammatical subject does not directly perform the action expressed by the past participle, but plans, intends, or wills it. For this reason, the causative *have* construction is frequent after *will* and *would* (Franz 1939: 501; Söderlind 1958: 215; Yamakawa 1958: 181; Ando 1976: 652–653). The agent of the action may be expressed explicitly in a *by* phrase (as in *I had my suitcase put in the corner by the porter*).

The causative *have* construction seems to be quite well established during Middle English, as evidenced by the examples given in Visser (1973: 2388), dating from 1205, and those in the *Middle English Dictionary* (s.v. *haven*, def. 10a), dating from 1175. (The first example in the *Oxford English Dictionary*, s.v. *have*, def. 17b, is 1390.) However, during this period, the order of object and participle is not yet fixed; the participle may precede or follow the object:

(7)   a. *He* hath slain *And* piked out *hire fader brain, And of the Skulle* had mad *a Cuppe* (1393, Gower, *CA* 1.2569; cited in the *Middle English Dictionary*, s.v. *haven*, def. 10a)

b. *Item, I will* have delyvered *to a gude trewman ... that weendes in pilgramege iiij marcas* (1429, *Will York* in *Sur. Soc.* 4 420; cited in the *Middle English Dictionary*, s.v. *haven*, def. 10a).

Ando (1976: 652–653) finds causative *have* to be more frequent than causative *make* or *see* in Marlowe, and in Shakespeare, Franz (1939: 501) considers the construction "ziemlich geläufig"; in both authors, the participle is always postposed. The causative is the most frequent of the *have* + object + past participle constructions in the Helsinki Corpus. In the seventeenth century, the participle is always postposed:

(8) a. *I must* have *more coals* laid in (1610, Ben Jonson, *Alchemist* [Everym.] III, ii p. 42; cited by Visser 1973: 2388)
 b. *To that end he furnish'd them, and* had *them* train'd *in Arms* (Milton, K. 3.473.9; Stern – Kollmeier 1985, s.v. *had*)
 c. *[We] will* have *all the benches of judicature* annex'd *to the throne* (Milton, RE. 7.460.25; Stern – Kollmeier 1985, s.v. *have*)
 d. *I will take care to correct the press; & to* have *it* printed *well* (Dryden, Let 62; cited by Söderlind 1958: 215)
 e. *I'll* have *him* cudgelled *by my footman* (Dryden, Limb 37; cited by Söderlind 1958: 216)
 f. *But Solon very well replyd to a fond parent that would not* have *his child* corrected *for a perverse trik but* excused (Locke, Directions Concerning Education 50; Helsinki Corpus).

The construction undergoes little change in the eighteenth century:

(9) a. *some persons who thought it their interest to* have *it* suppressed (1702, Farquhar, *Twin-rivals*, Preface; cited by Visser 1973: 2388)
 b. *The country members are violent to* have *past faults* inquired *into* (Swift, *Journal to Stella*, 121; cited by Jespersen 1940: 22)
 c. *how he was pleased and affected to* have *that noble Writer* call'd *his Adversary* (Swift, Apol. 6 4; Kelling – Preston 1984, s.v. *have*)
 d. *I was vain enough to* have *the whole story* inserted *in the news* (1748, Smollett, *Roderick Random* [Tauchn.] VI, p. 27; cited by Visser 1973: 2388)
 e. *I must not suffer to* have *the laws* broken *before my face* (1764, Goldsmith, *History of England* [in Lett. 1771] II, p. 308; cited by Visser 1973: 2388.

The meaning of "allow" is common in this construction (see 8f, 9c, 9e), especially following *would*. This meaning is noted in Modern English examples such as *I'll not have you say such things* (Poutsma 1905: 574).

In Modern English, *get* may replace *have* in the causative construction (see Kirchner 1952: 231; Yamakawa 1958: 185–187; Visser 1973: 2384–2385; *Oxford English Dictionary*, s.v. *get*, def. 28a). The earliest citations of the causative *get* constructions given in Visser and in the *Oxford English Dictionary* date from about 1500. Two eighteenth-century examples are the following.

(10) a. *she was provided with a warrant . . . to* get *me apprehended* (1741, Richardson, *Pamela* [Dent], p. 159; cited by Visser 1973: 2384)
 b. *Le Fleur . . . had* got *himself so gallantly array'd* (1768, Sterne, *Sentimental Journey* [1778] II, p. 120; cited in the *Oxford English Dictionary*, s.v. *get*, def. 28a).

This construction also develops the meaning "allow" (see Kirchner 1952: 231).

4.2. Indirect passive

A second *have* + object + past participle construction is the indirect passive, where the indirect object or object of *to* of the active sentence becomes the subject of the passive, as in *I had a book given to me*. Grammarians frequently do not distinguish it from the passive of experience (see section 4.3), but the most distinct discussions of the construction may be found in Kirchner (1952: 397–398), Yamakawa (1958: 187–193), and Visser (1973: 2155–2157). According to several (Franz 1932: 501; Poutsma 1926: 136; Kirchner 1952: 398; Visser 1973: 2155–2156), the indirect passive with *have* is the preferred alternative to the similar construction with *be*, viz. *I was given the book,* which is often condemned by purists (see the illustrative quotations in Visser 1973: 2149–2150). It may also fill a gap by providing an indirect passive version for prepositional verbs which do not permit the construction with *be*, such as *I had the problem explained to me*, cf. **I was explained the problem to* (Poutsma 1926: 136; Kirchner 1952: 398; Visser 1973: 2156).

The indirect passive construction with *have* may pre-date that with *be* (for the history of the latter construction, see Visser 1973: 2143–2149). The *have* construction seems to be well established during the latter Middle English period (Kirchner 1952: 398n.; Yamakawa 1958: 189); Visser cites one example from the *Cursor Mundi* and numerous later Middle English examples, while the *Oxford English Dictionary* gives one Middle English example (the usage is not listed in the *Middle English Dictionary*). As is the case with the causative *have*, however, the order of the construction does not seem to be fixed during Middle English, when preposition of the participle was possible (11a), though postposition seems to have been more common (11b):

(11) a. *I myth* have sent *me home* ... *ij. peyir hose* (1422–1509, *Paston Letters* [Gairdner] no. 526; cited by Visser 1973: 2156)
b. *If I may* have *all thes money* payd *onto me* (1422–1509, *Paston Letters* [Gairdner] no. 526; cited by Visser 1973: 2156).

By the sixteenth century, however, the order of the construction is fixed with the past participle in end position, and the construction remains virtually unchanged in the seventeenth and eighteenth centuries, as the following examples show:[8]

(12) a. *Our servant ... humbly signified his desier to* have *som small tyme* granted *vnto him* (1582–1603, *Letters of Queen Elizabeth* [Camden Soc.; ed. Bruce], pp. 39, 67; cited by Visser 1973: 2150)
b. *I* had *myself twenty angels* given *me this morning* (1598, Shakespeare, *Merry Wives*, II, ii, 72; cited by Franz 1932: 502)
c. *The poor* have *the gospel* preached *to them* (1611, Bible, Mt. 11, 5; cited by Visser 1973: 2157)
d. *they that loue the Lord Iesus* haue *a sweet lesson* giuen *them how to strengthen & stablish themselues in the faith* (Hooker, Two Sermons 2; Helsinki Corpus)
e. *But Adam who* had *the wisdom* giv'n *him to know all creatures* (Milton, T. 2.593.16; Stern – Kollmeier 1985, s.v. *had*)
f. *Slaves, when they were set free,* had *a cap* given *them, in sign of their liberty* (Dryden, NSat 255; cited by Söderlind 1958: 215)
g. *Accordingly they* have *a subaltern court* paid *to them by persons of the best rank* (Swift, *Gulliver's Travels* [Riverside ed.], p. 206)
h. *Fame, who much frequented, and* had *a large Apartment formerly* assigned *to her* (Swift, BB. 152 31; Kelling – Preston 1984, s.v. *had*)
i. *the desire that she should* have *justice* done *her* (1778, Burney *Evelina* [London 1904], p. 128; cited by Visser 1973: 2157).

Visser notes (1973: 2156) that *to* appears to be optional nowadays. In fact, the construction without *to* seems to predominate at all times; the preposition *unto* is used in rare instances in the sixteenth century (as in 12a), while *to* appears for the first time in the seventeenth century (as in 12c, 12g, and 12h). Finally, Jespersen (1940: 15) notes the frequency of *have ... left*;

this concatenation appears as early as the sixteenth century and is common thereafter:

(13) a. *So I may* have *some nooke or corner* left *him* (Marlowe, E 367; cited by Ando 1976: 654)
 b. *Churchman who* had *a competency* left *him* (Milton, Ar. 2.531.7; Stern – Kollmeier 1985, s.v. *had*)
 c. *They* have *this* left *perhaps to object further* (Milton, LM. 7.305.3; Stern – Kollmeier 1985, s.v. *had*)
 d. *and I shall not* have *a Remnant* left (Swift, XI.123 21; Kelling – Preston 1984, s.v. *have*)
 e. *his heart* had *scarce strength enough* left (Fielding, 3.572; cited by Jespersen 1940: 15).

This construction is, however, rarely a true passive (as in 13b); rather, it means 'have something remaining'; in the latter sense, it approaches the meaning of the conclusive perfect (see section 4.4; cf. Yamakawa 1958: 166) or the *have*-existential (see section 5; Kirchner 1952: 400).

An indirect passive with *get* is a more recent development (see Kirchner 1952: 229–230; Yamakawa 1958: 193–194; *Oxford English Dictionary*, s.v. *get*, def. 28a), though it is still less common than the indirect passive with *have* in Modern English. Examples of this construction may be found in eighteenth-century English:

(14) *Do you* get *them* told *you in your sleep?* (1725, Ramsay, *Gentle Shepherd* III, ii; cited by Visser 1973: 2157).

4.3. Passive of experience

A construction closely related to the *have* passive is the so-called "passive of experience" (Curme 1935: 22), in which the subject is represented as experiencing or suffering something (see also Poutsma 1905: 574; Curme 1931: 126; Kruisinga 1931: 386–387; Kirchner 1952: 395–397; Söderlind 1958: 215; Scheurweghs 1959: 167; Zandvoort 1966: 51; Quirk – Greenbaum – Leech – Svartvik 1985: 1207). The subject "is indirectly affected by the action" (Palmer 1987: 165–166; also Quirk – Greenbaum – Leech – Svartvik 1985: 1413). A pronoun co-referential with the subject of the sentence, usually in the genitive, normally appears in the construction, but even a definite or indefinite article will be interpreted as possessive (Kirchner 1952: 395n; Palmer 1987: 166):

(15) a. *he has* had *his appointment* terminated (BBC; cited by Kirchner 1952: 396)
   b. *The pilot* had *a leg* broken (BBC; cited by Kirchner 1952: 396) (Here *a* = 'one of his'.)
   c. *the plate is very nearly entire, merely* having *the edge slightly* chipped (W; cited by Kirchner 1952: 396) (Here *the* = 'its'.).

According to Kirchner (1952: 396), this construction foregrounds the genitive relationship of the subject.[9]

In surface order, the passive of experience is identical to the causative, leading to possible ambiguities (Curme 1931: 126; 1935: 220; Kirchner 1952: 396; Yamakawa 1958: 188–189; Quirk – Greenbaum – Leech – Svartvik 1985: 1207, 1413; Palmer 1987: 165). Taken out of context, the following eighteenth-century construction could, for example, be interpreted as either 'they caused their fortunes to be told', or 'they experienced the telling of their fortunes', but the context dictates the causative reading:

(16)   to have *their Fortunes* told *them* (1772, Defoe, *Plague* [1754], p. 32; cited in the *Oxford English Dictionary*, s.v. *have*, def. 17b).

In contrast, the following Shakespearian example must in context be interpreted as a passive of experience, though the *Oxford English Dictionary* classifies it as causative:

(17)   To haue *their Balmy slumbers* wak'd *with strife* (1604, Shakespeare, *Othello*, II, iii, 258).

In other instances, the nature of the subject or the character of the verb will dictate the reading given. For example, the following two examples, given by Visser (1973: 2388) as examples of the causative, can be read only as passives of experience, since in (18a) the inanimate subject cannot willingly bring about the action and in (18b) the action of the verb is not one which a person would intentionally bring upon himself:

(18) a. *the Packard is* having *something* done *to it* (Wodehouse, *Quick Service* [Penguin], p. 6)
   b. *Old Acton* had *his house* broken into *last Monday* (1894, A. Conan Doyle, *Memoirs Sherl. Holmes* 3, p. 233).

Curme (1931: 126; 1935: 220) argues that the two constructions are distinguished by stress: the participle is stressed in the passive of experience, while *have* is stressed in the causative construction. Yamakawa (1958: 188–189) suggests that the increased stress on *have* in the causative construction is due to the increased intentional or volition force of the verb.

The passive of experience appears to be contemporaneous with the indirect passive. Visser (1973: 2161) suggests that it is not to be found in Middle English, and the *Middle English Dictionary* contains no listing for it, but the *Oxford English Dictionary* dates it from the fourteenth century. Examples of the construction occur in sixteenth century, and by Shakespeare's time, it is fully established. Again, however, the order of object and participle is not entirely fixed:

(19) a. *I have* had slayne *mo then xx. M. Men* (1533, Ld. Berners *Huon* ciii, p. 343; cited in the *Oxford English Dictionary*, s.v. *have*, def. 18a)
   b. *Would it not grieue a King to be so abusde, And* haue *a thousand horsmen* tane away (Marlowe, 1T, p. 529; cited by Ando 1976: 653)
   c. *I* had *my pocket* pickt (Shakespeare, *Henry IV*, Part 1, III, iii, 113; cited by Jespersen 1940: 14)
   d. *A Wedded-Lady, That* hath *her Husband* banish'd (1611, Shakespeare, *Cymbeline*, I, vi, 3; cited in the *Oxford English Dictionary*, s.v. *have*, def. 18a)
   e. *The hedge-sparrow fed the cuckoo so long, That it* had *it head* bit off *by it young* (Shakespeare, *Lear*, I, iv, 214–215).

In the Helsinki Corpus, passives of experience and indirect passives with *have* are equally common. Seventeenth and eighteenth-century examples of the passive of experience are fully fixed with postposition of the participle. A co-referential pronoun in the genitive may or may not appear:

(20) a. *Some haue lost, some* haue *thinges* stollen *from them, some are vexed in their bodies* (Gifford, *A Dialogue Concerning Witches* E4R; Helsinki Corpus)
   b. *& after a while I was brought uppe before him againe to* have *sentence* pronounced *against mee* (*The Journal of George Fox*, p. 79; Helsinki Corpus)
   c. *[they]* had *their breath so* congeal'd *by the cold* (Milton, HM. 8.477.13; Stern – Kollmeier 1985; s.v. *had*)
   d. *having* had *three choice Horses* kill'd *under him* (Milton, B. 5.401.19; Stern – Kollmeier 1985, s.v. *had*)
   e. *when his upper-gallery fools discover they* have *tricks* put *upon them* (Dryden, Mor 402; cited by Söderlind 1958: 215)
   f. *So that man ... hath his heart all the day long* gnawed on *by feare of death* (1651, Hobbes, *Leviathan* XII, p. 52; cited by Visser 1973: 2388 [as a causative!])

g. *Is it not provoking to* have *the most ill-natured things* said *of one?* (Sheridan, *School for Scandal*; cited by Poutsma 1905: 574)
h. *Another* had *one of his hands* ... burnt (1719, Defoe, *Robinson Crusoe*, II, x; cited in the *Oxford English Dictionary*, s.v. have, def. 18a)
i. *I never* had *a robbery* committed *in my house* (Fielding 3.572; cited by Jespersen 1940: 15).

A similar construction with *get* seems to be of more recent origin, though examples do occur in the eighteenth century:

(21) a. *I* got *my right wrist* dislocated (T. Jefferson, *Writings* [1787]; cited by Yamakawa 1958: 194)
b. *That family had lately* got *their pictures* drawn *by limner* (1766, Goldsmith, *Vicar*, Ch. 16; cited by Visser 1973: 2384 as "passive", though it could also be causative).

4.4. Conclusive perfect

The development of the conclusive perfect is more difficult to establish than that of the indirect causative, indirect passive, or experiential passive. In part, this results from the view of grammarians that the conclusive perfect is a remnant form. Hence its occurrence in earlier stages of the language is often taken for granted, while its occurrence in Modern English is carefully documented. It is claimed that the conclusive perfect begins to decrease in frequency in the seventeenth century (Visser 1973: 2190), perhaps due to competition with the actional perfect and pluperfect (Visser 1973: 2187; Harris 1984: 322; 1985: 49), possible confusion with the comparable causative construction (Visser 1973: 2190), or the replacement of *have* by *have got*, especially in British English (Harris 1984: 322; 1985: 49). Today it is thought to be relatively infrequent, except in the more conservative dialects such as Anglo-Irish and American where it is better preserved. But Visser then makes the apparently contradictory observation that the conclusive perfect is now of "increasing frequency" in popular diction (1973: 2190) and appears mainly in the late modern period (1973: 2387). One may well ask, then, whether the conclusive perfect is increasing or decreasing in frequency in Modern English.

As argued in section 3, there is no evidence that the sequence *have* + object + past participle carries an exclusively stative meaning in Middle English; depending on context, it could be interpreted as a perfect or as stative/resultative. By the late sixteenth century, however, postposition of the object usually, though not always, seems to dictate a stative/resultative interpretation, as these examples of the conclusive perfect from Marlowe and Shakespeare show:[10]

(22) a. *To* have *this skirmish* fought, *let it suffice thee* (Marlowe, O 2.13.28; cited by Ando 1976: 654)
   b. *Any of all my Sisters wandring here?* having *a quiuer* girded *to her side* (Marlowe, D 185; cited by Ando 1976: 654)
   c. *And so* haue *I a noble father lost, A sister* driven *into desperate tearmes* (Shakespeare, *Hamlet*, IV, vii, 25–26; cited by Jespersen 1940: 15, who observes of the example that the first clause is "probably a simple perfect", while the second is a "nexus object", i.e., a passive of experience)
   d. *Thou* hast *thy father much* offended (Shakespeare, *Hamlet*, III, iv, 9; cited by Kirchner 1952: 402)
   e. *And when we* have *our naked frailties* hid (Shakespeare, *Macbeth*, II, iii, 128; cited by Kirchner 1952: 402)
   f. Have *you the lion's part* written? (Shakespeare, *Midsummer Night's Dream*, I, ii, 68; cited by Kirchner 1952: 402).

Since they occur in verse, many of the Shakespearian examples must be viewed with caution, for postposition of the participle puts it in rhyme position. Of the examples given here, only (22f) occurs in prose. Furthermore, perfect interpretations are certainly not impossible with examples such as (22a) and (22d). In the Helsinki Corpus, there are only two instances of conclusive perfects in the period 1500–1570, and one each in the periods 1570–1640 and 1640–1710.[11] Milton's prose offers a number of examples of the conclusive perfect, though it is certainly less frequent than the causative or passive constructions (Stern – Kollmeier 1985, s.v.v. *had, have*):

(23) a. *While thus Paulinus* had *his thought still* fix'd *before* (B. 5.76.5)
   b. *But Antoninus who* had *his wicked thought* tak'n up (B. 5.104.2)
   c. have *yet our hearts* rivetted *with these old opinions* (A. 1.705.3)
   d. *I* have *yet a store of gratitude* laid up (T. 2.579.18)
   e. *And thus we* have *their preface* supported *with three Reasons* (O. 3.321.22)

None of the constructions with postposed participles in Milton permits a perfect reading. It is interesting to note that, like the passive of experience, a co-referential pronoun in the genitive frequently occurs in this construction. In the eighteenth century, the conclusive perfect is somewhat more common:

(24) a. *I haue thy faythefull promised* redubled (*The Correspondence of Lady Katherine Paston* 65; Helsinki Corpus)
b. *That as soon as he* hath *the money* settled, *he believes a peace will be clapped up* (*The Diary of Samuel Pepys* VII, p. 411; Helsinki Corpus)
c. *I have another play just* finished, *but I want a plot for't* (1702 Farquhar, *Twin-Rivals*, III, i; cited by Visser 1973: 2190)
d. *upon this they* had *another charter* passed (W. Penn, Letter 1710 to J.W. Graham, W.P., 1917; 277; cited by Kirchner 1952: 402)
e. *this your lady* ... had *her talents* cultivated *among the venerable society of weeders, podders and hoppers* (Smollett, *Peregrine Pickle*, Chapt. 87; cited by Kirchner 1952: 403)
f. *as he walked the Street, he would* have *his Pockets* loaden *with Stones, to pelt at the Signs* (Swift, Apol. 8 12; Kelling – Preston 1984, s.v. *have*).

By the nineteenth century, however, examples of the conclusive perfect are more frequent, and the construction seems entirely natural and regular (see examples in Kirchner 1952: 403; Visser 1973: 2190).

Yamakawa (1958: 174–177) notes a comparable construction with *get* meaning 'succeed in bringing (the object) into the specified state'. The most common types are *get X done/finished*, but other verbs may occur, as in the following modern examples:

(25) a. *I* got *them* tied up *like a couple of girl friends in the convent* (Hemingway, *The Killers*; cited by Yamakawa 1958: 175)
b. *But they've certainly* got *it* fixed up *poetic* (Waugh, *The Loved One*; cited by Yamakawa 1958: 176).

Yamakawa (1958: 175) suggests that the construction with *get* is "unsupported in its development with any firm historical background", though he cites one example from Shakespeare. However, examples of the *get X done* type may be found already in the seventeenth century (26a–b), and other types occur in the eighteenth and nineteenth centuries:

(26) a. *who puts me in the best way how to* get *it* done (1660 Pepys i 80.20 [7 Mar])[12]
b. *About 9 a-clock I* got *all my letters* done (1660 Pepys i 126.15 [4 May])
c. *he has* got *you* turned away (1775, Sheridan, *The Duenna* I, v; cited by Visser 1973: 2384)[13]

d. *Then between them they* got *it* [sc. the opiate] swallowed (1888, Mrs. H. Ward *Rob. Elsmere* [Nelson] 563; cited by Visser 1973: 2384).

5. Related constructions

A number of similar constructions with *have* may shed light on the development and underlying meaning of the various *have* + object + past participle constructions.

5.1. *Have* + object + {adjective, prepositional phrase}

The "*have*-existential" (Quirk – Greenbaum – Leech – Svartvik 1985: 1411–1414) consists of *have* + object + adjective or prepositional phrase, as in *I have my article ready* or *He has his arm in a sling*. The *have*-existential construction is of modern origin (*Oxford English Dictionary*, s.v. *have*, def. 17a), occurring freely by the seventeenth century:

(27)   *and* has *large comely Volumes* ready (Swift, Epis. 20 28; Kelling – Preston 1984, s.v. *has*).

The relation of the *have*-existential to the passive, experiential, and causative *have* constructions has been noted by several grammarians (Kirchner 1941: 149; Ando 1976: 654; Quirk – Greenbaum – Leech – Svartvik 1985: 1412; Palmer 1987: 167).[14] Kirchner (1952: 399–400) believes that the *have*-existential bears closest resemblance to the conclusive perfect, and even points to examples in which a conclusive participle is conjoined with a pure adjective (1952: 408; Curme 1935: 320–321). Like the *have* + object + past participle construction, the *have*-existential may express indirect causation, as in *They had him slightly tipsy* (Kirchner 1952: 400), or indirect passive, with an 'affected' or recipient subject, as in *You have a taxi ready*, or active 'accomplishment', as in *The porter has a taxi ready* (Quirk – Greenbaum – Leech – Svartvik 1985: 1411–1412). The significant aspect of meaning of the *have*-existential comes out in contrast to the corresponding *there* predication, as in *There is a taxi ready*, or stative, as in *A taxi is ready*: an "extra participant" is introduced in the *have*-existential, namely the subject. Moreover, unless a genitive or dative is present, as in *His arm is in a sling* or *There is a taxi ready for you*, this subject cannot even be inferred from the corresponding stative (Quirk – Greenbaum – Leech – Svartvik 1985: 1411–1413).

5.2. *Have + object + infinitive*

The infinitive in the construction *have* + object + infinitive is termed a "retroactive infinitive" (Jespersen 1940: 203) since it is retroactive to something which is the object of *have*. Following van der Gaaf (see Visser 1969: 1474), such constructions are seen to carry a range of meanings from 'possession' to 'duty, obligation, compulsion'.[15] Visser notes that in constructions having a pure possessive meaning, as in *I have a nice warm coat to wear*, and in those having a mixed meaning of possession and obligation (in the sense 'have something or somebody to look after'), as in *I have a letter to mail*, "formerly the word order was rather free, but nowadays it is invariably have – object – infinitive" (Visser 1969: 1475, 1477). When the meaning of the *have* infinitive construction is that of pure obligation and *have* functions as an auxiliary, however, both orders are possible in Modern English.[16] Determining the semantic distinction between the variants, e.g. *I have to write a paper* and *I have a paper to write*, has caused grammarians great difficulty (see Kirchner 1952: 373–375). Rejecting van der Gaaf's notion that the latter retains more of the original meaning of possession, Visser (1969: 1482–1483) sees a subtle difference: he believes that the former order is preferred when the action is commanded by a person other than the subject, while the latter is preferred when the action is commanded by the subject himself. The construction with postposition of the infinitive has the meaning 'to be burdened with (often as the result of a self-imposed task)' or 'to feel it incumbent on oneself'.[17] Visser's earliest example of *have* + object + infinitive with the meaning of 'self-imposed obligation' dates from 1611; other seventeenth and eighteenth century examples are the following:

(28) a. *I* have *some letters* To write *and* send away (1611 Ben Jonson, *Cataline* [Everym. Libr.] II, i, p. 109; cited by Visser 1969: 1483)
   b. *I* have *one concluding Favor,* to request *of my Reader* (Swift, Conc. 134 7; Kelling – Preston 1984, s.v. *have*)
   c. *They* had *no more* to do *then* (Defoe, R. 2.18; cited by Jespersen 1940: 226)
   d. *he will moreover* have *various Accounts* to reconcile; *Anecdotes* to pick up; *Inscriptions* to make out; *Stories* to weave in; *Traditions* to sift; *Personages* to call upon ... (1759–1767, Sterne, *Tristam Shandy* [Everym.], p. 28; cited by Visser 1969: 1483).

Kirchner (1952: 386–390) also discusses a related group construction consisting of *have* + AcI (= accusative + infinitive) with or without *to*. This construction, like the *have* + object + participle construction, carries the meaning of cause, especially after *will* or *would* (e.g. *Vergil has Cupid say in the Aeneid*), of permission, now only in the negative (e.g. *I won't have you discuss my life*), and of experience, which Kirchner considers pleonastic (e.g. *I have had many scholars visit me*). In these cases, the infinitive is invariably postposed. Kirchner cites several Early Modern English examples, such as the following: *hate to have any new Wits rise* (Swift, J. to Stella).

5.3. *Have a* V

More distantly related is the *have a* V construction, e.g. *have a look, have a dip, have a sleep, have a try* (see Poutsma 1926: 394, 398). This construction is likewise of modern origin (Strang 1970: 101; Traugott 1972: 173; *Oxford English Dictionary*, s.v. *have*, def. 11b, first citation 1590). According to the *Oxford English Dictionary*, the *have a* V construction is used "when the action or proceeding is treated as something experienced, got at, attained, or enjoyed". Wierzbicka (1982: 753–799) accounts for this construction more completely in an insightful article. She argues that the verb *have* in this construction concentrates "the speaker's attention on the experiences of the person involved in the situation, to the exclusion of everything else" (1982: 760); the *have a* V frame "shifts the focus from the action to the potential effect of that action on the agent". Furthermore, *have* converts a predication about an object into an implicit predication about the subject; if one says *John had a walk* rather than *John walked*, one expresses the notion that John experienced something because of his walk. One ascribes something to, or characterizes, the subject (1982: 790–791). Among other things, then, the *have a* V construction is both agentive and experiencer-oriented (1982: 759).

In all of the related *have* constructions, therefore, the focus of interest appears to be directed to the subject.

6. The common meaning of *have* + object + past participle constructions

If the seemingly quite disparate uses of the *have* + object + past participle construction discussed in section 4 are historically related, there must be a common meaning underlying them. In fact, scholars make remarkably similar observations about the meaning of the various *have* + object + past participle constructions. Jespersen (1940: 14; also Kirchner 1941: 150), for example, says that in the passive and experiential *have* constructions, "the interest centres on the person", while Kruisinga (1931: 387; see also Kirchner 1952: 398n.) observes that these constructions enable the writer to "make the psychological subject the grammatical subject" of the sentence. Visser (1973: 2156) remarks of the *have* indirect passive that "the recipient – when he and not the thing given is the main topic – is effectively foregrounded by being mentioned twice". One can compare Strang's remark (1970: 151) that historically the indirect passive "is one aspect of a yet wider tendency, namely to prefer human, especially first person, subjects where possible". The passive *have* construction denotes an "affected subject", says Palmer (1987: 165), while according to Yamakawa (1958: 192), the "subjective experience [is] more stressed" in the *have* than in the *be* indirect passive. Furthermore, the meaning of subjective experience is thought to derive from one of the two basic meanings of *have*, from its "dynamic" meaning of 'experience, achieve, receive, suffer, etc.', rather than from its "stative" sense of 'possess, hold, retain, etc.' (Palmer 1987: 162, 163; also Kruisinga 1931: 41, 377, 386; Yamakawa 1958: 189).

The common meaning of the *have* + object + past participle constructions becomes clearer if one considers the *have* constructions in contrast to the corresponding stative expressions:

(29) a. *I* had *my house* painted. (indirect causative)
   My house is painted.
   b. *I* had *an award* given *to me*. (indirect passive)
   An award is in my possession.
   c. *I* had *my purse* stolen. (passive of experience)
   My purse is stolen.
   d. *I* have (have got) *my paper* finished. (conclusive perfect)
   My paper is finished.

In both cases, there is a shift away from the action (of "painting", "awarding", "stealing", and "finishing") to the effect of that action, which is the resultant state of the object. In addition, the *have* constructions foreground the animate subject by placing it in the position of grammatical subject, that is by topicalizing it. We can see this effect even more strongly in the passives corresponding to (29a–c): *My house was painted, An award was given to me, My purse was stolen*. However, the human subject in the *have* constructions is not an agent, as one can see by contrasting to following active counterparts (which answer the question "What did X do?"): *A friend painted my house, The council gave me an award, A thief stole my purse, I finished my paper*. Rather, the animate subject in the *have* constructions appears to undergo or experience the effects of the action and to be in a particular internal state as a consequence of the action. The *have* constructions answer the question "What happened to X?". There is a focus on subjective experience, whether the subject is willing the action (as in 29a), benefiting from the action (as in 29b), undergoing or suffering the action (as in 29c), or accomplishing the action (as in 29d). Note that even in contrast to the other indirect passive construction, *I was given an award*, (29b) seems to emphasize the internal experience of the subject (or the effect upon the subject) more strongly. Thus, all of the *have* + object + past participle constructions highlight the internal experience of a human subject as well as focus on the resultant state of the object.

The focus on subjective experience in the *have* constructions can be considered part of a larger process of "subjectification" observed in the semantic and syntactic development of languages. For example, Traugott (1989) details this process in semantic changes in modals, speech act verbs, and evidentials in English, while McCawley (1976) accounts for the syntactic change from impersonal constructions to personal construction by a drift toward "human experiencer subject".[18] The development of *have* constructions is consistent with two of the subjective tendencies that Traugott identifies (1989: 34–35). First, since *have* constructions, unlike simple statives, passives, or actives, focus on the internal experience of a human subject, there is a movement from an externally described situation to an internally (evaluatively, perceptually, or cognitively) described situation, as in *Someone sent a letter to Bill, A letter was sent to Bill, Bill was sent a letter, Bill had a letter sent to him*. Second, there is an increase in the extent to which the statement is based on the speaker's subjective belief state/attitude toward the proposition, or, in other words, an increase in epistemicity. For example, statements such as *I had my shoes repaired, I had my article rejected*, or *I have my bank book balanced* depend to a much greater extent on the speaker's knowledge or belief than do statements such as *My shoes were repaired, My article was rejected*, or *My bank book is balanced*.

7. The development of *have* + object + past participle constructions

Two different routes of development have been proposed for the various *have* + object + past participle constructions. Yamakawa (1958) argues that the original sense of the construction is perfective/possessive. At the end of the Middle English period, as the modern perfect is formed, "the older loose word-order '*have* + object + past participle' [comes] to have its functional sphere restricted and acquire the new derivative sense, causative or passival" (Yamakawa 1958: 167). The causative meaning develops because the construction is often equivocal: an Old English example such as *He hæfd man geworhtne æfter his onlicnesse* can mean either that God himself made man or that He had his workers make man after his image, and thus the construction is "destined sooner or later to have its ordinary sense specified into the causative ... one, or otherwise to be confirmed into the perfect tense form '*have*' + past participle" (Yamakawa 1958: 179–180). Furthermore, the older order is also often equivocal between a causative and a passive interpretation: *They had a special dinner given them* can mean either that 'they caused a special dinner to be given to them' or that 'they were given a special dinner', depending on the degree of volition of the subject. For Yamakawa, then, the meaning of the modern conclusive perfect is a remnant of the original perfective/possessive meaning, with the causative and passive meanings derived from it.

Ikegami (1986) sees the semantic development of these constructions as part of a larger drift towards intensification of the notion of agentivity, with concomitant dynamization of the verb. A construction such as *I had a book stolen* begins as 'stative', in which there is no agent ('the book is stolen'). In the next stage, there is an agent, but it is not the grammatical subject of the sentence: the meaning is 'indirect causation' if the agent is within the control of the subject (*I had the book stolen* – 'by someone over whom I had a control'), and 'adverse effect' (i.e. passive) if it is not (*I had the book stolen* – 'by someone else over whom I had no control'). In the last stage, the agent is the grammatical subject of the sentence, and the construction has the meaning of 'successful accomplishment' (i.e., conclusive perfect) or 'perfect' (Ikegami 1986: 383). It is only a "short step" from the meaning of 'successful accomplishment' (e.g., *I had the book stólen* – 'by me') to the final meaning of 'perfect' (*I had stolen the book*): the notion of agent is now explicit rather than merely implied (1986: 383). *Have* also undergoes a change in meaning from 'be in possession of' to 'become in possession of' to 'become affected by', while the past participle is dynamicized (1986: 382). Thus, Ikegami sees the conclusive perfect as derived from the causative and passive meanings and as the immediate source of perfect meaning.[19]

Both the dating of the various *have* + object + past participle constructions (discussed in section 4) and their meanings, as well as the nature of the perfect construction in Old and Middle English (see section 3), argue against the routes of development proposed by Yamakawa (1958) and Ikegami (1986). Although transitive *have* + past participle may originally have had a possessive meaning, it has developed a perfect meaning even by Old English. A second use of the transitive *have* + past participle construction arises, perhaps in late Old English, with the meaning of indirect causation; this second interpretation may result from the ambiguity between perfect and causative readings suggested by Yamakawa (see above): either the subject performs the action denoted by the participle or causes someone else to perform that action. In Middle English, a third use of transitive *have* + past participle develops, one with passive meaning. Again, this meaning may result from ambiguity between causative and passive readings (see above, section 4.3): either the subject causes the action of the participle to be performed or undergoes the action of the participle. Throughout the Middle English period, the position of the object in these three *have* constructions remains variable, either before or after the participle. By the sixteenth century, however, the order of the transitive perfect seems to become fixed with the object in end position, reserving the alternate order with the object in mid position for the causative and passive meanings. The fixing of these two orders in the early modern period seems to be part of a larger process of differentiation between perfects and statives, or, more broadly, between actions and states, since the causative and passive uses of the *have* construction are both clearly stative in meaning. The development of the conclusive perfect, another stative construction, follows from the regularization of the perfect-stative contrast in transitive *have* + past participle constructions. The conclusive perfect continues, and extends, the notion of subjective experience found in the causative and passive *have* constructions, and is possible only because of the prior existence of these constructions. The conclusive perfect can not have acquired currency, therefore, before the seventeenth century.

8. Concomitant developments: Loss of perfect *be* and rise of passive *get*

A further aspect of the differentiation of perfects and statives is the replacement of *be* by *have* in perfect constructions with mutative intransitives. This change has been attributed to a variety of causes: the ambiguity of '*s* = *has* or *is* (Jespersen 1932: 30; Visser 1973: 2043; Rydén – Brorström 1987: 197); the functional overload of *be* as both passive and stative (Söderlind 1951: 56; Traugott 1972: 145; McCoard 1978: 250–252; Rydén – Brorström 1987: 23, 287); attacks by eighteenth-century prescriptive grammarians (Visser 1973: 2043–2044; cf. Rydén – Brorström 1987: 210); and the use of *have* in various contexts, such as conditional, optative, iterative, durative, and negative contexts, as well as in perfect infinitives, the pluperfect, and the progressive and with adverbials of time, manner, or place (Fridén 1948: 43–57, 115–117; Johannisson 1958: 114–117; Rydén – Brorström 1987: 184–194). However, Rydén – Brorström (1987: 17, 26, 183; also Johannisson 1958: 107) see the "overarching distributional determinant" in the change from *be* to *have* as the distinction between action and state. This principle was recognized even by eighteenth-century grammarians (Rydén – Brorström 1987: 208). While this change seems to take place very gradually during the seventeenth, eighteenth, and even early nineteenth centuries (see examples of the alternation between *have* and *be* in Lannert 1910: 94–103 and Horton 1914: 122–124 [from Defoe]; Charleston 1941; 24–26, 43–44 [from the eighteenth century]; Phillipps 1970: 109–110 [from Austen]; Rydén – Brorström 1987 [from the period 1700–1900]), the end result is an exclusively stative interpretation for *be* + past participle constructions in Modern English.

The remaining *be* + past participle constructions with mutative intransitive verbs, such as *be gone, be retired, be begun, be finished*, and so forth, are all now exclusively stative, with the past participle functioning adjectivally (see Poutsma 1926: 215–216; Curme 1931: 359; 1935: 322; Jespersen 1932: 31; Visser 1973: 2042–2044; McCoard 1978: 228; Rydén – Brorström 1987: 26, 198–199, 211–212). Visser terms this construction the "resultative form", since it expresses the result of a preceding action. Thus, while it bears close resemblance to the conclusive perfect in meaning, it is unlike the conclusive perfect in being a survival of the older meaning of the construction and in being in gradual decline in the modern period.

The restriction of *be* + past participle constructions to stative or passive meaning is likely to have contributed to the development of a distinct form of the passive to express dynamic meaning, viz. the *get* passive. This construction is of colloquial origin and appears in written documents for the first time in the early nineteenth (Visser 1973: 2031–2033; *Oxford English Dictionary*, s.v. *get*, def. 34b).[20] Though the *get* passive is not yet fully standardized in English, its existence may ultimately lead to the restriction of the *be* form to stative or statal passive meaning and the *get* form to dynamic or inchoative passive meaning.

9. Standardization and the differentiation of statives and perfects

The general differentiation of stative and perfect constructions discussed here is one aspect of the process of language standardization which took place in English over the seventeenth and eighteenth centuries. A commonly held view of language standardization is that it leads to "minimal variation in form" (Haugen 1972: 107): "the chief linguistic characteristic of standardisation is suppression of optional variation at all levels of language" (Milroy – Milroy 1985: 36 and passim; Milroy [this volume]). Prior to the modern period, the *have* constructions treated in this paper provide a wealth of variant forms and meanings. Both the structures *have* + object + past participle and *have* + past participle + object can express perfect, conclusive perfect (resultative), indirect causative, indirect passive, and experiential meaning; context alone determines the appropriate interpretation. The consequent possibility of ambiguity (see section 7) undoubtedly provides some motivation for the regularization of the different *have* constructions. The first step in this regularization, which occurs by the end of the sixteenth century, is restriction of the *have* + past participle + object order to perfect meaning. The frequency of the perfect meaning in the *have* construction, especially in written discourse of a more objective or scientific kind, probably contributes to the early regularization of the perfect. A number of criteria may dictate the selection of the order with the past participle in mid rather than end position for perfect interpretation. First, with the gradual replacement of *be* by *have* with mutative intransitives (see section 8), the object becomes optional in the *have* + past participle construction. Second, the cohesiveness of *have* + past participle as a verbal periphrasis would favor this order. As Harris (1985: 48–49) points out, "The cohesion within the new verbal group is reflected in the diachronic movement of the participle to the immediate right of *have*, a position it had already in intransitive constructions, where the *have* perfect was replacing the older *be* perfect." Finally, there may be some objection among eighteenth-century grammarians, under the guise of lack of logic or awkwardness, to embraciated, or "split", constructions (see Leonard 1929: 94–95), though the split perfect does not seem to receive mention in this context.[21]

The alternate order, *have* + object + past participle, then becomes restricted in the seventeenth century to causative, passive, and experiential readings. A single sequence can serve as the exponent of all three readings because they are obligatorily transitive, share stative meaning, and have subject orientation (see section 6). The related infinitival constructions seem to follow a parallel course during the same period, with *have* + infinitive + object restricted to the meaning of (externally imposed) obligation, and *have* + object + infinitive restricted to the meaning of (internally imposed) obligation and stative/possessive meaning (see section 5.2).

While these changes are in part motivated by the principle of reduction of variation in form, another standardizing principle, namely, differentiation of forms, may be more important here. This is the principle, well represented in the eighteenth century, of one form/one meaning or function; logically, it is "directly contrary" to the suppression of alternate forms since it leads to the "retention of whatever variations in form English possesses, and even to the creation of new forms" (see Leonard 1929: 59–77). In a general way, it accounts for the distinction between perfect meaning in the *have* + past participle + object construction and stative (or passive) meaning in the *have* + object + past participle and *be* + past participle constructions. More importantly, it accounts for the development of the conclusive perfect as a separate syntactic/semantic construction. In the traditional view of the development of the perfect (see section 3) and conclusive perfect (see section 4.4), reduction of variation leads to the gradual loss of the conclusive perfect from the seventeenth century onward. In this view, *have* + past participle constructions in earlier English, whether with object in mid or end position, have an exclusively resultative meaning. The rise of a fixed word order with the object in end position is concurrent with the change from resultative meaning to perfect meaning. With this change, the alternate word order, with object in mid position, is gradually eliminated since, as resultative meaning is lost, it no longer makes any semantic distinction. However, I have argued above that both perfect and resultative meanings are possible in earlier English, the choice of interpretation being dependent upon context. As *have* + past participle + object is restricted to perfect meaning (for the reasons given above), *have* + object + past participle takes over the resultative meaning by a process of differentiation of forms. It is not gradually eliminated, for the elimination of variants, as Milroy and Milroy (1985: 66) point out, depends on a "principle of equivalence", "the assumption that the alternants are exactly equivalent", but as Harris shows for Hiberno-English (1982: 15–17; 1984: 311–313; 1985: 38–46; see also section 2), the perfect and conclusive perfect are not at all "referentially equivalent". Since the variant orders are functional, that is, they express real semantic distinctions, they are both retained. The existence of such functional variants is especially common in oral language and non-standard dialects (Milroy – Milroy 1985: 67–68; Milroy [this volume]; Cheshire [this volume]) so it is not surprising that the conclusive perfect is initially very rare in written texts, occurring primarily in texts of an oral nature,[22] nor that it is more common in regional varieties of English, where it seems to be increasing rather than decreasing in frequency.[23]

I think that two features of standardization as a process of language change emerge here. The first is that standardization is ongoing; languages are continually undergoing standardization (Milroy – Milroy 1985; Milroy [this volume]). The differentiation of statives and perfects in English has been a long process lasting over three centuries, and it is not yet complete. Furthermore, it may go on at different rates and in different ways in dialects of a language, leading to the creation of regional standards. The second feature that is apparent here is that standardization is not solely a conservative force which inhibits or prevents language change, as is traditionally claimed (Haugen 1972: 107; Milroy – Milroy 1985: 36), but may also be an innovative force which encourages or motivates certain kinds of change. It may lead not only the elimination of forms but also to their creation. In this case, standardization has created a newly distinct form to express resultative meaning, the conclusive perfect, and later a new form of the passive, the *get* passive, to express dynamic meaning. A similarly innovative example of standardization is the creation of the *its* neuter possessive form (Nevalainen – Raumolin-Brunberg [this volume]).

10. Conclusion

This paper has argued that the conclusive perfect, *have* + object + past participle constructions with the meaning of 'accomplishment of a state', is not a remnant of the older form of the perfect with possessive/stative semantics. In the pre-modern period, word order does not, in fact, distinguish the stative from the perfect form. Rather, the order *have* + object + past participle assumes an exclusively stative meaning in the modern period only after the fixing of the order *have* + past participle (+ object) with perfect meaning. The conclusive perfect develops in the seventeenth century with the impetus of earlier *have* + object + past participle constructions, the indirect causative, indirect passive, and experiential passive, with which it shares stative meaning and an emphasis on subjective experience. A concomitant modern change is the replacement of perfect *be* by *have* with mutative intransitives, which fixed *be* + past participle with exclusively stative (or passive) meaning. These changes are thus part of a general differentiation of perfects and statives which occurs as part of the standardization of English in the early modern period.

Notes

* I am grateful to the Social Sciences and Humanities Research Council of Canada and the University of British Columbia for financial support to attend ICEHL6 in Helsinki. This paper has benefited from comments and queries from Kathleen Carey, David Denison, and Lilita Rodman. I would also like to thank Merja Kytö, Terttu Nevalainen, and Matti Rissanen for their aid and hospitality while I used the Helsinki Corpus.
1. Palmer (1987: 168) admits that "most people would find it difficult to arrive at this interpretation" and suggests that it is most natural with verbs such as *beat*, as in *We had them beaten, and then they scored*.
2. Harris (1982: 6–8, 17–18; 1984: 319–320; 1985: 47–48) considers, but rejects, the possibility of this construction's being a calque on Irish, primarily because it is well-attested in earlier stages of English and in non-contact dialects outside Ireland.
3. Hoffmann (1934) identifies only seven instances of possessive *have* + past participle constructions in Old English. For fuller discussion of the development of the perfect, see Brinton (1988: 99–102).
4. Carey (1990: 374–375) argues that the *have* + past participle construction in Old English, while essentially stative, has developed from a purely adjectival construction to a "resultant state perfect". That is, rather than expressing a relation between a subject and an object, which is the final state of a past process, it has come to express the relation between a subject and a completed past process performed on an object. What is emphasized in this development is the change in the subject, not the change in the object. Furthermore, the subject is now necessarily the agent of the process. This increased focus on the subject and the effects of the action on the subject is consistent with the subsequent changes in the *have* + past participle construction discussed below (section 6).
5. For a description of the Helsinki Corpus of English Texts, Dialectal and Diachronic, see Kytö and Rissanen (1988) and references therein.
6. Under certain clearly-defined circumstances, the object may be moved from midposition. In questions and relative clauses, it assumes initial position, while if it is very lengthy or highly stressed, it may also assume end position in the sentence (see Kirchner 1952: 394, 399).
7. Harris notes in passing but does not pursue the notion that there is "a close structural relationship between PII with possessive/experiential *have* [i.e., the conclusive perfect] and with causative, benefactive or 'indirect passive' *have*" (1984: 311–312). Harris (1985: 42) analyzes all of these *have* constructions as involving raising.
8. The following seventeenth-century example shows an exceptional prepositioning of the participle: *I had then given me a roll, sealed, to comfort me* (Bunyan, *Pilgrim's Progress* I; cited by Yamakawa 1958: 190). This order may be dictated by the appositional participle *sealed* modifying the object *roll* (see n. 6).

9. Kirchner (1952: 397n.) argues that the difference between the *have* construction with the genitive and with the dative is that the former expresses perfective aspect, the action as completed, while the latter merely denotes an occurrence in the passive, with *have* expressing an imperfective character. A behavioral difference between the two constructions is that the dative structure can be transformed into an indirect passive with *be* (e.g., *I had a book given to me* > *I was given a book*), while the genitive cannot (e.g., *He had his leg broken* > **He was broken a/his leg*).
10. Visser (1973: 2190) cites the following example as a perfect, but queries whether it might not be a causative: "*Ay me, most wretched, That* haue *my heart* parted *betwixt two friends That do afflict each other*" (Shakespeare, Antony and Cleopatra III, vi, 76). In fact, this construction must in context be interpreted as a passive of experience.
11. In the texts of the third period of the Early Modern English period in the Helsinki Corpus, there are roughly 752 occurrences of *have* + past participle; of these 736 are regular perfects, 11 are indirect causatives, 3 are passives of experience, 1 is an indirect passive, and 1 is a conclusive perfect.
12. I am grateful to David Denison for the two examples from Pepys.
13. Visser claims that the distinction among causative, possessive, and passive interpretations of *get* + object + past participle constructions is "too subtle to form a criterion on which to base a classification", so he includes examples of all three types "pell-mell" under one heading.
14. Whether the *have*-existential leads to the spread of the conclusive perfect, or vice versa, is not clear to Kirchner (1941: 149): "Such expressions as '*they have got their facts wrong*' = 'they are mistaken' must have contributed largely towards extending the use of the 'Conclusive Perfect', if it is not the other way about".
15. Visser (1969: 1478) sees a slow semantic development from possession to obligation. Kirchner (1952: 372–374n., 376; also Jespersen 1940: 226), however, rejects the meaning of pure possession in this construction except where the infinitive is an attributive, as in *She was happy to have somebody to look after*. He considers the meaning of obligation to be original.
16. The date of origin of the variant orders is a matter of scholarly debate. According to Visser (1969: 1478–1479, 1485–1486), the order *have* + infinitive (+ object) dates from the thirteenth century, but Kirchner (1952: 381–382) thinks that it became common only at the beginning of the nineteenth century. The *Oxford English Dictionary* (s.v. *have*, def. 7c) dates the form without an object to 1579–1596 (with a subsequent gap to 1765). The order *have* + object + infinitive either derives from the earliest English, according to Kirchner (1952: 373–373), who claims that it is an example "bei dem die Wortstellung von der ältesten Zeit bis heute erhalten geblieben ist" or it is a modern innovation, according to Visser (1969: 1478, 1482), who considers the alternate order the usual means for expressing obligation without possession. Jespersen cites examples of *have* + object + infinitive from Shakespeare.

17. Jespersen (1940: 204) quotes the following lines from Trollope which contrast the two orders: "the writer, when he sits down to commence his novel, should do so, not because he has to tell a story, but because he has a story to tell". However, I believe that Jespersen glosses the two lines wrongly, saying that "the writer sits down to write not because he has something which he burns to tell, but because he feels it incumbent on him to be telling something."
18. Similarly, Thornburg (1986) explains the development of the indirect passive (with *be*) as involving the topicalization of "an inherently highly animate and definite NP, the [indirect object]".
19. Ikegami (1986) provides no historical data for this proposed development.
20. The *Oxford English Dictionary* cites an early example from 1652. However, a gap of over 140 years intercedes between this example and the next one cited.
21. The only mention of the conclusive perfect that I have found in eighteenth-century grammarians occurs in the context of an argument about whether the past participle is always passive in meaning. Pickbourn (1789: 13) cites Beattie's claim that the word order in sentences such as *I had a letter written* or *I have a letter written* (rather than *I had written the letter* or *I have written the letter*) "on some occasions, and on subjects that admit a more harmonious phraseology, might be tolerated in verse: and it will appear that the participle *written* belongs, not to the nominative *I*, the person *who acts*, but to the accusative *letter*, the thing *acted upon*, (or to give it in other words) the thing which in respect of the action is *passive*." Not only does Beattie accept this "split" construction in certain styles, then, but he also seems to recognize a semantic and syntactic distinction between the variant perfect orders. Interestingly, Pickbourn (1789: 13–14) does not seem to recognize Beattie's distinction between the two word orders, but argues that the interpretation that Beattie suggests is impossible in sentences such as *I have sent a letter to America* or *I have returned the book, which I borrowed*: "in what sense could I be said to *have* the book returned, i.e., to *have*, or possess, a book, which has been returned, and which I have no longer in my possession?"
22. In the Modern English period of Helsinki Corpus, the conclusive perfect occurs in a work of light fiction (*A Hundred Mery Tales*), in private correspondence (*The Correspondence of Lady Katherine Paston*), and in a diary (*The Diary of Samuel Pepys*).
23. Harris (1982: 19; 1984: 322; 1985: 49) considers the *have* + object + past participle construction to be losing ground to the regular perfect, while I see the construction as gaining ground, as it becomes more acceptable in the standard. At the same time, however, Harris notes (1982: 13–14) that the conclusive perfect is perceived as standard by almost 60% of his respondents, a much higher rate of acceptability than the other Hiberno-English features he considers.

References

Ando, Sadao
    1976   *A descriptive syntax of Christopher Marlowe's language.* Tokyo: University of Tokyo Press.

Brinton, Laurel J.
    1988   *The development of English aspectual systems: Aspectualizers and postverbal particles.* (Cambridge Studies in Linguistics.) Cambridge: Cambridge University Press.

Carey, Kathleen
    1990   "The role of conversational implicature in the early grammaticalization of the English perfect", in: Kira Hall – Jean-Pierre Koenig – Michael Meacham – Sondra Reinman – Laurel A. Sutton (eds.), 371–380.

Charleston, Britta Marian
    1941   *Studies on the syntax of the English verb.* Bern: Francke.

Chomsky, Noam
    1965   *Aspects of the theory of syntax.* Cambridge, MA: The MIT Press.

Curme, George O.
    1931   *A grammar of the English language, Vol. III: Syntax.* Boston: Heath.
    1935   *A grammar of the English language, Vol. II: Parts of speech.* Boston: Heath.

Franz, Wilhelm
    1939   *Die Sprache Shakespeares in Vers und Prosa.* (4th edition *Shakespeare-Grammatik*.) Halle/Saale: Niemeyer.

Fridén, Georg
    1948   *Studies on the tenses of the English verb from Chaucer to Shakespeare with special reference to the late sixteenth century.* Uppsala: Lundequistska.

Hall, Kira – Jean-Pierre Koenig – Michael Meacham – Sondra Reinman – Laurel A. Sutton (eds.)
    1990   *Proceedings of the sixteenth annual meeting of the Berkeley Linguistics Society.* Berkeley Linguistics Society.

Harris, John
    1982   "The underlying non-identity of English dialects: A look at the Hiberno-English verb phrase", *Belfast working papers in language and linguistics* 6: 1–36.
    1984   "Syntactic variation and dialect divergence", *Journal of linguistics* 20: 303–327.
    1985   "The Hiberno-English 'I've it eaten' construction: What is it and where does it come from?", in: Dónall P. O Baoill (ed.), 36–52.

Harrison, James A
    1887   "The Anglo-Saxon perfect participle with *habban*", *Modern language notes* 2: 268–270.

Haugen, Einar
    1966   "Dialect, language, nation", *American Anthropologist* 68: 922–935.
    [1972]   [Reprinted in: J. B. Pride – Janet Holmes (eds.), *Sociolinguistics*. Harmondsworth: Penguin, 97–111.]

Hoffmann, Gerhard
    1934   *Die Entwicklung des umschriebenen Perfektums im Altenglischen und Frühmittelenglischen*. [Ph.D. dissertation, Universität Breslau.]

Horten, Franz
    1914   *Studien über die Sprache Defoe's*. Bonn: Hanstein.

Ikegami, Yoshihiko
    1986   "The drift toward agentivity and the development of the perfective use of *have* + pp. in English", in: Dieter Kastovsky – Aleksander Szwedek (eds.), 381–386.

Jespersen, Otto
    1932   *A Modern English grammar on historical principles, Part IV (third vol.): Syntax*. London: Allen & Unwin.
    1940   *A Modern English grammar on historical principles, Part V (fourth vol.): Syntax*. Copenhagen: Munksgaard.

Johannisson, Ture
    1958   "On the *be* and *have* construction with mutative verbs", *Studia linguistica* 12: 106–118.

Kastovsky, Dieter – Aleksander Szwedek (eds.)
    1986   *Linguistics across historical and geographical boundaries. In honour of Jacek Fisiak on the occasion of his fiftieth birthday. Vol. 1: Linguistic theory and historical linguistics*. (Trends in Linguistics, Studies and Monographs 32.) Berlin: Mouton de Gruyter.

Kelling, Harold D. – Cathy Lynn Preston (eds.)
    1984   *A KWIC concordance to Jonathan Swift's A tale of a tub, The battle of the books, and A discussion concerning the mechanical operation of the spirit, a fragment*. New York-London: Garland.

Kirchner, Gustav
    1941   "The road to standard English. Two more cases in point: 'The Conclusive Perfect' and 'To be for + -ing' ", *English studies* 23: 143–153.
    1952   *Die zehn Hauptverben des Englischen im Britischen und Amerikanischen*. Halle/Saale: Niemeyer.

Kruisinga, Etsko
    1931   *A handbook of present-day English, Part II: English accidence and syntax 1*. (5th edition.) Groningen: Noordhoff.

Kytö, Merja – Matti Rissanen
    1988   "The Helsinki Corpus of English Texts: Classifying and coding the diachronic part", in: Merja Kytö – Ossi Ihalainen – Matti Rissanen (eds.), 169–179.

Kytö, Merja – Ossi Ihalainen – Matti Rissanen (eds.)
    1988   *Corpus linguistics, hard and soft. Proceedings of the eighth International Conference on English language research.* Amsterdam: Rodopi.
Lannert, Gustaf L.
    1910   *An investigation into the language of Robinson Crusoe as compared with that of other 18th century works.* Uppsala: Almqvist and Wiksell.
Leonard, Sterling A.
    1929   *The doctrine of correctness in English usage 1700–1800.* (University of Wisconsin Studies in Language and Literature 25.) Madison.
McCawley, Noriko A.
    1976   "From OE/ME 'impersonal' to 'personal' constructions: What is a 'subjectless S'", in: Sanford B. Steever – Carol A. Walker – Salikoko S. Mufwene (eds.), 192–204.
McCoard, Robert W.
    1978   *The English perfect: Tense choice and pragmatic inferences.* (North-Holland linguistic series, 38.) Amsterdam – New York – Oxford: North-Holland.
The Middle English Dictionary.
    1954–1966 Sherman Kuhn – John Reidy (eds.). Ann Arbor: University of Michigan Press.
Milroy, James – Lesley Milroy
    1985   *Authority in language: Investigating language prescription and standardization.* London – Boston – Henley: Routledge and Kegan Paul.
Mitchell, Bruce
    1985   *Old English syntax, Vol. 1: Concord, the parts of speech, and the sentence.* Oxford: Clarendon Press.
The Oxford English Dictionary.
    1989   Prepared by J.A. Simpson – E.S.C. Weiner. Oxford: Clarendon Press.
Nikiforidou, Vassiliki – Mary Van Clay – Mary Niepokuj – Deborah Feder (eds.)
    1986   *Proceedings of the twelfth annual meeting of the Berkeley Linguistics Society.* Berkeley Linguistics Society.
O Baoill, Dónall P.
    1985   *Papers on Irish English.* Irish Association for Applied Linguistics.
Palmer, Frank R.
    1987   *The English verb.* (2nd edition = 3rd edition.) (Longman Linguistics Library.) London: Longman.
Phillipps, Kenneth C.
    1970   *Jane Austen's English.* London: André Deutsch.
Pickbourn, James
    1789   *A dissertation on the English verb.* London: Davis.
    [1968] [Reprinted in: R. C. Alston (ed.), *English Linguistics 1500–1800* 107. Menston: Scolar Press.]

Poutsma, H.
  1905 *A grammar of late modern English, Part I: The sentence, Section II: The composite sentence.* Groningen: Noordhoff.
  1926 *A grammar of late modern English, Part II: The parts of speech, Section II: The verb and the particles.* Groningen: Noordhoff.
Rydén, Mats – Sverker Brorström
  1987 *The be/have variation with intransitives in English, with special reference to the late modern period.* (Stockholm Studies in English 70.) Stockholm: Almqvist and Wiksell.
Quirk, Randolph – Sidney Greenbaum – Geoffrey Leech – Jan Svartvik
  1985 *A comprehensive grammar of the English language.* London: Longman.
Scheurweghs, Gaston
  1959 *Present-day English syntax: A survey of sentence patterns.* London: Longman.
Söderlind, Johannes
  1951 *Verb syntax in John Dryden's prose, Part I.* (Essays and Studies on English Language and Literature 10.) Uppsala: Lundequistska.
  1958 *Verb syntax in John Dryden's prose, Part II.* (Essays and Studies on English Language and Literature 19.) Uppsala: Lundequistska.
Steever, Sanford B. – Carol A. Walker – Salikoko S. Mufwene (eds.)
  1976 *Papers from the parasession on diachronic syntax.* Chicago Linguistic Society.
Stern, Laurence – Harold H. Kollmeier (eds.)
  1985 *A concordance to the English prose of John Milton.* (Medieval and Renaissance Texts and Studies 35.) Binghamton, NY: Center for Medieval and Early Renaissance Studies.
Strang, Barbara
  1970 *A history of English.* London: Methuen.
Thornburg, Linda
  1986 "The development of the indirect passive in English", in: Vassiliki Nikiforidou – Mary Van Clay – Mary Niepokuj – Deborah Feder (eds.), 261–270.
Traugott, Elizabeth Closs
  1972 *The (A) history of English syntax: A transformational approach to the history of English sentence structure.* (Transatlantic Series in Linguistics.) New York: Holt, Rinehart and Winston.
  1989 "On the rise of epistemic meanings in English: An example of subjectification in semantic change", *Language* 65: 31–55.
Visser, Fredericus Th.
  1969 *An historical syntax of the English language, Part 3, first half: Syntactical units with two verbs.* Leiden: Brill.
  1973 *An historical syntax of the English language, Part 3, second half: Syntactical units with two or more verbs.* Leiden: Brill.

Wierzbicka, Anna
    1982   "Why can you *have a drink* when you can't *have an eat?*", *Language* 58: 753–799.

Yamakawa, Kikuo
    1958   "On the construction '*have* (or *get*) + object + past participle' ", *Anglica* 3: 164–196.

Zandvoort, Reinhard W.
    1986   *A handbook of English grammar*. (4th edition.) London: Longman.

Its strength and the beauty *of it*:
The standardization of the third person neuter possessive in Early Modern English

Terttu Nevalainen – Helena Raumolin-Brunberg

1. Introduction*

The Standard English system of personal pronouns was to a great extent fixed during the Early Modern English period (1500–1700). The process involved both simplification and innovation. On the one hand, the system was simplified as the second person plural pronouns were generalized into the singular, and *thou/thee* was gradually replaced by *you*. Partly concurrently, an opposite development took place which replaced the third person neuter singular possessive *his* by a new form *its*.

Quite a few studies have been devoted to the levelling of the second person pronouns, while much less has been written about the rise of the third person possessive apart from the standard textbook accounts. This analogical innovation may be largely attributed to the loss of grammatical gender in English. As the historically regular form *his* became associated with the animate masculine gender, its use in the neuter could result in ambiguity. At the beginning of seventeenth century, the neuter *his* still coexisted with *it*, *thereof* and the periphrastic *of it*, but the new form *its* was also already available. By the latter half of the century, it had gained a dominant position in the paradigm as the regular neuter possessive, and both *his* and *it* had almost disappeared from standard usage. What we see as a key element in this process of change is the role of *of it* as a periphrastic variant of the neuter possessive.[1]

Our paper focuses on the implementation and extraordinary rapidity of this change. Much longer time spans were required before a similar systemic stability was reached by some other Early Modern English changes, such as the *who/which*, *thou/you*, and the third person singular *-th/-s* variations.[2] We shall concentrate on three issues: the paradigm of the variant possessive forms in Early Modern English, their contemporary grammatical representations, and the empirical evidence for the process of change. Our data are derived from the Early Modern English section of the Helsinki Corpus of English Texts (see Kytö 1991; Nevalainen – Raumolin-Brunberg 1989). A systematic comparison of the alternative forms of the neuter possessive will make it possible to narrow down the linguistic and nonlinguistic circumstances that promoted the innovation.

The variationist approach also helps one to evaluate the position that the change occupies on the natural v. learned scale of language changes. Was it an innovation from above, or did it emerge from below the level of social awareness (Labov 1972: 290)? If *its* spread from below, how could it then replace *his* in the Early Modern English standard language so rapidly? The rise of *its* is further related to a number of broader issues. Two of them appear particularly interesting: the typological shift in the English noun phrase structure, and what looks like a semantic drift in the modern English gender system. Both will be considered in the course of our discussion.

2. The core paradigm and its variants

A standard account of Middle English personal pronouns would present the following paradigm for the third person singular neuter (see *Oxford English Dictionary*, s.v. *it*, pron.):

Nominative:	hit (stressed), it (unstressed)
Accusative:	hit (stressed), it (unstressed)
Dative:	him
Genitive:	his (hit)

By 1600, the difference between the stressed and unstressed forms in the nominative and accusative was apheretically reduced from *(h)it* to *'t*, while the dative would now have two and the genitive as many as three variants (*Oxford English Dictionary*, s.v. *it*, pron.; Barber 1976: 208):

Nominative:	(h)it
Accusative:	(h)it
Dative:	him, it
Genitive:	his, it, its

2.1. *His*

His is the historically regular genitive of the Old English third person masculine and neuter pronouns *he* and *hit*. As the English gender system shifted from a grammatical to a notional one, the position of *his* was also affected. In Middle English, *his* was frequently supplemented by pronominal adverbs, and the genitive form *it* was also introduced (see below). Nevertheless, *his* still persisted in Early Modern English in many contexts with inanimate antecedents. The following two instances are drawn from the Helsinki Corpus (for a bibliography of the corpus data, see Kytö 1991).

(1) *There followeth now in* his *place after these knowledges alreadie rehearsed, the ordering and gouernment of Dairies, with the profits and commodities belonging to the same.* (Markham 1615: 104)

(2) *WHICH IS THE ARCTIQUE CIRCLE, AND WHY IS IT SO CALLED? The Arctique Circle is that which is next to the North Pole, and hath* his *name of this worde Arctos, which is the great Beare or Charles wayne, which are seuen stars placed next to this Circle on the outside thereof.* (Blundeville 1597: 156)

The *Oxford English Dictionary* records its last instance of the neuter genitive *his* from the 1670s (*his*, poss. pron. B3). Our corpus evidence agrees with this in that there are no instances of neuter *his* in the third subperiod of the Early Modern English section of the Helsinki Corpus (1640–1710; most texts from the latter half of the period). In more general terms, the issue may turn out to be less straightforward, because it also involves gender distinctions that seem to shift slightly between the Early Modern English period and the present day. The different animate and personal gender classes will be reconsidered in sections 3 and 4.

2.2. *It*

The uninflected genitive pronoun *it* first appeared in the fourteenth century in texts of West Midland origin (*Middle English Dictionary*, s.v. *hit*. pron. 3a, *Oxford English Dictionary*, s.v. *it*, pron. III.10). Lehnert (1958: 23) describes it as an analogous formation that was based on the phonetic similarity between the genitive and oblique forms of the other personal pronouns in the singular:

> Da neben den meist schwachtonig gebrauchten flektierten Personalpronomina im Singular *mi* 'me' *ði* 'thee' und *her* 'her' die gleichlautenden schwachtonigen Possessivpronomina *mi* 'my', *ði* 'thy' and *her* standen, bildete man analog zu personalem *it* ein possessives *it* nach folgendem Muster:
> Give me my book
> I give thee thy book : I give it it – .
> I give her her book

Graband (1965: 257) suggests an alternative source of analogy for *it*, namely the reflexive pronoun with a nominal interpretation of the element *self*. On the model of *herself* the form *hisself* also appeared in Early Modern English. An analogous extension of this pattern would then give us the following paradigm:

    herself : her book
    hisself : his book
    itself   : it book

This suggestion may find support in the increased frequency of *it* around 1600, but it does not account for its Middle English origins.

A third possible source for the uninflected genitive *it* is suggested by regional usage in both Early Modern English and today. Besides the oblique forms mentioned by Lehnert (1958), it is not uncommon to find the nominative occurring in the genitive as well (see Wright 1905: 275). In other words, genitive *it* could have originated in a regional paradigm that had undergone a more radical loss of inflections than would be the case in standard English. An early levelling is, in fact, also implied by Lehnert's account since he is suggesting that the analogy was based on the oblique form *it*. Presumably it could not have taken place in a variety that still currently employed the dative form *him*.

As far as the developing Early Modern English standard is concerned, it appears difficult to substantiate the *Oxford English Dictionary* statement (s.v. *its*, poss. pron.) that *it* became very common about 1600. Regionally this may, of course, have been the case. In the Early Modern English section of the Helsinki Corpus (about 550,000 running words), a double check of all the tokens of the pronoun *it* and its spelling variants (c. 5,400 instances in all) yielded only one case from the manuscript edition of John Locke's *Directions Concerning Education* (1933: 45; written between 1684 and 1688). The genitive *-s* in angular brackets has been supplied by the modern editor.[3]

(3)   *for if loosnesse come to threaten either by* it<s> *violence or duration it will soone enough and sometimes too soone make a phisitian be sent for, and if it be moderate and short it is commonly best to leave it to nature.* (Locke 1684–1688 [1933]: 45)

The same passage in the first printed edition contains *its*.

(4)   *for if it come to threaten, either by* its *Violence, or Duration, it will soon enough, and sometimes too soon, make a Physician be sent for;*

> *and if it be moderate or short, it is commonly best to leave it to Nature.* (Locke 1693: 25)

Although available for a considerable time, *it* does not seem to have become the universal neuter genitive even in individual usage in Early Modern English. Variation seems to be the norm around 1600 (see Graband 1965: 257). To take one example, Gervase Markham, the prolific author of numerous handbooks, has the new form *its* and the recessive variant *his* side by side in his *Countrey Contentments* (1615; see examples 1 and 5). At the same time, Markham (or his printer) also uses the genitive *it* in *it damme* with reference to an ass (*Oxford English Dictionary*, s.v. *it*, pron. III.10). In addition to the three pronominal forms, Markham expresses the neuter genitive by means of the prepositional periphrasis *of it* and the pronominal adverb *thereof*, and bypasses it by using the definite article *the*.

2.3. *Its*

The *Oxford English Dictionary* records the first occurrence of the genitive form *its* in Florio's Italian-English Dictionary *A Worlde of Wordes* (1598).[4] It is specified as a Southern English (London and Oxford) form that had been colloquial for some time before it appeared in writing. The new form had two spelling variants, *its* and *it's* (*Oxford English Dictionary*, s.v. *its*, poss. pron.). Both of them are attested in the second period of the Early Modern English section of the Helsinki Corpus.

(5) *The best time for a Cow to calue in for the Dairie, is in the later ende of March, and all Aprill, for then grasse beginning to spring to* its *perfect goodnesse will occasion the greatest increase of milke that may be;* (Markham 1615: 107)

(6) *I was faine to wade ouer the Riuer of Annan in Scotland, from which Riuer the County of Annandale, hath* it's *name.* (Taylor 1630: 128)

An analogous source has been suggested for this new formation in the literature. Lehnert (1958: 24), among others, argues that *its* was modelled both by analogy with *his* (the spelling *its*) and the nominal possessives (the spelling *it's*):

he : his   =   it : its
cat : cat's =   it : it's

Although both sources are well established in the literature, it is difficult to see how they could have served as models for the two spellings. The apostrophe was not yet current in the nominal possessives in the first half of the seventeenth century.

The spread of *its* seems remarkably rapid. The *Oxford English Dictionary* relates its origins to colloquial language. The conservative Authorized Version of the Bible (1611), for example, does not yet admit *its*, but prefers the older form *his* (Partridge 1973: 118).[5] Neither does *its* appear in Shakespeare's writings during his lifetime. The first folio of 1623, however, has ten instances of *its* (Franz 1939: 287). This is still a relatively small number compared with the 8,000-odd instances of the pronoun *it* in other uses, 15 of which are, incidentally, in the genitive (see Spevack 1970, Vol. V, s.v. *it*; Lehnert 1958: 22).

The literature suggests that the breakthrough of *its* must have taken place during the first three or four decades of the seventeenth century. By the 1650s, *its* had gained a dominant position as the marker of the neuter genitive in the writings of Evelyn (about 1640), Lovelace (1649) and Baxter (1650), for instance (Knorrek 1938: 117). In the latter half of the century, *his* and *it* as good as disappeared from the standard language (Graband 1965: 257).

2.4. *The*

In some cases the neuter possessive could be left unexpressed, and the definite article would be used instead of the possessive pronoun. The *Oxford English Dictionary* (s.v. *its*, poss. pron.) records this usage but also adds that it only continued as late as the neuter *his*. The use of the definite article would seem to provide a convenient means of avoiding the selection of a genitive form particularly in a situation of rapid linguistic change (for absence of the possessive in Middle English, see Mustanoja 1960: 162–163). Contrary to the *Oxford English Dictionary*, however, the definite article is used even in Present-day English, especially where the speakers do not wish to commit themselves to either personal or nonpersonal pronominal use. That could be the case with higher animals, which can be referred to by the nonpersonal *it* or the personal *he* and *she*.[6] The following passage will serve as an illustration (cf. also the use of *the* with reference to body parts in Present-day English, Quirk et al. 1985: 270–272).

(7)   *Shetland Pony or Sheltie. This is the smallest of our ponies being about 101 cm high; the smallest one on record was only 66 cm high. The* colour may be black, brown, bay, grey, dun, or chestnut, and piebald and skewbald ones also occur. In winter *the* coat is of long hair with an undergrowth of wool. *(M. Nixon – D. Whiteley, The Oxford Book of Vertebrates, 1972: 152)*

The use of the definite article instead of the neuter possessive may be difficult to account for synchronically, let alone over a longer period of time during which English article usage is also changing (see section 4). We have made no attempt to include it in the neuter possessive paradigm in the present study, although it is not difficult to find good candidates for instances of the "possessive" *the*. To give an example, a passage from Markham can be cited. His reasons for using *the* in (8) would presumably be the same as in (7). If personified, the hare is feminine in Markham's usage. The possessive form *its* in this passage is also worth noting.

(8) *Touching the Hunting of the Hare, which is euerie honest man, and good mans chase, and which indeed is the freest, readiest, and most enduring pastime, and likewise in* its *owne kinde ful of good profit for mans Preseruation: for though the beast be but little, yet are* the *members worth inioyment, as* the *flesh, which is good for all manner of fluxes,* the *braines good to make children breed their teeth with ease,* the *wool excellent to stench blood.* (Markham 1615: 31)

The data in the *Survey of English dialects* suggest that this use of the definite article is widespread in present-day regional variants of English (see answers to questions IV.6.20 and VI.1.7). However, the questions have the drawback that they do not refer to inanimate things but to a chicken and a baby, respectively. The *Survey of English dialects* data may then not provide unambiguous evidence for the neuter (Wakelin 1972: 115–116). This would seem to support the point that, if necessary, the definite article may also be used as an avoidance strategy.

2.5. Pronominal adverbs: *Thereof* (*hereof*, *whereof*)

Another possessive alternative became popular in Middle English, as the neuter *his* began to be substituted by pronominal adverbs. More precisely, the combination *thereof* became equivalent to 'of it', while *hereof* could replace the demonstrative 'of this', and presumably also the personal 'of it' (see Mustanoja 1960: 424; Bourcier 1981: 211). The relative adverb *whereof* could be used for similar purposes in continuative relative clauses (*relativischer Anschluss*, see Reuter 1936, Görlach 1978: 118–119). In the present study, we shall be mainly concerned with *thereof*, partly because the other two are infrequent in our data, and partly because they may have broader spheres of reference than *thereof* in the neuter. All three continue to occur in Present-day English, but much less frequently than in Early Modern English.

In the neuter, *thereof*, *hereof* and *whereof* have two obvious advantages over the possessive pronoun: they are not marked for notional gender, nor are they marked for number. The two headings from Blundeville in (9) and (10) show the flexible use of *thereof* in parallel contexts in Early Modern English. Only the instance in (9) would, of course, count as a variant of the possessive neuter 'of it'.

(9)   OF THE MERIDIAN, AND OF THE VSES THEREOF. (Blundeville 1597: 11)
(10)   OF THE VERTICALL CIRCLES, AND USES THEREOF. (Blundeville 1597: 13)

2.6. Prepositional periphrases: *Of it* and *of the same*

Two other expressions that could replace the neuter genitive in Middle English are the prepositional periphrases *of it* and *of the same* (*Oxford English Dictionary*, s.v. *its*, poss. pron.). *Of it* is often cited in Early Modern English grammars as well (see section 3). While *of the same* is archaic in Present-day English, *of it* continues both in the standard and in regional varieties. The latter may also employ periphrastic *of him* in the neuter (Wakelin 1972: 115–116, Ihalainen 1985b: 155).

The literature offers practically no quantitative accounts of the relative frequencies of the postnominal variants of the neuter genitive. It is only suggested that the paraphrase *of it* was common in seventeenth-century colloquial language and poetic prose, while the use of *thereof* was limited to scientific prose, diaries and correspondence (Knorrek 1938: 115; see section 6.1). The use of *of the same* is not usually discussed at all.

Of the same has the same characteristics as *thereof* in that it does not mark gender or number. Hence it applies more widely than *of it*, which marks both. The wider applicability could also lead to referential ambiguity, but in practice this does not often seem to be the case. The example in (11) illustrates the use of *of the same* in our corpus.

(11)   so that the line A.B. standeth for the length of the square, and the other line C.D. for the breadth of the same. (Record 1551: 17)

As pointed out above, variation in usage was the rule rather than an exception in the first few decades of the seventeenth century. As the century wore on, the number of variants diminished, and the two main variants left were *its* and *of it*. The title of our paper is derived from Hooke's *Micrographia* (1665), in which he uses the two possessives contrastively in two consecutive paragraphs. In both *it* refers to a flea.

(12)   *THe strength and beauty of this small creature, had it no other relation at all to man, would deserve a description. For* its *strength, the Microscope is able to make no greater discoveries of it then the naked eye, but onely the curious contrivance of* its *leggs and joints, for the exerting that strength, is very plainly manifested, such as no other creature, I have yet observ'd, has any thing like it;*

* * *

But, as for the beauty of it, *the Microscope manifests it to be all over adorn'd with a curiously polish'd suit of sable Armour, neatly jointed, and beset with multitudes of sharp pinns, shap'd almost like Porcupine's Quills, or bright conical Steel-bodkins;* (Hooke 1665: 210)

Our corpus data indicate that *of it* is a significant possessive variant not only in quantitative terms but also qualitatively. Overall, the periphrastic *of it* seems to occupy a more central role in the process of the neuter possessive change than the literature would lead us to assume (but see Knorrek 1938: 115–117). In what follows we shall then be arguing, together with Sapir (1921 [1978]: 165), that the third person singular neuter *it* has the basic semantic properties which readily permit a posthead variant in the possessive. Our quantitative data indicate that it is put to full use during a time of paradigmatic instability. On the strength of this, *of it* could even be included in the neuter possessive paradigm proper as a marker of the tendency in modern English towards more analytic forms.

3. The evidence of contemporary grammars

The first half of the seventeenth century was the time during which the third person neuter possessive underwent its most radical changes in the standard language. A useful descriptive viewpoint on the process is provided by the early seventeenth-century grammars. This varied set of textbooks was intended either for foreigners learning English or to benefit the teaching of Latin grammar in England (see e.g. Vorlat 1975: 1–11). In contrast to early eighteenth-century grammars, they were on the whole descriptive and did not take it upon themselves to regulate contemporary usage.

Comments on usage began to appear in the latter half of the seventeenth century. Dryden was perhaps the first to condemn the use of the neuter *his* by labelling it as "ill syntax" in his *Defence of the Epilogue* (1672 [1962]: 175).

The comment was directed against Ben Jonson's use of *his* with reference to an inanimate entity in *Catiline*: "Though Heaven should speak with all *his* wrath at once, We should stand upright and unfear'd".

3.1. The neuter possessive and its variants

It seems that the accounts of the neuter possessive given in the early grammars reproduce some of the more established variants in the developing standard. Some scholars would even argue that, at least as far as *its* is concerned, the grammars follow the actual rate of the process of change (Graband 1965: 258). In most cases, both the dictionary sources and our corpus data lend support to this view. In his short *Pamphlet for Grammar* (1586: 20), William Bullokar cites *his* as a possessive form that is derived from *he* and from *it*. The new form *its* is not mentioned by Bullokar.

Alexander Gill's *Logonomia Anglica* (1621) has been seen as the first thorough grammatical work, a virtually complete grammar with extensive syntax and prosody (see e.g. Vorlat 1975: 15). Gill (1621 [1903]: 56) does not give any other neuter singular possessive forms than the periphrastic *of it*. His statement cannot, however, be taken as explicit evidence for the status of the periphrasis in the early 1620s because he also resorts to periphrastic forms elsewhere in the possessive paradigm. The possessive forms of the third person masculine and feminine, for instance, are similarly recorded as *of him* and *of her*. However, he does give examples of the possessives *his* and *her* on the following pages, while nothing more is said about the neuter possessive.

The first grammar book to cite the neuter possessive *its* is Charles Butler's *An English Grammar* (1634 [1910]: 40). Butler offers an explicit paradigm of the third person possessives with *his, her* and *its* in the singular and *their* in the plural. He does not provide any periphrastic forms. In his system, the third person singular neuter pronoun has only two other forms, the nominative *it* and the oblique *it*. Butler (1634 [1910]: 41) also mentions *itself* and *its own self* as compound possessives on a par with *him self, her self, he himself, she her self, his own self*, and *her own self* (spelling normalized). No mention is made of *hisself*.

Disappointingly, Ben Jonson omits the third person neuter pronoun altogether from his well-known *English Grammar* (1640). It is difficult to say whether we are here witnessing the author's avoidance strategy in an unstable linguistic situation, or simply an oversight. Oversights are not infrequent in Jonson; according to Vorlat (1975: 18): "The work is incomplete, sketchy and carelessly composed, it contains inconsistencies and omits essential data." There is nonetheless evidence for the avoidance argument as well. Jonson's grammar was first completed some time before 1623, when it was destroyed by fire, and the second version, published posthumously in 1640, was compiled around 1632 (Introduction to the Scolar Press facsimile edition of Jonson's grammar 1972). In fact Jonson was then writing his first version at a time when the usage was anything but settled. It does not seem impossible that under the circumstances he could have adopted the when-in-doubt-leave-it-out principle.

The same cannot perhaps be said of Joshua Poole's work, *The English Accidence*, which was published in 1646. Poole gives a full Latin-based case paradigm for *he* with the genitive *of him*, and a less complete one for *she*, but the singular *it* is left without any case assignment. Poole's grammar was obviously meant to provide the grammatical basis for teaching Latin grammar, and as such it did not provide an adequate description of English.

The first English grammar that is systematically based on an empirical analysis of actual language data is *Grammatica Linguae Anglicanae* (1653) by John Wallis (see Vorlat 1975: 28–30). Like Butler, Wallis (1653: 87) unambiguously gives the form *its* as the only alternative for the possessive of the neuter pronoun *it*. He also mentions that *hereof, thereof* and *whereof* are often used rather than *of this, of that* (*of these, of those*) and *of which*. However, not explicit mention is made of *thereof* corresponding to *of it*. Wallis has the reputation of being an acute observer. Among other things, he appears to have been the only grammarian in the seventeenth century even to consider the restriction of *which* to a nonpersonal antecedent in relative clauses, although the fact was already common enough in actual practice (Bately 1965: 249). We can then with relative confidence rely on his judgement on the possessive *its*.

The innovation *its* was subsequently adopted by the grammars of the late seventeenth century. Wallis alone was reprinted six times in his lifetime and continued to appear in successive editions up to 1767 (Bately 1965: 246). The fact that no seventeenth-century grammarian mentions *his* or *it* is of considerable value when assessing their relative positions in the language.[7] In the eighteenth-century grammars *its* appears as the unquestioned norm. The neuter *his* is mentioned in the context of earlier authors and historical use in general, for instance, by Robert Lowth and Joseph Priestley (Knorrek 1938: 118).

By way of a summary, Table 1 presents the neuter possessive forms given in the six early grammars discussed. Our assessment of the actual use of the forms is shown in the comments column.

Table 1. The neuter possessive in six early grammars

Grammar	Form(s)	Comments
Bullokar 1586	*his*	actual use
Gill 1621	*of it*	formal paraphrase?
Butler 1634	*its*	advanced use
Jonson 1640	none	avoidance?
Poole 1646	none	avoidance?
Wallis 1653	*its*	actual use

3.2. Gender distinctions

Because of the homonymy of possessive *his*, we cannot study the use of the Early Modern English neuter singular without determining some of the notional gender distinctions of the period (see section 4). In this respect the early grammars are perhaps less helpful than they are as a source for the neuter possessive paradigm. Most of them derive their classifications from Latin models, and some do not always make a distinction between a grammatical and a notional gender (Bullokar and Poole, for instance; see Vorlat 1975: 127, 223). However, even Bullokar (1586: 10–11) uses mainly semantic criteria when discussing the use of the neuter pronoun and the gender of its referents in English:

> And meaning neither mal nor femal reqyreth, It, and caled the Neuter-Gender. But meaning both mal and femal reqyreth som tym He, som tym She, and may be caled the Dobl-Gender, som tym mad manifest by the expresing of he, or she, according too the substantiu shewed, or antecedent rehearced by any of them: it, being mor-proprly applyed too a thing not hauing lyf. It being vsed Demonstratiuly iz accented, thus, it, being proprly of the neuter-gender singular number & third persn, yet som tym vzed in shewing other gender, number or persn: az, it iz I, it iz not thu,it iz they, it iz not we, that must doo it. (Bullokar 1586: 10–11; diacritics omitted and ash expanded to *ea*)

The Early Modern English notional gender system basically continues the Middle English one, but it also partly develops some of its own usages especially in literary language (Graband 1965: 140, 146). On the other hand, a number of the Early Modern English conventions have been altered since (see Quirk et al. 1985: 314–318). Some of these differences will be outlined in the remainder of this section.

Jonson (1640: 57) distinguishes six genders in English, four of which are of particular relevance here. His masculine gender comprises all males or representatives of the masculine species, such as angels, men, stars, months, winds and almost all planets. The feminine gender comprises women and female species including islands, countries, cities and some rivers. The neuter gender is defined by Jonson as the "feigned gender: whose notion conceives neither Sexe; under which are compriz'd all inanimate things, a ship excepted". Ships are feminine in Jonson's classification. He calls his fourth gender "promiscuous", because it comprises both masculine and feminine referents, although one of the two genders is assigned to them. Horses and dogs, for instance, are referred to in the masculine, although there may also be mares and bitches among them (Jonson 1640: 57).

Similar distinctions are commonly made in the early grammars although the details may vary. The partial disagreement among grammarians is particularly noticeable in the treatment of some higher and lower animals (for a list, see Graband 1965: 143). It reflects the context dependency of actual linguistic practice, which allows gender changes even within one and the same text. Greater human involvement may trigger such a change. When he gets very close to the flea under his microscope, Hooke, for example, abandons the neuter gender in favour of the masculine (example (13), direct continuation of (12), section 2.6).

(13) *the head is on either side beautify'd with a quick and round black eye K, behind each of which also appears a small cavity, L, in which* he *seems to move to and fro a certain thin film beset with many small transparent hairs, which probably may be* his *ears; in the forepart of* his *head, between the two fore-leggs,* he *has two small long jointed feelers, or rather smellers, M M, which have four joints, and are hairy, like those of several other creatures; between these,* it *has a small proboscie, or probe, N N 0, that seems to consist of a tube ...* (Hooke 1665: 210)

The animacy distinction was, however, usually observed with the higher orders on the gender hierarchy. Higher animals were only rarely considered neuter. The horse, for instance, consistently takes the masculine pronoun both in our corpus data and in early grammars. The higher animal distinction has a very long history.There do not even appear to be any instances of the neuter gender assigned to non-human mammals in Old English (Jones 1988: 9).[8]

Nonetheless, some notional shifts can be detected within the concept of animacy during the Early Modern English period. In our early and mid-sixteenth-century data, many parts of the human body can be regularly assigned the masculine gender (e.g. *brain, heart, liver, artery, ventricle,* and *stomach*). In the late seventeenth century, *stomach, belly* and *tumour,* for example, are systematically referred to by *it.* Even some notionally inanimate entities may vary according to the context and time of writing. Our corpus data contains a number of minimal pairs, including *tree*, *wind*, and *water*, all of which can be masculine in the first period data (1500–1570) but become associated with the neuter gender in the third period nonliterary texts (1640–1710).[9]

The attested variation has been attributed to a number of different sources. In literary language, the direct influence of French and Latin had continued in translations since the Middle English period (Mustanoja 1960: 45–51). Classical models were also imitated in allegorical personification, as a result of which the *moon*, for instance, was assigned to the feminine gender, and the *sun* to the masculine. The fact that some of these literary loans had made their way into common use by the end of the seventeenth century is recorded, for instance, in the grammars of Christopher Cooper (1685) and Guy Miège (1688) (Graband 1965: 144–146; but cf. Vorlat 1975: 131).

On the other hand, there is also the vernacular tendency to personify inanimate things that are of human relevance. Jonson's (1640) assignment of *the ship* to the feminine gender may reflect this tendency. In Chaucer's English a ship was still neuter, as was the Old English *scip* (Graband 1965: 151, Mustanoja 1960: 46). The use of the feminine gender was so widespread in this context in Early Modern English that it was also consistently applied to a *man-of-war* in Henry Manwayring's *Sea-mans Dictionary* (1644: 65).

If we compare notional gender use in Early Modern English and today, it is evident that some changes have taken place. The animacy criterion seems to be more highly weighted in the Early Modern English period. This may be partly attributed to differences in world views, and social and physical environments. Indicatively, present-day grammars replace the old neuter by nonpersonal gender. The choice between personal and nonpersonal gender is determined by whether a being is felt to possess characteristics associated with a member of the human race or not (Quirk et al. 1985: 341). This seems to imply that the third person neuter pronoun was of more restricted application in Early Modern English than it is today (but see section 4). Moreover, classically motivated gender assignments, including Jonson's planets, winds, islands and cities, for instance, have mostly disappeared from common use in Present-day Standard English. However, since there are practically no limits either to literary or informal sources of personification at any time, only an extensive comparison would do justice to the diachronic shift in notional gender.

4. The neuter possessive paradigm in the Helsinki Corpus

4.1. Formal selection criteria

We have based our analysis of the variant possessive forms in the Helsinki corpus on formal grounds of equivalence. More precisely, we have selected a number of criteria that should guarantee that the variant tokens included appear in equivalent contexts, and could thus be thought of, at least in theory, as interchangeable variants of the third person singular neuter possessive.

The basic requirement set for a variant is, of course, that it is either a member of the neuter possessive paradigm or one of its morphologically construed paraphrases discussed in section 3. This criterion excludes the instances of the definite article as a covert equivalent of the possessive. As pointed out in section 2.4, we consider this use of the definite article a convenient means of bypassing the selection of a neuter possessive proper. This use may also be in harmony with the tendency in English to restrict the use of inflected possessives with inanimate referents (Sapir 1921 [1978]: 165; see section 5). In our case, the inclusion of the definite article would take us too far afield from our purpose of tracing the history of its countertendency, the rise of *its*.

Like Altenberg (1982: 23–29) in his variational study of the genitive and the *of*-construction in the seventeenth century, we also excluded such invariant forms as quantitative partitives (see example 14), complex prepositions and other petrified idioms (example 15) from our corpus of neuter possessives.

(14)   ... *to forfaite at everye tyme so offending foure poundes, the oone haulfe* therof *to be to our Soveraigne Lorde the King, and thother haulfe* therof *to the partie that will sue for the same in any of the Kinges Courtes of Recorde,* ... (*Statutes of the Realm* 1542–1543: 11)

(15)   *Marry this is* the short, and the long of it: *you have brought her into such a Canaries, as 'tis wonderfull:* (Shakespeare 1597 [1623]: 45)

For the postnominal variants *thereof*, *of it* and *of the same*, we set a uniform criterion: their noun phrase (NP) heads had to be marked as definite by the use of the definite article. In other words, formal equivalence was established between "*its* + NP" and "the NP + *of it*". This criterion would rule out both independent genitives (*its* and *his* without a head noun phrase), sentential antecedents, and nonfinite clauses such as (16), which were common in our sixteenth century data.

(16)   That the Wolle whiche shalbe delyv<er>ed for or by the Clothier to any p<er>sone or p<er>sones for brekyng kembyng cardyng or spy<n>nyng of the same *the delyv<er>e therof shalbe by even just and true poise and weight of haberdebois sealid by auctorite not excedyng in weight after the rate of xij pounde Wolle* ... (*Statutes of the Realm* 1511–1512: 128)

The definiteness criterion would, on the other hand, include the use of posthead possessives in what can be called verbal nouns, as in (17), for example (see Quirk et al. 1985: 1290–1292).

(17)   *This first obseruation seemeth strange vnto me,* at the very naming of it. (Brinsley 1612: 41)

The number of posthead instances would have increased if we had relaxed the formal criterion of definiteness and allowed some diachronically comparable instances, for example, not only *by the authority of the same* (third period (1640–1710) Statutes) but *by auctoritie of the same* (first period (1500–1570) Statutes). The problem is perhaps most obvious with abstract and verbal nouns, which are undergoing a change in the Early Modern English period. It only illustrates the diachronic difficulties associated with socio-historical linguistics and its requirement of contextual invariance (see Nevalainen – Raumolin-Brunberg 1989). Our solution is to reconstruct the paradigm using the same criteria throughout the two-hundred-year Early Modern English period, and to take the source of error into account when interpreting the results of the analysis (section 4.3).

4.2. Notional selection criteria

Usually we encountered few problems in locating the instances of neuter possessives on notional grounds. With the exception of the overt neuters *it* and *its*, the neuter gender had to be established for all instances of neuter possessives contextually on the basis of (pro)nominal forms. Where referential opacity concerning the gender of the pronoun antecedent appeared in our data, it came in three kinds: (1) divided usage, (2) mixed usage and (3) uncertain usage of the neuter gender.

Divided gender usage concerns instances like those in (12) and (13), where the neuter gender changes in the middle of the text. They are normally unproblematic, as they establish a clear one-to-one chain of pronominal reference, for instance, *it – its* followed by *he – his*.

Mixed usage is a special case of divided gender assignment. It introduces a pronominal change which results in a one-to-many situation, where there can be an overlap of two pronouns referring to the same noun within one sentence. Instances like this occur in our first period data, as in (18), where the pronominal chain consists of *he – it – him – it – it – it – his – his*. They are all used with reference to the brain in Vicary's *The Anatomie of the Bodie of Man* (1548). Where the neuter pronoun is present in the immediate context, as in our example, the possessives are also interpreted as neuter.

(18)   *Also, why* he *is moyst, is, that* it *should be the more indifferenter and abler to euery thing that shoulde be reserued or gotten into* him: *Also, why* it *is soft, is, that* it *should geue place and fauour to the vertue of stering: And why* it *is meanely viscous, is, that* his *sinewes should be strong and meanely toughe, and that they shoulde not be letted in their working throughe* his *ouermuch hardnes.* (Vicary 1548: 32)

Finally, there are some cases of uncertain gender usage, where the context fails to provide the necessary pronominal anchorage. They involve nouns that can be assigned either the masculine or the feminine gender, or which may also be used in the neuter. Since we are mostly dealing with nonliterary texts, the animacy hierarchy discussed in section 3.2 was applied here. All instances that were notionally inanimate or represented lower animals were interpreted as neuter. This is, for instance, the case in (19). The literature suggests that, in spite of some early grammarians' statements to the contrary, cities were frequently assigned the neuter gender (Graband 1965: 147).

(19)   *And hauing viewed and seen this great and rich Citie of Agra with the pleasures and Commodities thereof; on the 18. day of Ianuarie, my selfe with Ioseph Salebancke and Iohn Frenchan, went to the King* ... (Coverte 1612: 41)

Although some of these cases might count as instances of pronoun avoidance, they also reveal the flexibility of the referentially less specific possessive expressions.

4.3. The quantitative paradigm

In order to see how the third person neuter possessive forms are distributed in our data, we have calculated the mean frequencies of the variant totals per 1,000 words in our three Early Modern English periods. A further comparison is established between the possessives and the occurrence of the neuter pronoun form *it* in the same set of Early Modern English data. Finally, these figures are contrasted with those of the Lancaster – Oslo/Bergen Corpus of

Table 2. Mean frequencies of the neuter pronoun *it* and the neuter possessives in Early Modern English and present-day written English

Period	Pronoun *it* N/1,000 words	Possessive forms* N/1,000 words
Period I 1500–1570	1,624 / 9.06	117 / 0.66
Period II 1570–1640	1,834 / 9.69	107 / 0.57
Period III 1640–1710	1,950 / 12.11	175 / 1.10
Present-day English	10,503 / 10.50	1,514 / 1.51

(* The Early Modern English figures include all the neuter possessive variants, the LOB ones only the form *its*.)

Present-day written British English (LOB; Johansson – Hofland 1989). These figures are shown in Table 2.

If we consider the neuter possessive frequencies, we notice that there is a drop in their occurrence in Period II, and a remarkable rise in Period III. That the frequency in the Lancaster – Oslo/Bergen Corpus is higher still might indicate that the process of change was not completed by the end of the seventeenth century. This argument is supported by the fact that there are only some 50 instances of the periphrastic *of it* in the Lancaster – Oslo/Bergen Corpus. But change need not be the only factor responsible for the difference.

There may be a number of reasons for the differences in the possessive distributions in Table 2. Structural reasons include the increase in the use of the definite article in the course of time. As pointed out above (section 4.1), our data provide evidence to the effect that this was particularly the case with abstract and verbal nouns in Early Modern English. That this need not distort the trend of the pronominal change, however, appears from the distributional details of Table 3, below.

Another factor that may be reflected in the figures is the change in gender distinctions discussed in section 3.2. It would seem that, parallel to the restriction of relative *which* to impersonal referents and *who* to 'persons (men and spirits)' (see Butler 1634 [1910]: 41), there was a similar shift in the use of the non-neuter personal pronouns. This then allowed the wider spread of the neuter form to inanimates and lower animals in Period III. The overall distribution of *it* supports this view. The relative frequency of *it* in Period III in fact exceeds its present-day frequency in Table 2.

When comparing the overall figures we should not lose sight of the fact that they are also affected by the subject matter of the texts. Although the three Early Modern English periods by and large contain the same selection of genres, their subject matter has not been regulated except in so far as the genre itself would naturally limit it (e.g. medicine in science, husbandry in handbooks). It appears from our detailed comparison of the genres in section 6 that genres and genre groups nonetheless differ in much the same way across time in their general use of the neuter possessive. Unfortunately, the LOB genres do not correspond to the Early Modern English ones, which complicates their direct comparison in Table 2.

Even if the figures in Period III were partly the result of a difference in neuter subject matter, including the added effect of a semantic shift, there still seems to be some room left for avoidance strategies. While the overall frequency of *it* slightly rises in Period II, that of the possessives goes down. This cannot be properly accounted for by any of the above sources of error, and we seem to be left with the avoidance hypothesis. Our data would agree with Lehnert (1958: 25), who makes the point that both avoidance and paraphrase are common where a linguistic system is undergoing rapid change. With these caveats in mind we can now turn to the actual neuter possessive variants in our data.

Table 3. The neuter possessive paradigm in the Helsinki Corpus

Period	*his* (%)	*its/it* (%)	*thereof* (%)	*of it* (%)	*of the same* (%)	N
Period I 1500–1570	31 (26%)	–	41 (35%)	35 (30%)	10 (9%)	117 (100%)
Period II 1570–1640	22 (21%)	2 (2%)	40 (37%)	38 (35%)	5 (5%)	107 (100%)
Period III 1640–1710	–	107/1 (62%)	13 (7%)	49 (28%)	5 (3%)	175 (100%)

Table 3 shows the relative incidence of the different forms of the neuter possessive in the Helsinki Corpus. We can see that the paradigm that emerges from the corpus data reveals two cases of discontinuity. The prehead variants *his* and *its* seem to be in complementary distribution diachronically. *His* still common in Period I (first half of the sixteenth century), but is no longer found in III, while, after a modest start in the middle period II (around 1600), *its* already dominates in Period III (latter half of the seventeenth century). The only variant whose frequency noticeably increases during the crossing-over period is the periphrastic *of it*. The old synthetic variant *thereof* is well represented until the third period, where it clearly loses ground. The third posthead variant *of the same* looks like a minor alternative throughout the Early Modern English era, but it also appears to be on the wane in Period III.

The figures in Table 3 also indicate something that will partly relieve us of our worry over the structural changes that were taking place in English during the Early Modern period. If we had relaxed the formal selection criteria stated in section 4.1, the first period posthead variants would have been even better represented than they are at the moment. This would only have increased the difference between Periods I and II without having much effect on the quite striking difference between II and III. In other words, the process of change would have looked even more radical than it does within the present framework.

5. Structural factors and semantic roles

5.1. Paradigmatic gap

The previous sections confirm Lehnert's claim (1958: 27) that the paradigm of the third person singular possessive in sixteenth-century English virtually contained a systemic gap in the sense of Anttila (1989: 184–189), as no exclusive neuter item existed. With the change from grammatical to notional gender, *his* became less and less appropriate for inanimate reference, and no other prenominal alternative existed. Instead, several postposed paraphrases were in use. According to Table 3, during the first half of the sixteenth century, *his* was still chosen in 26% of the cases, and in the rest of the cases, posthead alternatives were employed.

The figures in Table 3 indicate how drastic the change in fact was between Periods II and III. While during Period II the prehead items (*his/its*) accounted for only 23% of the possessive instances, the last subperiod showed a clear majority of *its/it* (62%). The most obvious explanation for this change is the rapid filling of the gap immediately after the introduction of a suitable variant. Another factor may also be mentioned within the noun phrase structure in general, although its influence is far more general and supposedly only secondary as compared with the previous one. Between the first half of the sixteenth century and Present-day English, it is possible to discern a development from postmodification towards premodification or combined pre- and postmodification (Raumolin-Brunberg 1991: 189, see further section 8.1).

Table 3 shows that a gap indeed existed in prenominal position until a paradigmatic adjustment filled it with *its* during the second half of the seventeenth century. How then could this situation persist for such a long time? It is obviously connected with the general tendency of placing items with animate reference before the head, and those with inanimate reference after the head (see e.g. Altenberg 1982: 146–149). As the neuter possessive had come to refer to inanimate things, its natural position was postnominal (see also Sapir 1921 [1978]: 165).

5.2. Reflexive use

Although on the basis of Table 3 it is easy to argue that a gap existed in the possessive paradigm in sixteenth-century English, it is equally easy to point out that the hole in the pattern cannot be postulated in absolute terms. During Periods I and II, *his* still accounted for more than twenty percent of all instances of the neuter possessive. Some occurrences of *his* can certainly be attributed to changing views on gender and animacy, as discussed in section 3.2, but other constraints on its use can also be detected.

The general choice of a prenominal variant appears to be conditioned to a large extent by a relatively strong grammatical factor, viz. the reflexive use of the possessive pronoun. Reflexive possessives can be characterized as items referring to the subject of the (finite or nonfinite) clause (examples 20 and 21). Here they parallel reflexive pronouns in their basic use (Quirk et al. 1985: 356–357). The distinction between reflexive and nonreflexive possessives is grammatically coded in various languages (e.g. in Swedish and Russian; see also the Government and Binding approach to anaphora, Chomsky 1981). Swedish, for instance, distinguishes between the reflexive *sin*, *sitt*, *sina* and the nonreflexive third person possessive pronouns *hans*, *hennes*, *dess*, *deras*.[10] It should also be remembered that Old English had a similar reflexive possessive, *sin* (see Mitchell 1985: 119–120).

(20)   Also there is an other Pannikle that couereth the Ribbes inwardly, that is called Plura, of whom the Midriffe taketh his beginning. (Vicary 1548: 60)
(21)   ... may force it to spend its effluviable matter, if I may so call it, so plentifully. (Boyle 1675–76: 38; it refers to Electrical Substance of the Stone)

An analysis of the pre- and postnominal variants shows that the posthead possessives were seldom used reflexively. They are occasionally found in passive clauses and complex expressions with a long distance between the subject and the possessive. Example 17 above, represents a case where the semantic role (OBJECT) is a stronger constraint in the choice of the variant than reflexivity (see section 5.3 below). In contrast, among the prenominal pronouns the reflexive use was frequent, as the following percentages indicate:

	Reflexive use (% of all instances)
Period I (1500–1570) *his*	65%
Period II (1570–1640) *his/its*	58%
Period III (1640–1710) *it/its*	47%

The above makes it evident that at least one prehead alternative was to be expected, because the reflexive use of the postnominal paraphrases was not the norm in the language. This was indeed an important factor supporting the use of *his* despite the changes in the gender system. It was no surprise, either, to find the first two instances of *its* in the Helsinki Corpus in reflexive use (examples 5 and 6). Furthermore, a look at Shakespeare's First Folio of 1623 shows that nine out of the ten instances of *its* are in fact reflexive.

Nevertheless, although the reflexive use can be regarded as a route through which *its* entered the language, it seems that the connection between the reflexive use and prenominal possessives should not be exaggerated. The above percentages make it clear that even the nonreflexive use of the pronouns *his* and *its* was extensive. We might characterize *his* and *its* as items with a dual function in this respect, while the postnominal paraphrases retained or assumed a strictly nonreflexive character. Present-day English lends support to the latter claim, as all the instances of *of it* in the LOB Corpus are nonreflexive.

5.3. Semantic roles of the possessives

Studies discussing the use of the genitive as compared with the *of*-phrase confirm that there are certain semantic roles that are usually connected with the use of the former and others which most often appear with the latter (Altenberg 1982: 151–244; Taylor 1989). There are, no doubt, parallel choices as regards the possessive pronouns as compared with their corresponding posthead alternatives.

An analysis of the semantic roles that the variants represent was carried out in order to find out whether any general changes could be observed before and after the introduction of *its* in Early Modern English. A rough three-alternative system was set up: AGENTS, POSSESSORS and OTHERS.

AGENTS (AG) are instigators of the action identified by the verb or verbal noun (see Fillmore 1968: 24; examples 22 and 23).

(22) *On the other side costiveness has too* its ill effects *and is much harder to be dealt with by physique, purgeing medicines which seeme to give releife rather increasing then removeing the evill.* (Locke 1684–88: 45)

(23) *I perseave you have had an acc^t of* the most sad and lamentable efects of it *heere in England, not only in the losse of our shipping, but about 1500 men in the Queen's shipps.* (Haddock Correspondence 1703: 45)

POSSESSORS (PO) are understood in very broad terms as something belonging or pertaining to somebody or something. Possession is what Taylor (1989: 679–684) calls the semantic prototype of the construction involving a noun phrase in the genitive as a determiner, or its pronoun counterpart (examples 24 and 25).

(24) *the town did not extend it self to the sea but now* its ruines *sets it 3 mile off*; (Fiennes 1698: 143)

(25) *Otherlesse then it as you se D, whose right lines make a sharpe corner, or greater then a quadrate, as is F, and then* the right lines of it *do make a blunt corner.* (Record 1551: 4)

OTHERS (OT) represent roles that are neither AGENTS nor POSSESSORS. The most frequent role is an effected or affected OBJECT (Altenberg 1982: 160–170), syntactically corresponding to the object in a nominalization (examples 26 and 27).

(26) *Likewise every Form should have a Repository near unto it, wherein to lay such Subsidiary books as are most proper for* its use. (Hoole 1660: 224)

(27) *And for* the better atcheving thereof, *requested Langland, Bishoppe of Lincolne, and ghostly father to the kinge, to put a scruple into his graces head, that itt was not lawfull for him to marry his brothers wife;* (Roper 1556: 31)

The results of the analysis of the three semantic roles are presented below in Table 4.

As expected, Table 4 shows that the variants mostly represent the possessive role. The low number of AGENTS is not surprising because the items

Table 4. Semantic roles of the neuter possessive variants

	Prenominal his, it, its				Postnominal thereof, of it, of the same			
Period	AG %	PO %	OT %	N	AG %	PO %	OT %	N
Period I 1500–1570	10	90	0	31	2	63	35	86
Period II 1570–1640	4	96	0	24	5	67	28	83
Period III 1640–1710	13	80	7	108	6	57	37	67

under examination hardly ever refer to human or higher animate beings, which have a natural connection with AGENTS (see e.g. Fillmore 1968: 24).

The share of the group OTHERS is relatively high among the postnominal paraphrases during all the three subperiods. A postnominal variant is expected in English, in particular in nominalizations and verbal nouns, where a word order corresponding to the clausal SVX-order is preferred.

5.4. Modification and position of the possessive construction

In the comparisons of the use of the genitive and the *of*-phrase, structural factors are usually given considerable emphasis. It is argued that heavy modification of the head is a factor favouring the use of the genitive (Altenberg 1982: 76–115). An investigation of the use of the different possessive variants with structurally varying heads (simple versus pre- and postmodified heads) in the corpus did not reveal any significant differences. On the whole, simple (unmodified) heads were preferred by both the pre- and posthead items (70–80% of the cases), which would indicate that pronouns do not behave in a similar fashion with genitive nouns or *of*-phrases.

We also examined the distribution of the different variants in pre- and postverbal position in the clause. In general terms, the preverbal position diminishes in Early Modern English (33%, 24% and 20% for our three periods, respectively), which is likely to be connected with the development of the SVX word order with fewer preverbal noun phrases in general. During all the three periods, *thereof* had the largest number of preverbal occurrences (33% to 47%), while the preverbal instances of the prehead items *his* and *its* at most amounted to 19% of the cases. Preverbal *thereof* was often employed in anaphoric reference which crossed clause boundaries. On the other hand, the frequency of *thereof* in preverbal position can also be attributed to the complex syntax of legal writing, the genre where this variant was used most.

6. Textual factors

6.1. Textual differences

The first instances of *its* in the Helsinki Corpus are found in Period II in a handbook and a travel book (1615 and 1630). By the latter part of the seventeenth century, the use of *its* had spread into other instructive, narrative and expository genres (see Appendix I), but not into legal writing and official correspondence. Neither is it found in private diaries, fiction and trial recordings. Some instances occur in comedies and personal letters.

At the same time as *its* becomes frequent, *his* disappears from the corpus. It is important to note that the range of text types that made use of *his* the first two periods in our corpus was not as extensive as that of *its* during the last subperiod. The use of *his* was mainly limited to scientific treatises, handbooks and the Bible with a very small number of cases elsewhere. The remaining genres relied on paraphrases or had no occurrences at all (e.g. fiction in the whole corpus; see Appendix I).

On the basis of the exclusive use of the postposed variants *thereof* and *of the same*, the most formal genre, viz. legal language, seems to develop in a direction which could be characterized as archaic, even at this stage. After being used in various text types during Period I, the periphrastic form *of the same* seems to become a special feature of legal English in the second and third subperiods. Both *thereof* and *of the same* are very useful in reference to lists including items both in the singular and the plural, such as are often found in the *Statutes of the Realm* (see sections 2.5 and 2.6 above).

According to Knorrek (1938: 115), the use of *thereof* in the seventeenth century was limited to scientific writing, letters and diaries. Our material only partly confirms this statement, as there are no instances of *thereof* in scientific texts at the end of the seventeenth century. Knorrek seems to have missed the fact that it is the language of law that for a long time retained *thereof* as its main possessive variant.

The above seems to motivate a conclusion that at the end of the seventeenth century, legal language could no longer be regarded as a good representative of the standard norm, as was the case with Chancery English a century and a half earlier and even at the beginning of the sixteenth century (Samuels 1981;

Fisher 1977; Gómez Soliño 1981, 1985; Raumolin-Brunberg – Nevalainen 1990). As a matter of fact, the above might rather indicate that the language of law was on its way to becoming an LSP (language for specific purposes) and thus gradually disappearing from the registers generally commanded by well-educated Englishmen.

The Bible sample (Authorized Version of 1611) does not contain any instances of *its*. Lehnert (1958: 23) and the *Oxford English Dictionary* (s.v. *its*, poss. pron.) mention that it contained one case of possessive *it*, which in 1660 was transformed into *its* (*of it/its own accord*, Leviticus XXV, 5). As no attempts were made to change the instances of *his* into *its*, the Bible came to represent conservative language even in this respect. It is noteworthy that the Authorized Version contains more instances of *his* and *thereof* than Tyndale's version, although the passages chosen for the corpus are the same. The corpus shows, however, that the conservatism of the Bible did not prevent clergymen from using *its* in their sermons during the third subperiod.

Scientific treatises permit good comparisons because of a continuity in subject matter. For instance, Vicary's *Anatomie of the Bodie of Man* (1548), in which several body parts are referred to with the pronouns *he*, *it*, and *his* (see example 18 above), is followed by Clowes's book on struma (1602) with no instances of similar use. Robert Record's work on geometry (1551) contains several occurrences of *his* with clearly inanimate referents (e.g. *square, line*), and Blundeville's book on navigation (1597) follows the same pattern. It is worth pointing out that the above examples are almost unique in the corpus, as here the use of *his* cannot be explained by broadly interpreted animacy, personification or fixed collocation. As to reflexivity, the usage in these books is divided. Hence the use of *his* with inanimate reference might either be considered a special characteristic of early scientific writing, or it represents conservative tradition in general or the dialectal background of the authors.[11] In any case, this usage was discontinued in the treatises by Hooke (1660) and Boyle (1675–1676).

One of the most puzzling questions in our material is the rareness of *its* in genres representing informal or speech-based types of text: private diaries, fiction (merry tales, jest books and other predecessors of the novel) and personal letters. Trial recordings lack *its* completely. Only comedy, the other genre generally held to contain features of spoken language, makes exclusive use of *its* (8 instances) during our last subperiod.

The rareness of *its* in informal writing might be understood as counterevidence to the colloquial origin of *its* (*Oxford English Dictionary*, s.v. *its*, poss. pron.; Wyld 1920: 331; Graband 1965: 257). However, our findings are in harmony with Lehnert's (1958: 25–26) observation on the infrequency of *its* in the private letters of the Verney family. Lehnert explains this as linguistic insecurity and the strategy of avoidance. In the corpus all the variants of the neuter possessive are rare in these informal genres during all the three periods. This would support the idea of avoidance to such an extent that not even the postnominal paraphrases were eligible. People would use the plural form instead or the definite article alone (see section 2 above).

Another, more likely explanation for the rareness of *its* would be a difference in the subject matter. Informal discussions most likely deal with human beings and hence there is only a limited need to use pronouns that refer to inanimate beings. It might be even more unusual to have noun phrases with inanimate reference promoted to subjects in these texts, a phenomenon that would be necessary for the reflexive use of *its*.

6.2. The colloquial origin of *its*?

It is generally argued in the literature that *its* originated in colloquial language. As mentioned above, textual comparisons indicate very low frequencies with any of the variants in informal or speech-based genres. Hence we could not compare individual text categories separately. Instead, a study of the role of the more "oral" text types in the process of change was carried out (on the dichotomy between "oral" and "literate", see Tannen 1982; Biber 1988: 104–108; Biber – Finegan 1989).

The following genres were classified as representatives of the oral type of writing: private correspondence, comedies, fiction, diaries, biographies and travel books. They either consist of private writing or their purpose is entertainment. All the instances of the five variants of the neuter possessive in these texts were counted and their relative shares compared with the total number of the instances of each variant in the whole corpus. The results are given in Table 5.

It is worth pointing out that the possessive total shows remarkable stability all through the three subperiods: about 20% of all the instances of the neuter possessive are found in the oral genres. Table 5 indicates that *his* is very rare in this type of writing and that the shares of *thereof* and *of the same* radically diminish with time.

On the other hand, the relative share of *of it* is much larger than the average during the first two subperiods (31% and 41%). It is obviously this form that the oral genres and hence the colloquial language prefers before the introduction of *its*.

What then makes *of it* a "better" alternative than the others? Its major advantage is an unambiguous semantic marking: *Of it* is the only variant

Table 5. The neuter possessive in oral genres

Period	his (%)	its/it (%)	thereof (%)	of it (%)	of the same (%)	total (%)
Period I 1500–1570	1 (3%)	0	10 (24%)	11 (31%)	2 (20%)	24 (21%)
Period II 1570–1640	0	1 (50%)	4 (10%)	15 (41%)	0	21 (20%)
Period III 1570–1710	0	25 (23%)	1 (8%)	11 (22%)	0	37 (21%)

Note to Table 5. The percentages given indicate the proportion of the figure from the corresponding total in the Corpus, e.g., in the oral genres the share of *it/its* in period II, 50%, corresponds to 1 occurrence out of the total of 2, and in period III, 23%, to 25 instances out of the total of 107. For the absolute frequencies, see Appendix I.

with an exclusive singular neuter reference. *His* is connected with masculine animacy, *thereof* and *of the same* can also refer to plural noun phrases (see section 2 above). The semantic content of the pronoun *it* is obviously decisive in the choice of *of it*, and later in the adoption of *it* and *its*. Also, *of it* is an analytic form at a time when a typological change from synthetic to analytic has been continuing for several centuries. Thirdly, it is a postnominal alternative and thus well suited for inanimate reference.

Nevertheless, *of it* was not suitable enough to be established as an only alternative. It was a postnominal form, and the reflexive use as well as some semantic roles favoured a prehead item. As the other persons had possessive pronouns of their own, there was a systemic gap in the neuter. In addition, the preposition *of* had a large variety of uses in Early Modern English and a risk of ambiguity was imminent.

The figures in Table 5 can be taken to indicate indirectly that the emergence of *its* indeed originated in colloquial language. We might classify this change as a specimen of systemic regulation, where the empty slot left by the specialization of *his* to masculine animate reference was filled (e.g. Samuels 1972: 64–87). Its first filler was *of it*, although it could not be employed in every case. *Of it* was followed by the generally applicable *it* and *its*. *Of it* could be regarded as a vehicle pulling *it* and *its* into Standard English as its prenominal counterparts. Of these two *it* was introduced first, but its functional load was too heavy as it already represented both the subjective and objective forms. Consequently, *it* was modified into *its* on analogy with *his* and the genitive, and the new form rapidly spread into the literate genres as well.

Although the absolute frequencies in Appendix I might motivate an interpretation of this very rapid and relatively late Early Modern English change as a learned one with a close relation to the general standardization process, our evidence in Table 5 points to the opposite direction, to the oral genres and thus towards a natural change or a change from below in Labovian terms (Labov 1972: 178–181). Our analysis is supported on the one hand by the fact that neither *of it* nor *it/its* appear in the most formal genres (law and official correspondence) and on the other by the appearance of other gender-related changes during the same period (Poussa 1992). The case may be rather that the change was successful because it took place before extensive implementation of standardization policies in Late Modern English.

Table 5 further shows how the frequency of *of it* in oral genres dropped to 22% after the emergence of *its*, which also had a similar percentage, viz. 23%, corresponding to the possessive average of the oral genres. These figures indicate that during the latter half of the seventeenth century, the system had found new stability and the oral and literate genres both used the forms *its* and *of it* with similar frequencies.

7. Socio-historical aspects of the change

7.1. Standard versus dialect

In the compilation of the Early Modern English part of the Helsinki Corpus, we relied on extralinguistic criteria in the choice of the texts, which on the whole should represent the evolving standard language. This method was applied in order to avoid circular reasoning (Nevalainen – Raumolin-Brunberg 1989: 89–95). The conclusion was reached that a combination of the author's high rank or profession and a formal text type would most likely guarantee the standardness of the text.

In the corpus the users of *its* were mostly gentlemen or professional men in Period III.[12] As the text types in which *its* is found also largely belong to the more formal types of writing (see Appendix I), there is no doubt that *its* was used in the standard language at this time (see Nevalainen – Raumolin-Brunberg 1989: 95). Because of the small number of users in Period II, no conclusions can be drawn on the basis of their backgrounds.

We can thus see that the Present-day Standard English usage with *its* as the main variant and *of it* as its postnominal alternative had become standard by the end of the seventeenth century. A few sporadic instances of *thereof* could still be found, and, as mentioned above, legal language followed a different pattern.

The literature (*Oxford English Dictionary*, s.v. *its*, poss. pron.; Lehnert 1958; Graband 1965: 258) agrees that the variants *it* and *the ... of it* (pronounced *o't*) and the use of *his* with inanimate reference appear in regional dialects both before and after the innovation of *its*. Of these, *of it* has become part of the written standard, *his* has disappeared from standard written usage, and *it* was only briefly used in standard texts before the introduction of *its*.

The *Oxford English Dictionary* (s..v. *its*, poss. pron.) mentions that *its* first appeared in the south of England, in particular in London and Oxford. It is generally agreed that the language of London and its surroundings functioned as a model in the standardization process (Nevalainen – Raumolin-Brunberg 1989: 86–89), and this might provide an explanation for the very rapid establishment of *its* as the standard form. There is no evidence of *its* in regional dialects or stigmatized social varieties before its use in the standard, but later on it found a position in nonstandard varieties as well.

7.2. Socio-historical connections with the rapid adoption of *its*

The rapidity with which *its* spread in written English is remarkable. According to the literature, *its* began to be frequent in the 1630–1640s, it was the usual variant in the middle of the century, and in 1672, Dryden could call its main competitor *his* "ill syntax" (see section 3.1 above).

This development is in agreement with our relatively small corpus, collected so that the middle period (1570–1640) mainly represents texts from the decades around the turn of the century, and the last period (1640–1710) concentrates on materials from the last few decades of the seventeenth century (see Nevalainen – Raumolin-Brunberg 1989: 76). Consequently, the corpus contains a gap for the years 1630–1660. But from the 1660s onwards, *its* is definitely the main variant (62% of all instances, see Table 3).

In practical terms, the change appears to have taken place within the time span of one generation. In this connection, it is interesting to relate this change to the social realities of the day and see if some explanations for its rapidity can be found there. Milroy – Milroy (1985: 375) advance a model of the connectedness of linguistic change and social stability: "Linguistic change is slow to the extent that the relevant populations are well established and bound by strong ties, whereas it is rapid to the extent that weak ties exist in populations."

In Nevalainen – Raumolin-Brunberg (1989: 78–81), we discussed the social and economic conditions in Early Modern England and came to the conclusion that the following factors contributed to an increase in weak ties in social networks: population growth causing migration, urbanization, commercial farming and economic diversification, better communication networks and increased educational opportunities. We may say that all these factors were in operation until the last decades of the seventeenth century, when the period of Restoration gradually created conservative stability in society. In addition, the Civil War in 1642–1646 caused disorder, increasing sporadic contacts between people.

The Early Modern English section of the Helsinki Corpus has provided material for studies of some interesting linguistic changes, such as Rissanen (1989, development of the conjunctions *for* and *for that*), Rissanen (1991a, the auxiliary *do*), Rissanen (1991b, the clausal link *that* v. zero). All these analyses seem to indicate that it is particularly the middle subperiod (1570–1640) in which many linguistic changes culminate (see also Lass in this volume). It would seem to us that it is possible to connect these patterns of change to the frequencies of weak ties in social networks. At the same time, there are also other well-attested developments such as the regularization of the third person singular suffix *-s* (v. *-th*) in the more formal registers around 1600 (see Stein 1987). The period thus proves interesting both from the viewpoint of increased variation and stabilization in the emerging standard language (for further discussion, see Raumolin-Brunberg – Nevalainen forthcoming).

The question of social prestige cannot be neglected in studies of linguistic change. As far as the rapidity of the acceptance of *its* is concerned, we may suggest that the London origin of the form was of importance at a time when London English represented "the best spoken English" or the written standard (for a discussion of standardness of pronunciation and London English, see Milroy in this volume). It is important to bear in mind that in 1550–1650 one out of eight and in 1650–1750 one out of six English adults had some experience of life in London and were thus in one way or another exposed to the variety used in the capital. We also know that the general lifestyle of the upper ranks was imitated by others, and there is no reason to believe that this would not include language as well (see Nevalainen – Raumolin-Brunberg 1989: 88–89). On the other hand, recent research has shown that such phenomena as the consumption habits of the middle ranks could also develop independently (Weatherill 1988).

8. Discussion and conclusions

8.1. Complexity of the change

In the previous sections we have shown the complexity connected with the introduction of *its*, which on the surface may look like a rather simple change from *his* to *its*. This change has not only proved to be one which involves a number of different factors, but it has also indicated how difficult it can be to find constants, viz. factors which remain unchanged over a longer period of time. Both the linguistic and extralinguistic constraints change. As regards the linguistic ones, it is not only the grammatical issues (e.g. the use of the definite article) but also semantic principles (e.g. the gender system) that undergo change during the Early Modern English period.

In this final section, the major constraints connected with the development of the neuter possessive paradigm, both linguistic and extralinguistic, are examined separately. In most of them we can find a general trend, but factors working in the opposite direction can also be traced. This discussion will indicate that especially in the study of a linguistic change taking place in unstable environments, it is of crucial importance to find evidence both within and outside a corpus. The risk of missing important factors increases if materials are restricted to one type only (see Lass and Tieken in this volume).

The very emergence of the peculiar situation of the neuter possessive is a result of a change in the English gender system, which is closely linked with morphological levelling in English. As has been shown in section 3.2, in broad terms, the system of personal and possessive pronouns underwent a change from a stage where the animacy of the referent was decisive for the choice of the pronoun towards a stage where the humanness or personal reference was the most imporant criterion. We might call this a change upwards in the gender hierarchy (see Quirk et al. 1985: 314–318; Taylor 1989: 668–669; see also Poussa 1992).

However, this change did not proceed in a linear manner, but was impeded or influenced by various factors. The whole concept of animacy is problematic, and it is difficult for us to decide, for instance, whether the users of *his* when referring to wine, wind or water regarded these items as animate or whether they only employed the receding neuter possessive for other reasons. We may speculate about man's changing relation to nature and animacy, but to corroborate this would demand more research. Another factor opposing the change is conscious or unconscious application of personification, which could and can be employed for many purposes in different styles and genres in the English language.

A further large-scale change in English has been the typological drift from synthetic to analytic (see Sapir 1921 [1978]: 165–168). A change from pronominal adverbs to prepositional phrases, such as replacing *thereof* by *of it* can be taken as a typical instance of this development. But this typological change is not all-pervading either. The innovation *its* is more synthetic than *of it*, as it is a word with an inflectional suffix. Again, there are exceptions to the general drift.

In the structure of the noun phrase, there was and still is a tendency towards the restriction of the inflected possessive to animate nouns and pronouns. This involves a placement of items with animate reference prenominally and phrases with inanimate reference postnominally. This principle explains the extensive use of the posthead paraphrases during the relatively long period of instability that obtained before the introduction of *its*.

If this positional tendency connected with animacy had been implemented in English with maximal consistency, *its* would hardly have come about. Apparently, this trend was not so strong in Early Modern English that the other factors, such as the "need" for a prenominal reflexive possessive or systemic regulation in filling a gap, could not have worked against it. In addition, a very general tendency in the noun phrase structure operating in the opposite direction may have had an effect, viz. the development from posthead modification towards more compact prenominal or combined pre- and posthead modification (Raumolin-Brunberg 1991: 189).

8.2. Standardization

We now turn our attention to the main topic of this volume, viz. standardization. In practical terms, standardization can be characterized as the gradual reduction of variant forms in language or the specialization of certain items to specific uses or varieties. Although a totally new element was introduced into the neuter possessive paradigm in Early Modern English, the period ended with only two major variants in the standard language, *its* and *of it*, as compared with four variants in Period I, viz. *his*, *thereof*, *of it* and *of the same*. In Early Modern English, *thereof* and *of the same* became textually marked, as their use was restricted to the most official type of language, mainly the language of law.

As regards textual variation, Early Modern English represents the period that followed the invention of the printing press. Consequently, the repertoire of genres and text types increased all through the period. This versatility together with intrageneric changes does not necessarily help a researcher in his or her attempts to make diachronic textual comparisons. In this context, it is particularly important to point out that the texts representing the standard norm appear to have changed during the Early Modern English period, as described in section 6.1.

Despite certain enduring patterns of life (e.g. social order and family relations) Early Modern England experienced extensive economic, social and educational changes, including a relative increase in literacy. As the social order in broad terms remained unchanged, the social status of the corpus informants can be utilized in the discussion of the standardness of the language used. On the other hand, the relative instability in society seems instrumental in the rapid diffusion of *of it* and *its*.

A further interesting question in the discussion of standardization can be raised on the basis of the suggested colloquial origin of *its*. As mentioned in section 6.2, no evidence is presented in the literature of the use of *its* in regional varieties before its introduction into the standard. On the other hand, the *Oxford English Dictionary* (s.v. *its*, poss. pron.) states that *its* was used in colloquial language before being employed in writing. These statements would imply that there was a nonregional colloquial variety which was apparently used in London and elsewhere in southern England, as this area was mentioned as the origin of *its*. This situation would not contradict what is known about the general status of the language of London, but further research is needed especially in order to trace the differences between this nonregional colloquial variety and the true local dialect of London.

We have above subscribed to the view that the origin of *its* lies in colloquial language, in other words, that its introduction can be regarded as a natural change rather than a learned one. However, this interpretation is obviously oversimplified if the whole paradigmatic shift is taken into consideration. Standardization can essentially be taken as a force that opposes changes coming from below, and its effects can hardly be ruled out in the process of restricting the number of variant forms in the neuter possessive paradigm. The role of learned and literary language with Latin and French influence can be detected in the development of the English gender system and the spread of certain types of personification (see section 3.2 above). On the other hand, contemporary grammars assumed a descriptive rather than a prescriptive role, and provide an important source of evidence for dating the change.

8.3. Parallel changes

On the whole, the introduction of *its* can be characterized as a linguistically conditioned change rather than one of purely extralinguistic initiation. The linguistic issue in this change is the emergence of a hole in the pattern and the consequent adjustment that filled it with a new item. Although the final phase of the change, the innovation and spread of *its*, is very rapid, the process as a whole, which is mainly based on the gradual change from grammatical to notional gender or what Poussa (1992) calls the "Great Gender Shift", lasted for centuries. The extralinguistic factors cannot, however, be ruled out, because they, together with the fact that the new item *its* suited the paradigm very well, probably bear the main responsibility for the rapid general adoption of the new form.

Interesting parallels to the possessive paradigm are offered by contemporary developments of other pronouns, viz. relative pronouns and second person pronouns. The conditioning factor in the development of the distinction between *who* and *which* was the same change in the English gender system as that which influenced the possessive paradigm. But here we face a more gradual change leading to a division of labour by 1700, with *which* ending up with nonpersonal reference, *who* with personal reference and *that* with both (Dekeyser 1984). It is evident that the changes within the possessive and relative systems supported each other, but the processes were different: the possessive paradigm experienced an abrupt readjustment, while the relative pronoun system evolved in a rather smooth and orderly manner. On the other hand, Poussa (1992) argues that in the singular demonstrative pronouns *this* and *that*, the gender gap is still there, as these pronouns cannot refer to human beings, except when used pejoratively.

The process which leads to the disappearance of *thou/thee* from standard language is different from the ones discussed above. It is a change where one variant form, *you*, becomes the sole representative of the paradigm. As forms of address, these items have clear associations with extralinguistic factors, viz. social stratification, although the social conditions in Early Modern England can hardly be assigned the whole responsibility for this change, because similar stratification also prevailed in other societies where languages retained the distinction. Nevertheless, it does not seem incorrect to characterize this change as a process which was constrained by extralinguistic rather than linguistic factors.

The questions of pronominal gender are by no means all settled in Present-day English. Growing uneasiness is felt about the use of *he* as the neutral third person pronoun with personal reference. As in the case of *his* in Early Modern English, speakers' attitudes are changing rapidly (see e.g. Mühlhäusler – Harré 1990: 228–247). Gillian Brown's *Listening to Spoken English* was first published in 1977. What she writes in her preface to the second edition (1990) gives an insight into how change may affect an individual speaker. Without pressing the parallel too far, we may perhaps assume that something similar was felt about the neuter possessive *his* around the turn of the seventeenth century.

> I should make a stylistic point. I remember holding the opinion when I wrote this book originally that the masculine third person pronoun was properly to be interpreted as neutral as between male and female where no question of different gender was involved. I find, somewhat to my surprise, that my feelings (note that I do not say "my thoughts") have changed radically. I now find the insistence on the masculine pronoun dated and repetitive. You will be able to recognize those parts of the book which have been rewritten, by the elaborate lengths I go to avoid using the singular pronoun. (Brown 1990: xii–xiii)

Notes

* We would like to thank the participants of the workshop for their valuable comments on the first version of *its*. Our especial thanks are due to Matti Rissanen for reading and commenting on the draft version in detail. The remaining shortcomings are our own joint responsibility.

1. For textbook accounts, see e.g. Barber (1976: 208ff), Bourcier (1981: 211), Pyles – Algeo (1982: 157, 190–192). Our approach is couched in traditional paradigmatic terms, and personal pronouns are considered a closed system of variants. The fact that at one point a variant such as the neuter possessive *his* falls out of use is clearly something that historical linguists should account for. For descriptive purposes we shall adopt the position that "if in the middle of an otherwise perfect pattern an 'expected' unit is missing, one speaks of a hole in the pattern" (Anttila 1989: 184). In our case, the expected unit was never totally missing, as the periphrastic possessives testify. Our question then is why *its* was the form to fill this particular systemic position better than any of its well-established rivals.

2. For *who/which*, see Bately 1965, Meier 1967, Rydén 1983, Dekeyser 1984, Rissanen 1984, Romaine 1984, and von Bremen 1987; for *thou/you*, Mulholland 1967, Barber 1981, Wales 1983, Brown – Gilman 1989: 176–179; and for *-th/-s* Samuels 1972: 174–176, and especially Stein 1987.

3. A similar occurrence of *it* was found by Knorrek (1938: 116) in Locke's *Essay Concerning Human Understanding* (1690: 16): "not need any Truth, nor want any Reason to gain *it* Approbation". Knorrek regards it as an obvious printer's error.

4. It is interesting that *its* is not given as a neuter possessive pronoun equivalent by Florio. It is used to disambiguate gender in the English gloss for *spontaneamente* ('willingly, naturally, without compulsion, of himselfe, of his free will, for *its* own sake'). At the same time, the earlier attestation of *its* from Nicolas

Yonge's translation of Italian madrigals referred to by Baugh (1951: 295), is a later emendation. All the British Library copies of Yonge's *The Second Booke of Madrigalles* (1597), shelf-marked BL.K.3.k.20, have the form *his*. The first version of the seventh Cantus, for instance, begins "Browne is my Loue but gracefull ... and each renowned whitenesse ... looseth his brightnesse".

5. Gleason (1965: 384) points out that the Authorized Version of the English Bible seems to be deliberately avoiding *his* in some passages by several devices, and quotes the following parallel verses:

(i) *And they shall make an ark of shittim wood: two cubits and a half shall be the length* thereof, *and a cubit and a half the breadth* thereof, *and a cubit and a half the height* thereof. (Ex. 25: 10)

(ii) *And Bazaleel made the ark of shittim wood: two cubits and a half was the length* of it, *and a cubit and a half the breadth* of it, *and a cubit and a half the height* of it: (Ex. 37:1)

6. We would like to thank Mary Hatakka for drawing our attention to this alternative in Present-day English.

7. Graband (1965: 33, 259) refers to Edward Richardson's bilingual textbook *Anglo-Belgica* (1677) as the last grammar to mention the possessive *it*, attributing it to the Yorkshire background of the author. However, the pronoun table in the British Library copy of Richardson (1677: 278), shelf-marked 12972.a.15, unambiguously gives only the neuter possessive *its* on a par with the masculine *his* and feminine *her*. A similar inaccuracy occurs in Graband (1965: 258) with Bullokar's neuter possessive paradigm. Bullokar (1586: 20) states that *his* is derived from both *he* and *it*, but does not actually give the form *of it* as a periphrastic variant of *his*, as Graband would have us believe.

8. Some neuter instances are, however, cited in *Middle English Dictionary*, s.v. *hit*, pron. 1 (b), with reference to a horse and a steed, for instance.

9. The masculine pronoun *he* is still used, for example, in South-Western British English dialects to refer to inanimates; one of the restrictions on its use is that the referent will have to be countable (see Ihalainen 1985a: 69). We are grateful to Professor lhalainen for information on regional variation in pronoun use.

10. The following examples illustrate the distinction between the reflexive and non-reflexive possessives in Swedish:

Peter tog sin bok. 'Peter took his (Peter's own) book.'
Peter tog hans bok. 'Peter took his (some other boy's) book.'

11. Record was from Pembrokeshire (Wales) and Blundeville from Norfolk. We must not forget that in the literature there is evidence of *his* with neuter reference in other types of and sixteenth- and seventeenth-century texts as well (see section 2.1 above).

12. 1570–1640: professional men   1   1640-1710:   gentlemen   3
            other   1   professional men   7
            total   2   gentlewomen   1
                                                       other   1
                                                       unknown (man)   1
                                                       total   13

Appendix I. The neuter possessive in the Early Modern English section of the Helsinki Corpus (prefinal version)

Genre	his	it/its	thereof	of it	of the same	total
Period I (1500–1570)						
Law			13		3	16
The Bible	4		2	11		17
Sermons	1		2	1		4
Educational treatises			2	1	1	4
Scientific treatises	23		2	8	1	34
Handbooks	2		3	1	1	7
Chronicles, histories			4		1	5
(Auto)biographies			3	1		4
Travel books	1		2	8	1	12
Diaries			1	1		2
Private correspondence			4	1	1	6
Official correspondence			3		1	4
Trial proceedings			1	2		3
Fiction						0
Comedies						0
Total	31		42	35	10	118
Period II (1570–1640)						
Law			6		5	11
The Bible	14		5	6		25
Philosophical treatises	1					1
Sermons				6		6
Educational treatises	1			5		6
Scientific treatises	5		14			19
Handbooks	1	1	4	1		7
Chronicles, histories			3			3
(Auto)biographies						0
Travel books		1	3	9		13
Diaries				2		2
Private correspondence				2		2

Genre	his	it/its	thereof	of it	of the same	total
Official correspondence						0
Trial proceedings			1	4		5
Fiction						0
Comedies				2		2
Total	22	2	36	37	5	102
Period III (1640–1710)						
Law			9		5	14
Sermons		21		14		35
Educational treatises		1/10		3		14
Scientific treatises		38		13		51
Handbooks		12		5		17
Chronicles, histories		1	4	1		6
(Auto)biographies		3		3		6
Travel books		13		3		16
Diaries			1	1		2
Private correspondence		1		4		5
Official correspondence			1			1
Trial proceedings				2		2
Fiction						0
Comedies		8				8
Total		1/107	15	49	5	177

References

Aijmer, Karin – Bengt Altenberg (eds.)
    1991   *English Corpus Linguistics: In honour of Jan Svartwik*. London: Longman.
Altenberg, Bengt
    1982   *The genitive versus the* of-*construction. A study of syntactic variation in 17th century English* (Lund Studies in English 62). Lund: CWK Gleerup.
Anttila, Raimo
    1989   *Historical and comparative linguistics*. (2nd edition.) Amsterdam & Philadelphia: Benjamins.
Bach, Emmon – Robert T. Harms (eds.)
    1968   *Universals in linguistic theory*. London: Holt, Rinehart & Winston.
Barber, Charles L.
    1976   *Early Modern English*. London: Deutsch.

1981 "'You' and 'thou' in Shakespeare's *Richard III*", *Leeds Studies in English*, N.S. XII, 273–289.
[1987] [Reprinted in Vivian Salmon – Edwina Burness (eds.) *A reader in the language of Shakespearean drama*. Amsterdam & Philadelphia: Benjamins, 163–179.]

Bately, Janet M.
1965 "*Who* and *which* and the grammarians of the 17th century", *English Studies* 46: 245–250.

Baugh, Albert C.
1951 *A history of the English language*. (2nd edition.) London: Routledge & Kegan Paul.

Benskin, Michael – Michael Samuels (eds.)
1981 *So meny people, longages and tonges. Philological essays in Scots and mediaeval English presented to Angus McIntosh*. Edinburgh: Middle English Dialect Project.

Biber, Douglas
1988 *Variation across speech and writing*. Cambridge: Cambridge University Press.

Biber, Douglas – Edward Finegan
1989 "Drift and the evolution of English style: A history of three genres", *Language* 65: 487–517.

Bourcier, Georges
1981 *An introduction to the history of the English language*. English adaptation by Cecily Clark. Cheltenham: Stanley Thornes.

Brown, Gillian
1990 *Listening to spoken English*. (2nd edition.) London & New York: Longman.

Brown, Roger – Arthur Gilman
1989 "Politeness theory and Shakespeare's four major tragedies", *Language in Society* 18: 159–212.

Bullokar, William
1586 *Pamphlet for Grammar*. London.
[1980] [*The Works of William Bullokar*. Vol. II. *Pamphlet for Grammar* 1586. London. Facsimile edition. (Leeds Texts and Monographs, N.S. I.) The University of Leeds, School of English.]

Butler, Charles
1634 *English Grammar*. London.
[1910] [Reprinted in: Albert Eichler (ed.), *Charles Butler's English Grammar*. (Neudrucke frühenglischer Grammatiken 4: 1.) Halle: Niemeyer.]

Caie, Graham – Kirsten Haastrup – Art Lykke Jakobsen – Jørgen Erik Nielsen – Jørgen Sevaldsen – Henrik Specht – Arne Zettersten (eds.)
1990 *Proceedings from the 4th Nordic Conference for English Studies*. Vol. I, Department of English, University of Copenhagen.

Chomsky, Noam
    1981   *Lectures on government and binding.* Dordrecht: Foris.
Cooper, Christopher
    1685   *Grammatica linguae Anglicanae.* London.
Dekeyser, Xavier
    1984   "Relativizers in early Modern English: A dynamic quantitative study", in: Jacek Fisiak (ed.), 61–87.
Dryden, John
    1672   Defence of the epilogue to the second part of *The Conquest of Granada.* London.
    [1962] [Reprinted in: G. Watson (ed.), *Of dramatic poesy, and other critical essays.* London: Dent.]
Eaton, Roger – Olga Fischer – Willem Koopman – Frederike van der Leek (eds.)
    1985   *Papers from the 4th International Conference on English Historical Linguistics.* (Current Issues in Linguistic Theory 41.) Amsterdam & Philadelphia: Benjamins.
Fillmore, Charles J.
    1968   "The case for case", in: Emmon Bach – Robert T. Harms (eds.), 1–88.
Fisiak, Jacek (ed.)
    1984   *Historical syntax.* (Trends in Linguistics: Studies and Monographs 23.) Berlin: Mouton de Gruyter.
Fisher, John H.
    1977   "Chancery and the emergence of standard written English in the fifteenth century", *Speculum* 52: 870–899.
Florio, John
    1598   *A Worlde of Wordes, or Most Copious, and Exact Dictionarie in Italian and English, collected by Iohn Florio.* Printed at London, by Arnold Hatfield for Edw. Blount.
Franz, Wilhelm
    1939   *Die Sprache Shakespeares in Vers und Prosa.* (*Shakespeare-Grammatik*) (4th edition.) Halle: Niemeyer.
Gill, Alexander
    1621   *Logonomia Anglica.* London.
    [1903] [Reprinted in: Otto L. Jiriczek (ed.), *Alexander Gill's Logonomia Anglica.* Strassburg: Trübner.]
Gleason, Henry Allan Jr.
    1965   *Linguistics and English grammar.* New York: Holt, Rinehart & Winston.
Gómez Soliño, José S.
    1981   "Thomas Wolsey, Thomas More y la lengua inglesa estándar de su época", *Revista Canaria de Estudios Ingleses* 3: 74–84.
    1985   "William Caxton y la estandarización de la lengua inglesa en el siglo XV", *Revista Canaria de Estudios Ingleses* 10: 95–118.

Görlach, Manfred
    1978   *Einführung ins Frühneuenglische.* Heidelberg: Quelle & Meyer.

Graband, Gerhard
    1965   *Die Entwicklung der frühneuenglischen Nominalflexion. Dargestellt vornehmlich auf Grund von Grammatikerzeugnissen des 17. Jahrhunderts.* Tübingen: Niemeyer.

Ihalainen, Ossi
    1985a   "Synchronic variation and linguistic change", in: Roger Eaton – Olga Fischer – Willem Koopman – Frederike van der Leek (eds.), 61–72.
    1985b   "*He took the bottle and put'n in his pocket*: The object pronoun *it* in present-day Somerset", in: Wolfgang Viereck (ed.), 153–161.

Johansson, Stig – Knut Hofland
    1989   *Frequency analysis of English vocabulary and grammar, based on the LOB Corpus.* Vol. I. Oxford: Clarendon Press.

Jones, Charles
    1988   *Grammatical gender in English: 950–1250.* London, New York & Sydney: Croom Helm.

Jonson, Ben
    1640 [1972]   *The English grammar.* A Scolar Press facsimile. Menston: Scolar Press.

Kastovsky, Dieter (ed.)
    1991   *Historical English syntax.* (Topics in English Linguistics 2.) Berlin: Mouton de Gruyter.
    Forthcoming   *Early Modern English.* Berlin: Mouton de Gruyter.

Knorrek, Marianne
    1938   *Der Einfluss des Rationalismus auf die englische Sprache, Beiträge zur Entwicklungsgeschichte der englischen Syntax im 17. und 18. Jahrhundert.* Breslau: Paul Plischke.

Kytö, Merja (comp.)
    1991   *Manual to the diachronic part of the Helsinki Corpus of English Texts. Coding conventions and lists of source texts.* Helskinki: Department of English, University of Helsinki.

Labov, William
    1972   *Sociolinguistic patterns.* Philadelphia: University of Pennsylvania Press.

Lehnert, Martin
    1958   "Die Entstehung des neuenglischen *its*", *Zeitschrift für Anglistik und Amerikanistik* 6: 22–28.

Locke, John
    1933   *Directions concerning education.* Being the first draft of this *Thoughts concerning education*, now printed from Additional MS. 38771 in the British Museum. Oxford: The Roxburghe Club.

Manwayring, Henry
    1644 [1972] *The Sea-mans dictionary*. A Scolar Press facsimile. Menston: Scolar Press.

Middle English Dictionary
    1954   Hans Kurath – Sherman Kuhn *et al.* (eds.) Ann Arbor: University of Michigan Press.

Meier, Hans Heinrich
    1967   "The lag of relative *who* in the nominative", *Neophilologus* 51: 227–288.

Miège, Guy
    1688   *The English grammar*. London.

Milroy, James – Lesley Milroy
    1985   "Linguistic change, social network and speaker innovation", *Journal of Linguistics* 21: 339–384.

Mitchell, Bruce
    1985   *Old English Syntax*. I–II. Oxford: Clarendon Press.

Mühlhäusler, Peter – Rom Harré
    1990   *Pronouns and people: The linguistic construction of social and personal identity*. Oxford: Blackwell.

Mulholland, Joan
    1967   " 'Thou' and 'you' in Shakespeare: A study of the second person pronoun", *English Studies* 48: 1–9.
    [1987]   [Reprinted in Vivian Salmon – Edwina Burness (eds.) *A reader in the language of Shakespearean drama*. Amsterdam & Philadelphia: Benjamins, 153–161.]

Mustanoja, Tauno
    1960   *A Middle English syntax* (Mémoires de la Société Néophilologique, 23). Part I. Helsinki: Société Néophilologique.

Nevalainen, Terttu – Helena Raumolin-Brunberg
    1989   "A corpus of Early Modern standard English in a socio-historical perspective", *Neuphilologische Mitteilungen* 90: 67–110.

Oxford English Dictionary, The
    1989   J.A. Simpson – E.S.C. Weiner (comps.). (2nd edition.) Oxford: Clarendon Press.

Partridge, A.C.
    1973   *English biblical translation*. London: Deutsch.

Poole, Joshua
    1646 [1969]   *The English Accidence*. London. A Scolar Press Facsimile. Menston: Scolar Press.

Poussa, Patricia
    1992   "Pragmatics of *this* and *that*", in: Matti Rissanen – Ossi Ihalainen – Terttu Nevalainen – Irma Taavitsainen (eds.), 401–417.

Priestley, Joseph
   1761   *The rudiments of English grammar.* London.

Pyles, Thomas – John Algeo
   1982   *The origins and development of the English language.* (3rd edition.) San Diego, New York & Chicago: Harcourt Brace Jovanovich.

Quirk, Randolph – Sidney Greenbaum – Geoffrey Leech – Jan Svartvik
   1985   *A comprehensive grammar of the English language.* London: Longman.

Raumolin-Brunberg, Helena
   1991   *The noun phrase in early sixteenth-century English. A study based on Sir Thomas More's writings* (Mémoires de la Société Néophilologique, 50). Helsinki: Société Néophilologique.

Raumolin-Brunberg, Helena – Terttu Nevalainen
   1990   "Dialectal features in a corpus of Early Modern standard English?" in: Graham Caie – Kirsten Haastrup – Art Lykke Jakobsen – Jørgen Erik Nielsen – Jørgen Sevaldsen – Henrik Specht – Arne Zettersten (eds.), 119–131.
   Forthcoming   "Social conditioning and diachronic language change." In: Dieter Kastovsky (ed.), forthcoming.

Reuter, Ole
   1936   *On continuative relative clauses in English.* (Societas Scientiarum Fennica. Commentationes Humanarum Litterarum 9: 3.) Helsingfors.

Richardson, Edward
   1677   *Anglo-Belgica, The English and Nederdutch Academy.* London.

Rissanen, Matti
   1984   "The choice of relative pronouns in 17th century American English", in: Jacek Fisiak (ed.), 417–435.
   1989   "The conjunction *for* in Early Modern English", *North-Western European Language Evolution (NOWELE)* 14: 3–18.
   1991a   "Spoken language and the history of *do*-periphrasis", in: Dieter Kastovsky (ed.), 321–342.
   1991b   "On the history of English object clause links", in: Karin Aijmer – Bengt Altenberg (eds.), 272–289.

Rissanen, Matti – Ossi Ihalainen – Terttu Nevalainen – Irma Taavitsainen (eds.)
   1992   *History of Englishes. New methods and interpretations in historical linguistics* (Topics in English linguistics 10). Berlin: Mouton de Gruyter.

Romaine, Suzanne
   1984   "Towards a typology of relative-clause formation strategies in Germanic", in: Jacek Fisiak (ed.), 437–470.

Rydén, Mats
   1983   "The emergence of *who* as relativizer", *Studia Linguistica* 37: 126–133.

Samuels, Michael L.
- 1972 *Linguistic Evolution, with Special Reference to English*. Cambridge: Cambridge University Press.
- 1981 "Spelling and dialect in the Late and Post-Middle English Periods", in: Michael Benskin – Michael Samuels (eds.), 43–54.

Sapir, Edward
- 1921 [1978] Language, an introduction to the study of speech. London - Toronto - Sydney: Granada.

Survey of English Dialects. The basic material.
- 1962–1971 Ed. by Harold Orton et al. 4 vols. Leeds: University of Leeds.

Spevack, Marvin
- 1969–1974 *The Harvard concordance to Shakespeare*. Cambridge, MA: Belknap Press of Harvard University Press.

Stein, Dieter
- 1987 "At the crossroads of philology, linguistics and semiotics: Notes on the replacement of *th* by *s* in the third person singular in English", *English Studies* 68: 406–431.

Tannen, Deborah
- 1982 "Oral and literate strategies in spoken and written narratives", *Language* 58: 1–21.

Taylor, John R.
- 1989 "Possessive genitives in English", *Linguistics* 27: 663–686.

Viereck, Wolfgang
- 1985 *Focus on: England and Wales.* (Varieties of English around the World 4.) Amsterdam & Philadelphia: Benjamins.

Von Bremen, Klaus
- 1987 *English wh-relativization: Cross-linguistic perspectives, diachrony, synchrony and linguistic theory*. Bloomington, IN: Indiana University Linguistics Club.

Vorlat, Emma
- 1975 *The development of English grammatical theory 1586–1737, with special reference to the theory of parts of speech*. Leuven: Leuven University Press.

Wakelin, Martyn F.
- 1972 *English dialects, an introduction*. London: Athlone Press.

Wales, Kathleen M.
- 1983 "*Thou* and *you* in Early Modern English: Brown and Gilman re-appraised", *Studia Linguistica* 37: 107–125.

Wallis, John
- 1653 [1969] *Grammatica Linguae Anglicanae*. London. A Scolar Press Facsimile. Menston: Scolar Press.

Weatherill, Lorna
- 1988 *Consumer behaviour and material culture*. London: Methuen.

Wright, Joseph
    1905   *The English dialect grammar*. Oxford: Clarendon Press.

Wyld, Henry Cecil
    1920   *A history of modern colloquial English*. London: T. Fisher Unwin Ltd.

Yonge, Nicolas (transl.)
    1597   *Musica Transalpina, CANTVS, The Second Booke of Madrigalles, to 5. & 6. voices*. London: Thomas Este.

Standard and non-standard pronominal usage in English, with special reference to the eighteenth century

Ingrid Tieken-Boon van Ostade

1. Introduction

One of the numerous points of conflict among eighteenth-century normative grammarians concerned the pronominal system. Leonard (1929: 263–264) lists constructions such as *between/told you and I, it is me/us/him, my father and him have* ... , *who should I meet, who is it for, whom do men say that I am*, and *whom he thought was* ... , all of which had their opponents and equally strong advocates. Other points of discussion involved the use of *you* as the subject pronominal, and the question which form of the pronominal should be used after the conjunctions *as* and *than*. Together, these questions relate to a single phenomenon, namely that of pronominal case. It appears from the many discussions over these problems at the time that usage differed from the rules provided in many of the grammar books; furthermore, there was no consensus among grammarians on the extent to which different usages were to be tolerated. In the eyes of many, eighteenth-century English seemed to have deteriorated greatly compared to an earlier, more correct state of its grammar, and, what was even worse, when compared to Latin. This particular debate, therefore, is one instance of a more fundamental discussion about whether to allow usage to be the basis for grammatical description, or whether to superimpose a grammatical system on usage patterns which were more often than not in disagreement with it. In the pronominal system, as in the grammar of Latin, a fairly complete set of forms was preserved which reflect full opposition between case, number, and gender, including the second person pronominals singular and plural *thou/you*, which are still found in most grammars of the period when they treat the morphology of the verb.

One of the things I intend to discuss in this paper is the question of to what extent the pronominal system advocated by some of the more important eighteenth-century grammarians, and still accepted as part of the grammar of standard English today, is in conflict with actual usage at the time. In doing so, I shall concentrate largely on constructions in which the subject pronominal appears in object position, as in *between you and I* and *they don't mind you and I*, and, conversely, on those in which an object pronominal functions as the subject or as part of the subject of the sentence, for example *Lady Browne and him had better be married*. For my analysis of eighteenth-century English I have concentrated on fairly informal written English, such as it occurs in private letters, not intended for publication, between friends and relatives, and in journals. I have done so because it may be assumed that if constructions such as those illustrated here are likely to appear at all, they will sooner do so in the more informal, relatively spontaneous styles of writing than elsewhere, these being the styles of writing in which usually less attention is given to grammatical correctness. Some of the authors studied seem to have been aware of the informal nature of their style of writing, and of the effect this might have on their grammar. Boswell, for example, notes in the opening pages of his London journal: "I shall not study much correctness, lest the labour of it should make me lay it aside altogether" (Pottle 1950: 40). See also Walpole:

> From partiality to me, you won't allow my letters to be letters – Jesus! it sounds as if I wrote them to be fine and to have them printed, which might be very well for Mr Pope ... Therefore if you have a mind I should write you news, don't make me think about it; I shall be so long turning my periods, that what I tell you will cease to be news. (Vol. 9: 29–30).

(On Betsy Sheridan making similar observations, see Tieken 1990a: 79). My analysis of eighteenth-century English will have its bearings on present-day pronominal usage, too, one obvious reason being that present-day English grammar to a large extent has its basis in the normative rules drawn up in the course of that period. Moreover, as English was in the process of being standardized, pronominal usage being to a certain degree similar then and now, it is the aim of the present paper to try and shed some more light on notions such as appropriateness and inappropriateness of usage, correctness and incorrectness, standard and non-standard usage. The term "standard", though strictly speaking, according to Milroy and Milroy (1985), it may not be applied to language as such, still serves a useful function in a discussion of the relationship between normative rules of grammar and actual usage.

2. "A female inaccuracy"

Not only grammarians were concerned over the question of "correct" pronominal usage. In adapting some of Shakespeare's plays, Dryden also corrected a number of pronominal "mistakes" – as they must have appeared to him – in Shakespeare's language (Tieken 1990b). Another instance may be found in a footnote to the second edition of Archibald Campbell's *Lexiphanes* (1767: 67), in which the author defends his use of *between you and I* in the first edition, for which he had been, it seems, severely criticized by the reviewers of the book (quoted by Leonard 1929: 187–188). Moreover, one of the problems which continually baffled Fanny Burney, according to Bloom (1979: 384–385), concerned the form a pronominal was to have in particular constructions, as appears from the two revised versions of her novel *Camilla*.

Walpole regards the occurrence of pronominal "mistakes" as typically characteristic of the language of women:

> You will be diverted to hear that a man who thought of nothing so much as the purity of language, I mean Lord Chesterfield, says, "you and *me* shall not be well together," and this not once, but on every occasion. A friend of mine says, it was certainly to avoid that female inaccuracy *they don't mind you and I*, and yet the latter is the least bad of the two (as quoted by Leonard 1929: 188).

It seems unlikely that Walpole's claim bears any relationship to reality; moreover, the instance he quotes was produced by a man, Lord Chesterfield. Even so, it seems worthwhile to try and discover whether "incorrect" pronominal usage is indeed found more with women than with men, and if not, to determine what may have given rise to this pronouncement in the first place.

To this end, I have analyzed the writings of the following four women to begin with: Lady Mary Wortley Montagu (1689–1762), Mrs Thrale (1741–1821), Fanny Burney (1752–1840), and Betsy Sheridan (1758–1837).[1] Only a small number of instances were found:

Lady Mary:
and them ought to be excusable to you (Vol. I: 73)[2]
We are both, the child and me, in health (Vol. I: 185)

Mrs Thrale:
Miss Owen says so as well as me (Vol. II: 167)[3]

Fanny Burney:
but she – he found – "a poor modest common wofull affair –" said He (Vol. I: 20)

> ... they who will nobly dare to be above submitting to Chains their reason disapproves, they shall I always honour – if that will be any service to them! (Vol. I: 72)
> & if the signorine *(Hetty, Sue & me)* were all my Father's (Vol. I: 235)
> to talk Nonsence to We fair sex (Vol. I: 288)[4]
> They Live but next Door to us, & came out this morning, as well as Mrs R. & me, to see ... (Vol. I: 306)

Alternatively, Fanny Burney's first instance might be interpreted als a sentence in which the verb *to be* has remained unexpressed: *but she [was] – he found – ...* ; following the latter interpretation, the use of *she* would be, of course, grammatically correct. Betsy Sheridan's journal produced no instances at all.

If instances with "incorrect" pronominal usage were not found to be particularly common, the use of a different kind of pronominal was, *viz.* that of what I shall here refer to as non-reflexive *-self* pronominals,[5] especially with Fanny Burney:

> *Miss Allen & myself went to an Auction* (Vol. I: 6)
> *Mrs. Allen ... has presented Hetty, Mary, Susette & myself with Tickets* (Vol. I: 25).

The use of *myself* occurs most frequently in subject position, occasionally even without the possessive *my*:

> *my sister & self lately spent the Evening at* ... (Vol. I: 71).

From the number of instances recorded, it would appear that the use of *myself/self* in coordinated subject phrases presents an alternative to the grammatically more correct use of *I* (26 instances with *myself/self* as against 35 with *I*). Though whether Fanny Burney resorted to this alternative so frequently in order to avoid the "incorrect" use of *me* as subject, as has been suggested by some scholars (cf. Ilson 1985: 176, Mittins *et al.* 1970: 64 and Erdmann 1978: 72),[6] remains to be discussed. Only Mrs Thrale did not make use of *myself* in coordinated subject or object phrases. I shall return to this phenomenon in section 5.

Next, I analyzed the language of the following men: John Wesley (1703–1791), Thomas Turner (1729–1793), William Cowper (1731–1800), and James Boswell (1740–1795).[7] With the exception of Cowper, the "incorrect" use of pronominals was found in the writings of all the men, though least in those of Wesley[8] and Boswell:

> Wesley:
> *Araspes ... was extremely delighted as well as me* (Vol. 25: 277)

Turner:
which I see Wm. Weller and he cancel today in my kitchen (15)
for my wife and I (30)
between Mr. Laugham and I (44)
for my wife and I to go to ... (45, 63)
between my brother and I (116)
gave my wife and I an invitation (131)
and found she, Mr. Porter, Mr. Fuller and his wife (138)
and him, myself and Joseph Fuller Jr. went to ... (252)
Mr Goldsmith ... *swore Mr. Carman and I to appraise* ... (285).

Boswell:
This was a day eagerly expected by Dempster, Erskine, and I (152)
I wish you were as good a patient as me (181).

(For the instance from Wesley and the second one from Boswell, see note 3.) Non-reflexive *-self* pronominals are used by most of the men, too: in the case of Turner and Cowper both in subject and object position, and with Boswell only in object position, though not very frequently. Moreover, Turner, like Fanny Burney, makes use of *self*, both as subject and as object pronominal:

My wife, self, Ann Slater, and maid very busy (3)
my mother's cruelty against my wife and self (3).

Cowper uses the non-reflexive *-self* pronominal even for the second person singular, as in

and He but little taller than yourself (Vol. I: 470),

and so does Wesley, though only once in the letters analyzed. Here, however, the device was obviously not resorted to by these authors as an avoidance strategy, *you* being the same whether functioning as subject or as object of the sentence.

From all this, it is clear that the "incorrect" use of pronominals is found with men and women alike, though with some writers more frequently than with others, while yet with others no instances were found at all. It would seem, therefore, that there is no justification in Walpole's label "a female inaccuracy" for the phenomenon. The question then is, what made him attribute the misuse of pronominals to women to begin with? One possible solution to this problem might be that among Walpole's own acquaintances it is the women more than the men who are guilty of "mistakes" in pronominal usage, in which case Walpole's label would be justified after all. However, before pursuing this particular question any further, Walpole's own pronominal usage may be considered, as it is found in his letters to one of his closest friends, Montagu,⁹ in order to find out if in his practice he is true to his own principles. Not surprisingly, I have not come across a single sentence in which he uses a subject for an object pronominal or vice versa. Nor did he use any non-reflexive *-self* pronominals, as a possible means of avoiding the issue. Only *yourself* was found several times, though as in the case of Cowper, the use of this form cannot have served as an avoidance strategy. Walpole, in fact, is almost scrupulously correct in his pronominal usage, as may be concluded from the following, syntactically complex sentences:

> *as if I had obliged him, not he me* (Vol. 9: 182)
> *We met at Northumberland House at five, and set out in four coaches; Prince Edward, Colonel Brudenel his groom, Lady Northumberland, Lady Mary Coke, Lady Carlisle, Miss Pelham, Lady Hertford, Lord Beauchamp, Lord Huntingdon, old Bowman, and I* (Vol. 9: 273).

Walpole clearly appears to have taken care to avoid the use of what were regarded – particularly by himself – as stigmatized constructions.

In order to discover if any more "mistakes" – from a purist point of view – in pronominal usage were made by Walpole's female acquaintances than by the women discussed above, I have analyzed the letters written to him by a number of women, which were included among his own collected letters. These women include Lady Ailesbury, Henrietta Seymour Conway, Lady Hertford, the Duchess of Gloucester, Lady Waldegrave, Lady Hervey, and Hanna More. I have also studied extracts from the diaries of Mary Hamilton and Lady Mary Coke, which were included among Walpole's letters because of the references they contain to their friendship with Walpole.¹⁰ The letters and journal extracts produced no more than three instances:

> Lady Ailesbury:
> *by Mr Conway and I* (Vol. 37: 466)
>
> Lady Hertford:
> *and both Mr Fitzroy and her were vastly liked here* (Vol. 39: 38)
>
> Lady Mary Coke:
> *Lady Browne and him had better be married* (Vol. 31: 180)¹¹

Most of the women make use of the non-reflexive *-self* pronominals: *myself* as subject (only Lady Mary Coke uses *myself* as object as well); *yourself;* even unreflexive *himself* occurs once:

> Lady Waldegrave:
> *I saw Lord Thurlow when I was in town who notwithstanding the events that have happened to himself appeared as warmly interested about* ... (Vol. 36: 284).

However, instances are likewise found in the language of some of Walpole's male correspondents:[12]

Conway:
but what might very probably have happened to anybody but you or I (Vol. 37: 16)

Hertford:
Lady Mary Coke and her have conversed upon it (Vol. 38: 86)
Both him and Lady Holdernesse dined with us yesterday (Vol. 38: 236).

Walpole's close friend Montagu is equally scrupulous in his pronominal usage as Walpole himself, as the following examples show:

An hundred and forty miles out of my way and I not very well into the bargain, I look over ... (Vol. 9: 355)
We always meet at supper, I with my broth and he with his wine and water (Vol. 9: 391).[13]

It is clear, therefore, that Walpole's label "a female inaccuracy" for mistakes in pronominal usage is completely unfounded. Not only do women use "incorrect" forms sparingly; men are found to use them, too. It would seem that his observation represents no more than a folklinguistic belief, and an example of what Coates (1986: 15) calls "The Androcentric Rule": "Men will be seen to behave linguistically in a way that fits the writer's view of what is desirable or admirable; women on the other hand will be blamed for any linguistic state or development which is regarded by the writer as negative or reprehensible". That constructions such as *between you and I* are incorrect by the norms of standard English is beyond dispute; but to regard such incorrectnesses as characteristic of the language of women only, while men are "guilty" of them, too – and Walpole himself, when discussing the problem, quotes from the language of a man – is yet another example of sexual disparagement, stemming from the belief in the primacy of the language of men, and in the conviction that women use a derived form of it (cf. Baron 1986: 87–88). Walpole's attitude, in fact, expresses a fear of the corrupting influence women's language is often believed to have on language generally. A similar fear lies at the basis of many arguments offered by, for example, Simon (1980: 27–28, 40–41 and elsewhere) when explaining the downhill course on which the English language is apparently bent in our day and age.

3. A case of hypercorrection?

If sex differentiation does not have anything to do with the confusion of pronominal forms, what does? Education as a possible explanatory factor does not seem to be the solution either. While in the eighteenth century women were on the whole less well educated than men, this distinction is not reflected in a difference in usage, as has become clear from the evidence in section 2. Even among the women studied here there are some, like Lady Mary Wortley Montagu, who are much better educated than others, such as Fanny Burney (see Tieken 1987a: 144–146); yet no significant difference in usage is found. The authors' regional backgrounds are perhaps of more interest here. Duncan (1972) describes the use of *her* as subject pronominal as a characteristic of present-day dialects spoken in the southwest of England; it may have been so in the eighteenth century, too. Among the authors analyzed, Thomas Turner, who lived in Sussex most of his life, is the only one whose connections are not more or less centred around London society, which generally condemned the use of non-standard, regional forms of English (see, e.g., Tucker 1967: 46–48). He is the only author in whose language the "confusion" of pronominals seems more common than in that of any of the others.[14] The absence of any instances from the language of Betsy Sheridan and their extreme rarity in that of Boswell[15] confirms the importance of regional background as a factor correlating with the occurrence of "incorrect" pronominal forms. Betsy Sheridan, like Walpole and Montagu, is scrupulously correct in her use of subject and object pronominals. I have argued elsewhere that she tended, even in her most informal writing, to adhere almost too strictly to the rules of grammar (Tieken 1990a). Betsy Sheridan is of Irish origin, and from her journal it appears that she was well aware of the biased attitudes in her day towards speakers of any dialect other than standard English. She appears to have attempted to modify her language in the direction of standard English, one result being an almost overscrupulous adherence to the grammar of standard English, even when writing at her most informal to her sister in Dublin. Boswell was similarly aware of the existence of prejudices towards speakers of non-standard English at the time (cf. Tieken 1987b: 169), and it is his linguistic insecurity in this respect which may have caused him to strive after grammatical correctness in spite of his claim to the contrary (see section 1). Neither uses the non-reflexive *-self* pronominals very much.

In the eighteenth century, confusion of pronominal forms may have been more common in non-standard forms of English than in standard English – as it is today. But even in standard English it was not uncommon either, as the illustrations provided above clearly demonstrate. Nor is it uncommon today, as the following quotation from the *Observer* (Sunday 23 July 1989) shows (see also Erdmann 1978 and Kjellmer 1986):[16]

> *Failure of economic reform would almost certainly require he [i.e. Gorbachov] or his successor to slam the brakes back on and re-assert central control* (29).

An example representing standard spoken usage is the following sentence produced by a BBC announcer introducing an instalment of the popular series *Moonlighting* (BBC2, 25 January 1988): "... with her in Chicago and he in LA". Kjellmer (1986: 448) and Lass (1987: 152) attribute the confusion of pronominal forms to hypercorrection (see also Harris 1981):

> The pedagogical emphasis on the quite un-English nominative after *be* [as in *It is I* instead of *It is me*] has led to a common hypercorrection: the use of nominatives after prepositions (*as for my wife and I*, and so on). The origin is simple: people have been taught that *me* is "bad", so they avoid it except where they can't possibly (nobody yet says *give it to I*) (Lass 1987: 152).

However, this explanation meets the problem only halfway: it does not explain the occurrence of object forms in subject position, as in the sentence *Lady Browne and him had better be married* quoted in section 2. Further on in his book, Lass observes that "this phenomenon occurs elsewhere in Germanic: thus Afrikaans has *ons*, an old oblique form, for both 'we' and 'us' – cf. Dutch *wij* vs. *ons*; and *hulle* (also oblique for both 'they' and 'them': cf. Dutch *zij* vs. *hulle*" (Lass 1987: 231). Very common in non-standard Dutch (and also in Dutch children's language) is the use of oblique *hun* as subject: *hun hebben* 'them have'. Furthermore, there is the use of *her* as subject in several southwestern British dialects, as well as the sporadic occurrence of *them* for *they* in Sussex and parts of the Midlands (Duncan 1972: 190). To all this may be added the Quaker use of *thee* – formerly dative and accusative – as subject pronominal, and a similar development in the case of the standard English second person pronominal *you*. The confusion of pronominal forms is clearly a widespread phenomenon, which is not confined to English dialects, standard or non-standard, alone.

4. A natural change

The question remains why pronominal forms should be confused in the first place. For most of the pronominals, including *you/ye*, the *Oxford English Dictionary* provides illustrations of the confusion of forms from around the sixteenth century onwards.[17] As all pronominals are undergoing the same kind of formal/functional confusion at approximately the same time, it would seem that they are all subject to a single general process. This process may perhaps be described as a continuing loss among speakers of English of their sense of case distinction. The beginnings of this development are already apparent at the end of the Anglo-Saxon period, and by the sixteenth century it is likewise affecting the pronominal system, the only part of English grammar in which the old case system had been preserved (cf. Kjellmer 1986: 447–448). That English grammars today still prescribe a pronominal system which distinguishes between subject and object forms is due to the codification process the English language underwent since the late seventeenth, early eighteenth centuries. Not only was a more or less complete set of pronominals thus preserved, a set which neatly exhibited differences in case, number and gender (cf. the inclusion in grammars of English of the second person singular pronoun in the description of the verb for a long time after this pronominal had ceased to be in common use); attempts were also made to "regularize" the use of this set of pronominals. Instances of such attempts are the discussions at the time, and still continued today (cf. Simon 1980: x, 20), as to whether it should be *it is I* or *it is me*, and *taller than I* or *than me*. Each construction has its opponents and advocates (Leonard 1929: 263, 264), and both parties are able to provide sensible arguments to defend their preference.[18]

Kjellmer (1986: 447) observes that in most Indo–European languages the distinction between subjecthood and objecthood has disappeared in nouns, having remained in the pronominal system only. In non-standard English, as well as in less formal types of standard English, this loss of distinction has apparently affected the pronominal system, too. Moreover, what is true for English may also be true for other Germanic languages. Dutch and Afrikaans have already been referred to. In the case of Dutch, the use of *hun* as subject has largely become accepted as a characteristic of non-standard usage, though it is not any the less stigmatized as such. In children's language, pronominal forms are regularly confused until a fairly late stage (age 5 and upwards; see also Schaerlaekens and Gillis 1987: 164):[19] besides *hun hebben* "them have", I have frequently observed constructions like *bij hij* 'with he' and *voor Casper en ik* 'for C. and I' in my own family. Constructions such as these do not appear to be the result of hypercorrection: they are too common to be regarded as such (cf. Chiat 1981: 87–89). It is only after continued exposure to standard adult usage and as the result of persistent correction that the grammatically correct forms begin to appear more regularly. This seems true for gender distinctions in pronominals, too.[20] The set of pronominals in which case, number and gender are distinguished therefore has to be actively acquired as part of the process of first language acquisition. This is the case for Dutch, and it seems not unlikely that it is also the case for English (cf. Chiat 1981).

All this suggests that the loss of case distinction in the history of English must be the result of a natural process. By contrast, acquiring the pronominal system that is described in the grammars of English is to a large extent a conscious process. In order to illustrate to what extent this acquisition process may have been only partially completed among the large variety of speakers and even among speakers of standard English, the case of Thomas Turner may be discussed in greater detail. Of all authors discussed above, Turner's language produced the largest number of instances both with and without pronominal confusion. As shown in section 2, I came across ten instances of pronominal confusion in Turner's diary, all of which are coordinate constructions and nine of which have a subject for an object pronominal; the remaining one has an object for a subject pronominal. The instances may be given here once more:

> which I see Wm. Weller and he cancel today (15)
> for my wife and I (30)
> between Mr. Laugham and I (44)
> for my wife and I to go to ... (45, 63)
> between my brother and I (116)
> gave my wife and I an invitation (131)
> and found she, Mr. Porter, Mr. Fuller and his wife (137–138)
> and him, myself and Joseph Fuller Jr. went to ... (252)
> Mr Goldsmith ... swore Mr. Carman and I to appraise ... (285).

In absolute terms, the number of instances found is not very large. However, when viewed against the instances with "correct" pronominal usage, a different picture emerges. Coordinate constructions in object position are fairly rare: I have come across only 38 instances in the diary against 310 subject constructions. Thus, by virtue of frequency of occurrence the probability for a subject construction to appear in Turner's written language is far greater than an object construction, as indeed turns out to be the case: as many as nine out of the 38 object constructions recorded is grammatically incorrect. Furthermore, seven of the above ten instances are of the construction "a name/nominal *and I*", the nominal usually being *my wife*.[21] In the diary, this construction appears with very great frequency in subject position: "a name *and I*" was attested 118 times, and "a nominal *and I*" 78 times, of which *my wife and I* was by far the most frequent (59). Again, it is only to be expected in view of the general rareness of the object construction in the diary, that, for example, *my wife and I* is used irrespective of its function in the sentence.

My wife and me as object does not appear at all, *me and my wife* occurs only once. Coordinate constructions in object position with more than two legs are likewise relatively rare: only eleven instances were found, as against 71 in subject position.

Though it looks like another example of the construction "name *and* personal pronominal", the first of Turner's ten instances must be explained differently. The nominal *Wm. Weller and he* functions as the subject of the embedded sentence. One result of the embedding process would have been for this subject to be changed into an object construction, *Wm. Weller and him*. Apparently, the embedding process was left incomplete, possibly on analogy with the extremely frequent construction of the type *my wife and I*. Such incomplete transformations are not uncommon today – see for example the sentence from the *Observer* quoted in section 3. For an instance showing the opposite effect, see the sentence produced by Lady Mary Coke, discussed in note 11.

It is clear, therefore, that the choice between a subject and an object pronominal in Turner's language is not merely determined on sentence level, that is in its function either as subject or as object of the sentence. More often than not, the selection process seems to occur at the level of the nominal itself. The choice of the pronominal is apparently largely determined by collocationary factors. Thus, in the construction "a name/nominal *and* first person singular pronominal" the pronominal *I* is automatically selected, irrespective of its function at sentence level. It even seems likely that it is the coordination process which makes the author lose sight of the overall structure of the sentence; further evidence for this suggestion will be provided in section 5 below. This is not only true for Thomas Turner: most of the examples of pronominal confusion provided in section 2 above are instances of coordination. If they are not, as in the case of the second instance from Fanny Burney's journal, the author has apparently lost control over the syntax of the sentence as a result of its too great complexity (see, for example, the instance from Lady Mary Coke provided in section 2 above). The present-day English instances provided above may be explained similarly: the *Moonlighting* one is an example of a coordinated sentence; and the one from the *Observer*, like the first instance from Thomas Turner discussed above, seems to be the result of an incomplete conflation of the embedded sentence (*he or his successor slams the brake back on . . .*) with the embedding sentence (*failure of economic reform would almost certainly require him to . . .*). In this day and age such a mistake seems typically the result of working with a word processor: in the course of editing the text, the author may well have been too intent on the conflation process to remember to look at the sentence level afterwards.

5. A modesty device

Another interesting characteristic of Turner's pronominal usage in general is his use of the non-reflexive *-self* pronominal, mostly with the first person singular. This usage has also been found in the language of Boswell, Fanny Burney, Cowper, Lady Mary Wortley Montagu and Betsy Sheridan. As observed in section 2, it has been suggested that this pronominal is used as part of an avoidance strategy, to avoid the choice between the correct subject or object form of the pronominal. However, evidence from Turner's language suggests that this is not entirely the case. There are so many instances of the non-reflexive *-self* pronominal in Turner's journal, and this is true for Fanny Burney and Cowper as well, that it seems unlikely that this device is used solely to avoid possible mistakes. Furthermore, within the space of a single page (e.g., Turner: 171, 209), both the standard pronominal and a non-reflexive *-self* pronominal may occur in constructions that are virtually identical (see also Fanny Burney, Vol. I: 267). This suggests that Turner must have been perfectly capable of selecting the "correct" pronominal form, and that there must therefore have been a different reason for selecting the *-self* pronominal. The figures below indicate that in coordinated constructions with two legs *myself* and *I* are used almost as variants of each other, irrespective of their function in the sentence.[22]

Table 1. Subject and object pronominals in coordinated nominals

		coord. 2 legs	coord. >2 legs		coord. 2 legs	coord. >2 legs
subject:	*myself*	78	56	object:	15	9
	self	5	12		3	2
	I	222	3		8	—
	me	—	2		—	—

This is true only for coordinated constructions with two legs; in those with more than two legs, *myself* and *self* are predominantly found. I shall come back to this type of construction below. *Myself* even occurs in uncoordinated constructions: I have come across fifteen instances of *myself* used as subject, as in *myself at church*[23] and *myself being the bondman*, and two as object. Usually, however, *I* or *me* are found, depending on their function In the sentence.

From all this it is clear that Turner used *myself* as an alternative for *I* and *me* alike: when all the instances in Table 1 are taken together, *myself* or *self* is found in more than half of them (57%). A similar use of non-reflexive *-self* pronominals, including *yourself*, examples of which were supplied above, has been discussed for present-day English by Churchward (1955). Wood (1956: 103), in a criticism of Churchward, observes that the usage is frowned upon but that it is nevertheless very common, mostly in coordinated constructions and after prepositions. He disagrees with Churchward that *-self* forms are preferred because "the unnecessary use of the word *I* or *me*, particularly *I*, is apt to sound unpleasantly egotistic" (quoted by Wood 1956: 104); instead, Wood suggests a number of other reasons for their use, such as euphony. However, on the strength of the findings presented here, I tend to agree with Churchward. The non-reflexive *-self* pronominals are usually found with the first person singular, the author him/herself, and it seems only natural, given polite human behaviour, that they might want to make their own presence, say in a list of names, somewhat less obtrusive. The use of *myself* may therefore be regarded as a kind of modesty device. One result of the use of *myself* rather than *I* is that the stress falls on the second syllable, thus deflecting attention from the "I". This tendency is stronger with some writers, such as Turner and Fanny Burney, who seem naturally modest people, than with others like Boswell, who was quite the opposite, and who does not use any non-reflexive *-self* pronominals in the *London Journal* at all. Moreover, in Turner's language as well as in that of Fanny Burney, *myself* is frequently reduced to *self*, either because *my* appears in an earlier leg of the coordination and thus apparently includes *self* in the later leg in its scope (e.g., *My wife and self at church*, 38)[24] or as a tendency to reduce the first person pronominal even further in order to make the "I" yet more unobtrusive.[25]

Non-reflexive *-self* pronominals other than *myself* are rare in Turner's language, but one would not normally expect non-reflexive *yourself* to occur in a journal such as his. In the letters analyzed, however, I did come across this pronominal several times. Its use often seems to have a kind of lighthearted or even playful effect, possibly resulting from the fact that it would normally be unusual or discourteous for the speaker to deflect attention from the addressee. Its use seems to derive from the speaker placing himself, out of a kind of inverted modesty, into the shoes of his addressee, and acting as he himself would presumably have done in the circumstances. The following example, in a letter from Walpole to Montagu, may serve as an illustration: ... *the Triumvirate, composed of yourself, Charles and Your sincere Friend* (Vol. 9: 4). It is revealing from the point of view of Walpole's character that in lists of names in which he himself appears he always uses *I*, never *myself*, though in those in which his friend Montagu is involved he invariably writes *yourself*. It would seem that the only type of modesty Walpole is capable of showing is inverted modesty. At the same time, this indicates that the use of *myself* as a modesty device is not a characteristic of the language of politeness, as discussed by Klein and by McIntosh elsewhere in this volume. Had it been so, the pronominal would certainly have been used by Walpole and Boswell.

Table 1 above shows an interesting difference in Turner's language between the occurrence of non-reflexive *-self* pronominals in coordinated constructions with two legs and with more than two legs. It appears that in a coordinated subject with more than two legs *I* is used only very rarely (in 4% of the instances), while in object constructions neither *I* nor *me* are used at all (though it should be observed that only eleven instances were recorded). This suggests that while in coordinated subject or object constructions with only two legs *I* is the more usual pronominal for the first person singular, irrespective of its function in the sentence (it occurs in precisely two-thirds of the instances recorded), in coordinated constructions containing more than 2 legs the pronominal selected in the majority of the instances (93%) is either *myself* or *self*. Thus, apart from the possibility of *myself* and *self* being used as a modesty device even in coordinated constructions with more than two legs, these pronominals may also have been selected to avoid the choice between *I* and *me*. This provides further support for the suggestion, made in section 2, that the decision as to which pronominal to select occurs at a level well below that of the sentence: the higher the number of coordinated nominals, the more the speaker or writer tends to lose control over the syntax of the sentence as a whole, and the sooner he or she will deploy the avoidance strategy at their disposal in this context.

Apart from *myself* and *yourself*, *himself* also occurs in the letters and other texts analyzed, though more rarely; however, it is in any case often hard to distinguish non-reflexive *himself* from the reflexive pronominal. Non-reflexive *herself* and *ourselves* are used even more sparingly still: I have come across only two instances of the first pronominal, one in Conway's letters to Walpole and one in Fanny Burney's journal; and no more than a single instance of *ourselves*, likewise in the letters by Conway. Of the other non-reflexive pronominals (*yourselves*, *themselves*) I have not found any instances at all, though this obviously need not imply that they did not occur. From Baker's (1770) objection to the construction *themselves and Families*, discussed by Leonard (1929: 175), it is clear that in any case *themselves* occurred frequently enough to attract his attention. These pronominals clearly are not used as part of a modesty device or even an inverted modesty device. According to Baker, "it is mere Shopkeepers Cant ... and will always sound contemptible in the Ears of Persons of any Taste" (1770: 118). This lends further support to the observation made above, that the use of non-reflexive -*self* pronominals is not characteristic of the language of politeness.

6. Non-standard and standard usage

It has been suggested that the use of non-reflexive -*self* pronominals instead of the more regular pronominals is particularly characteristic of Anglo-Irish (Bliss 1979: 287 and Todd 1989: 72). However, this suggestion tells only part of the story. The evidence presented in this paper, in addition to the fact that non-reflexive -*self* pronominals are also very common in everyday informal, usually spoken English today (Wood 1956: 103–104), indicates that they are commonly used in most varieties of English, possibly with the sole exception of the most formal types of standard English. Verheyen (1983: 46) calls the use of non-reflexive -*self* pronominals a peripheral phenomenon, but it is only so from the point of view of standard English. However, even within standard English it is less than merely peripheral. Furthermore, the usage has been attested since the late Middle English period (Visser 1963: 95). In informal standard English the use of non-reflexive -*self* pronominals seems to have developed into a modesty device, while in Anglo-Irish the pronominals would seem to occur more generally. Here, but here only, Irish influence may have played a role (cf. Bliss 1979: 287).

The same applies to what has throughout this paper somewhat tentatively been referred to as pronominal "confusion", which has likewise been called characteristic of Anglo-Irish (Bliss 1979: 285). In addition, Bliss has observed it in the language of Scottish Highlanders and in the speech of Welshmen. Again, the phenomenon is common in other forms of English, too (see also Duncan 1972), including informal standard English. While by the rules of standard English, such as they have been laid down in grammar books, a construction like *between you and I* as well as the sentence quoted from the *Observer* and the announcement of *Moonlighting* must be regarded as mistakes, it may well be that in certain informal speech situations these constructions, with the exception of the one from the *Observer* (see section 3), can only be regarded as appropriate to the context in which they occur (cf. Kjellmer 1986: 445). This is even more true for constructions like *it is I/me* and *taller than I/me*, for if the grammatically more correct *It is I* were to appear in an informal speech situation, such as a chat between close friends, the effect would be rather stilted or unduly formal.[26] In other words, its use would be distinctly inappropriate.[27] This appears to have been so even in the eighteenth century, as I have argued in the case of Betsy Sheridan discussed in section 3 (see also Tieken 1990a).

7. Conclusion

All this suggests that to speak of a double standard, a written and a spoken one, as some scholars do (e.g., Baugh – Cable 1978: 313), does not do justice to the patterns described here. Nor does abolishment of the term standard, underlying Milroy (this volume), appear to provide a useful solution either, mainly because a standard form of the language, an artifact though it may be, provides a realistic norm for many speakers. This norm can be found in all well-known usage guides like those by Fowler, Partridge, Gowers and others, and it provides the background to publications such as Simon (1980). Rather than speaking, as Milroy does, in terms of vernaculars, which are characterized by patterns of variation appropriate to them, I prefer to regard the patterns discussed in this paper from the point of view of a continuum, ranging, even in the spoken language, from a pronominal usage which adheres to the rules set down in grammars of English to one in which constructions like *between you and I* are the rule rather than the exception. In between these two extremes, different degrees of variation occur, depending to a large extent on the speaker in question. Whether this speaker would tend more in one direction than in the other depends on a variety of sociolinguistic factors, such as style, medium (speech/writing), social background and the prestige of one or another linguistic norm.

From this point of view, the standard English system of pronominal usage represents no more than one system out of several, and one which is in effect a formalized, tidied-up relic of past usage, which presumably represented a situation in which case was still meaningful, and in which the formal/functional opposition between different pronominal forms was still fully employed. With the disappearance of case from the nominal system, the possibility to distinguish similarly between subject and object pronominal forms must have lost much of its significance. In spite of this, the old system was kept alive, first, possibly, as a result of Latin influence,[28] and subsequently through the teaching of grammar. It is therefore first and foremost a characteristic of the written language, though many speakers use the system regularly in their spoken styles, too, largely as a result of an increase in literacy, both historically and generally. The use of non-reflexive *-self* pronominals as an avoidance strategy must be viewed as an indication of the fact that the speaker is somehow aware of the importance of case, but is at the same time hesitant as to the syntactic function of different pronominal forms in the sentence. This usage must be distinguished from the use of the *-self* pronominals as part of a modesty device, which, as I have argued above, is probably most characteristic of users of those pronominal systems which tend towards the direction of the standard (e.g., Fanny Burney and Turner).

The development described here, *viz.* the loss of the distinction between subject and object pronominals correlating with their different functions in the sentence, is part of the more general loss of case distinctions in the history of English. This development has been described as reflecting a natural process of change, part of a much larger process leading towards the evolution of early modern standard English (Poussa 1982). By contrast, the acquisition of the standardized pronominal system is part of a learned process, as evidence from the language of very young children bears out. As such it is unlikely, as Kjellmer (1986) predicts, that the subject pronominals will eventually disappear. Though there are strong tensions between what is regarded as grammatically correct and actual usage, prescriptivist forces will see to it that the pronominal system, having survived in the grammars of English, will be kept in tact. Whether these tensions will grow any stronger will depend on future developments in the position of formal standard English, written and spoken, with regard to that of less formal as well as non-standard varieties of the language.

Notes

1. For Lady Mary Wortley Montagu, I have analyzed all letters to her lover, who later became her husband, in Vol. I of her collected letters (1710–1716), ca. 66,500 words; for Mrs Thrale, all letters to her close friend Dr. Johnson, as they appear in Chapman's edition of Dr. Johnson's letters (1772–1784), ca. 27,000 words; for Fanny Burney, the early journals (1768–1773), Vol. I of her collected letters and journals, 327 pages; and for Betsy Sheridan, her journal letters, addressed to her sister (1784–1786, 1788–1790), 195 pages.
2. This type of sentence is possibly related to another peculiarity in the language of Lady Mary Wortley Montagu. In her letters to Wortley, her husband to be, I repeatedly came across sentences like

    Them admirers you speak of (Vol. I: 61)
    How much wiser are all them women ... (Vol. I: 83).

    In these sentences, the pronominal *them* is used instead of the more standard demonstrative *those*. Nowadays, this use of *them* is regarded as non-standard

(it does not even appear to be a "usage problem"; cf. Ilson 1985); whether or not it would have been so in the eighteenth century is hard to say with any certainty, though it does seem to have been the case, as the construction is found in the language of non-standard English speaking characters in a number of contemporary novels (Burney, Smollett). Demonstrative *them* is not mentioned by Leonard as an object of discussion among the grammarians of the period. It is possible that Lady Mary uses this demonstrative out of a kind of linguistic affectation. Cf. the dual status of *he don't* as both a feature of non-standard English (see e.g. Cheshire 1978) and of the language of speakers belonging to the upper middle classes and upwards: it is used by Lady Mary, but also by Betsy Sheridan (cf. Tieken 1990a), Mrs Thrale, Walpole and many of the latter's aristocratic friends (e.g. Lady Dysart and Lady Suffolk, and also Montagu), but not by any of the other writers whose language I have analyzed here.
3. Erdmann (1978: 71–72) observes that in his analysis of about forty novels published between 1930 and 1970 the subject and object pronominals are almost equally frequent in this position. *Me*, he notes, occurs "almost exclusively in spoken or quasi-spoken discourse", the subject forms being "used in polished, formal styles of speech and writing". Judging from eighteenth-century comments on the construction, this may well have been so at the time, as well.
4. According to Kjellmer (1986: 448), this would be an instance of hypercorrection.
5. Verheyen (1983: 13), basing himself on Poutsma (1926), distinguishes two kinds of *-self* pronominals, reflexives and intensifiers. They can be recognized by their function in the sentence – they must be either direct object, indirect object, prepositional object or adverbial adjunct – and by the fact that they must be coreferential with the subject. Furthermore, the intensifying *-self* pronominals have a small number of fixed positions in the sentence: following the nominal or pronominal they modify (*as we ourselves also acted*), as part of the predicate (*he had never been himself a student*) and following the predicate (*as if he had been shot himself*) (1983: 3–6). Verheyen notes that "there are some apparent exceptions to the alleged rule that reflexives cannot appear in subject position" (1983: 46). For these, as well as for any other *-self* forms that do not fit the criteria presented above, I have adopted the term "non-reflexive *-self* pronominals". Contrary to what is suggested by Verheyen, who rejects any instances of this usage as "exceptions" that are part of "an extremely peripheral phenomenon", it will be shown in the course of this paper that they are in fact highly common.
6. For another example of an avoidance strategy, relating to the use of the definite article instead of the innovative form *its*, see Nevalainen and Raumolin-Brunberg (this volume).
7. For John Wesley, I have analyzed all letters to his mother, father and brothers, as well as to a close friend, Mrs Mary Pendarves, as they appear in Vols. 25 and 26 of his collected works (1721–1739), ca. 37,000 words; for Thomas Turner, the extracts from his journal (1754–1765) as they appear in Vaisey's edition, 323 pages (130,000 words); for Cowper, all letters to his very close friend Joseph

Hill, as in Vol. I of his collected letters (1750–1781), ca. 27,000 words; and for Boswell, the *London Journal* (1762–1763), 333 pages.

8. Cf. Wesley's brother Charles, who in a letter to Wesley produces the following sentence:

   what's between you and I only ... (Vol. 25: 238).

9. I have analyzed all letters to Montagu as they appear in Vol. 9 of Walpole's collected letters; 1736–1761, ca. 60,000 words.

10. I have analyzed the following letters and journal sections: Lady Ailesbury: all letters in Vols. 37–9 (1751–1793), ca. 4000 words; Henrietta Seymour Conway: all letters in Vols. 38–39 (1759–1768), ca. 2300 words; Lady Hertford: all letters in Vols. 37–39 (1757–1780), ca. 6200 words; the Duchess of Gloucester: all letters in Vol. 36 (1772–1789), ca. 3800 words; Lady Waldegrave: all letters in Vol. 36 (1785–1795), ca. 2800 words; Lady Hervey: all letters in Vol. 31 (1763–1766), ca. 2000 words; Hannah More: all letters in Vol. 31 (1784–1793), ca. 15,000 words; extracts from Lady Mary Coke's diary in Vol. 31 (1766–1790), ca. 9000 words; extracts from Mary Hamilton's journal in Vol. 31 (1783–1785), ca. 1600 words.

11. This clause is part of a larger sentence:

    Mr Walpole told her, to facilitate the affair, Lady Browne and him had better be married.

    Lady Mary Coke's use of *him* instead of the grammatically more correct *he* may well have been prompted by the object function of the entire clause *Lady Browne and him had better be married* in relation to the sentence as a whole.

12. For Conway, I analyzed all letters in Vols. 37–39 (1737–1790), ca. 11,000 words; for Hertford, all letters in Vols. 37–38 (1755–1765), ca. 40,000 words; and for Montagu, all letters in Vol. 9 (1745–1761), ca. 17,000 words.

13. Cf. the following present-day example, cited by Erdmann (1978: 69):

    We sat in the pub, she at tomato juice and me with a brown ale (Sillitoe, *A Start in Life*, 151).

14. It should be observed that it is hard to draw any definite conclusions here as to the frequency of occurrence of constructions, as the amounts of text analyzed are of highly disparate length, ranging from approximately 1600 words (Mary Hamilton) to over 60,000 (Fanny Burney, Lady Mary Wortley Montagu, Betsy Sheridan, Boswell, Thomas Turner, Walpole and Wesley).

15. The *London Journal* contains by far the largest number of instances in which pronominal confusion might have occurred (149); cf. Fanny Burney with the next largest number (99).

16. I am grateful to Dr. C.C. Barfoot, not merely for supplying me with this quotation and others, but particularly for the many useful discussions we had on the topic of this paper.

17. Barber (1976: 204) observes that "the first examples of nominative *you* go back to the 14th century, but in the standard literary language its encroachment is not rapid until the 1540s".
18. Even the use of a subject for an object pronominal was defended at the time. See Ann Fisher (2nd ed. 1750: 119):

    Sometimes the leading State [i.e. nominative case] of a Relative is set after the Preposition; but then a Verb is understood, as, *they came before we*, i.e. before we came. Here *before* is turned into an Adverb, and *we* belongs to the Verb; but when the Verb is not understood, we say, *they came before us*. (Almost *verbatim* in Kirkby 1746: 116.)

19. Alternatively, at least according to the information provided by my four-and-a-half year old son, *hun* is used in *hun hebben* as the masculine form, the standard Dutch *zij* 'they' being reserved for girls, by analogy with the singular *zij* 'she'. This suggests that the pronominal system in Dutch children's language is structured differently from that in the language of adults. On the basis of this evidence it seems that further investigations into the structure of Dutch children's language might produce interesting results.
20. I therefore disagree with Poussa (1985), who attributes the confusion between masculine and feminine pronominals in the language of a Finnish-English bilingual girl to contact with Finnish. From observing the language of my own monolingual Dutch children I can only conclude that grammatical gender is a concept that has to be learnt, and that is acquired considerable time after children have learnt to distinguish between the sexes. (I also disagree with Schaerlaekens and Gillis (1987: 150), who seem to suggest that these two processes take place more or less simultaneously.) In this light, I would suggest that the data provided by Poussa might be reinterpreted as part of a monolingual, not bilingual, language acquisition process.
21. Had Turner's wife lived longer (228), it stands to reason that more instances of the construction would have occurred in the latter part of the diary.
22. It should be noted that these figures do not include sentences with a coordinated nominal after a form of *to be*, as in

    The overseers chosen for the year ensuing are myself and Mr. Tho. Carman ... (Turner: 268).

    As observed above, both *I* and *me* might have been used instead of *myself*.
23. Turner preferred this construction to, e.g., "at church", a sentence typically characteristic of journal language. However, the latter type is also found: "gave 6*d*" (129).
24. Cf. the following sentence, which demonstrates that *self* in Turner's language may often, indeed, be interpreted as such: *between my mother and self, but why do I say myself* (129).

25. According to Carol Percy (personal communication), *myself*, both as subject and as object pronominal, occurs in the journal of Captain Cook (1768–1771) even more frequently than the regular pronominals. Apparently, Cook does not "confuse" *I* and *me* in subject or object position, which seems to suggest that he did not use *myself* in order to avoid selecting the wrong pronominal form. His usage of the non-reflexive *-self* pronominal, therefore, provides further evidence of its being a modesty device. On the language of Captain Cook generally, see Percy (1990).
26. See Milroy and Milroy (1985: 117): "the choice appropriate to the more formal occasion is usually said to be the 'correct' form of the language". By implication, it is in many instances probably also true that the "rejected" form is more appropriate in colloquial, informal speech situations.
27. Erdmann (1978: 74) observes that his analysis has yielded no more than three instances of *it is I* as against 54 with the object pronominal.
28. The construction *It is I* and its variants appears to be fairly common in late Middle English texts. I have come across instances in Chaucer's *Miller's Tale* (*It am I*, l. 3766) and the *Wife of Bath's Tale* (*I am she*, l. 1092), as well as in the *Second Shepherds' Tale*: cf. *It is I, Mak, your husband* (Rose 1961: 189) and *I am he that him got* (Rose 1961: 195). Especially the first and last instances are incongruous with Mak's lowly origins. As the texts of the mystery plays are generally accepted to be the product of the clergy, it seems likely that these instances are the virtually inevitable result of Latin influence on the language of the play.

References

Baker, Frank (ed.)
    1980–1982 *The works of John Wesley*. Vols. 25–26. Oxford: Clarendon Press.
Baker, Robert
    1770 *Reflections on the English language*. London
    [1967] [Reprinted in: Robin C. Alston (ed.) *English linguistics, 1500–1800* 18. Menston: The Scolar Press.]
Barber, Charles
    1976 *Early modern English*. London: Deutsch.
Baron, Dennis
    1986 *Grammar and gender*. New Haven: Yale University Press.
Baugh, Albert C. – Thomas Cable
    1978 *A history of the English language*. (3rd edition.) Englewood Cliffs, N.J.: Prentice Hall.
Bliss, Alan
    1979 *Spoken English in Ireland, 1600–1740*. Dublin: The Dolmen Press.

Bloom, Lillian D.
    1979   "Fanny Burney's *Camilla*. The author as editor", *Bulletin of research in the humanities* 82: 367–393.

Boswell, James
    See Pottle, Frederick A. (ed.).

Bunt, Gerrit H.V. – Erik S. Kooper – John L. Mackenzie – David R.M. Wilkinson (eds.)
    1987   *One hundred years of English studies in Dutch Universities*. Amsterdam: Rodopi.

Burney, Fanny
    See Troide, Lars E. (ed.).

Campbell, Archibald
    1776   *Lexiphanes*. London.

Chapman, Robert W. (ed.)
    1952   *The letters of Samuel Johnson*. 3 vols. Oxford: Clarendon Press.

Chaucer, Geoffrey
    See Robinson, Fred N. (ed.).

Cheshire, Jenny
    1978   "Present tense verbs in Reading English", in: Peter Trudgill (ed.), 52–68.

Chiat, Shulamuth
    1981   "Context-specificity and generalization in the acquisition of pronominal distinctions", *Journal of child language* 8: 75–91.

Churchward, C. Maxwell
    1955   "Personal pronouns ending in -self or -selves", *English language teaching* 9: 125–131.

Coates, Jennifer
    1986   *Women, men and language*. London: Longman.

Cowper, William
    See King, James – Charles Ryskamp (eds.).

Duncan, Pauline
    1972   "Forms of the feminine pronoun in modern English dialects", in: Martyn F. Wakelin (ed.), 182–200.

Erdmann, Peter
    1978   "It's I, It's me: A case for syntax", *Studia Anglica Posnaniensia* 10: 67–80.

Fisher, Ann
    1750   *A new grammar*. (2nd edition.) Newcastle-upon-Tyne.
    [1974]   [Reprinted in: Robin C. Alston (ed.), *English linguistics, 1500–1800* 130. Menston: Scolar Press.]

Greenbaum, Sidney (ed.)
    1985   *The English language today*. Oxford: Pergamon.

Halsband, Robert (ed.)
    1965   *The complete letters of Lady Mary Wortley Montagu.* Vol. 1. Oxford: Clarendon Press.

Harris, Martin
    1981   "It's I, It's me: Further reflections", *Studia Anglica Posnaniensia* 13: 17–20.

Ilson, Robert F.
    1985   "Usage problems in British and American English", in: Sidney Greenbaum (ed.), 166–182.

King, James – Charles Ryskamp (eds.)
    1979   *The letters and prose writings of William Cowper.* Vol. 1. Oxford: Clarendon Press.

Kirkby, John
    1746   *A new grammar.* London.
    [1974]   [Reprinted in: Robin C. Alston (ed.), *English linguistics, 1500–1800* 297. Menston: The Scolar Press.]

Kjellmer, Göran
    1986   " 'Us Anglos are a cut above the field': On objective pronouns in nominative contexts", *English studies* 67: 445–449.

Lass, Roger
    1987   *The shape of English. Structure and history.* London: Dent.

LeFanu, William
    1960   *Betsy Sheridan's journal. Letters from Sheridan's sister. 1784–1786 and 1788–1790.* Oxford: Oxford University Press.
    [1985]   [Reprinted Oxford: Oxford University Press.]

Leonard, Sterling Andrus
    1929   *The doctrine of correctness in English Usage, 1700–1800.* Madison: University of Wisconsin.

Lewis, Wilmarth S. (ed.)
    1941–1974   *The Yale edition of Horace Walpole's correspondence.* Vols. 9, 31, 36, 37, 39. New Haven: Yale University Press.

Milroy, James – Lesley Milroy
    1985   *Authority in language. Investigating language and standardisation.* London: Routledge & Kegan Paul.

Mittins, William H. – Mary Salu – Mary Edminson – Sheila Coyne
    1970   *Attitudes to English usage.* Oxford: Oxford University Press.
    [1975]   [Reprinted Oxford: Oxford University Press.]

Montagu, Lady Mary Wortley
    See Halsband, Robert (ed.).

Oxford English Dictionary, The
    1989   Prepared by J.A. Simpson – E.S.C. Weiner. Oxford: Clarendon Press.

Percy, Carol
    1990   The language of Captain James Cook: Some aspects of the syntax and morphology of the Endeavour Journal, 1768–1771. [Unpublished Ph.D. dissertation, University of Oxford.]
Pottle, Frederick A. (ed.)
    1950   *Boswell's London journal, 1762–1763.* New York: McGraw-Hill.
Poussa, Patricia
    1982   "The evolution of early standard English: The creolisation hypothesis", *Studia Anglica Posnaniensia* 14: 69–85.
    1985   "The development of the 3rd person singular pronoun system in the English of a bilingual Finnish-English child", *Scandinavian working papers on bilingualism* 5 (mineograph).
Poutsma, H.
    1926   *A grammar of late modern English.* Groningen: Noordhoff.
Robinson, Fred N. (ed.)
    1974   *The complete works of Geoffrey Chaucer.* (2nd edition.) London/Oxford: Oxford University Press.
Rose, Martial (ed.)
    1961   *The Wakefield mystery plays.* London: Evans Brothers.
Schaerlaekens, Anne M. – Steven Gillis
    1987   *De taalverwerving van het kind.* (Revised edition.) Groningen: Wolters Noordhoff.
Sheridan, Betsy
    See LeFanu, William (ed.).
Simon, John
    1980   *Paradigms lost. Reflections on literacy and its decline.* Harmondsworth: Penguin.
Thrale, Mrs Hester
    See Chapman, Robert W. (ed.).
Tieken-Boon van Ostade, Ingrid
    1987a   *The auxiliary do in eighteenth-century English: A sociohistorical-linguistic approach.* Dordrecht: Foris.
    1987b   "Negative *do* in eighteenth-century English: The power of prestige", in Gerrit H.V. Bunt – Erik S. Kooper – John L. Mackenzie – David R.M. Wilkinson (eds.), 157–171.
    1990a   "Betsy Sheridan: Fettered by grammatical rules?", *Leuvense bijdragen* 79: 79–90.
    1990b   "Drydens versies van *De tempest* en *Troilus and Cressida*: de bewerker als purist", *Traditie & progressie. Handelingen van het 40ste Nederlands filologencongres.* 's-Gravenhage: SDU Uitgeverij, 161–169.
Todd, Loreto
    1989   *The language of Irish literature:* London: Macmillan.

Trudgill, Peter (ed.)
    1978   *Sociolinguistic patterns in British English*. London: Arnold.
Tucker, Susie I.
    1967   *Protean shape. A study in eighteenth-century vocabulary and usage*. London: The Athlone Press.
Turner, Thomas
        See Vaisey, David (ed.).
Vaisey, David (ed.)
    1985   *The diary of Thomas Turner, 1754–1765*. Oxford: Oxford University Press.
Verheyen, Cornelis R.
    1983   *Reflexives and intensifiers in modern British English*. [Unpublished Ph.D. dissertation, University of Leiden.]
Visser, Fredericus Th.
    1963   *An historical syntax of the English language*. Part I. Leiden: Brill.
Wakelin, Martyn F. (ed.)
    1972   *Patterns in the folk speech of the British Isles*. London: The Athlone Press.
Walpole, Sir Horace
        See Lewis, Wilmarth S. (ed.).
Wesley, John
        See Baker, Frank (ed.).
Wood, Frederick T.
    1956   "Further thoughts on the pronouns in *-self*', *English language teaching* 10: 97–108.

The critic and the grammarians: Joseph Addison and the prescriptivists

Susan Wright

1. Introduction

It is a popular assumption that modern standard English is the product of the later eighteenth century, and particularly associated with its most famous grammarians. Dr Johnson and Robert Lowth. But if one looks closely at the welter of contemporary prescriptive grammars which sought to codify and regulate the English language, it is striking that the work most frequently held up to exemplify "good" English does not belong to the literary figures of the late eighteenth century. So who then, of the 'best writers' clearly epitomize the language that the prescriptivists were urging on the later eighteenth-century student? Not all the grammarians adopted literary examples to illustrate their Rules of good usage. Those who did – among them, Lowth, Fell, White, Fogg, Baker and Ward – range widely across a corpus of prose (and more frequently verse) spanning the sixteenth, seventeenth and eighteenth centuries, drawn from the giants of English literature – from Shakespeare to Milton, Locke and Bacon, to Pope, Dryden and Swift.

Yet while of enormous stature, these writers do not, for the most part, form the bulk of the exemplification in the grammars mentioned above. William Ward's *Essay on Grammar* (1765) and Fogg's *Principles of English Grammar* (1792–6) are two specific examples of corpus based grammars of the second half of the eighteenth century. They cite a wide range of writers – from the translators of the Bible, Shakespeare and Milton, to Sheridan, Blair, Goldsmith and even, in the case of Fogg, Byron. But the text most frequently referred to is the *Spectator*, and of its contributors, the most frequently cited is Joseph Addison. William Ward's favorite sources are actually the authorized versions of the Old and New Testaments (88 and 85 citations each), but immediately following these comes the *Spectator* with 59 citations. More than half of the *Spectator* extracts consists of the writing of Joseph Addison. In addition, Addison's prose and verse is separately mentioned no fewer than 38 times, making his contribution to Ward's corpus no fewer than 67 illustrations. Steele, the other principal contributor to the periodical, is not cited individually at all.[1] Fogg (from a corpus of at least 57 authors) places Addison (39 citations) second only after Pope (48 citations). He also cites eight extracts from the *Spectator*, which he does not attribute to Addison or Steele.[2] Table 1 gives league positions for the writers most frequently cited by Ward and Fogg.

Table 1. Frequency of citations by Ward and Fogg

Ward (1765)	[38 authors]	Fogg (1792–6)	[57 authors]
Old Testament	(88)	Pope	(48)
New Testament	(77)	Addison (inc. Spect)	(39)
Spectator (unattrib)	(59)	Milton	(37)
Addison (separate)	(38)	Shakespeare	(33)
Shakespeare	(37)	Dryden	(30)
Dryden	(31)	Johnson	(21)
Milton	(18)	Goldsmith	(14)
Locke	(18)	Blair	(13)
Pope	(12)	Locke	(11)
Bacon	(10)	Swift	(10)
Swift	(7)	Steele (Spectator)	(9)
		Spectator (unattrib)	(8)

Fogg sets down his criteria for the selection of his illustrative material in his advertisement to the second volume of his *Principles*: "... the choice of examples has been, in some degree, regulated by beauty of expression, and excellence of sentiment; and they have been generally extracted from approved authors." (1796: iii) But not content to illustrate good usage to the exclusion of bad, he also cautions that "many of the instances of bad English are likewise taken from authors, after the manner of Lowth, but more fully."[3]

Now, judging from the prominence of Addison, Pope, Dryden, Swift and other eighteenth-century writers in these lists, the roots of the standard may perhaps be no more than a body of texts situated mainly at the beginning of the eighteenth century. Moreover, the composition of my league table of writers raises the question of the content of this standard. If the standard is a matter of high literary style, we could reasonably expect explicitly literary works to be the most constantly cited models, but they are not. Notice, for instance, the positions of Shakespeare, Milton, Dryden and Swift in relation to Addison. The Bible is heavily referred to perhaps because it carries the weight of authority in spheres other than the use of language, and not because it symbolizes literariness. It is a text that is widely used as day-to-day reading and it is accessible and popular, in the sense that it is an obligatory aspect of the education of any child at this time. On the other hand, if the standard is a matter of modern usage, we would expect the later eighteenth-century grammarians to cite more contemporary authors such as Johnson, and later ones like Blair and Goldsmith far more frequently. But they do not. So we are left with the problem of why they seem to be virtually ignored in contrast to the early eighteenth-century writer Joseph Addison; and if it seems then that the early part of the century is pre-eminently important as a source for the prescriptive enterprise, why should it be Addison, of all the early eighteenth-century writers, who is most frequently invoked by the grammarians?

To discover the reasons for the apparent prominence accorded to Addison in the construction of standard English in the late eighteenth century, it is necessary to consider what it is about his use of particular forms that qualifies him as a suitable model. Definitive criteria of standard English are very rarely explicitly or consistently given by the grammarians themselves. They are, however, concerned that good English should be "correct" (Lowth uses the expressions "right" and "proper" among others). Another desirable feature of good English is that it should be "modern", although this particular expression is remarkable for its virtual absence in the grammars. But a potent clue to the identity of modernity as a criterion of good English is ever present in the grammarians' injunctions to their readers to emulate the best in polite conversation. Ward's preface contains a further clue to the unstated importance of modernity: "It is farther urged, that *mode and custom* must be the only rule of speech, because every living language is perpetually changing by their sole influence" (1765: ix). [my emphasis – SW]

The issues of modernity and correctness are complicated. Comparatively few of the prescriptivists discuss the language of their contemporaries and that of their antecedents in terms of their temporal distance. They frequently omit explicit mention of usage in the "wells of English undefil'd" as being archaic or obsolete. The reason for this overall failure to discriminate between older and more modern patterns of usage may well be that following Dr Johnson, the later eighteenth-century grammarians believed the test of time had not yet qualified the moderns to rank among the best writers. Their inclination to observe the tradition of valuing established, time-honored literary texts above contemporary ones seems to percolate to the treatment of language itself. The tendency to avoid temporal discrimination leads to an approach which can be construed as essentially ahistorical on the one hand. On the other, it sometimes gives the impression that the grammarians hallow older patterns of usage as much as they do their users.

This rather ambiguous attitude then complicates the assessment of the importance of modern patterns of usage to the grammarians. For example, it sometimes results in a kind of purblindness when it comes to compiling and setting down actual patterns of current usage. So many grammarians end up listing paradigms which are hardly ever countenanced in the writing of their chosen models, still less in that of their own age.[4] But there are exceptions. For instance, Lowth's references to Milton suggest that for him, modernity is an inescapable aspect of the new standard. He uses Milton principally in order to point out the antecedents of more modern patterns of expression and construction. Fell (1784) offers extracts from Chaucer in order to demonstrate even earlier stages of the language.

The practice of using literary illustration and exemplification seems to have two functions. One is to impress upon the reader the greatness of those texts most highly revered – Shakespeare and the Bible. The other is more practical in its aim; for the grammarians also believed that readers should be given practical models of the constructions that they thought eighteenth-century speakers ought to be able to control with ease and confidence in conversation and writing. So within the constraints imposed by the acceptability of selecting older, established texts and the dubious wisdom of selecting those unproven by time, they drew strongly from the literary canon of the late seventeenth and early eighteenth centuries for their perfect practical models. James White, in the advertisement to *The English Verb*, fears that his sources are not sufficiently modern:

> The present Piece might have been much improv'd, had the Author, in reviewing his Collections, had time to enrich them from the works of Swift, and some productions *still more modern*, which are of Classic excellence; particularly the Pleasures of the Imagination by Dr Akenside, the Art of preserving Health by Dr Armstrong, and the Leonidas of Mr Glover. (1761: xii) [my emphasis – SW]

But while we can speculate about the possible rationale for using different parts of the canon for different purposes, the selection of texts alone does not supply us with the means of identifying the criteria of modernity or correctness. For it appears that the grammars contain a paradox. There is a strong tendency to champion the traditional: the conservative and established literary texts. This tendency is polemical rather than practical, since it sits beside the evident impulse to use as models of appropriate usage, Addison and (near) contemporaries like Pope, Dryden and Swift. It strikes me that the paradox is simply resolved if we treat these as complementary tendencies. Quite clear about the kinds of literature that ought to be valued, the grammarians are less easily able to identify the actual forms which they believe ought to be adopted by ordinary speakers. Hence, while explicit about the texts, the criteria for good usage are left unstated or at best, implicit in the examples chosen.

Some hint of the modern substance of the language in which the grammarians are unavoidably immersed does emerge in the form of definitions and discussions of increasingly rare or retreating constructions which become more and more confusing and vague as the century progresses. Constructions like the so-called *be*-perfect, and the passive progressive, or indeed the use of what Johnson had condemned as "superfluous" (unemphatic) *do* in affirmative declarative sentences, receive scant attention and even less comment from grammarians after Johnson and Lowth. Gough and Dilworth, and even James White, who devoted his book entirely to the verb, tend to avoid any mention of these constructions at all.

Picking up this hint, I shall select some linguistic features which are either contentious innovations or prestigious patterns in the usage of the time, and examine their treatment by the grammarians themselves, and their usage by Addison and his contemporaries. This method will provide a basis for assessing the reasons for Addison's prominence among the early eighteenth-century examples, and suggest some fruitful areas for speculation on the nature of the thing that standard English was perceived to be.

The degrees of modernity and correctness can be measured by comparing the incidence of some of these controversial constructions in a range of contemporary works. To this end, I have taken samples of 41,000 words each from eight works published in 1711 – the same year as the launch of the *Spectator*. The point about them is that they are contemporary. In assessing admittedly thorny issues such as modernity and propriety, it seemed unadvisable to apply to their selection criteria usually associated with the discrimination of text-type – such as communicative purpose or genre. These variables, if adopted as determinants of textual patterning, can act to preclude considerations of other factors which may turn out to be more influential in language change, such as idiolect. By defining this corpus solely in terms of date of publication, the analysis avoids circularity and admits the possibility of considering the impact of such variety in relation to their audience (a subject for later exploration).

Nevertheless, it is a matter of information to situate both authors and texts in relation to one another and to the time of publication.[5] As it happens, the texts fall into two groups broadly distinguished in terms of genre or communicative purpose. The first is topical, polemical and colloquial in impulse: its members include two comedies by Susannah Centlivre, William

Whiston's (personal) historical preface to his translation of ancient Greek Epistles and Abel Boyer's newsletter *The Political State of Great Britain*. Boyer's newsletter and Whiston's preface both include a large number of letters; and since Boyer's also contains reports of Parliamentary speeches, it has something in common with the 'speech-based' Centlivre comedies. The other group contains texts which in principle are more uniform with respect to style (familiar, 'easy') and to general audience. Anthony Ashley Cooper's (Shaftesbury) *Characteristicks of Men and Manners*, Jonathan Swift's *Miscellanies in Prose and Verse*, and of course both Steele's and Addison's *Spectator* essays together make up a putative genre themselves. This is the literary 'miscellany', being reflective and speculative rather than narrative in impulse, containing verse, and prose that is frequently presented in an epistolary frame.[6] Stylistically, the texts in my corpus range across a spectrum – from the explicitly colloquial, speech-based comedies, to the established literary genre of the miscellany essays of Shaftesbury. The diversity of these works affords the investigation of particular linguistic features across a set of contemporary texts.

2. Linguistic indicators of correctness and modernity

The linguistic features that I have selected for examination are intended to situate Addison's status among his contemporaries as an exemplum of modernity on one hand, and a model of linguistic propriety or correctness on the other. They concern the treatment of auxiliary *do* and the control of relative markers; both of which have been demonstrated to be important issues in the history of English in the eighteenth century (Visser 1969–73; Austin 1985 and this volume, Tieken-Boon van Ostade 1987, to name but a few extended treatments).

The propriety or correctness of Addison's language will be assessed according to the extent to which his language shows a preference for patterns accepted in his own time as being prestigious, above those perceived to be less appropriate. (See Leonard 1929). The feature is the choice of relative clause marker, whose variants each have different social and stylistic values. This is not a feature undergoing change as such in the eighteenth century. On the contrary, the stylistic stratification of its variants provides a solid basis on which to assess its use by Addison and his contemporaries. Addison's eminence as a model of linguistic modernity compared with his contemporaries will be judged in terms of the extent to which he eschews obsolescent linguistic forms. In their place, he either adopts the patterns of present-day English or indeed, opts for a completely alternative construction. The features examined as evidence are the use of negative sentences with *do*-support and the use of emphatic *do* in affirmative declarative sentences. The radical changes in the verb phrase that occur in the seventeenth century do not characterize the eighteenth century. Rather, there is a gradual stabilization of the new patterns, for instance, the so-called "regulated" use of auxiliary *do*, principally in negative sentences.[7]

2.1. Auxiliary *do* and negation

Tieken's (1987) study of the use of dummy auxiliary *do* in the eighteenth century provides a tantalizing indication of Addison's status as a modern. She examined the use of the dummy auxiliary in interrogative, negative and affirmative declarative sentences in the different writing styles of a group of authors throughout the century. Her figures demonstrate that Addison's use of the regulated auxiliary (interrogative and negative) is distinctly modern when compared with many of his successors.[8] So how modern does he turn out to be when compared with some of his exact contemporaries?

The focus of my analysis rests on the use of *do*-less negative sentences relative to those with *do*.[9] Table 2 shows the proportions as percentages, together with the total numbers found in each sample.

Table 2. Percentages of *do* vs ∅ (*do-less*) negatives: (N = 41,000)

Do	Shaftes.	Swift	Boyer	Whiston	Addison	Steele	Centlivre
do + neg	28	69	89	86	87	71	69
∅ + neg	72	31	11	14	13	29	31
100%	18	42	55	71	97	109	122

Notice that the absolute number of negatives which could have *do*-support varies widely across writers, with Shaftesbury and Swift each having fewer than fifty in their 41,000 word samples. The *Spectator* authors are remarkable for having the largest number of negative sentences, surpassed only by the dialogue-based comedies of Centlivre. What is most striking about the figures in Table 2 is that apart from Shaftesbury, the next greatest proportion of *do*-less negatives in Centlivre's corpus (31%) is shared by two writers whose texts occur at opposite ends of the stylistic spectrum – Swift's literary miscellany and Centlivre's colloquial comedies. Over half of the *do*-less negatives in Centlivre's corpus (53%) are used with the first person singular pronoun, with highly expressive verbs – *care, believe, understand, doubt, fear, see*. The verb *know* accounts for no fewer than half of these personal constructions. In contrast, Swift has just less than half (46%) with the first person singular pronoun, and of these, half are accounted for by *know*. Swift tends to use the *do*-less negative with first person in parentheses as it were, as a comment subordinated to the main point being made. For example:

(1) a. *Having long observed and lamented these, and a hundred other Abuses of this Art, too tedious to repeat, I resolved to proceed in a new way, which* I doubt not *will be to the general Satisfaction of the Kingdom* (1711: 215).
   b. *The Reason of my Doubt is, because I have been so very idle as to Read above Fifty Pamphlets, written by as many Presbyterian Divines, loudly disclaiming this Idol Toleration, some of them calling it* (I know not *how properly) a Rag of Popery, and all agreeing, it was to establish iniquity by Law.* (1711: 341).

For Centlivre, it is possible that the *do*-less negatives are being used in a different way from what might seem to be relics of an older syntactic pattern. Indeed, the inverted verb + *not* form might well be considered to have a particular pragmatic function – especially in the context of the dramatic, performative situation of comedy. This pragmatic function would not be dissimilar to the new eighteenth-century use of declarative *do* as an emphatic or contrastive element. In the comedies, the function of the personal *do*-less negative is direct and declarative rather than parenthetical:

(2) a. *Frederick: Did he see you?*
       Lissardo: I believe not, *Sir.* (1714: 33)
   b. *Felix: What means my Father?*
       Frederick: I understand you not, *Sir!* (1714: 33)
   c. *Pedro: ... You are enough to spoil your Lady Housewife, if she had not abundance of Devotion.*
       Violetta: I am all Obedience, Sir, I care not *how soon I change my Condition.* (1714: 55–56)

The broader distinction between Addison, Steele, and the "colloquial" authors on one hand and Shaftesbury and Swift on the other can be interpreted in terms of the verbs which appear to resist *do*-support, and the context in which these verbs occur. For Addison, the only verbs that are consistently exempted from the modern rule are *question* and *doubt* (which tend to be used as speech act verbs, taking first person subjects).[10] Whiston and Centlivre have a high proportion of *do*-less negatives in imperative contexts. Whiston also uses them in declaratives but in a rather formulaic epistolary way. Only Boyer has any notable instances of the somewhat transitional negative construction, *not* + *V* in which the negative precedes the main verb, without the *do* auxiliary: *it not appears*, in which the negative adverb *not* is placed before the main verb, rather than following it, as in the older construction: *it appears not*.[11]

The grammarians' discussion of the negative and *do*-support is generally sparse. Many simply content themselves with the observation that *do* may be used to construct negative and interrogative sentences. Fogg distinguishes between negative and interrogative sentences with *do* and those without, but in terms of the stylistic contrast of solemn and familiar writing:

> 302. The present and past times of the indicative mode are made by the same times of the auxiliary *do* with the original state of the primary verb in the following cases. ... 2. When a question is asked *in familiar language*. 3. When a thing is denied, as They *do* not see; *but in the solemn style* the negative particle is put after the simple primary verb, as, They see not. (1792: 154) [my emphasis – SW]

Modern sociohistorical studies of the history of the language have established the equivalence of stylistic oppositions such as Fogg's with the historical distinction between conservative and advanced constructions. But the general tendency for the prescriptivists to express historical differences as stylistic ones makes the scrutiny of the illustrative texts all the more important. But Lowth provides a pivotal statement on the modern regulatory use of auxiliary *do* which Fogg can only hint at by contrasting solemn and familiar styles. Quite neatly and succinctly, he notes that "*Do* and *did* ... are of frequent and almost necessary use in Interrogative and Negative Sentences" (1762: 57).

With the exception of Boyer, Addison has the largest proportion of negative sentences with *do*-support, followed immediately by Whiston. Boyer's total number of sentences which could have *do*-support is virtually half of Addison's. Now the Whiston and Boyer texts are clearly not literary in the same way that Swift and Shaftesbury are definably so. I have suggested that the former are more informal, even speech-based on occasion. The high proportion of negative sentences with *do*-support could be ascribed to the fact that they are less tightly constrained by the conventions of literary discourse than the miscellanies of the accomplished Swift and Shaftesbury. Fogg's identification of what we know to be the older construction with the "solemn style", presumably that which characterizes the literary prose of Shaftesbury and Swift, suggests that by the end of the eighteenth century, these authors are viewed as markedly conservative in their usage. This conservatism may account for the fact that Shaftesbury's prose, unlike Addison's, is absent from the grammarians' list of citations. For Addison appears to be adhering more to patterns of negation that are novel or innovative in the context of literary writing in the early part of the century. His usage is also non-literary and popular – inclining towards the usage of the speech-based texts without losing the gravity which places his work in the literary genre of the essay. On the basis of these samples, Addison appears to be an excellent candidate for a model of modern writing.

2.2. Emphatic *do*

The other marked change which affects the use of the dummy auxiliary verb *do* in the eighteenth century is the replacement of its unemphatic or unregulated use in affirmative declarative sentences by a more restricted (contrastive, emphatic) use. This gradual transition is particularly difficult to identify with absolute certainty, since the impact of a putatively emphatic *do* is controlled by pragmatic factors more than by syntactic ones. That is, the transition is not marked by a change in the formal expression of the construction. However, since contextual factors may provide important pragmatic clues to the function of the auxiliary, I have taken particular account of adverbial and other modifying expressions which pattern with the auxiliary.

The problem of distinguishing emphatic from plain unemphatic *do* in eighteenth-century writing is not confined to twentieth-century interpretations. The grammarians themselves offer a rather mixed bag of comments on the use of auxiliary *do* in affirmative declaratives. This suggests that the construction was indeed in transition, and that the distinction was contingent and pragmatic, not absolute and formal. The most explicit comments on the transitional status of affirmative *do* are offered by Samuel Johnson, who noticed by the time he came to write his grammatical preface to the *Dictionary*, that unemphatic, "superfluous" *do* was increasingly rare. He is, moreover, proscriptive when it comes to the question of using *do* as a dummy auxiliary verb without emphatic force in declarative sentences. He declares it to be a "vitious expression", and condemns its use in Waller's poetry for example. He suggests that it is a marker of deficiency in poetic expression that poets must resort to such devices. Yet he is cautious: "I know not whether it is not to the detriment of our language that we have rejected these expletives *do* and *did*". In spite of the fact that Johnson's comments are generally based on the analysis of much earlier texts, and consequently are somewhat dated, he can also be innovative, unlike the grammarians who follow him.[12] It is also striking that it is only following Johnson that grammarians comment on this use of *do*, which suggests that he might have served as an example for the subsequent treatment of auxiliary *do* more or less in the same terms.[13] He makes no bones about his own feelings regarding the constructions involving the unemphatic, superfluous use of auxiliary *do*, and declares in his dictionary entry: "*I do* is sometimes used superfluously ... but this is considered as a vitious mode of speech ... It is sometimes used emphatically ... It is frequently joined with a negative ... Its chief use is in interrogative forms of speech." (1755: sig. b2) Setting the trend for grammarians after him, Johnson does not distinguish between the genres in which the construction is employed, assigning general functions to the verb rather than discriminating between its use in verse or prose. So he includes in his dictionary entry for the "dummy" verb, an extract from Bacon's prose *Holy Wars*, as well as excerpts from the poetry of Dryden and Pope.

Lowth, in contrast to Johnson, is uncharacteristically brief on the use of *do* in declarative sentences. While he makes no explicit distinction between emphatic and unemphatic functions, the substance of his prescription indicates that he is directly concerned with the dummy auxiliary. The apparent omission of what Johnson condemned as the "superfluous" use of *do* suggests that his treatment is more rooted in current practice than Johnson's: "*Do* and *did* mark the Action itself, or the Time of it, with greater force and distinction" (57–58). Many of those whom Alston called the "schoolmaster" grammarians, like Gough, Dilworth and Ussher for instance, follow Lowth very faithfully in their definitions, and only very rarely do they expand into discussion.[14] One who does not slavishly follow the Lowth model is William Ward. He appeared to be somewhat perplexed about the proper use of *do* in affirmative declaratives. In particular, he associates what is presumably the emphatic use of *do* with activity verbs. This speculation, of course, cannot be used to account for the colligation of *do* with non-activity verbs. The result is singularly misleading: "The signs *do* and *did* manifestly denote the exertion of the effort, by which action is produced at some time, present or past. But, by analogy, they are also prefixed to verbal states which require no exertion of effort; as, *I do resemble – thou didst suffer*." (1765: 210) However, most of the late eighteenth-century grammarians content themselves with a straightforward observation of current practice. Fell (1784), for instance, merely includes discussion of *do* as an auxiliary verb together with *have* and *be*. He concerns himself with its formal use, paying no attention at all to the pragmatic contrasts which arise from its choice.

This descriptive insecurity on the part of the grammarians is amply reflected in the practice of the writers in my corpus. The status of emphatic *do* does seem rather uncertain in the writing of the early eighteenth century. Table 3 shows the frequency of plain affirmative sentences with *do*, with some indication of the proportion which may be construed as emphatic.[15]

Table 3. Declarative sentences with *Do*

	Shaftes.	Addison	Steele	Centlivre	Swift	Boyer	Whiston
Do decl	1	9	12	18	29	32	87
+ Emph	–	7	3	15	15	20	80
%	0%	77.8%	25%	83.3%	51.8%	62.5%	92%

The clearest cases of emphatic auxiliary *do* are those which occur in contrastive or contradictory utterances. The most unambiguously emphatic examples are provided by Centlivre and Boyer. It is worth bearing in mind that these writers are concerned with the dramatic or quotative representation of speech respectively, and so it is reasonable to assume that each attempts to capture something of the flavor of verbal argument or conflict.

(3)   a. *Violante: 'Tis harder to Pardon an injury done to what we love than to our selves, but at your request, Felix, I* do *forgive her*; (Centlivre: 1714: 52).

       b. *Felix: was you asleep, Sirrah, that you did not hear me call? Lissardo: I* did *hear you, and answer'd you, I was coming Sir.* (Centlivre: 1714: 32)

       c. *The eyes of the People have been for some time open'd, they will observe, they will judge of our Votings in the Cause, and* do *expect from us, as we have put a Stop to unjust and exhorbitant Power Abroad, that we should neither suffer nor endure it at Home.* (Boyer 1711: 52)

       d. *I must declare I don't remember that the Earl ever apply'd himself to me in particular upon that subject; if he had, the Answer must naturally have been, that Matter depended not upon me to grant or refuse, but upon the King of Spain, under whose Command I was. But I* do *remember the Earl propos'd this at some General Council,* ... (Boyer 1711: 89).

These examples are fairly unequivocal. Some difficulty arises, however, when other modifying material intervening between *do* and the main verb is itself emphatic, or strongly emotional in import. The difficulty lies in identifying the actual site of emphasis in the sentence. It could be argued that the dummy auxiliary simply indicates that we should expect emphasis which may not necessarily centre on the auxiliary. Tieken-Boon van Ostade (1987: 49) was concerned with the same issue, citing Steele's use of *do* as illustrative of the problem.

(4) a. I do assure You *I am not ashamed* ... (Steele, *Corr.*, 334). [emphasis – IT]

Rather similar problematic cases are instanced by the following, in which emphasis is probably located in those phrases and words which I have italized:

(4) b. ... *so there is another [source of Wit] of a quite contrary Nature to it, which* does *likewise branch it self out into several Kinds. For not only the Resemblance but the Opposition of ideas* does *produce Wit*; (Addison, *Spectator* No. 62).

In this particular example, the first *do* prepares the reader for the emphatic force of the adverbial *likewise* which immediately follows it. The second instance has a more clearly emphatic function as it indicates the contrast of two aspects of Wit. But notice that although its function is to signal emphasis, the locus of emphasis occurs elsewhere in the sentence; in particular, on the two elements contrasted. For Swift, the inclusion of auxiliary *do* is dictated by intrusive adverbs of time or manner between *do* and main verb. While the auxiliary itself is ostensibly non-emphatic, the adverb in the sequence *do* + adverb + main verb does convey some emphatic force:

(5) do *of themselves* divide; did *immediately* usurp; did *at several times* aim; did *soon* take *occasion*; did *soon after* get *many lengths*; do *seldom* appear; does *likewise this month* gain.

But we are more inclined to treat these problematic uses of *do* as close to the modern use of emphatic *do* when we compare them with those encountered in Boyer and Whiston. The kinds of expression adopted in Boyer's reports of speeches, and Whiston's letters are strikingly formulaic and conventional. They seem to be fixed phrases, inserted wholesale at appropriate moments in the discourse.

(6) a. *So we* do, *with equal Joy and Gratitude, reflect on the Wisdom of Your Councils at Home* ... (Boyer 1711: 12)
b. *We ... the Commons of Great Britain in Parliament assembled,* do *joyfully appear before Your majesty, to return our most humble Thanks* ... (Boyer 1711: 42)
c. *I did, by my Letter of the 15th September last, prepare your Expectations of the great Alterations* ... (Boyer 1711: 1)

d. *The Court of aldermen* did *on the eleventh chuse Sir Gilbert Heathcote, Lord Mayor for the Year coming*; (Boyer 1711: 11).

Actually, in view of the quite rigid nature of these formal expressions of thanks and request, some of Addison's apparently unemphatic uses of declarative *do* become quite explicable.[16] Addison's appropriation of the formulaic is generally used without serious intent – the formulae are used with mock solemnity, with tongue very firmly in cheek. Thus, his phrases *I do hereby enter*, and *I do promise* strike one as acknowledging, even aping the unemphatic, yet clearly solemn intent which accompanies the formulae observed in the speeches reported by Boyer.

The declarative use of *do* lends itself to the rhetorical organization of sentences for some authors. Swift controls the construction to balance a contrastive negative clause: *that the stars do only incline, and not force*. This is a skilful combination of balance and emphasis. Whiston's use is slightly different, landing between the formulaic and the emphatic function of *do*. He uses it to balance the juxtaposition of two adverbs preceding the main verb. This strategy results in a somewhat conventionalized phrasing in his letters, which are nevertheless very sincere.

(7)   "*I always* did *and freely* do *assent*;
      I always did *and always shall heartily wish*"

Some of the *do*-declarative sentences include the construction of *do* + *but* + main verb.[17] This is in fact the only guise in which *do*-declarative occurs in Shaftesbury: *If it does but keep us sober and honest ... and if we can but be trusted* (1711: 19). And notice here that it is tightly controlled, rhetorically balanced against the almost identical construction with the modal verb *can*. The auxiliary *do* occurs in inverted sentence structures too, in which it is also intended to have strong emotional force. Swift has a large variety of these: for example: *in vain does the busie Art of Man pretend*. Steele too makes use of *do* in inverted declarative sentences, to emphatic effect in the following, mainly owing to the comparative phrase that he employs: *does but the more recommend*.

Declarative *do* then occurs in many guises and apparently with many functions in my corpus. Yet with the exception of Whiston, it is not overall particularly numerous. Whiston demonstrates a strikingly modern pattern of usage, as regards both the overall frequency of *do*-declaratives, and the proportion of emphatic constructions. It is worth remembering that the bulk of the Whiston sample is made up of letters, most of which are pleading, persuasive or argumentative, with very little narrative content. Overall then, his style is markedly emphatic, as illustrated in the extracts in (8):

(8) a. *I found that in the very same Justin, who affirm'd, That Christ in his entire Person* did *include the* ... , did *just as expressly affirm, That Man* does *include just the same Number of Parts*, (1711: vi).
b. *For, as I have not done without great Evidence what I have done already, so* do *I verily believe I have strong, very strong Evidence, for the Genuine and Apostolick Authority of the Constitutions. And if you are once convinced of that, tho' you will not hear me, yet* do *I hope you will hearken to the Apostles of our Lord in these Matters*, (1711:: I xxxi).

Shaftesbury keeps to my initial expectation of conservatism, and Steele, when he has *do* in affirmative declaratives, appears to be most happy with the older unemphatic use.

Addison, in this context, is markedly cautious – he uses very few *do*-declaratives. Yet he inclines very strongly towards the emphatic use, proving closer to the patterns adopted in the "speech-based" genres than the literary ones. So what is he doing with this innovation? Notwithstanding its very low incidence in his prose, Addison is clearly a consistent exponent of the modern construction. It could be that Addison effectively produces a style that is recognizably colloquial while still being part of the literary tradition that includes Swift and Shaftesbury. But while the latter authors symbolize a mode of writing that is conservative and consequently increasingly inaccessible to the young of the late eighteenth century, Addison's interpretation, and therefore treatment of the literary miscellany as a much more colloquial medium is not. In this light the value of Addison as a linguistic model may well be that he effectively mediates in the construction of the standard as a popular and accessible product that has solid literary underpinnings.

This mediating role between the colloquial and the literary then provides some basis for Dr Johnson's assessment of Addison's importance as the champion of the "middle" style.[18] In terms of the discussion of the use of the auxiliary *do*, Addison's caution in using the emphatic declarative parallelled with his consistent use of negative *do* suggests that he is indeed an exemplar of a modern standard – tracking a path between the conservative literariness of the high stylists like Swift, and the strongly colloquial modernism of Whiston, Boyer and Centlivre. This balance of the literary and the popular may be instrumental in assuring the longevity of the linguistic influence of Addison's prose. It also accounts for his prominence as a model of modernity for the grammarians of the latter half of the century. "In an age when conversation was regarded as a refinement of class, not divorced from the ethical" as the Blooms (1984: 5) aver, Addison together with Steele, "translated the tone of civilized oral discourse into print" better than any preceding writers in English: "The easy flow of written speech" became Addison's "literary signature".

2.3. Correctness and relative clause markers

The discussion of an innovative linguistic feature – the control of auxiliary *do* in negatives and emphatic sentences – suggests that Addison's language is midway between his literary colleagues like Swift, Shaftesbury and Steele, and the plain colloquialism of Centlivre, Boyer and Whiston. Yet how "correct" is his use of language? Do the grammarians select him so frequently exclusively because he is modern, or does he also represent a standard of correctness which they sought to prescribe? After all, if the grammarians' avowed task was to educate the public (both adult and young) in the art of "polite" speaking and writing, we should expect the notion of correctness to be pertinent to the choice of appropriate models of good usage.

This issue involves then the question of the perceived correctness of Addison's language – the extent to which his prose embodies the practice of the standard as it was beginning to be identified and defined by the grammarians. The focus of this part of my analysis does not involve a feature undergoing change as such. Instead, it is a feature whose appropriate use arouses very definite views that are vigorously expressed by virtually all the grammarians. It is the marking of restrictive relative constructions. The appropriate use of the *wh*-relative pronouns, in particular, *who*, *which* and *whose* was a controversial issue for eighteenth-century grammarians (see for instance, Grijzenhout 1992).

One sign of the relevance of relative clause marking in the matter of the appropriate use of language for even ordinary speakers of the language is that the *Spectator* itself had occasion to comment on it. Steele and Addison published two issues on the usage of the *wh*-pronouns, casting the pieces as letters from characters representing the pronouns *which* and *that* respectively. In the first piece (*Spectator* 78), *Which* argues that it is ignored at a writer's peril, since the frequent replacement of *which* by the "jacksprat" *that* commonly results in confusion and ambiguity. In the second piece, *That* retaliates (*Spectator* 80), pointing out the rhetorical advantages of using the demonstrative *that* (but has nothing to say on the choice of relative markers). In this context, it is worth reminding oneself firstly that Mr *Spectator* (here, Richard Steele, not Addison) got the comparative chronologies of relative *that* and the *wh*-relative pronouns wrong: *Which* accuses *That* of being a vulgar modern upstart. Secondly, he fails to distinguish between the different guises of *that* as relative marker and as demonstrative.

Before examining the ways in which Addison and his contemporaries reflect the apparently general acceptance of the prestige norms governing use of the relative pronouns, it is useful to consider the later grammarians' comments on the issue.[19] Lowth's discussion is one of the more detailed that I have encountered.[20] In common with most of the other grammarians, he is principally concerned with the appropriate pronoun for personal and non-personal antecedents. The establishment of the person distinction separating *who* and *which* in the course of the seventeenth century prompts him to give something of the earlier usage of the *wh*-pronouns.

> The RELATIVES *who*, *which*, *that*, having no variation of gender or number, cannot but agree with their Antecedents. *Who* is appropriated to persons; and so may be accounted Masculine and Feminine only: *which* is used of things only; and so may be accounted Neuter. But formerly they were both indifferently used of persons: "Our Father, *which* art in heaven." *That* is used indifferently both of persons and things: but perhaps would be more properly confined to the latter (1762: 133–134) [my emphasis – SW].

Unlike many of his contemporaries, Lowth does countenance the zero-relative (which I have represented as ∅-relative). But he levels the charge of obscurity and ambiguity against the use of *that* or ∅ in place of the *wh*-pronouns: "The accuracy and clearness of the Sentence depend very much upon the proper and determinate use of the Relative, so that it may readily present its Antecedent to the mind of the hearer or reader without any obscurity or ambiguity". And although he does concede to contemporary practice in mentioning the zero-relative, it does not pass without some hint of disapproval:

> The Relative is often understood, or omitted: as, "The man I love;" that is, "*whom* I love".[note]
> [NOTE: "Abuse on all he lov'd, or lov'd him, spread." Pope, Epist. to Arbuthnot. That is, "all *whom* he lov'd, or *who* lov'd him:" or to make it more easy by supplying a Relative that has no variation of Cases, "all *that* he lov'd, or *that* lov'd him." *The Construction is hazardous, and hardly justifiable, even in Poetry.* "In the temper of the mind he was then." Addison, Spect. No. 549. "In the posture I lay." Swift, Gulliver, Part 1, Chap 1. In these and the like Phrases, which are very common, there is an Ellipsis both of the Relative and the Preposition; which were much better supplied: "In the temper of the mind *in which* he was then." "In the posture *in which* I lay." In general, *the omission of the Relative seems to be too much indulged in the familiar style; it is ungraceful*

in the serious; and of whatever kind the style be, it is apt to be attended with obscurity and ambiguity.] (1762: 137) [my emphasis – SW]

Although Lowth makes no bones about the fact that he sees the non-*wh* relative construction as rather ungraceful, he displays his concern with description by relegating his expressions of disapproval to footnotes. In these footnotes, it is clear that his regard for writers like Pope, Swift and Addison does not exempt their linguistic infelicities from his scrutiny. Others are not so restrained. Baker condemns Swift for his misuse of the relatives *that* and *which*, lamenting that Swift's "Stile is far from being so excellent as it is often asserted to be. In some Parts of his Works it is exceedingly good; but in many others it is flat, low, and shamefully incorrect" (1770: 77). And he complains that "The Nominative of the Relative Pronouns *Who, That, Which,* is frequently omitted by bad writers (and sometimes, tho' rarely, even by good ones) and left to be supposed" (1770: 3). But apparently unhappy with the force of his condemnation, he notes,

> There are, however, in Shakespeare and other great Writers, some few Instances, where the omission adds to the Spirit of the Sentence, without causing any Obscurity. It may likewise now and then be borne with in common Conversation. Yet in general it has a bad Effect in Conversation, and a still much worse in Writing. (1770: 3).

Most of the grammarians who follow Lowth are generally content to let his definition stand. But some, like Ussher, actually provide rules guiding the proper use of *that* as a relative marker in preference to *who* or *which*.

28. *First,* that *is more proper than* who *or* which *after an Adjective in the superlative degree; as,* he was the ablest minister that James ever had.
29. *Secondly,* that *is more proper than* who *or* which *after the Pronouns* same *and* who; *as,* he is the same man that you saw before. Who, that has any sense of religion, could have argued thus.
30. *Thirdly,* that *is more proper than* who *or* which *when it serves as a relative to two antecedents, the one a person the other a thing; as,* have you seen the man and the Coach that I met in the road. (1785: 18)

So how do Addison and his contemporaries measure up to the norms set by Lowth and the other grammarians of the later eighteenth century? The *Spectator* discussions as well as recent sociohistorical linguistic work on the relative clause (Romaine 1982, Nevalainen 1987) support the grammarians' observations that the *wh*-options were more prestigious than *th*- and ∅ in writing at the beginning of the century. Using the same samples scrutinized for the previous section, I concentrated on restrictive relatives because it is in these constructions that the choice between *wh*-pronouns and *that* is most relevant. The main issues of correctness are how assiduously the 1711 writers incline towards the use of the *wh*-pronouns *who* (labelled wh1) and *which* (labelled wh2) in preference to the *that* (th) and zero (∅) options. Table 4 below gives the total number of relatives per 41,000 words for each author, and a breakdown of choice of markers expressed as percentages.[21]

Table 4. Percentages (restrictive) relative clauses: personal antecedents (per 41,000 words)

	Shaftes.	Swift	Steele	Addison	Boyer	Whiston	Centlivre
wh1	93	80	71	60	55	50	24
th+	–	15	21	35	39	43	50
∅+	7	5	8	5	6	7	26
100%	85	158	335	348	67	74	91

The first thing to notice is that Addison has far more restrictive relatives than any of this contemporaries. It is perhaps to be expected that the speech-based genres represented have fewer relatives than the "miscellanies", and that of those, Centlivre's comedies have fewest *wh*-pronouns. Addison's essays are situated in the middle, as it were, with respect to the proportion of *wh*- to non-*wh* forms. Together with Swift, he has fewest zero-relatives. Table 5 compares the incidence of *who* against *which* to refer to personal antecedents. The dilemma raised by the choice of *which* in place of *who* for personal antecedents is how far it may be an indication of conservatism, or indeed, whether it is better considered to be a deviation from the polite norm, a barbarism.

Table 5. Personal antecedents

	Steele	Addison	Swift	Shaftes.	Whiston	Boyer	Centlivre
who	238	210	127	79	40	37	22
which	–	–	1	1	3	–	4

Addison, Steele and Boyer are not guilty of conservatism or of stylistic viciousness on this count. For Whiston and Centlivre, however, it is tempting by the fact that with respect to the use of the *wh*-relative markers, they are clearly the most "correct" members of the group. Yet their prose style poses particular problems. In particular, they tend to write sentences with heavily punctuated phrase boundaries. Further, the punctuation conventions very rarely distinguish between the strength of syntactic boundaries, so that restrictive and nonrestrictive relative clauses are separated from their antecedents in identical ways. The consequence of this pausal style of punctuation is that it is sometimes difficult to identify the antecedent of a relative marker, for example, in Swift:

> ... and the Collectors and other officers throughout the Kingdom are generally appointed by the Commissioners, which give them a mighty influence in every Country. (1711: 331)

Note that the plural form of *give* indicates that the antecedent of *which* must be *Commissioners* but from a modern perspective, this reading is potentially obscured by two factors – first, the choice of the nonpersonal pronoun for a personal antecedent, and second, the separating comma, which could be construed as a signal of a nonrestrictive relative, and the consequent identification of *which* with the whole preceding clause. Both Swift and Shaftesbury each have comparatively few restrictive relatives. This is not the case for Steele and Addison. While Steele inclines towards Swift and Shaftesbury in his use of *wh*-pronouns, Addison pursues a middle course. His pattern of usage reflects the observations of the grammarians concerning the use of *that* and the familiar style.

Let us consider the group's comparative handling of nonpersonal antecedents (Table 6).

Table 6. Percentages of nonpersonal restrictive relatives[22]

	Shaftes.	Addison	Steele	Whiston	Swift	Centlivre	Boyer
wh2	78	49	47	42	38	29	22
∅-	17	10	29	30	26	45	39
wh3	3	3	9	5	12	2	4
th-	2	38	15	23	24	30	29
N = 100%:	134	646	430	228	206	111	216

at the same time, fewest relatives marked by what I have labelled *wh3*, like *when* and *where*. These take the place of the most formal phrasal markers, such as *in which*, *of which*. The realization of these *wh3* markers varies considerably. Steele, for instance, differs from Addison consistently using distinctively archaic words like *wherein*, *whereof*, *whereon*.

Again, Shaftesbury's choice of relative pronouns marks him out as the most "correct" as well as the most formal member of the group. Swift, however, is far less stringent about the selection of markers for nonpersonal antecedents than he is about personal antecedents. Indeed, his profile has more in common with the more colloquial (speech-based) writers like Whiston, than with the periodical writers. Steele and Addison are roughly similar with respect to their control of the *wh*-pronoun, but Steele tends to adopt the zero-relative far more frequently, in line with the other writers.

What of Addison's handling of restrictive relative marking overall? First, it is evident that he and Steele are inclined to use the construction more than their contemporaries, Swift and Shaftesbury. Indeed, the extent to which Addison's usage in particular surpasses them is very striking – we might think especially so since the *wh*-relative markers are highly prestigious and more significantly, indicative of formal or distinctly literary styles. But note that while the choice of relative clause *markers* is more usually associated with formal styles, the use of relative clauses as a subordinating strategy per se is not. To be able to assess more completely the significance of the relative clause strategy of subordination compared with others, it would be necessary to examine the patterns most favoured by Swift and Shaftesbury in some detail – a task well beyond the scope of the present paper. Yet the structure of the sentence used by Swift and Shaftesbury is an aid to speculation. Unlike the *Spectator* writers , they tend to write long sentences with heavy noun phrases, typically concatenated rather than subordinated. Consider this example of Shaftesbury's sentence construction.

> I can hardly forbear fancying, that if we had a sort of Inquisition, or formal court of Judicature, with grave officers and Judges, erected to restrain Poetical Licence, and in general to suppress that Fancy and Humour of Versification; but in particular that most extravagant Passion of Love, as it is set out by Poets, in its Heathenish Dress of Venus's and Cupid's: if the Poets, as Ringleaders and Teachers of this Heresy, were, under grievous Penaltys, forbid to enchant the People by their vein of Rhyming; and if the People, on the other side, here, under proportionate Penaltys, forbid to hearken to any such Charm, or lend their Attention to any Love-Tale, so much as in a Play, a Novel, or a Ballad; we might perhaps see a new Arcadia arising out of this heavy Persecution, (1711: 20–21).

This long sentence consists of a string of three conditional clauses, made up of heavy noun phrases. These are connected by a combination of (mainly) infinitive subordination strategies and conjunction. The measured use of punctuation contributes both to the balanced weight of the conditional clauses, and to the obscurity of the consequent clause. In this light, Addison's use of the relative clause has the effect of differentiating the weight of information, making the sentence structure more transparent. Compare his strategy as found in the following quotation:

> As I love to see everything that is new, I once prevail'd upon my Friend, Will. Honeycomb to carry me along with him to one of these Travell'd Ladies, desiring him, at the same time, to present me as a Foreigner who could not speak English, that so I might not be obliged to bear a Part in the Discourse. (*Spectator*, No. 45: 192).

While still more heavily punctuated than any present-day English sentence, the weight of the clauses in this sentence is varied by a combination of relative clauses and infinitive subordination. This strategy enables Addison to foreground the main (narrative) point of the sentence. I highlight the relative markers and other subordinating markers, and the narrative locus of the sentence to illustrate more clearly the weighting of information:

> As I love to see everything that is new, *I once prevail'd upon my Friend, Will. Honeycomb* to *carry me along with him to one of these Travell'd Ladies, desiring him,* at the same time, to *present me as a Foreigner* who could not speak English, that so *I might not be obliged to bear a Part in the Discourse.* (*Spectator*, No. 45: 192).

Addison is also very flexible with respect to his choice of relative marker. While there is a predominance of the polite (or prestige) *wh* markers, he is equally comfortable with the *th* and ∅ relatives. Now the fact of this flexibility is explicitly noted by Lowth, albeit in not altogether favorable terms in his comments above. Yet, of my group of writers, Addison is the most assiduous in avoiding the zero-relative for both personal and nonpersonal antecedents. This point suggests that while Addison may not be the most formal in anticipating the prescriptions of the grammarians, he is possibly the most strictly "correct" in avoiding the viciousness of the zero-relative. Alternatively, he could be interpreted as being the most explicit, in the sense that he aims to avoid ambiguity of expression. In Lowth's terms, Addison presents himself as an exemplar of the "proper" use of relative markers.

It may be instructive to dwell for a moment on the performance of Centlivre and Whiston. As noted before, these two works, together with Boyer, represent speech-based or at least less formal styles than the essayists' work. On the basis of what Romaine (1982: 201–209) has observed with respect to the distribution of *wh-* v. *th-*relative markers in Middle Scots and in Modern American and Scottish English, we should expect there to be a continuum according to style in the eighteenth century too. And so there is; as the style becomes less formal (more speech-based, epistolary, dialogistic) so the proportion of *th-* and zero-relatives increases. Constructing a continuum of this sort, we would expect Addison's handling of relative marking to be situated somewhere in the middle – consonant with the general characterization of his style in his own time as easy, or familiar. Taking the overall proportions of *wh-* as opposed to other relative markers (to indicate both personal and nonpersonal antecedents), we find that Addison is placed exactly in the middle of a continuum (Figure 1).

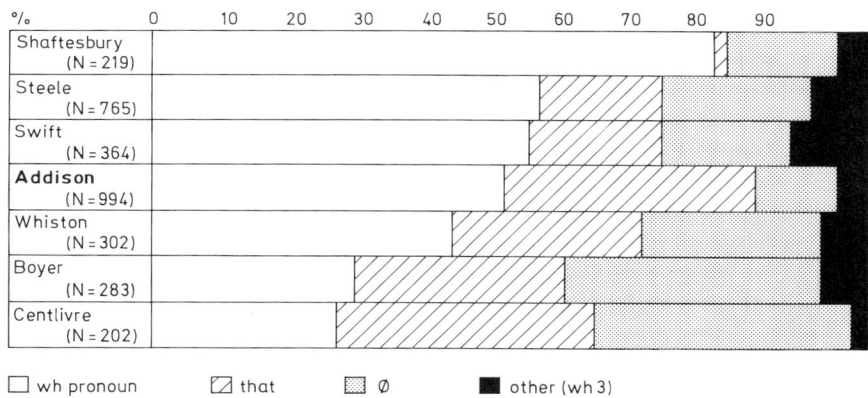

Figure 1. Relative Clause Markers (overall proportional percentages)

The examination of two linguistic features – one innovative and one an index of propriety – provides a clear sense of the grounds for Addison's eminence as an exemplar of the new standard. Indeed, Addison's prose possesses qualities which seem, with the benefit of hindsight, to be criterial in the codification of the new standard English and correctness. His ease with the *do-*negative demonstrates that he was at the forefront of the establishment of the periphastic negative, and his cautious control of emphatic *do* suggests that he reflects the transitional status of the construction. And his treatment of relative markers identifies his orientation towards the colloquial without abandoning the degree of correctness or propriety deemed important in literary texts. Modernity and correctness (propriety) are thus balanced in Addison's prose to the extent that his language appears to occupy the centre of a stylistic continuum. In fact, if we plot aspects of innovation (e.g. incidence of *do* in negative sentences) against propriety (e.g. incidence of *wh*-pronouns) for all the authors in my corpus, Addison turns out to be distinctly innovative while maintaining the middle ground in propriety.

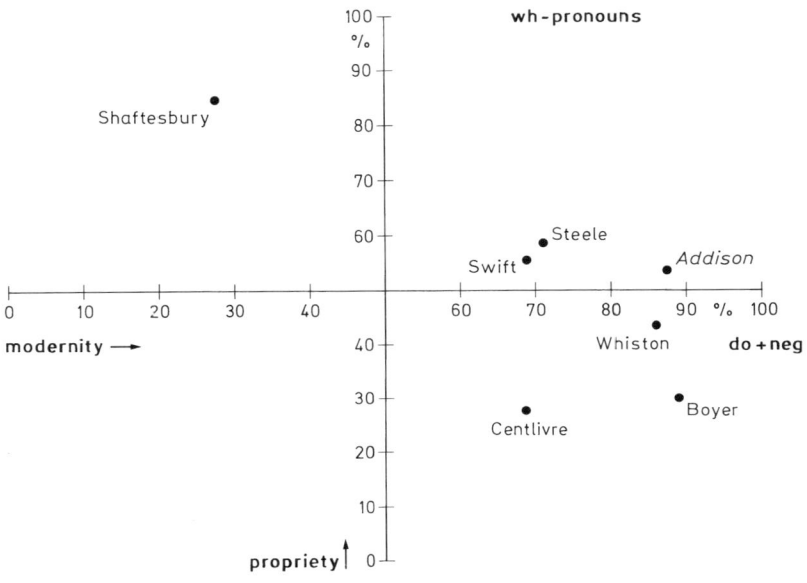

Figure 2. Addison in the matrix of propriety and modernity[23]

The graphic impression of Figure 2 adds some explicit linguistic substance to Dr Johnson's description of Addison as the champion of the "middle style".[24] On my analysis, Addison embodies a middle style, not because his writing embraces extremes of formal and informal features (as suggested by Biber – Finegan, 1990), but because he treads a middle line between them. According to the choice of *wh*-pronouns as an indicator, Addison is just on the right side of the axis of propriety (53%). He stands between his literary contemporaries and the colloquial writers. In terms of his usage of *do*-negatives (along the axis of modernity), he is closest to the colloquial writers. What is striking here is that Shaftesbury is isolated as markedly conservative (28%) from all the others. This isolation perhaps accounts for the fact that he is excluded from the grammarians' lists while his literary contemporaries Swift and Steele, are not. This matrix of modernity and propriety and Addison's position within it seem to justify his prominence in the construction of the standard. Dr Johnson's characterization of Addison's writing as an exemplar of the "middle style" was perhaps more precise than he could know. It forms a compromise between an explicitly literary mode of writing on the one hand (where the extreme would be in the nature of Shaftesbury) and a more popular, colloquial mode on the other.

3. Addison in pursuit of the middle style

Addison's place as a trend-setter of a particular kind of polite standard is further highlighted by the issue of his editing practices. When Addison and Steele collected the folio issues of the *Spectator* for a collected edition, published in 1714, they each subjected their own contributions to rigorous editing. In Bond's (1965) edition of the *Spectator*, the consistent comparison of the folio and collected versions of individual numbers indicates that the patterns of editing practised by Addison and Steele were quite different. While the alterations made by Steele mainly concerned matters of lexis and phrasing, Addison applied himself to the very syntactic fabric of his papers. For example, among the stylistic alterations that Addison made in the folio issues of the paper for the collected volumes of the *Spectator*, was the substitution of many of the instances of relative *that* by *which* or *who*. I have restricted my focus to the alterations made to markers of restrictive relative clauses.

The question which concerns me in looking at the pattern of Addison's editing is how far he can be viewed as a practical disseminator of linguistic taste. Could he have been as conscious of norms and standards in language, as he was in the more general area of aesthetic taste? If Addison was conscious of the prestige values attached to *who/which* in preference to *that* or indeed zero (∅) as a relative marker, we might expect there to be a tendency to "correct" the Folio in the direction of the *wh*-standard.

The actual extent of the alteration to relative marking is not great, but it is worth examining because of the pattern which asserts itself. The apparent trend was to replace relative *that* with a *wh*-form (in both restrictive and nonrestrictive relatives). Tables 7a and 7b illustrate the changes made to personal and nonpersonal relative markers respectively, in the correction and stylistic editing of *Spectator* Folio editions for the collected volumes.

Notice that the zero relative, ostensibly the most informal strategy of expressing relative constructions, increases at the expense of the *that* relative, gaining by 23%. Thus, Addison appears to be not so much inclining towards the *wh*-options as moving away from the potentially repetitive and ambiguous

Table 7a. Editing of personal relative markers

Spectator (41,000 words)	Folio	Collected edition
who	190	210 (+ 10.5%)
that	145	122 (− 15.9%)
∅	13	16 (+ 23.1%)

Table 7b. Editing of nonpersonal relative markers

Spectator (41,000 words)	Folio	Collected edition
which	300	318 (+ 6%)
that	264	242 (− 3.3%)
∅	61	65 (+ 6.6%)

that. This trend is replicated in the case of the nonpersonal markers. Here again, both *which* and the zero strategy benefit at the expense of *that* as relative markers.

So what do these breakdowns suggest about Addison's practical awareness of the prestige value of the *wh*-relative markers? In fact, the pattern of alteration reflects neither a blind application of the prestige variant nor indeed an overwhelming concern for grammatical appropriateness. The motivation for alteration is both aesthetic and contingent; a question of an appropriate stylistic perspicuity rather than grammatical correctness.[25] Recall that Addison tends to use *that* far more frequently than his contemporaries, and his editing practices do not change this. But he does replace *that* as a relative marker for the sake of clarity, with the consequence of greater ease of expression. The following quotation from the collected edition of the *Spectator* illustrates Addison's consciousness of the potential for the ambiguous construal of *that* (the form used in the folio is given in square brackets): "The Shepherd's Pipe may be said to be full of Musick, for it is composed of nine different kinds of Verses, *which* [F: that] by their several Lengths resemble the nine Stops of the [F: that] old musical Instrument, *that* [F: which] is likewise the Subject of the Poem", (Bond 1965: 246). In this example, the first alteration is the replacement of *that* (nonrestrictive relative marker) by *which*; the second is the replacement of the demonstrative determiner *that* by the definite article, and the last is the substitution of relative *which* by *that*.

Addison seems to anticipate the prescriptivists, but with respect to the issue of perspicuity rather than the more clearly prescriptivist notions of correctness. He is aware of a particular grammatical aesthetic however, and he corrects his own stylistic barbarisms and viciousness. Addison is more explicitly an exponent of "proper" patterns of speaking and writing (as declared by Dryden in his *Essay on Dramatic Poesy* (1667)), which came to be codified as correct or standard in the later part of the century. He is, however, faithful to the demands of his style – judicious in his avoidance of those features that would be considered vicious, yet confident in his adoption of those he considers pertinent and appropriate.

4. The *Spectator* and the foundation of the standard

I have established that Addison's prominence above his contemporaries for the prescriptive grammarians is vindicated by the balance of modernity and correctness in his language. But it still remains for us to account for the choice of Addison's language as the apparent embodiment of the new standard. Here, we must turn to consider his medium, the *Spectator*, and its contribution to the evolution of eighteenth-century perceptions of the standard, as crystallized in the work of the grammarians.

Addison produced the highly respected daily periodical *Spectator* (1711–1714), with Richard Steele (and a few others like Tickell, Hughes and Budgell). It had a wide and faithful readership which was carefully targeted and catered for.[26] It is arguable that one of the reasons for the enduring popularity and influence of Addison's writing (and Steele's less explicitly so) was the paper's overtly stated concern with educating the taste of its audience. In effect, Addison launched a cultural project with the *Spectator*. Addison himself declared the nature of this venture in *Spectator* (No. 10): "... I shall be ambitious to have it said of me, that I have brought Philosophy out of Closets and Libraries, Schools and Colleges, to dwell in Clubs and Assemblies, at Tea-Tables, and in Coffee-Houses." He is not concerned only with the Wits and Gentlemen, but aims to reach "all well regulated families" and advises them "for their Good to order this Paper to be punctually served up, and to be looked upon as a Part of the Tea Equipage". The Blooms (1984: 11) argue that Addison became "a formidable shaper of public taste", making his presence strongly felt "in the provinces and the colonies as well as in the town and the marketplace": "His essays became a meeting ground for the great and the modest – politicians, financiers, merchants; for women galore, public officials, and professional writers. In many homes the *Spectator* had pride of place alongside the Bible and the works of John Locke."

In fulfilling his aims. Mr *Spectator* is at pains not to lose sight of the needs of this target audience. So Addison takes up the issue of taste in *Spectator* No. 409 because the word itself arises so often in conversation; an indicator of the fact that aesthetic matters were of immediate topical interest as well as of more general concern. He defines it as "that faculty of the soul, which discerns the beauties of an author with pleasure, and the imperfections with dislike". The test of the faculty, he comments, can be determined according to the reader's response to the ancients and to the moderns "which have the sanction of the politer part of our contemporaries". He concludes that the reader ought to discover his lack of taste if he fails to discern the greatness of the greats. The remedy of such lack is, he admits, difficult since (good) taste is a faculty that one is born with, but he signals some hope – "the most natural method for this purpose is to be conversant among the writings of the most polite authors".[27] Ironically, perhaps Addison's own comments on taste serve to place him as an automatic choice as a model of polite writing: "As the great and only End of these my Speculations is to banish Vice and Ignorance out of the Territories of Great Britain, I shall endeavour as Much as possible to establish among us a Taste of polite Writing" (*Spectator* 58, ed. Bond, Vol. 1, p. 245). Addison's writing style was not only accessible to the polite classes; what he wrote was also popular. For the "middle style", as exemplified by Addison's language, is inextricably linked to this other eighteenth-century keyword, "politeness". The word *polite* and its variant *politeness* pervade the discourse of the period, frequently used as a term of satire as well as critical judgement or discernment (see Klein, this volume, for an extended discussion). Johnson's *Dictionary* construes *polite* as simply "elegant of manner", but gives the nominal *politeness* a broader application: "Elegance of manners; gentility; good breeding". Here the definition carries the term from the description of what can be acquired (manners) to what is innate (breeding). Johnson quotes Swift for elaboration: "I have seen the dullest men aiming at wit, and others, with as little pretensions, affecting politeness in manners and discourse". Politeness then grows into a catchall term for social grace and good manners in opposition to barbarism and vulgarity. Frequently, in its broader usage, it is applied to those parts of metropolitan society most in command of social graces – the well bred, the gentlemen and ladies of fashion (and leisure). This association gives rise to the commonplace expression "polite society".[28]

The eighteenth-century grammarians were by no means explicitly agreed on the literary counterpart of politeness. For some, the criterion of propriety was far more important than modernity, which frequently smacked of dubious fashion, of corruption and barbarism. So we are familiar with Dr Johnson's unequivocal declaration that the Elizabethans pre-eminently embodied the "wells of English undefil'd" (though less so with his inconsistency in applying this dictum); and many grammarians followed his lead. Yet the figures at the outset of this paper suggest that Shakespeare alone of the Elizabethans survives the rigours of the prescriptivist movement. On the whole, the literary giants of the seventeenth and early eighteenth centuries, Milton, Swift and Dryden, fare little better. This treatment reflects, as Berger (1978) and Stein (1990) suggest, an effective, if still poorly understood, change in the perception of what can be construed as "polite" at the beginning of the eighteenth century. As the match of conversation was ignited as the domain of polite conduct and practice, the rules of elegance began to shift, from a concern with formality and solemnity, to an aim of comfortable communication in a social context marked by familiarity and ease.

So figures like Swift, Dryden and Milton were increasingly associated with the seventeenth century, and effectively distanced from the new age of the eighteenth. One reason might be that few of them use the language in ways that most ordinary speakers could or would aspire to. Each is highly distinctive; at times they are severe and formal; and all are idiosyncratic exemplars of the diversity of which contemporary English is capable. They each had an élite readership, their detractors as well as their admirers. In short, while highly regarded, they were never populist in the mid-eighteenth century. So while these giants provided plenty of grist for the mills of the prescriptive grammarians, none of them could satisfy the need for a literary model that was accessible to and popular with the metropolitan bourgeoisie – the readership of the *Spectator* for instance. Perhaps this is why Joseph Addison's place as a model of politeness survives the eighteenth century (even into the nineteenth century)?[29]

5. Conclusions and speculations

In conclusion, it may be worth reviewing some basic assumptions which underlie the notion "standard" as it applies to the emergence of "standard" English in the eighteenth century. On one current interpretation, "standard English" is just one of many dialects which characterize the manifestation of "English". As such, it is as distinct from say Norwich English as Northumbrian English is from Norwich English. Yet it is widely and popularly accepted that "standard English" stands quite apart, as uniquely different from all other dialects of English. The nature of this contrast is nonlinguistic. Simply put, standard English is the most prominent external symbol of Englishness. It is a kind of totem, conjuring up images as diverse as the royal family, Churchill, West End theatre, the BBC World Service and the Henley Regatta. It is perceived to be an authentic marker of polite English society in a way that no other English dialect is. The division of standard and non-standard Englishes has its roots in the eighteenth century – when one variety was invested with an authority which both distances it from and raises it above all others. The criterial features of this authority are that it is unchallenged, highly valued and influential.[30] More strikingly, it is immensely popular in its impact. The agents of authority then, must themselves reflect its qualities. They must be in a position to initiate trends and communicate them to a group that is anxious to identify itself as socially pre-eminent. To this extent, the agents must themselves be popular, influential and highly valued.

Traditional approaches to the rise of the standard (for example Leonard 1929), tend to take the social and political impetus towards standardization for granted and instead home in on the linguistic consequences of this process. After all, that is the clearest and most fixed manifestation of the age. It is easy to be seduced by Lowth's stated aim of grammar (to enable the student "to judge of every phrase and form of construction, whether it be right or not" (1762: x)) into accepting that a doctrine of correctness pervades the eighteenth-century concern with language. But judging from the accounts of the grammarians, the term "correctness" itself subsumes many things, ranging from notions of prestige to views of propriety. And as I have demonstrated, the grammarians themselves are neither entirely secure nor sufficiently consistent in their own definitions and observations of current usage for us to take their pronouncements and judgments as a convincing statement of what the standard is. Indeed, they differ quite strikingly among themselves as regards their awareness of current patterns of usage, their views of current linguistic change, and even their basic knowledge of the syntax of the language. In short, while they express definite views on the principles which they believe ought to underlie good English – propriety, elegance, custom – they have no explicit inventory of forms on which to anchor these principles.

My study of Addison's language prompts the speculation that the basis of modern standard English was hibernating, as it were, in a literary style at the beginning of the century. The practitioners of this style, exemplified chiefly by Addison, were not interested primarily in linguistic authority – yet they set authoritative aesthetic standards in art, literature and conversation for a wide cross-section of readers. The style is characteristic of the essay genre – not commonplace journalism, but a literary form nominally shared with more elevated, solemn exponents like Shaftesbury. Its medium is not the private miscellany, but the popular periodical, published daily or weekly, and circulated in clubs and coffee houses, drawing rooms and salons.

Addison's popular periodical essay presents the prescriptive grammarians of the mid and late eighteenth century with a potential model of a standard to which all English speakers could aspire. More precisely, his "middle style" satisfies the balance of modernity and propriety which the prescriptivists sought in the new standard English. The fact that it is anchored in the essay genre ensures the literary propriety of its popular and colloquial inclinations. Consequently, Addison provides a suitable literary style from which the grammarians could then select and codify apposite patterns of usage; compiling the linguistic indices of good taste.

This new standard (in the sense of an authoritative totem) came to encapsulate a way of speaking and writing that was discernibly modern and sophisticated; what Dryden would have said was more elegant than the writing and conversation of earlier ages, and more pure (or "correct") than it had ever been. If my speculations turn out to approach the truth of the matter, Addison's style has an influence on the century's ideal use of language that is at least as great as the influence he has as a cultural figure on the century's notion of taste. He is then undoubtedly one of the agents of the authority which marks the pre-eminence of standard English.

Notes

* An extensive and very helpful list of eighteenth-century grammarians is given in Tieken-Boon van Ostade (1987) and (1990). Thanks are also due to Sylvia Adamson and Roger Lass for comments on earlier drafts of this paper.

1. Ward cites 59 examples from the *Spectator* without attributing them to a particular author. Addison contributes 29, Steele 21, Budgell 5, and Tickell 3. One extract is not given the issue's number.
2. Four of these are not numbered, one issue (401) was written by Budgell, and three extracts are of uncertain authorship (from Nos. 425 and 404).
3. It must be pointed out that Addison is also the most prominent contributor to Fogg's list of what he terms "promiscuous" examples. The league table of the contributors of bad English consists of the following: Addison (8); Shakespeare (7); Milton (6); Pope (6); Dryden (3).
4. Examples of these grammarians are notably who Alston labels the "schoolmaster" grammarians, like Gough (1751) and Dilworth (1754), who tend to list obsolete forms next to current ones, without comment. See Note 14.

5. See Appendix for a brief biographical profile of each author.
6. I have not included verse for analysis in the samples from these miscellanies.
7. The other emerging construction of most note is the progressive (or expanded) construction, which I will not discuss in this paper.
8. Tieken-Boon van Ostade's figures (1987: 128–130) indicate that Addison has a comparatively low incidence of *do*-less negative sentences for the century – only 12.2% (in a sample of 25,000 words from the *Spectator*). Tieken divides her authors into two groups: the first consists of those authors who have a low relative frequency, the second has those with a high relative frequency. I highlight those who are active in the first half of the century, and are thus roughly contemporary with Addison:
   a. *Lady Mary Wortley Montagu* (1.85%); Burke (3.57%); Smollett (8.33%); Walpole (9.42%); *Steele* (9.68%); *Addison* (12.2%); Boswell (13.51%); *Johnson* (14.29%); Gibbon (16.67%); Paine (19.44%); *Fielding* (22.22%);
   b. Goldsmith (38.46%); *Defoe* (45.24%); *Swift* (52.38%); *Richardson* (52.94%); Burney (75%). I assume that the discrepancy between my figures and hers for Addison, Steele and Swift is not significant, resulting possibly from different size samples.
9. Tieken-Boon van Ostade (1987) deals with the *do*-less negative construction in considerable detail as type 1 of her ten target constructions. For a detailed discussion and survey, to which I am indebted, and a different perspective, see in particular, pages 35–39.
10. One of the verbs which seems to be overall most resistant to the support of *do* – *know* – receives a rather mixed treatment from Addison. The other authors have a far wider range of verbs which occur without *do*: *guess, name, come, deny* (Steele); *value, let* (Swift); *meddle* (Whiston); *mistake, disdain, reach, enter, discover, fail* (Shaftesbury); *deserve, discharge, bring, find, see, start; forgive* (Centlivre). Many of them share the verbs *care* and *think*.
11. This construction tallies with Tieken-Boon van Ostade's type 4 negative (1987: 45–47). Masatomo Ukaji (1990) presents an exploratory paper on the "transitional" or "bridging" historical status of this construction. I await his development of that paper with interest.
12. Tieken-Boon van Ostade (1987: 217) points out that Johnson is one of the few mid eighteenth-century commentators on language who does isolate novel forms from his observations of contemporary practice; and that he is the first to comment on the use of *do* as a pro-verb (to refer anaphorically to an activity already mentioned in the text). "To Do is used for any verb to save the repetition of the word; as, *I shall come, but if I do not, go away*, that is, *if I not come* [sic]." His comment is supported by illustrative quotation from Sidney and Tillotson; more pertinently, he includes evidence from eighteenth-century authors – Arbuthnot (for *do*) but also Pope. This point should not altogether surprise, since Johnson was also engaged in explicitly literary criticism of the work of (at least near) contemporaries. For further discussion comparing Johnson's comments

with those of contemporary and near contemporary grammarians on dummy *do*, see in addition, Tieken-Boon van Ostade (1988).
13. See for instance, the treatment of dummy auxiliary *do* by White (1761), Fenning (1771), Webster (1784), Fogg (1792) and Murray (1795).
14. See Alston's prefatory note to Dilworth's *A New Guide to the English Tongue* in the Scolar Facsimile Edition (English Linguistic Number 4).
15. Table 3 is presented here with a list of some of the verbs which feature prominently in the declarative sentences with *do* for each author:

Do decl	Addison	Steele	Swift	Shaftes.	Whiston	Centlivre	Boyer
	9	12	29	1	87	18	32
	promise	destroy	reason	*do but	profess	belye	believe
	confess	murder	vary	keep	believe	content	affirm
	put	want	endeavour		pray	look	assure
	propose	resolve	imagine		endeavour		take
	apprehend		deserve		assert		perform
	produce	stay	overthrow				thank

16. Tieken-Boon van Ostade remarks on some of these expressions in Addison as "an instance of legal or semi-legal language, comparable to a formulaic expression such as *I do promise and solemnly swear*" (1987: 69).
17. The use of an adverbial with declarative *do* is another of Tieken-Boon van Ostade's ten construction types (1987: 119–121). She argues that the occurrence of *but* in this construction is common in the "language of direct speech" and therefore appears to be "particularly characteristic of the medium speech in writing" (1987: 120).
18. *The Lives of Dryden, Pope and Addison with Critical Observations on their Works* (pp. 66–67). Johnson comments: "His prose is the model of the middle style; on grave subjects not formal, on light occasions not grovelling; pure without scrupulosity, and exact without apparent elaboration; always equable, and always easy, without glowing words or pointed sentences. ... It was apparently his principal endeavour to avoid all harshness and severity of diction; he is therefore sometimes verbose in his transitions and connections, and sometimes descends too much to the language of conversation; yet if his language had been less idiomatical, it might have lost somewhat of its genuine Anglicism. ... His sentences have neither studied amplitude, nor affected brevity; his periods, though not diligently rounded, are voluble and easy. Whoever wishes to attain an English style, familiar but not coarse, and elegant but not ostentatious, must give his days and nights to the volumes of Addison." (Edition printed in 1777, by J. Parker & Co., Oxford.)
19. First worth noting is the fact that none makes any distinction between restrictive and nonrestrictive relative clauses. The consequence is very often that the

examples that they use to illustrate both proper and improper usage include nonrestrictive and well as restrictive relatives. The question of even identifying the distinction between restrictive and nonrestrictive relatives in the eighteenth century is a vexed one. For one thing, it is completely inappropriate to allow punctuation to act as a simple guide to the distinction between restrictive and nonrestrictive relatives, since it appears to function prosodically rather than syntactically. Lowth's practical guide to punctuation (incidentally using Addison as a model) demonstrates the folly of relying solely on punctuation. He praises Addison for his measured and well-judged use of punctuation, including in his text for analysis, restrictive relatives separated from their antecedents by commas and semi-colons. Consequently, I have tried to rigorously apply a combination of syntactic, semantic and punctuation criteria, but admit that there may yet be some equivocal examples in the sample.

20. Fell (1784) for example, is comparatively unknowledgeable on relative clauses. Not only does he not mention zero-relatives; he also lumps together restrictive and nonrestrictive relatives as a matter of course. This is evident in the following comment, which is concerned with agreement and government: "Sometimes another verb, with its nominative case, will come between the relative and that verb, to which the relative is nominative case; yet the agreement between the relative and its proper verb will be evident; thus, it was said, that the people, *who*, whilst they fought for their own interest, *had been* invincible, being enslaved, were grown sordid and base" (109).

21. *Table 4a.* (Restrictive) relative clauses: personal antecedents: raw figures

	Shaftes.	Swift	Steele	Addi.	Boyer	Whist.	Centliv.
wh1	79	127	238	210	37	40	22
th+	–	23	23	122	26	32	45
∅+	6	8	27	16	4	2	24
100% =	85	158	335	348	67	74	91

22. *Table 6a.* (Restrictive) relative clauses: nonpersonal antecedents: raw figures

	Shaftes.	Addi.	Steele	Whist.	Swift	Centli.	Boyer
wh2	105	318	204	96	78	32	47
th–	2	242	64	53	50	33	63
∅–	23	65	124	69	53	43	97
wh3	4	21	38	11	25	3	9
100% =	134	646	430	228	206	111	216

23. The axis of modernity is based on the percentage proportion of *do*-negative sentences for the writers in my corpus; see Table 2. The axis of propriety is based on the percentage proportion of *wh*-pronouns (both personal and nonpersonal) of

overall relative markers. The values for *wh*-pronouns are as follows: Shaftesbury: 84%; Steele: 58%; Swift: 56%; Addison: 53%; Whiston: 45%; Boyer: 30%; Centlivre: 27%.
24. See above, Note 18.
25. It is worth pointing out that Addison not only alters markers of restrictive relative clauses; he also changes nonrestrictive relative markers and demonstrative pronouns. His evident concern with replacing the word *that*, whether relative or demonstrative pronoun, suggests that he is more concerned with the word itself than with the structure of relative clauses per se. The following examples (from Bond's 1965 edition of *The Spectator*) illustrate this point, suggesting that the overall concern is to avoid repetition of *that* on the one hand, and *which* on the other:

> The Shepherd's Pipe may be said to be full of Musick, for it is composed of nine different kinds of Verses, *which* [F: that] by their several Lengths resemble the nine Stops of the [F: that] old musical Instrument, *that* [F: which] is likewise the Subject of the Poem, (Bond 1965: 246).

Flavors of alteration (variation, avoidance of repetition):

> (a) Several Hours of the Day hang upon our Hands, nay we wish away whole Years, and travel through Times as through a Country [F: *that is*] filled with many wild and empty Wastes, *which* we would fain hurry over, *that* we may arrive at those Several little Settlements or imaginary Points of Rest *which* are dispersed up and down it.
> (b) There is another kind of Virtue *that* [F: which] may find Employment for those Retired Hours in *which* we are altogether left to ourselves, and destitute of Company and Conversation; I mean, that Intercourse and Communication *which* every reasonable Creature ought to maintain with the great Author of his Being. (Bond 1965: 395).

26. *The Spectator* first appeared in folio, as a daily periodical. Bond (1965: Introduction) reports that it sold for a penny until the imposition of stamp tax forced the price to rise to tuppence in August 1712. Circulation up until the stamp tax was approximately 4000 daily. Afterwards, the average print run was 1700. Different issues were more popular than others – No. 384 had a circulation of more than 14,000. Copies were delivered to homes, as well as being sold by street vendors, and at booksellers and "newsshops". Back copies were made available after its first month. Addison and Steele edited and published the folios as a collected edition in 1714.
27. He is careful to guide his readers away from the mistaken assumption that formal "forced" conceits, epigrams and turns of wit are indices of good literature. And he urges them towards the work of the critics who can discourse more on "the very Spirit and soul of fine Writing" rather than simply enumerate the mechanical

rules ("which a man of very little taste" but presumably some formal instruction may discourse upon) (*Spectator* 409).

28. Yet while elegance and good breeding may appear necessary preconditions for having taste, they are by no means sufficient. Johnson is scathing about the merely fashionable gentleman who, "instead of endeavoring at purity or propriety, has no other care than to catch the reigning phrase and current exclamation, till by copying whatever is peculiar in the talk of all those whose birth or fortune entitle them to imitation, he has collected every fashionable barbarism of the present winter." (*Rambler* 194, Jan. 1752). Swift too, targets polite fashionable society for satirical treatment in his *Polite Conversations* (1737). See Matthews (1937) for an informal but suggestive discussion.
29. In his own time, Lowth and Fell among many eighteenth-century grammarians, and Johnson and Blair among the century's critics valourize Addison as a graceful exponent of the polite, easy style. In the nineteenth, Lucy Aikin in her *Life of Addison* (1834) exemplifies the later appreciation that his work receives in the nineteenth century. She quotes too, from early nineteenth-century purists like Anna Laetitia Barbauld, who published a selection of articles from the *Spectator*, *Tatler*, *Guardian* and *Freeholder* for the instruction and edification of young women (1804). This quotation is interesting for the reassessment it contains of Addison in the light of Samuel Johnson's waning popularity as a prose writer. I am indebted to Professor Carey McIntosh for pointing out Barbauld's concern with Addison.
30. For extensive discussion of the relation between authority and standardization, see Milroy – Milroy (1985).

Appendix: Biographical Sketches
(Principal source: *Chambers Encyclopaedia of English Literature*)

Joseph Addison. Born 1672, educated at Charterhouse (with Steele) and Magdalen College, Oxford. He was elected to a Fellowship (1698), which he held (mainly out of residence) till 1711. He prepared for a diplomatic career by travelling Europe (1699–1703). He wrote opera, Latin and English poems. He became Under-Secretary of State (1706–1708), and then Secretary to the Lord Lieutenant in Ireland (1709). He joined Steele on the *Tatler* and the *Spectator*. He wrote a play *Cato*, the Grand Tour memoirs: *Letter from Italy*. Died 1719.

Abel Boyer. Born 1667, in Languedoc. Protestant refugee who wrote histories of William III, and of Queen Anne, a Life of Sir William Temple, and other historical and miscellaneous works. He founded the monthly magazine *Political State of Great Britain*, which ran to 38 volumes (1711–1729). Pope hated him, and gave him a place in the *Dunciad*. Died in London 1729.

Susannah Centlivre (née Freeman). Born 1670 in Ireland. Runs away from home at fifteen and becomes a strolling player. Her first play: *The Perjur'd Husband*, or, *The Adventures of Venice* premiered at Drury Lane in 1700. In 1707, she married Joseph Centlivre, "Yeoman to the Mouth of Queen Anne". She had sixteen comedies performed between 1702–1722, including the hits *Busie-Body* (475 performances in London theatres 1711–1800) and *Wonder! Mar-Plot*, the sequel to *Busie-Body*, was a comparative flop, with seven performances in the 1711 season. She also published poetry and contributed occasionally to the *Female Tatler*. The accession of George I (1714), brought her an increase in Royal patronage. She died in 1723.

Anthony Ashley Cooper (third Earl of Shaftesbury). Born 1671. He was first tutored by John Locke, and then attended Winchester School. He took his place in the Commons before succeeding to his title in 1699. He suffered from ill-health and withdrew from public life, eventually retiring to Italy in 1711. His main work is *Characteristicks of Men, Manners and Opinions* (1711). Died in 1713.

Richard Steele. Born 1672, educated at Charterhouse and Merton College, Oxford. He left university without taking his degree to enlist in the Duke of Ormonde's regiment of horse guards in 1694. While Captain of the Tower Guard, he wrote his first book, *The Christian Hero* (1701). He produced comedies, contributed poetry to monthly miscellanies like *The Muses Mercury* (1707). He went into politics, and wrote the official *Gazette* (1707–1710). He then started his periodical writing with the *Tatler*, and then followed the *Spectator, Guardian, The Reader* (1714), *Town-Talk* (1715–1716), *The Tea Table* (1715–1716) and *Chit Chat* (1716). In 1719, he was expelled from Parliament, and his politics lost him the post of Governor of Drury Lane Theatre. He turned to invention and died in 1729.

Jonathan Swift. Born 1667, educated at Trinity College, Dublin. He came to England in 1688 as secretary to Sir William Temple. He returned to Dublin in 1694, and was ordained an Anglican priest. He became chaplain to the Earl of Berkeley (1700) and published *Tale of a Tub* and *Battle of the Books* (1704). He moved to London (1708) and became involved in ecclesiastical politics, writing many of his pamphlets – *Conduct of the Allies* (1711), *Remarks on the Barrier Treaty* (1712). He was appointed Dean of St Patrick's Cathedral, Dublin (1713), and there wrote his *Drapier's Letters* (1724), *Gulliver's Travels* (1726). Pope edited four volumes of Swift's work as Miscellanies (1727–1732). He died in 1745.

William Whiston. Born 1667 in Leicestershire. An accomplished but eccentric theologian. Elected a Fellow of Clare's College, Cambridge (1693), then appointed chaplain to the Bishop of Norwich and (1698) rector of Lowestoft. His *Theory of the Earth* (1696) led to his election in 1703 as Newton's successor as Lucasian Professor of Mathematics, Cambridge. His exponence of Arianisim led to his professorship being taken away from him (1710) and his eventual expulsion from the University. Patrons included Addison, and admirers included Lady Mary Wortley Montagu. His *Primitive Christianity Revived* is the clearest expression of his theology, in which he argued that the doctrine of the Trinity was unscriptural. He spent the remainder of his life in London, and died in 1752.

References

Adamson, Sylvia – Vivien Law – Nigel Vincent – Susan Wright (eds.)
    1990   *Papers from the 5th International Conference on English Historical Linguistics*. Amsterdam, Philadelphia: Benjamins.

Addison, Joseph
    See   Bond, Donald F. (ed.)

Aikin, Lucy
    1843   *Life of Joseph Addison* (2 vols). London.

Anderson, Howard – J.S. Shea (eds.)
    1967   *Studies in criticism and aesthetics 1660–1800: Essays in honor of Samuel Monk*. Minneapolis: University of Minnesota Press.

Atkins, John W.H.
    1951   *English literary criticism, 17th and 18th centuries*. London: Methuen.

Austin, Frances O.
    1985   "Relative *which* in late 18th-century usage: The Clift family correspondence", in: Roger Eaton – Olga Fischer – Willem Koopman – Frederike van der Leek (eds.), 15–29.

Baker, Robert
    1770   *Reflections on the English language*. London.
    [1968]   [Reprinted in: Robin C. Alston (ed.), *English Linguistics, 1500–1800*. 87. Menston: Scolar Press.]

Barrell, John
    1983   *English literature in history, 1730–80: An equal, wide survey*. London: Hutchinson.

Berger, Dieter A.
    1978   *Die Konversationskunst in England, 1660–1740. Ein Sprechphänomen und seine literarische Gestaltung*. München: Fink.

Biber, Douglas – Finegan, Ed
    n.d.   "Drift in five 'spoken' and written English genres since the seventeenth century". [Paper presented at the Sixth International Conference on English Historical Linguistics, May, Helsinki.]

Bloom, Edward A. – Bloom, Lillian D. (eds.)
    1980   *Addison and Steele: The critical heritage*. London: Routledge & Kegan Paul.

1984 "Joseph Addison: The artist in the mirror", in: *Educating the audience: Addison, Steele and eighteenth century culture*. California: William Andrews Clark Memorial Library, UCLA.

Bogel, Frederic
 1987 "Johnson and the role of authority", in: Felicity Nussbaum & Laura Brown (eds.), 109–209.

Bond, Donald F. (ed.)
 1965 *The Spectator*. Vol. I. Oxford: Clarendon Press.

Boyer, Abel
 1711 *The political state of Great Britain*. London.

Centlivre, Susanna
 1711 *Mar-Plot*. London.
 1714 *The wonder! A woman keeps a secret*. London.

Chambers Encyclopaedia of English literature
 1902 Vol. 2. Edinburgh.

Cooper, Anthony Ashley (Shaftesbury)
 1711 *Characteristicks of men and manners*. Vol. I. London.

Cowler, Rosemary (ed.)
 1988 *The prose works of Alexander Pope*. Volume 2. 1725–1744. Oxford: Blackwell.

Crowley, Tony
 1989 *The politics of discourse: The standard language question in British cultural debates*. London: Macmillan.

Dilworth, Thomas
 1751 *A New Guide to the English Tongue*. London.
 [1974] [Reprinted in: Robin C. Alston (ed.), *English Linguistics* 4. Menston: Scolar Press.]

Dobson, Eric J.
 1955 "Early Modern standard English", *Transactions of the Philological Society*: 25–54.

Eaton, Roger – Olga Fischer – Willem Koopman – Frederike van der Leek (eds.)
 1985 *Papers from the 4th International Conference on English Historical Linguistics*. (Current Issues in Linguistic Theory 41.) Amsterdam: Benjamins.

Fell, John
 1784 *An essay towards English grammar*. London.
 [1974] [Reprinted in: Robin C. Alston (ed.), *English Linguistics* 16. Menston: Scolar Press.]

Fogg, Peter Walkden
 1792–96 *Elementa Anglicana or The Principles of English Grammar*.
 [1974] [Reprinted in: Robin C. Alston (ed.), *English Linguistics* 25. Menston: Scolar Press.]

Gough, James
   1754   *A Practical Grammar of the English Tongue*. Dublin.
   [1974] [Reprinted in: Robin C. Alston (ed.), *English Linguistics* 13. Menston: Scolar Press.]

Grijzenhout, Janet
   1992   "The change of relative *that* to *who* and *which* in late seventeenth century comedies", *NOWELE* 20: 33–52.

Johnson, Samuel
   1755   *Dictionary* (including *Grammar*). London: Rivington.
   1777   *The lives of Dryden, Pope and Addison with critical observations on their works*. Oxford: Parker.

Kahlas-Tarkka, Leena (ed.)
   1987   *Neophilogica Fennica*. (Mémoires de la Société Néophilologique de Helsinki 45). Helsinki: Société Néophilologique.

Kirkby, John
   1746   *A New English Grammar*. London.
   [1974] [Reprinted in: Robin C. Alston (ed.), *English Linguistics* 297. Menston: Scolar Press.]

Leonard, Sterling A.
   1929   *The doctrine of correctness in English usage, 1700–1800*. Madison: University of Wisconsin.

Lowth, Robert
   1762   *A short introduction to English grammar*. London.
   [1967] [Reprinted in: Robin C. Alston (ed.), *English Linguistics, 1500–1800*. 18. Menston: Scolar Press.]

Matthews, William
   1937   "Polite speech in the eighteenth century", *English*. Vol. 1, No. 6: 493–511.

Milroy, James – Lesley Milroy
   1985   *Authority in language*. London: Routledge.

Nevalainen, Terttu
   1987   "Change from above: A morphosyntactic comparison of two Early Modern English editions of *The Book of Common Prayer*", in: L. Kahlas-Tarkka (ed.), 295–315.

Nussbaum, Felicity – Laura Brown (eds.)
   1987   *The new eighteenth century*. London: Methuen.

Pickbourn, James
   1789   *A dissertation on the English verb*. London.
   [1974] [Reprinted in: Robin C. Alston (ed.), *English Linguistics* 107. Menston: Scolar Press.]

Priestley, Joseph
    1761   *The rudiments of English grammar*. London.
    [1974] [Reprinted in: Robin C. Alston (ed.), *English Linguistics* 210. Menston: Scolar Press.]
Romaine, Suzanne
    1982   *Sociohistorical linguistics*. Cambridge: Cambridge University Press.
Sedger, John
    1798   *Structure of the English language*. London.
    [1974] [Reprinted in: Robin C. Alston (ed.), *English Linguistics* 237. Menston: Scolar Press.]
Steele, Richard
    See   Bond, Donald F. (ed.)
Stein, Dieter
    1990   *The semantics of syntactic change: Aspects of the evolution of "do" in English*. (Trends in Linguistics; Studies and Monographs 47.) Berlin: Mouton de Gruyter.
Swift, Jonathan
    1711   *Miscellanies in prose and verse*. Facsimile Reprint. London.
    1735   *A proposal for correcting the English tongue, polite conversation, etc..* London.
    [1964] [Reprinted Oxford: Blackwell.]
Sykes Davies, Hugh – George Watson (eds.)
    1964   *The English mind: Studies in the English moralists*. Cambridge: Cambridge University Press.
Tieken-Boon van Ostade, Ingrid
    1987   *The auxiliary do in eighteenth-century English: A sociohistorical-linguistic approach*. Dordrecht: Foris Publications.
    1988   "Dr Johnson and the auxiliary *do*". *Hiroshima Studies in English Language and Literature* 33: 22–49.
    1990   "Exemplification in eighteenth-century grammars", in: Sylvia Adamson – Vivien Law – Nigel Vincent – Susan Wright (eds.), 481–496.
Ussher, George Neville
    1785   *The elements of English grammar*. Gloucester.
    [1974] [Reprinted in: Robin C. Alston (ed.), *English Linguistics* 27. Menston: Scolar Press.]
Visser, Fredericus Th.
    1969–73 *Historical syntax of the English language*. 3 vols. Leiden: Brill.
Ward, William
    1765   *An essay on grammar*. London.
    [1974] [Reprinted in: Robin C. Alston (ed.), *English Linguistics* 15. Menston: Scolar Press.]
Whiston, William
    1711   *Primitive Christianity revived*. Vol. 1. London.

White, James
    1761   *The English verb*. London.
    [1974] [Reprinted in: Robin C. Alston (ed.), *English Linguistics* 135. Menston: Scolar Press.]
Williams, Raymond (rev. ed.)
    1983   *Keywords: A vocabulary of culture and society*. London: Fontana Press.

The effect of exposure to standard English: The language of William Clift

Frances Austin

1. Introduction

By the end of the eighteenth century a standard form of written English had been almost fully established. That this was used by all people of education is axiomatic. But how far would it have been known to and espoused by the general working populace, especially those who did not live in London, the hub of polite society?

It is an accident that the letters of a family of the artisan class, living in the remote south western county of Cornwall, have survived. It is no accident that such letters existed. That both men and women of the humbler classes, in Cornwall and elsewhere, could read and write and that these accomplishments were considered a matter of course is well attested in the Clift letters. Elementary education outside the traditional grammar schools was more widespread, at least for boys, than is generally assumed (Austin 1969: 19–21). This was often provided by Writing Schools that concentrated on "reading, writing and casting accounts". Such schools undoubtedly helped to make young boys of the lower classes aware of a standard form of the language that was quite far removed from their own regional and "non-standard" speech. Most girls, on the other hand, almost certainly had no formal schooling but somehow they, too, acquired the rudiments of reading and writing. Perhaps they were taught by the lady of the local squire or the wife and daughters of the clergyman. However they learned, they could more often than not read and write after a fashion.

When I first began to analyze the Clift letters I believed that they would reveal a language similar to speech or as near speech as we could now reasonably hope to find. Over the years I have become convinced that this is not the case. It is clear that as soon as these people took up a pen they framed their minds to a formal mode of thinking. Of course they would retain the grammatical habits of their speech, but no glossary of the dialect is needed to understand what they wrote as is sometimes required for reconstructions of dialect in writing. To a greater or lesser degree, according to their individual capabilities, they aspired to the standard form of written English of the time. Their mastery of spelling, vocabulary and sentence structure varies but their letters are neither markedly dialectal nor colloquial. The level of writing is erratic but they are literary even if in a sense illiterate. There are flashes of vivid immediacy and drama that match anything written by the novelists of the day. These are naturally not sustained but the letters are composed in the true sense of that word.

The letters of William Clift, the youngest and most able of the family, may, therefore, seem surprisingly standard even at the time when he had barely left behind his provincial and humble home. However, it is possible to see a quite distinct move in certain areas towards the accepted standard, as minor dialectisms and non-standard or archaic usages are dropped and replaced by standard or prestige forms. This applies only to Clift's letters, because the other members of the family remained at their original social level while he moved inexorably up the social scale. His letters, therefore, are of interest for tracing the influence of sustained exposure to standard English on someone of a social class below those whose writings are more usually available.

2. Background

William Clift was born in Bodmin in Cornwall, the farthest west of the southern English counties, in 1775. His father was a journeyman miller, who eked out a livelihood for his large family by making walking sticks and fishing rods and by setting hedges. He was, therefore, little more than a laborer, although according to Clift he could "read well, and write very tolerably" (see Austin 1991: 19). He died when Clift was seven years old. Thereafter, his mother supported the family, helped by his two sisters, working for fourpence a day spinning and carding wool. Out of this meagre income, Clift's mother managed to save the few pennies a week needed for his schooling. It seems likely that he went to a Writing School, where he was evidently a bright pupil and excelled in handwriting. In later life he boasted in a letter to his daughter that he "beat" his schoolmaster and all his family at "print hand by their own unanimous confession" (21–22 August 1841; unpub. ms). In the evenings, however, he had to help augment the family income by winding the wool spun during the day. Schooldays came to an abrupt end when he was eleven and his mother died. An apprenticeship to a nurseryman did not work out. It lasted possibly two years at most. He was dismissed for drawing a caricature sketch of the irascible nurseryman, who informed the young Clift that he was "not in want of a Botanical draughtsman" (Austin 1991: 22). There followed four or five years of casual employment, mainly the running of errands for a Bodmin businessman. Clift's leisure hours were spent in the kitchen at the Priory, the home of the Squire, where he amused the servants by drawing pictures. His skill attracted the notice of Nancy Gilbert, the Squire's lady, and it was through her good offices that at the age of seventeen he was apprenticed to John Hunter. Hunter was the most eminent surgeon and anatomist of his day – he was the founder of modern surgery – and in 1792 he was in need of an amanuensis to make drawings of his biological specimens and take notes at dictation. Clift, therefore, was removed from his humble background in a remote county town and transported to one of the largest and most cultivated households in London.[1] Here he would have come into daily contact not only with Hunter himself but with all the eminent medical men and natural scientists of the day, even though he lived mainly in the servants' quarters. After eighteen months, in October 1793, Hunter died and the household was broken up. Although his letters contain references to the two executors, Dr. Matthew Baillie and Everard (later Sir Everard) Home, and to other medical "gentlemen" who came to stay in the house, Clift's principal companions were again servants and people of the lower orders.

If we consider Clift's humble background and rudimentary education, which he might well have forgotten during his rather idle early teens, it is surprising that his language was as standard as it appears from the first letters he wrote home in 1792. He rarely uses a dialect word, although traces of dialect usage can be found in his grammar and idiom. His spelling has occasional aberrations but is virtually standard and he could write lively coherent prose from the beginning. Nonetheless, in the first years that he spent in London his use of English moved increasingly towards the accepted norm. His anxiety to improve himself influences the tone and attitudes of all his letters, even though the only thing which he commented on explicitly was his progress – or lack of it – in drawing. His extant letters to his brothers and sisters run continuously from 1792 to 1801. After that, apart from one letter in draft, there is a gap of some eighteen years. For the years 1799 to 1801 only one letter remains for each year.[2] One or two features from different areas of his language have been selected to illustrate the progression towards a standard form.

3. William Clift's language

3.1. Grammar

3.1.1. Verb forms

Grammatical usage is one productive area for examining Clift's shift towards a standard. Verb forms, in particular, are useful here. One of these, although there are relatively few occurrences, is the 3rd person singular of the verb *do* (see Table 1). In his early letters Clift occasionally uses the form *do* beside *does*. The only other member of the family to use this form is Elizabeth Clift and it is probably dialectal. *Do* is a regular form for the 3rd person present singular in all south western dialects. It is still used periphrastically in affirmative statements in West Wiltshire and Dorset and Central and West Cornwall (Wakelin 1986: 36–38). It is probable that these two regions originally extended across the whole of the South western dialect area (Wakelin 1986: 38; Wright 1905: 296–297). There is only one example of a periphrastic *do* in an affirmative clause in Clift's letters and this is doubtful. Nearly all of his uses of 3rd person singular *do* or *does* are necessarily auxiliary verbs and, not surprising in letters in which questions are infrequent, all of these are in negative statements. There is variation between the full form *does not* and the contracted form *don't*. There is also one occurrence of *do not* in a letter of 1794 but this is closely followed by the form *does not* in an identical construction:

> Please to tell her from me that if she do not write in a Short time I shall give her up and strike her off my lists for I am sure if she does not write oftener than she writes to me she will soon forget to write at all (27 September 1794).

Table 1. Clift's use of *do/does* variation in 3rd person singular

	does	does not	do	don't
1792				
1793		xxxxx	xx	x
1794	x	xx	x (not)	xxx
1795		xxx		
1796		xxx		
1797	x			
1798	x		x	
1799–1801				

Altogether there are only four instances of *don't* against twelve of *does not*. The last use of *don't* occurs in 1794, and even in 1793 (there are no examples of either form in 1792) Clift prefers *does not*, using it five times and *don't* only once. The preference for the uncontracted form may be part of Clift's rejection of abbreviations (see section 3.6). Not surprisingly, there is no instance of a contracted form *doesn't*, as this did not appear until the mid-nineteenth century (Dykema 1947: 371). Of the total number of eight *do* forms, five are auxiliaries. One is an affirmative pro-form and the remaining two are contrastive uses of the verb, although one could be, as stated earlier, a dialectal non-emphatic use:

> It is by acting contrary to our reason that all the mischief which happens to mankind do arise ... (9 January 1798).

This, however, occurs in a letter written in 1798, long after Clift had abandoned most of his dialectal idioms and usages. It seems more likely that it is an example of an emphatic *do* of "implicit contrast" (Osselton 1983: 471; Tieken-Boon van Ostade 1987: 48). The contrast is "hidden" and must be recovered from the context, although, in this case, it is also indicated by the cleft form of the sentence. Two of Clift's three uses of affirmative *does* are main verbs. Nowhere does he use *do* as a main verb in the 3rd person singular.[3] The third use of affirmative *does* is as a pro-form. One question remains. Why, if Clift abandoned *don't* as part of his rejection of contractions generally, did he prefer *does not* rather than *do not* as early as 1793? As we shall see later, he quickly discarded other dialect forms, and this is the likely answer. However, he seems to have retained the form *do* for particular functions, notably to indicate emphasis.

The preterite forms of the verb *be* illustrate Clift's tendency towards the current standard rather more clearly, partly because they occur more frequently (see Table 2). Generally, the members of the family show a tendency to level the preterite forms of this verb under either *was* or *were*. Rogers (1979: 41) says that in south western dialect "both *was* and *were* can be used for all subjects". John (b. 1759) and Joanna (b. 1755) favor *were* for all persons, both singular and plural, and Elizabeth (b. 1757) uses *was*. Clift is closer, at least initially, to his elder sister Elizabeth. His usage following directly after pronouns differs significantly from other subject forms. Clift uses *was* only once in the first person plural after *we*, and that is in his first letter in 1792. In the same letter he uses *we were* three times. A co-ordinate 1st person plural subject with *were* occurs once in 1797. No instance of a plural 2nd person subject occurs until 1794 when Clift uses *were*. The subject is a co-ordinate one, as are all instances of the 2nd person plural, and *were*

Table 2. Clift's use of preterite plural forms of *to be*

		was	were
1792	we	x	xxx
	you	(x)	
	they	x	
	3 plural	x x^c x^{rel}	
1793	we		
	you		
	they	x	xxxxx
	3 plural	xxx xx^c xx^{there}	xx xxx^c x^{rel} x^{there}
1794	we		
	you		x^c
	they		xxxxx
	3 plural	x	x^c
1795	we		
	you	(x)	
	they		
	3 plural		
1796	we		
	you	(xxx)	x^c
	they		xxxxxxx
	3 plural	x^c	x x^c x^{rel}
1797	we		x^c
	you	xxxxxxx	(xx) x^c
	they		x
	3 plural	x^{there}	
1798	we		
	you		(x)
	they		
	3 plural		xx xx^{rel}
1799	we		
	you	(xx)	(xx)
	they		
	3 plural		(x)
1800			
1801	we		
	you	(x)	
	they		x
	3 plural		

(x) = singular subject
^{c} = co-ordinate subject
^{rel} = in relative clause
^{there} = foll. initial *there*

is invariable in this position. With the 3rd person after the pronoun *they*, however, a shift in usage is marked. In 1792 there is only one example and Clift uses *was*. In 1793 there are five instances of *were* to one of *was*. The last example of *was* after *they* occurs in 1794 and then it is distanced from the verb:

> they both came out in their night gowns and was very glad to see me (16 March 1794).

Other instances of 3rd person plural subjects vary, partly according to the form of the subject. In 1792 there are three instances of a plural subject with *was* and none with *were*. By 1793 the forms have levelled up: seven examples with *was* and seven with *were*. Thereafter very few instances with *was* and a plural subject occur, and then only if the subject is at a distance from the verb or if two single co-ordinate subjects are used. The last occurrence in Clift's letters, in 1797, is particularly understandable, following initial *there* and continuing "there was but one or two of ...". After 1794 there is no instance of a single word plural subject, e.g., *gentlemen* with a following *was*, and the last occurrence (27 September 1794) is itself accounted for by the distance between subject and verb and the attraction of a singular object:

> the men that did help this old bawd was drest in soldiers Clothes ...

In the preterite plural of the verb *be*, therefore, Clift's usage changed rapidly after his arrival in London and by 1794 was virtually standard.

The 2nd person singular *you was* follows a rather different pattern. This is not surprising in view of its widespread usage among speakers of standard English at the time. *Was* for the 2nd person singular was almost universal from the sixteenth to eighteenth centuries. It is found in the later eighteenth century in letters of such literary writers as Cowper, Gray and Gibbon. According to Wyld (1936: 356–357), however, in Jane Austen's novels only the vulgar characters, such as Lucy Steele, use *you was*. Phillipps (1970: 159) comes to the same conclusion, adding that it was the result of the strictures of the eighteenth-century grammarians. The opinion of the grammarians was, however, divided. A few, such as Blair (1783) and Webster (1789, 1798), condoned the use and Campbell (1776) admitted it in colloquial language – perhaps on the strength of its appearance in letters. Lowth (1762), Priestley (1761) and Withers (1788) were strongly against the form. Lowth, in particular, attacked it as an "enormous Solecism", although he admitted that "Authors of the first rank have inadvertently fallen into it" (Lowth 1762: 35, n.7). Clift uses *you was* regularly up to 1797. In that year he has two instances of singular *you were*, although one could be a subjunctive: "*If you were ...*". This is unlikely, however, as he rarely, if ever, uses the subjunctive elsewhere. In 1798 and 1799 he has three examples of *you were* for the singular, but there are two instances of *you was* in 1799 and one of *you was* in 1801. There does, therefore, seem to be a slight shift to what was becoming the standard form in the late eighteenth century, but Clift's adherence to *you was* is not altogether surprising. He must have heard a number of older educated speakers using the form and it is, of course, still widespread among non-standard speakers today.

3.1.2. Relative pronouns[4]

Clift's use of relatives is much more complicated than his use of verbs but it also shows the way in which he attempted to conform to what he believed to be correct usage (see Table 3). The more obvious non-standard use of *which* as a personal relative, which other members of the family use,[5] appears only twice in his letters, once in 1793 and once in 1795. It is possible that he used it more frequently than the corpus indicates, but the very occasional instances seem to be slips rather than any consistent practice. More important is the variation between the WH- forms and *that*. This was a subject of much controversy among the eighteenth-century grammarians, and, generally, the usage of *that* was condemned. Probably the best-known argument against the use of *that* appears in issue no. 78 (1711) of *The Spectator*, entitled 'The Humble Petition of Who and Which' (Bond 1965: I, 334–336). Hornsey is tentative in his view on the matter; he states: "*That* is perhaps better expressed with who and which" (Hornsey 1793: 24). Lowth takes a slightly different approach, allowing *that* for things but not for persons: "That is used indifferently of persons and things; but perhaps would be more properly confined to the latter" (Lowth 1762: 100). James Buchanan is more dogmatic: "That is often used, but inelegantly, for *who, whom* and *which*" (Buchanan 1767: 74). William Ward on the other hand accepts the use of *that* as a matter of course: "Either sort of objects with 'the powers of speech and intelligence' or without may be represented by the relative 'that'" (Ward 1765: 136).

In his early letters Clift uses both *which* and *that* about equally. *Who* is noticeably lacking from the letters until 1796. There are no occurrences in 1792 and just two or three for each of the following three years. For the first three years of his time in London Clift never uses restrictive *which*. All restrictive clauses, both personal and non-personal, are introduced by *that* or, very occasionally, *who*.[6] In 1795 he first uses *which* for restrictive clauses and this is the first year in which the uses of *which* outnumber those of *that*. The figures for the following year, 1796, are the most surprising. The number

Table 3. Clift's use of relatives

	who	which	that	prep. rel.	s. which	and which	and who
1792							
rp			xxxx	x (whom)	xxx	xx	
rnp			xxxxxx (5)				
nrp			?x				
nrnp		xxxxxxxx					
1793							
rp	x		xxxxx	x (which)	xxx+1rx		
rnp			xxxx (1)	xxx (that)			
nrp	xx						
nrnp		xxxxxx?x (2)					
1794							
rp	xx (1)		xxxxx	x (whom)	xxx	x	x
rnp			x				
nrp	xxx						
nrnp		xx					
1795							
rp	x			x (s which)	x	x	
rnp		xxx	x (1)				
nrp	xx	x (1)	x				
nrnp		xxxx (1)					
1796							
rp	xxxxxxxxxxxxxx	x	xxx	xxxx (which)	xxxxxx	xxxxx	x
rnp		xxxxxx (3)	xx				
nrp	xxxxxxxxxxxxx						
nrnp		xxxxxxxxxxx (4)					
1797							
rp	xxxxx		x (1)	x (which)	xx	xx	
rnp		xx	xxx (1)	x (and which)			
nrp	xxx		x				
nrnp		xx					
1798							
rp	xxxxxx			xx (which)	x		
rnp		xxxx (1)	xx (1)	x (s which)			
nrp							
nrnp		xx					
1799-1800							
rp				xx (which)	x	x	
rnp				x (that)			
nrp	xxx						
nrnp		x					

Note: The number of relatives with object function is shown in brackets following the total, e.g. (2).

rp = restrictive personal
rnp = restrictive non-personal
nrp = non-restrictive personal
nrnp = non-restrictive non-personal
lr = loosely restrictive *which*
?x = not clear if r or nr
s which = sentence antecedent

of relative clauses increases dramatically and the instances of *who* and *which* in both restrictive and non-restrictive clauses almost eclipse *that* altogether. There are, indeed, only five instances of *that*, three in restrictive clauses with a personal antecedent and two in non-restrictive with a non-personal antecedent. Beside these there are six instances of restrictive and eleven of non-restrictive *which*. In this year Clift also uses one *which* with a personal antecedent. More startling still is the use of *who*, which had scarcely occurred at all before this year. There are fifteen instances introducing restrictive clauses and fourteen introducing non-restrictive clauses. The increase in the amount Clift wrote during this year (even more than during his first two years in London) cannot wholly account for this upsurge in his use of relative clauses generally and WH- clauses in particular. Following this peak, relative clauses fall off markedly in the letters of the remaining years. This can be partly accounted for by the fewer numbers of letters, but not completely. In 1797 *that* even makes a slight comeback in proportion to the WH- forms. *Who* appears eight times, *which* four and *that* five.

Apart from one instance in a letter by Elizabeth, Clift is the only one of the family to use *and which* in a non co-ordinate position:

> I told you some time ago that I knew a person onboard the St George and which I think may be very lucky for him ... (3 January 1796).

An example with *and who* is:

> it has been brought forward again in the Parliament House, who appointed a Committee of 30 Gentlemen of the House of Commons to examine a Committee of Medical Men on the worth, and use, of the Collection to the Nation and who have spoke much in its praise (21 March 1796).

Jespersen (1927: 78) notes that, although this form is usually considered an error, it is heard frequently in colloquial English. It was also used in literary writing in the eighteenth century, and Jespersen cites examples from Defoe and Fielding among others; these are two writers whose works Clift was buying in 1793. It is also frequent in Dickens, although usually confined to lower-class characters, and this would seem to indicate that it was a feature of lower-class London speech. Brook (1970: 246) notes the occurrence of *and which* in some of Dickens's lower-class Cockney characters: "The use of *and* together with *which* produces a clause which is neither co-ordinate nor subordinate". He cites Sarah Gamp in *Martin Chuzzlewit* (ch. 40):

> *I maintain my independency with your kind leave, and which I will till death.*

It would be tempting, therefore, to assume that Clift picked up the usage in London, perhaps from the servants or his London acquaintance, or that he came across it in reading. However, it occurs twice in the letters of the first half of 1792 and there is also Elizabeth's one example. It could not, therefore, have been confined to the London area. However, after 1792 it does not appear in Clift's letters again until September 1794 and, as with the other relatives, its occurrence is most frequent in the year 1796, when there are five instances of *and which* and one of *and who*. It occurs most frequently when there is an intervening adjunct – phrase or clause – between it and its antecedent. It is possible that Clift's usage was reinforced by its occurrence in London dialect. It does not appear in the letters after 1800.

Generally, it seems that Clift believed that WH- forms were to be preferred and that this is reflected in his increasing use of them. However, it must also be said that all the Clifts use WH- forms more than they do *that*, in a ratio of between 3:1 and 2:1, with the exception of Elizabeth whose usage is just under 2:1 (Austin 1985: 25, 28). This is not what might be expected from dialect-speaking writers of little or no formal education.[7] However, it must be remembered that as soon as they put pen to paper the Clifts would, consciously or unconsciously, have adopted a formal attitude to the language they were writing. The letters by this kind of writer do not have the easy colloquial style of those by educated correspondents, who differentiate between formal or official letters and those to friends and relatives. The use of opening formulas, which we shall come to later, indicates the frame of mind in which the Clifts set about their epistolary composition. *Which* and *who* have generally been considered more literary and formal relatives than *that*. It has been suggested that at about the beginning of the eighteenth century WH-forms began to preferred in colloquial English,[8] and this could be one reason why Clift's letters to his brothers and sisters, as he began perhaps to be able to differentiate between formal and informal writing, show a marked increase in the WH- forms. On the other hand, he may have been following the more prescriptive grammars and the increase could be a determination to use the "correct" form. For whatever reason, his family letters show an increasing preference for WH- forms over *that* as the years go by.

3.2. Dialect

I have selected two dialectal usages to demonstrate how Clift rejected these very quickly after his arrival in London (see Table 4). The first is the use of the conjunction *where* for *whether*. An example from an early letter is:

> Be pleased to let me know in your next letter, where you have had any letter from Brother Thomas ... (5 March 1792).

Table 4. Clift's use of dialect forms

(1)	was a week	a week ago	last week	
1792	xxxx	xx		
1793	xx	xxx	xx	
1794	x	x	x	+x (mixed) *tomorrow was a Month ago*
1795		xx		27 September 1794
1796			x	
1797		x		

No instances of any form after 1797.

(2)	where	whether
1792	xxxxx	xx
1793	x	xxx
1794		xxxxx
1795		x
1796		xxxxxx
1797		xxx
1798		xx
1799		xxxxxx

Where is a contracted form of *whether* and existed in literate English until the seventeenth century. It was used occasionally by Chaucer and later by Shakespeare. The last instance of its use in standard English recorded in the *Oxford English Dictionary* is in 1660, but according to *The English Dialect Dictionary* it persisted in all western counties. Clift's use is therefore almost certainly dialectal. The only other member of the family to use the form in the letters is Elizabeth, although the others may have used it alongside the standard form elsewhere. Clift has both forms in the letter quoted above and so he was clearly familiar with the variants, although in the first year his preference seems to be for *where*. Five instances occur beside two of the full form *whether*. In 1793, however, he uses *where* only once (*whether* occurs three times, once in the same letter of September as *where*), and he drops it thereafter. Apart from the obvious danger of confusion with the adverb or interrogative *where*, it is possible that he was laughed out of the usage by his fellow servants.

The second idiomatic or dialectal usage is an adverbial expression used to indicate time. I call this "yesterday was (a) week". An example is "the Footman left us last monday was Sennight" (6 April 1792). The usual way of expressing this in present-day English is to use a phrase incorporating the adverb *ago* or something like "on Monday last". Sometimes one expression fits more readily than the other, although at times either can be used according to the cast of the sentence. The second edition of the *Oxford English Dictionary* (1989) notes that the idiom as used by Clift is no longer current but the first edition (1888-1928) gives no indication that it was obsolete then, although it does say, "*Was* is now generally omitted". Literate examples, however, are given only up to the eighteenth century, the last being from the *London Gazette* (1725): "About two or three Days after Holy Rood last was Twelve Month". I have found a later use by Alexander Pope, in a letter of 1744: "ever since Novr was twelvemonth" (Sherburn 1956: IV, 492). The *Oxford English Dictionary* also records a nineteenth-century example from George Eliot in *Adam Bede* (1859). This, however, is intended to convey dialect. It may be this late example that deters the *Oxford English Dictionary* from recording its disappearance from standard English by the late nineteenth century. Clift's early usage is clearly dialectal, since he gradually abandons the form. Again, only Elizabeth's letters afford further examples of the expression. Clift uses it regularly to the exclusion of any other form in his first letters. It is not until October 1792, after he had been in London for nine months, that he first uses a form incorporating *ago*: " it was about three weeks ago" (11 October 1792). The same letter also has "he has given me some lessons 2 or three days ago". The insecure syntax here – the present perfect with *ago* – may reflect Clift's relative uncertainty about the way the expression was used. He reverts to his usual idiom until the following year when, on 24 May, he writes: "Mr & Mrs Gilbert arrived in town on last monday fortnight" (again the inclusion of the preposition *on* betrays an uncertainty in handling the expression) and "I went there last sunday week". Both of these could have been expressed in his usual way: "I went there last sunday was a week". From this point, the dialect form disappears fairly quickly, although not so abruptly as *where*. In 1793 he has two instances of the "was a week" form against three using *ago* and two with *last*. The following year also shows an equal usage of the three expressions. The last example of "was a week" occurs in July of 1794. In the September letter he uses a mixture of the two idioms: "tomorrow was a Month ago". This is the last time that the expression occurs. From 1795 there is no further instance of the dialect form. This idiom survived for a longer time in Clift's language than the conjunction *where* but, generally speaking, by 1795 he had dropped virtually all his native dialect forms and expressions.

3.3. Epistolary formulas

I shall comment here only on the opening formulas of Clift's letters. These show not so much a change towards a standard as a move towards linguistic independence.[9] The formulaic openings and closings of letters that date back to the fourteenth and fifteenth centuries (and possibly earlier to the eleventh century in certain cases) had largely disappeared from letters written by literary and literate persons by the 1720s (see Austin 1973). That they still survived in letters by people such as the Clifts is evidence of their continued use among the lower classes, and this went on well into the present century in a much eroded form.

By the late eighteenth century the formulas had already been modified from their earlier wordings and the opening formula in the Clift letters can be expressed, in its fullest form, thus:

> I have taken this opportunity of writing these few lines to you hoping they find you in good health as it leaves me at present thanks be to God.

Note the lack of concord between *these few lines*, followed by the deictic *they*, and *it* of "as it leaves me at present". This is regular. For convenience, I shall divide the lengthy opening into four parts: (1) the statement of intention to write – the wording of this varies considerably but the above example is the most basic; (2) a wish for the recipient's health; (3) mention of the state of the writer's health at the time of writing; (4) "thanks be to God".

In most of his letters up to September 1794, Clift uses some parts of this opening formula, although he is inclined to omit (4). His first variation comes quite early, in his third letter, in fact, written in March 1792:

> I am not willing to loose [sic] any opportunity of sending you a few lines at any time when I can catch it ... (10 March 1792).

Even here he starts with an inversion of the normal form of (1), the statement of intention to write. In October 1793, he again starts with an accepted variant of (1) but quickly breaks off:

> I have now taken pen In hand to write but am at a loss for words to express my Ideas ... (18 October 1793).

This is probably because he is announcing the death of his master, John Hunter. He is clearly in an agitated state and conventional phrases are not adequate, although at the end of the letter he uses four of the five elements of the closing formula. In his next two letters to Elizabeth he reverts to the full opening formula, including (4): "thanks be to God for it". It is as if he needs to cling to the familiar stability of the formulaic approach in this time of personal upheaval. In January 1795 he first shows complete independence of the formulas, and this was fairly quickly to become habitual. He writes:

> I have been expecting to hear from you for a long time past, as it was your turn to write ... (3 January 1795).

His next letter reverts to the usual formulaic phrasing, omitting (4) and he then abandons the opening formula again until May 1796. Again he omits (4), which indeed he had not used since September 1794. Although he still occasionally uses the formulaic "I have received your letter of ... " after May 1796 – and how many people even now never use some similar phrase when embarking on a letter? – after this date he abandons the full formulaic opening altogether.

To summarize the openings of Clift's letters: in his first twenty letters, up to and including September 1794, he uses the full formula, parts (1), (2), (3) and (4) in nine letters; parts (1), (2) and (3) in six further letters; at least some variant of part (1) in four others; and parts (2) and (3) in the remaining one.

The other regular formula is the closing one and Clift's letters show a similar move away from the stereotyped wording. In addition there are a number of other formulaic phrases that frequently occur in the main body of the letters. Just before the closing formula Clift's letters usually contain a wish to be remembered to certain people mentioned by name and the list invariably finishes with "and all inquiring friends". In a letter to his daughter Caroline of 14 July 1845 Clift makes fun of this formula of his youth by ending his letter thus:

> Give our kindest remembrance to Mrs Poyser and Young Ladies, and to the Doctor and his Lady with a thousand thanks for their kindness and hospitality, and the young Lady who resides with them *"and all inquiring friends"*.

3.4. Punctuation

Clift's increasing command of punctuation is less easy to quantify. Although his use of punctuation increased and grew more certain during his first years, and even months, in London, he remained somewhat careless in the letters up to 1800 and, indeed, to the end of his life.

The first letter of February 1792 contains commas and dashes but no full stops. There are apostrophes in preterites in which the *-ed* ending has been abbreviated: *look'd* and *reach'd*. Apostrophes also occur in the abbreviated forms *cou'd* and *wou'd*. The possessive apostrophe appears for the first time in April 1792 when we find *St James's*, and a letter of May has *Mr Ough's*. Apostrophes for possessives are fairly regular from this time on, even in expressions such as *a week or two's time*. In the letter of 6 April 1792 there is an apparent apostrophe in the word *God's*, which is in fact a simple plural. Clift makes this mistake at least twice and one wonders if he was over-anxious in his use of the possessive apostrophe, having perhaps just acquired it. To return to the very first letter, there are punctuation marks beneath abbreviations: *Willm* and *Leices^r*. He also has, quite correctly, a parenthetical clause in brackets. Capital letters appear to be used somewhat haphazardly and continue to be for some time. By the end of 1793 capitals are mostly reserved for nouns, following the earlier eighteenth-century literary convention, and by the last quarter of 1796 they are mostly dropped except for emphasis. A letter of March 1792 has a semi-colon used for a full stop and the letter of 6 April has two full stops and a semi-colon used correctly. In May the first real evidence of paragraphing appears. A year later, in the May of 1793, Clift uses full stops followed by a capital fairly frequently. His preference, however, is still for a comma or a dash to mark a sentence ending. In the letter announcing Hunter's death in October 1793 he appears to have a complete command of standard punctuation. However, the competence shown in this letter is not maintained and he continues to use commas for full stops, to start sentences with lower case letters,[10] to use a capital after a comma, and so on, for the whole of the period covered by these letters. Very often a letter starts with correctly punctuated short sentences, using full stops, but, as Clift gets into his stride and ideas are obviously flowing fast, the punctuation becomes less regular and more careless. Nevertheless, his knowledge, if not his use, of standard punctuation seems to have been acquired quite rapidly – if, indeed, he had not come up to London with the rules already fully learned but not established in his writing.

3.5. Spelling

Generally, Clift could spell adequately when he left home. Mistakes in spelling are rare and even some of these are simply slips that anyone might make. In the very first letters he sometimes doubles the *r* in *verry* but this does not occur after the end of 1792. Erratic use of double or single letters is his most usual aberration from the norm. *Cabbin* appears in his very first letter. Later, he still occasionally uses a double *ll* in the derivatives *fruitfull* and *gratefull*. A couple of instances of *defer'd* occur, again in the early letters. There is an instance of *harrangue* as late as 1798 when this kind of irregularity had virtually disappeared. Some of these, notably the *ll* in derivatives, were earlier spellings that by the eighteenth century had disappeared from print but frequently remained in private spelling (Osselton 1984: 132). Clift does not always follow the rule of changing *y* to *i* in derivatives. Examples are *mercyfull* and *busyly*. In the first letter of February 1792 he muddles *straits* and *straights*, using both spellings for the geographical "straits" when describing the sea journey to London. In 1793 there are two instances of *years* for 'ears', presumably reflecting his pronunciation. He uses the spelling *practice* for the verb and occasionally muddles an *-ence* ending, spelling 'superintendence' both correctly and as *superintendance* in the same letter in 1798. Apart from a few other similar examples there seems to be little deviation from standard spelling. The fact that the deviant spellings can be listed shows how relatively few there are. Clift has a few typical eighteenth-century spellings, acceptable at the time (see Dr. Johnson's *Dictionary*, 1755) *Publick* and *staid* for 'stayed' are two such. In his first letters he retains the old-fashioned *cloaths* but by 1793 it has been replaced by *clothes*, which was becoming the more usual form at the time. Unlike many literary writers, such as Gray, Addison and even Johnson, Clift does not have a "private" spelling that is different from the standard or printers' spelling for domestic letters (Osselton 1984: 125).[11] This is not surprising. He would not have their casual approach to literary matters and desired above all to be correct, He, therefore, adhered to the spelling he had probably learned at school and perhaps even used a dictionary. In a letter of January 1798 he shows his obsession with correct spelling by reprimanding his unfortunate sister, who almost certainly had had no formal education and who spelt phonetically:

> I shall never be convinced to the contrary of what I now think, by you, unless you learn to mend your orthography or spell better; because No person on earth I am very certain can understand the true meaning of what they read unless they read it right ... Now you surely do not understand the true definition and derivation of the words Lutheran, Calvinist, Methodist, &c, otherwise you could not spell them wrong ... (9 January 1798)

An interesting fact that bears recording is his method when transcribing letters he received from his brothers and sisters in the early years. All the extant letters from Cornwall up to 1794 exist only in a letter book, transcribed by Clift into a simple numerical code. For some reason he must have thrown the originals away. His practice in these letters is to retain the morphological forms of the writers (forms such as *hath*, which he never used himself) but to normalize the spelling to conform with his own.

3.6. Contractions

Of particular interest in Clift's letters is his use of contractions and abbreviations.[12] Contractions of all sorts flourished in the seventeenth and early eighteenth centuries. Of those used by Clift the *-'d* ending for preterite and past participle verb forms is the most common. This is mentioned in grammars as early as the sixteenth century and was widespread in printed texts throughout the 1700s. Other contractions appear in the letters: *I'll*, usually without the apostrophe; proclitic *'tis* and *'twas*; contractions involving *not*; *can't*, *don't*, etc, which according to Jespersen (1917: 117) first appeared in writing around 1660 but were already criticized implicitly by Cooper in 1687 (1687: 77–78), and later *tho'* and *thro'*, *I'd* and one instance of *e're*.

The first outright attacks on contractions came from Addison in the *Spectator* 135 (1711, Bond 1965: 32–36) and Swift in the *Tatler* 230 (1710, Davis 1957: II, 174–177) and again in his *Proposal* (1712, Davis 1957: IV, 11). Both Addison and Swift seem to confuse spelling and pronunciation and this confusion continued in much of the succeeding debate.[13] Many of the grammarians began to repudiate contractions altogether. The first criticism of contracted verbal inflections found by Haugland (personal communication) is in an anonymous grammar of 1724. Strangely, contractions can sometimes be found in the same grammars that purport to reject them but this may be the work of the printers. Revisions of some of the later editions, such as Greenwood's of *A practical English grammar* (1711), have the full forms. From about 1750 most contractions disappeared from printed works. Some people also ceased to use them in private writings. For instance, Haugland has found no -*'d* abbreviation in preterites and participles in the first 100 pages of *The journals and letters of Fanny Burney* written in 1791–1792 (Hemlow et al. 1972), although in her early journals of 1768–1773 (Troide, I: 1988) they occur in a ratio of just under 1:2.[14] There is at least one instance of -*'d* in the later letters but the habitual form is the unabbreviated -*ed*.[15] Her later letters contain other contractions, such as *'tis*, *don't* and abbreviations using raised letters: w^d and wch. Johnson also dropped the -*'d* abbreviation in his private letters after 1738 (Tieken-Boon van Ostade 1991: 54), and Swift, as might be expected, showed a preference for the full forms in his later writings, both public and private. Barbara Strang (1967: 1951) notes how the abbreviated forms begin to disappear from his letters after 1726.

Clift's first letter, of 19 February 1792, is full of contractions. There are fourteen instances of -*'d* (the apostrophe is dropped about 50% of the time); eight examples of *Cou'd/Coud*; four of *Cant*; one of *Dont*; two of *Ill* [*I'll*] and one each of *twill* and *tis*. Less than a month later, 5 March 1792, there are only eleven contractions or abbreviations altogether. For the rest of 1792 contractions are virtually absent. Then, in the first letter of 1793, written in February, -*'d* abbreviations appear once more in larger numbers. This letter has five examples and one with a raised letter: rec^d. There is also an instance of *don't*.

The -'d forms in preterites and past participles and the short form *cou'd* (which extends to *wou'd* and *shou'd*) are the abbreviations used most often in the first letter of 1792 and the ones that are dropped most quickly. They are, therefore, worth examining in more detail. The -'d preterites and participles continue in considerable numbers until 1797. One reason for the absence of -'d in the later letters of 1792 is that these contain very few preterites and past participles of regular verbs. However, even with the small numbers available a distinct change is apparent after the first letter of 1792. The pattern is completely reversed, with fewer abbreviated forms to full ones. In the letter of 5 March 1792, written less than a month after Clift had been in London, full forms occur in a ratio of 3:1, compared with 1:3.5 in the first letter. Only once does the ratio rise to 1:1, occasionally it is 1:0 and in some letters there are no instances of regular verb preterites or past participles at all. Even in the letter of February 1793 cited above there are ten full forms to five abbreviated ones, a ratio of approximately 2:1. The proportion of abbreviated forms gradually decreases. Isolated examples occur up to 1800 but after January 1795 Clift virtually ceases to use then. The abbreviated forms of *would*, *could* and *should* are discarded even more rapidly. In the first letter of 1792 there are eight examples of *Cou'd/Coud* and none of a full form. The second letter, of 5 March, has *wou'd* four times, *twou'd* once; *cou'd* twice and *shou'd* once. There is also the first example of a full form: *would*. Five days later, on 10 March, *woud* occurs twice but there is one instance of *would* and two of *should*. No abbreviations of this type appear at all after this letter except for an isolated use of *twoud* in May 1793.

That Clift came to London using abbreviations and contractions is understandable. His teacher in Bodmin, the parish clerk and wigmaker, probably retained the spelling conventions of his own youth and passed them on to his pupils. More puzzling at first glance is why the abbreviated forms should begin to disappear less than a month after Clift came to London. The answer to this may be important for some of Clift's other practices. The following suggestion is conjecture but seems a very real possibility. Part of Clift's duties was to take notes from Hunter's dictation. Hunter would surely have wanted to assure himself in those first days that his new apprentice was performing his work satisfactorily. It is almost a certainty, therefore, that he looked over what Clift had taken down. If Clift's writing habits were old-fashioned, Hunter's certainly would not have been and the notes he was dictating were, in any case, formal – probably destined eventually for print. What more likely than that he would have directed his young apprentice to avoid the abbreviations he was apparently using? Clift, anxious to please, would equally certainly have obeyed and with a thoroughness (such was his admiration for

Hunter even in these early days) that caused him to eradicate them from all his writing, including his letters home. The fact that he began to use rather more abbreviations and contractions in his letters a year later may indicate a dawning realization that a distinction could be made between private and public spelling. Did Hunter, indeed, intimate that such contractions might be used in private writing?[16] If Hunter's is the guiding hand behind Clift's use of contractions, it may also be a factor influencing his spelling and punctuation generally. This is a possibility that must be borne in mind. After 1800 Clift stops using abbreviations altogether, even in letters that exist only in draft form.

3.7. Syntax

Punctuation and spelling both have a bearing on syntax and sentence structure. Clift's first letters tend to have lengthy, rather loose clauses, frequently but not always co-ordinate, and these, in the first few letters, are barely punctuated at all. By the end of the period, in 1799, his sentences tend to be shorter and to show more syntactical control. Around the years 1794 to 1795, when his use of subordination increases markedly, Clift's control of syntax is still often rather shaky. This may well be a result of his more adventurous experimentation in structure. A comprehensive study of his syntax would be profitable but is beyond the scope of this paper. Similarly, his increased command of vocabulary would make an interesting study but is, again, impossible to quantify. Two sentences – or parts of sentences – taken from an early and a later letter will show the extent to which Clift's powers had increased in both vocabulary and sentence structure. The first comes from his very first letter, in which he describes how he left the quay at Fowey on his journey by ship to London:

> Just as we was getting out of the Harbour I saw you and Cousin Polly out at St Cathrines and I look'd at you till I saw you get out at the Castle and sit down upon the Bank the other side and I look'd and look'd and look'd again till you look'd so small that I Cou'd not discern you scarcely only your red Cloak ... (19 February 1792)

The co-ordinate clause structure and relatively limited vocabulary is obvious here. There is also a double negative of a type found not infrequently in educated writing and not markedly non-standard. Already, however, working within a comparatively limited framework, Clift has a certain command of style. The way in which he represents how he watched his sister until she was out of sight is surprisingly effective and adequately conveys the feelings of the young boy bidding farewell to the last link with home. The second example comes from a letter of 1797, when Clift and his sister are engaged in a quarrel over religious opinions, set off by the departure of some of the Fowey cousins on a missionary venture to the South Seas:

> Religion is on its last legs indeed when such ignorant pretenders who have not even had a common education, ... shall superciliously arogate to themselves a knowledge of things above human capacity & in which the greatest men are lost whenever they resume the subject to trace it to its source/ Every one may see there is a divine providence attendant on all the creation, the different motions and movements of all bodies celestial and terrestrial are guided and performed in a wonderfull manner but by what means we shall be for ever ignorant, at least on this side of what we call eternity ... (1 July 1797)

The homily continues with many abstract ideas, expressed in abstract vocabulary. The syntax is still not perfectly under control (there is an example of a redundant *and* before the prepositional relative), perhaps because of the level of the subject matter, and punctuation is rather minimal. Again, this is probably because, Clift was concentrating on putting his thoughts down on paper and his brain was working more quickly than his pen could keep up with niceties of composition. These factors probably account too for the one spelling mistake. It should be stressed, perhaps, that Clift did not so much change his way of writing as increase his range of styles. Some of the letters of his later years contain passages similar to the first example given here but he could move easily from one style to another as his subject matter dictated.

4. Conclusion

From 1792 onwards, changes in Clift's written English show a fairly clear pattern of movement towards a standard. By the end of 1793, some eighteen months after his arrival in London, he had probably shed the majority of his dialectal usages, the most obvious non-standard features of his language. The shift from general non-educated non-standard followed slightly later, from the end of 1794 to the early months of 1795. This at first seems puzzling. Why did the change take place a year or more after Hunter's death when the influence of the master might be assumed to be waning? By then Clift was cut off from the professional and cultural circle of the Hunters and thrown back on the company of the servants in Castle Street where Hunter's Collection was housed. A number of other factors, however, none of them striking in itself, work together to offer a possible explanation of this problem.

After Hunter's death, Clift was still in contact with scientists interested in the Collection. Among them were Everard Home, Hunter's brother-in-law, and Dr. Matthew Baillie, the Trustees of the Collection. Then in October 1794, by a lucky chance for Clift's future career, Robert Haynes, who was responsible for the Collection with Clift as his assistant, was dismissed for petty theft and Clift was left "cock of the walk", as he wrote to his sister. He was in charge of a unique scientific Collection worth some £20,000 and he was still only nineteen years old. There can be no doubt that he took his responsibilities seriously. Among his duties was showing the Collection at a minute's notice to prospective purchasers and *cognoscenti*. One of these was William IV, Prince of Orange. Clift, therefore, had every incentive to ensure that his speech and general conduct were suited to the level of those to whom he was required to show the Collection and explain its significance.

Earlier still, during the eighteen months in which they worked together day by day, his initial liking for Hunter had grown into hero-worship. This in itself might lead one to expect that he would have adjusted his language to a greater extent somewhat earlier. Perhaps his spoken language changed more rapidly and it required some little time to show in his writing. Be that as it may, we know that after Hunter's death, Clift had a premonition that some accident might befall his master's writings, without which the Collection would be meaningless. Clift set about copying as many of Hunter's papers as he could. As it happened his fears were justified and very many of the papers were destroyed. Owing to Clift's uncanny foresight, the Royal College of Surgeons of England in Lincoln's Inn Fields still houses cupboards full of Clift's copies of Hunter's manuscripts. Scientific writing is, of course, very different in many respects from other varieties but it is nonetheless possible and even likely that certain forms repeated over and over, as the young scribe diligently copied his master's work, would have entered either consciously or unconsciously into his own usage.

Clift's knowledge of English was not confined to the utilitarian, however. As early as September 1793 he wrote to his sister that he had been buying novels: *Tom Jones*, *Tristram Shandy*, *Roderick Random*, *The Vicar of Wakefield*, *Joseph Andrews*, and *Robinson Crusoe*. There is no reason to suppose that he did not continue to buy and read more books when his slender means allowed. Reading undoubtedly influenced his own language. Indeed, by 1793 these novels were somewhat old-fashioned in expression and this could account for the fact that Clift retained certain older forms, such as the past participle *wrote*, longer than might have been expected. Unluckily, there is no record of his buying a grammar. It is hard to believe that he did not at some time use one or more of the many grammars that were readily available at the time. Their title pages often advertised them as specially adapted to the needs of young men who had been denied an education in their earlier years, and this might have had a strong appeal for Clift. Or perhaps his increasingly good opinion of himself would have drawn him to Lindley Murray's *English Grammar* (1795), which boasted of "assisting the more advanced students to write with perspicuity and accuracy".

By whatever means and whichever of the factors in his circumstances influenced him most, William Clift finally attained a fluent standard English. There is little doubt that initially he was motivated to adjust his language by the environment into which he was thrust at the age of seventeen and by his desire to emulate Hunter and the Hunter household. He is a supreme example of someone who strove consciously to acquire what he believed was the standard language of the day. To say that he had "social aspirations" would be misleading. If there was any driving force in his life it was intellectual. Even this is doubtful. He seems to have had his sights raised almost by accident and thereafter he gravitated towards the recognized norms of the day in language and every other aspect of life. By 1800 the period of uncertainty following the death of Hunter was over. In December 1799 the Government agreed to buy Hunter's Collection and entrusted it to the Corporation of Surgeons, which was reconstituted as The Royal College of Surgeons of London. William Clift was appointed the first Conservator at a salary of £80 a year. He was not yet twenty-five years old. Within the space of eight years the street urchin from one of England's most remote provincial towns was ready to take his place among the international scientists of the nineteenth century. In this sphere no reference ever seems to have been made to his country upbringing and by the time of his death in 1849 it had apparently been forgotten outside the family. Neither his speech nor his writing can have drawn attention to his humble origins. Less than ten years after he left Bodmin he had adapted his boyhood language to the late eighteenth-century standard of the educated élite of London.

Notes

* I am grateful to the British Academy for a grant enabling me to attend the workshop at Helsinki. I wish to record my thanks to Professor X. Dekeyser for sending me copies of his articles on relativization and explanations; also to Nadine van den Eynden for likewise supplying material and answering my

queries. I am grateful to Kari E. Haugland, who not only made available to me the paper on abbreviations and contractions that she read at the 6th ICEHL in Helsinki (May 1990) but elaborated it with much additional information. She is not, of course, responsible for any deductions I may have drawn or any material that I have added.

1. For more details of William Clift's early life see Austin (1991).
2. The approximate number of words for each year is as follows:

    | 1792 | 5,124 |
    | 1793 | 5,592 |
    | 1794 | 3,528 |
    | 1795 | 2,784 |
    | 1796 | 6,612 |
    | 1797 | 2,952 |
    | 1798 | 1,464 |
    | 1799–1801 | 1,764. |

3. This corresponds with Cheshire's deductions (1978: 57–58) that earlier forms of *do* had an "invariant suffixed form for the main verb".
4. Only the variation between WH- forms and *that* on a very basic level of analysis have been dealt with here as these are of particular importance for accepted standard usage at the time. Prepositional relatives have been included in Table 3 but not in the numbers in the text. Two instances of genitive relatives have not been shown.
5. See Austin (1985: 15–29). Grijzenhout (1992: 34) cites Rydén's (1983: 132–133) observation that *who* was preferred to *which* for personal antecedents by 1600; by the beginning of the eighteenth century personal *which* was rare.
6. Clift's use of *which* in restrictive clauses is less frequent than that shown by Dekeyser (1984: 68, Table VI) for the period 1600–1649 overall. Quirk (1957: 106) says that WH- forms preponderate in restrictive clauses in present-day educated spoken English. Even after 1795 when Clift first uses *which* in restrictive clauses, the numbers are insufficient to show a preference for *which* over *that*. On the other hand, *who*, which first appears in 1793, is used far more than *that* in both restrictive and non-restrictive personal clauses. In fact, there are only two clear examples of non-restrictive personal *that* altogether in the letters and only one of restrictive personal *that* after 1796.
7. This is a difficult area. Wright (1905: 280–281) does not record *which* as a relative in south western dialect. This does not mean it did not exist. Wright's observations on dialect are no more complete than present-day dialect surveys. Additionally, there are no genuine written regional dialects in English: they are spoken varieties of the language. Even if the Clifts did not generally use WH- forms when speaking, it does not mean that these were outside their competence.

   WH- forms have continued to gain in frequency in both restrictive and non-restrictive clauses in English since 1600 (Dekeyser 1984: 66; Quirk 1957: 102, 105–107). For letters in the period 1600–1649 Dekeyser (1984: 77, Table XVII) shows a ratio for WH- forms to *that* of 5:1, whereas for narrative/descriptive and informative prose the ratio drops to 2.2:1. The Clifts' unexpectedly frequent use of WH- forms is more understandable if it is part of a general pattern for epistolary prose. Their use is actually less frequent than that discovered by Dekeyser for the early seventeenth century and nearer to his ratio for other prose writing. This, too, seems acceptable in the light of their background.

8. See Grijzenhout (1992). The evidence for the theory that WH- forms began to replace *that* in colloquial English about 1700, however, is based exclusively on plays and may or may not reflect actual speech. As far as the Clifts are concerned – apart from William – it is important not to confuse colloquial English with formal but non-educated English.
9. For full details on the Clifts' use of epistolary formulas of various kinds see Austin (1973: 9–22, 129–140).
10. These could be late examples of the "semi-period" noted by Salmon (1988: 298). A small letter after a full stop when the following sentence was closely linked to the previous one was advocated in 1566 by Aldus Manutius. The first reference to this punctuation in England was by Christopher Cooper (1687: 114). Salmon found it in printed books until the mid-sixteenth century and in manuscripts until the later seventeenth century. There are about a dozen instances of it in Clift's letters up to 1800 and in every case the two sentences are closely linked semantically.
11. The hypothesis concerning Clift's changes of direction in using abbreviations, discussed later, should however be noted.
12. For details of the history of contractions in the eighteenth century I am indebted to Kari E. Haugland (1990 and personal correspondence).
13. Osselton (1984: 130) calls Swift's remarks on spelling at this time "disorganized splutterings".
14. Tieken-Boon van Ostade (1991: 53–54) . I am also indebted to Ingrid Tieken-Boon van Ostade for information on the usage of -'d in the early journals of Fanny Burney.
15. For example, Hemlow et al. (1972: 107), in a letter from Fanny Burney to her younger sister, Charlotte, but there are numerous full forms in the same letter and many hundreds in the collection as a whole.
16. See Osselton (1984) for the attitude to a double standard of spelling by men of education and letters.

References

Austin, Frances
    1969   Studies in the language of the Clift family correspondence. [Unpublished Ph.D. dissertation, University of Southampton.]

1973 "Epistolary conventions of the Clift family correspondence", *English Studies* 54: 9–22, 129–140.
1985 "Relative *which* in late 18th-century usage: The Clift family correspondence", in: Roger Eaton – Olga Fischer – Willem Koopman – Frederike van der Leek (eds.), 15–29.
1991 *The Clift family correspondence* (Occasional Publications 5.) Sheffield: Centre for English Cultural Tradition and Language.

Blair, Hugh
1783 *Lectures on rhetoric and belles lettres.* 2 vols. Second American edition [1793]. Philadelphia.

Blake, Norman F. – Charles Jones (eds.)
1984 *English historical linguistics: Studies in development.* (Occasional Publications 3.) Sheffield: Centre for English Cultural Tradition and Language.

Bond, Donald F. (ed.)
1965 *The Spectator.* 5 vols. Oxford: Clarendon Press.

Brook, George L.
1970 *The language of Dickens.* London: André Deutsch.

Buchanan, James
1767 *A regular English syntax.* London

Burney, Fanny
See Hemlow, Joyce et al. (eds.) and Troide, Lars (ed.)

Campbell, Archibald
1776 *Lexiphanes.* London.

Cheshire, Jenny
1978 "Present tense verbs in Reading English", in: Peter Trudgill (ed.), 52–67.

Cooper, Christopher
1687 *The English teacher.* London.

Davis, Herbert (ed.)
1939–1959 *The prose writings of Jonathan Swift.* 14 vols. Oxford: Blackwell.

Dekeyser, Xavier
1984 "Relativizers in Early Modern English: A dynamic quantitative study", in: Jacek Fisiak (ed.), 61–87.

Dykema, Karl W.
1947 "An example of prescriptive linguistic change: 'don't' to 'doesn't'", *The English Journal* 36: 370–376.

Eaton, Roger – Olga Fischer – Willem Koopman – Frederike van der Leek (eds.)
1985 *Papers from the 4th International Conference on English Historical Linguistics.* (Current Issues in Linguistic Theory 41.) Amsterdam: Benjamins.

Fisiak, Jacek (ed.)
1984 *Historical syntax.* (Trends in Linguistics: Studies and Monographs 23.) Berlin: Mouton de Gruyter.

Greenwood, James
    1711   *A practical English grammar.* London.
Grijzenhout, Janet
    1992   "The change of relative *that* to *who* and *which* in late seventeenth-century comedies", *NOWELE* 20: 33–52.
Haugland, Kari E.
    1990   Contraction in seventeenth and eighteenth-century grammars and spelling books. Unpublished paper read at the 6th International Conference on Historical Linguistics, Helsinki, 1990.
Hemlow, Joyce – Curbis D. Cecil – Althea Douglas
    1972   *The journals and letters of Fanny Burney.* Vol. I, 1791–1792. Oxford: Clarendon Press.
Hornsey, John
    1793   *A short English grammar in two parts.* York.
Jespersen, Otto
    1917   *Negation in English and other languages.* Copenhagen: Host.
    1927   *A modern English grammar on historical principals.* Part III: Syntax. London: Allen & Unwin.
    [1961] [Reprinted London: Allen & Unwin.]
Johnson, Dr. Samuel
    1755   *A dictionary of the English language.* London: Rivington.
Leonard, Sterling A.
    1929   *The doctrine of correctness in English usage 1700–1800.* Madison: University of Wisconsin.
    [1962] [Reprinted New York: Russell & Russell.]
Lowth, Robert
    1762   *A short introduction to English grammar.* London.
Murray, Lindley
    1795   *English grammar.* York.
Osselton, Noel E.
    1983   "Points of modern English syntax, LXV. 200", *English Studies* 64: 469–472.
    1984   "Informal spelling systems in Early Modern English: 1500–1800", in: Norman F. Blake and Charles Jones (eds.), 123–137.
Oxford English Dictionary, The
    1888-1928 Ed. James A.H. Murray – Henry Bradley – W.A. Craigie – C.T. Onions. 12 vols. Oxford: Clarendon Press.
    1989   Prepared by J.A. Simpson – E.S.C. Weiner. 2nd edition. Oxford: Clarendon Press.
Phillipps, Kenneth C.
    1970   *Jane Austen's English.* London: André Deutsch.
Priestley, Joseph
    1761   *The rudiments of English grammar.* London.

Quirk, Randolph
    1957   "Relative clauses in educated spoken English", *English studies* 38: 97–109.
Rogers, Norman
    1979   *Wessex dialect*. Bradford-on-Avon: Moonraker Press.
Rydén, Mats
    1983   "The emergence of *who* as relativizer", *Studia Linguistica* 37: 126–134.
Salmon, Vivian
    1988   "English punctuation theory 1500–1800", *Anglia* 106: 285–314.
Sherburn, George
    1956   *The correspondence of Alexander Pope*. 5 vols. Oxford: Oxford University Press.
Strang, Barbara
    1967   "Swift and the English language: A study in principles and practice", in: *To honor Roman Jakobson: Essays on the occasion of his 70th birthday, 11 October 1966*. Janua Linguarum, Series Maior 33. Vol. 3: 1947–1959.
Swift, Jonathan
    See Davis, Herbert (ed.)
Tieken-Boon van Ostade, Ingrid
    1987   *The auxiliary do in eighteenth-century English: A sociohistorical-linguistic approach*. Dordrecht: Foris.
    1991   "Samuel Richardson's role as linguistic innovator: A sociolinguistic analysis", in: Ingrid Tieken-Boon van Ostade – John Frankis (eds.), 47–57.
Tieken-Boon van Ostade, Ingrid – John Frankis (eds.)
    1991   *Language, usage and description: Studies presented to N.E. Osselton on the occasion of his retirement*. Amsterdam: Rodopi.
Troide, Lars (ed.)
    1988   *The early journals and letters of Fanny Burney*. Vol. I, 1768–1773. Oxford: Clarendon Press.
Trudgill, Peter (ed.)
    1978   *Sociolinguistic patterns in British English*. London: Arnold.
Wakelin, Martyn
    1986   *The southwest of England*. Amsterdam: Benjamins.
Ward, William
    1765   *An essay on grammar*. London.
Webster, Noah
    1789   *Dissertations on the English language*. Boston.
    1798   *A letter to the governors ... of the Universities*. New York.
Withers, Philip
    1788   *Aristarchus*. London.

Wright, Joseph (ed.)
    1898-1905 *The English dialect dictionary.* 6 vols. London: Henry Frowde.
    1905   *The English dialect grammar.* London: Henry Frowde.
    [1968] [Reprinted Oxford: Clarendon Press.]
Wyld, Henry C.
    1936   *A history of modern colloquial English.* Oxford: Blackwell.
    [1953] [3rd edition reprinted Oxford: Blackwell.]

Index

Aberdeen, as developing urban center 51
acceptance: *see* standardization process
Addison, Joseph 248, 258, 260, 272-273, 278, 280, 301
   cited by normative grammarians 107, 243, 244, 245, 246, 247, 252, 259-260, 266, 267, 269, 273, 276, 278
   on contractions 302
   as editor 267-269, 277
   as a model of modernity 11, 257, 265, 267-269, 269-271; *see also* modernity
   usage of periphrastic *do* 249, 250, 251, 254, 256, 257, 266, 274, 275
   on relative pronominals 258-259, 292
   usage of relative pronominals 261, 262, 263, 264, 265, 266, 267-269, 276, 277
American English:
   conclusive perfect in, 136, 149
   nonstandard weak verb forms in, 117, 125
   relative pronominals in, 265
   standard 3, 6
   variant verb forms in, 127, 128, 130
anglicization 56
Anglo-Irish: *see* Hiberno English
article, definite 177, 185, 188, 197, 202, 235, 268
   see also personal pronominals, possessive *the*
Australian English:
   aspectual distinction 128
   nonstandard weak verb forms in, 117, 125, 126
avoidance strategy 177, 180-181, 189, 197, 220, 222, 225, 229, 231, 233, 235, 238

Bacon, Francis 243, 244, 253
Baker, Robert 243
   citing contemporary authors 260
   on dynamic/stative distinction 129
   on pronominals 231, 260
   on strong verbs 126
be 289-292
   +past participle: *see* perfect, *be*
   with mutative intransitive verbs 138
Beattie, James 57-60, 165
Belfast 20, 21, 22
Bible, cited by normative grammarians 243, 244, 246, 261
Blair, Hugh 57, 60, 278, 291
   cited by normative grammarians 243, 244, 245
Boswell, James 42, 53, 218
   usage of pronominals 220-221, 224, 229, 230, 231, 236
   usage of periphrastic *do* 274
Boyer, Abel 248, 258, 278
   usage of periphrastic *do* 249, 251, 254, 255, 256, 257, 266, 275
   usage of relative pronominals 261, 262, 265, 266, 276, 277
British English
   conclusive perfect in, 136, 149
   variant verb forms in t/ed 127, 128
   verb forms in /ʌ/ 130

Buchanan, James 292
Bullokar, William
  on gender 182
  on neuter possessive 180, 182, 207
Burney, Fanny 235
  usage of contractions 302, 309
  usage of periphrastic *do* 274
  usage of pronominals 219-220, 221, 224, 228, 229, 230, 231, 234, 236
Butler, Charles
  on gender   188
  on neuter possessive 180, 181, 182

Campbell, Archibald 40, 66, 131, 219, 291
case 181, 233, 234
  loss of case distinction 226, 227, 233, 234
  pronominal case 217, 226, 234
  see also genitive; personal pronominals, subject/object pronominals
causative 147
  indirect 141, 149
  see also get; *have*
Centlivre, Susannah 247, 248, 258, 279
  usage of periphrastic *do* 249, 250, 254, 257, 266, 274
  usage of relative pronominals 261, 262, 264-265, 266, 276, 277
Chancery English 195
Chancery Standard 3, 4, 6
change, linguistic:
  from above 172
  from below 172, 199, 204
  external 11, 12-13
  internal 11, 12
  learned 199, 204, 227, 234
  and literacy 74
  natural 172, 199, 204, 227, 234
  and the normative grammarians 272
  and politeness 74

  orderly 205
  rapid 11, 200-201, 204, 205
  S-curve 12
  slow 200-201
  and standardization 162
  see also drift
children's language 118, 119, 124, 225, 226, 234, 237
Clift, William 286-287, 305-307, 308
  syntactic control 305
  usage of:
    contractions 301-304
    dialectal forms 295-297
    punctuation 299-300, 309
    relative pronominals 292-295
    spelling 300-301, 305
    verb forms 288-292
codification: *see* standardization process
colloquial language 176, 178, 196, 197-199, 204, 238, 252, 257, 258, 261, 263, 265, 266, 275, 285, 286, 291, 294, 295, 309
contractions: *see* Clift, William
conservatism:
  in language 11, 196, 251, 252, 257, 261, 266
  in society 201
convergence 2, 20, 25
  see also standardization
conversation 33, 34, 41
  the art of, 33, 257-258, 271
  linguistic models of, 246
  polite conversation 8
  see also the gentleman
Cook, Captain 238
Cooper, Anthony Ashley: *see* Shaftesbury
Cooper, Christopher 100-103, 106, 108, 110
  on codification 101
  on gender 184
  on punctuation 302, 309

and standardization 103
  on strong verbs 101-103, 104, 105, 108
Cooper, William 220-221, 222, 229, 235
  and pronominal usage 291
corpus studies 83, 109, 202, 219-223, 246-267
  see also Clift, William; Helsinki Corpus; Lancaster-Oslo/Bergen Corpus
corpus-based grammars 243
correctness 3, 5, 6, 8, 9, 12, 31, 44
  Addison as a model of, 257, 264, 265, 273
  doctrine of, 67, 272
  grammatical correctness 218, 219, 224, 229, 232, 244, 245, 246, 247, 248, 258, 264, 265-266, 272, 276, 292, 295
  and pronunciation 54, 55
  standard of, 258, 269, 270-271
courtesy books 72, 73, 74
cultivated speech 118
  see also norms; prestige patterns

decorum 68
  see also cultivated speech; the gentleman; politeness
Defoe, Daniel 118, 294
  usage of *do* 274
demonstrative pronominals:
  gender gap in, 205
  them 234-235
dialect: *see* regional varieties
dialectal variants 65, 120
  see also variation; variants
Dilworth, Thomas 247, 273, 275
  on periphrastic *do* 253
divergence 25
Dobson, E.J., and the standard language 23

drift, semantic 172
  typological 203
Dryden, John 34, 179, 273
  cited by normative grammarians 106, 107, 243, 244, 246, 253, 271, 273
  and correctness 219, 269
  on neuter possessive 179, 200

Edinburgh:
  as developing urban center 51
  anglicized literati 56
  educated upper-class speakers 55
  polite accent 55
elaboration: *see* standardization process
exocentric norms: *see* norms, supralocal

Fell, John 243, 246, 278
  on periphrastic *do* 253
  on relative pronominals 276
Fenning, Daniel 275
Fisher, Ann:
  on pronominal usage 237
Fogg, Peter Walkdenn 243, 244
  citing contemporary sources 273
  on periphrastic *do* 251, 275
formulas, epistolary 295, 297-299, 309

gap, paradigmatic 190-191, 198, 203, 205
gender 179, 186, 206
  distinctions 173, 182-184, 259
  drift in gender system 172-173
  grammatical 182, 237
  loss of, 171, 173, 190, 205
  natural (notional) 178
    changes in, 184, 188, 191, 192, 199, 202, 204
  in pronominals 226

genitive, the 172, 173, 174, 175, 176, 178, 181, 185, 192, 193, 194, 199
gentleman, the:
   as bearer of cultural standard 35, 37, 38, 269, 270, 278
   characteristics of, 41
   and conversability 33, 37, 40, 42, 43
   urban 41
   urbane 40, 43
   see also conversation; politeness
gentility 33, 35, 43
   elite 36, 42
   models of, 71
   pursuit of, 37
   see also conversation; politeness
get:
   causative 144
   conclusive perfect 151
   indirect passive 146
   passive 159
   passive of experience 149
Gill, Alexander 180
   on neuter possessive 180, 182
Glasgow, as developing urban center 51
Goldsmith, Oliver 65, 67, 70-71, 72
   cited by normative grammarians 243, 244, 245
   usage of periphrastic *do* 274
Gough, James 247, 273
   on periphrastic *do* 253
grammarians, descriptive 14, 117, 119, 126, 129, 179-184
   on gender 183
   on neuter possessive 180, 204
grammarians, normative 10, 13, 44, 60, 66, 76, 98-108, 117, 122-123, 125, 129, 179, 181
   on *be/have* periphrasis 158, 159, 160
   on conclusive perfect 165
   on contractions 302
   and illustrations of usage 244-245, 258, 266
   influenced by Lowth 253, 260
   on periphrastic *do* 251, 252
   on the pronominal system 217, 235
   and politeness 270, 271
   on relative pronominals 258, 262, 264, 269, 292, 295
   and standardization 245, 269-271, 271-273
   and strong verbs 98-108, 129
   and usage 122, 125, 179, 246, 260, 272, 291
   see also Cooper, Christopher; Dilworth; Fell; Fenning; Fisher; Gill; Gough; Greenwood; Johnson; Jones; Kirkby; Lowth; Murray; Priestley; Ussher; Wallis; Ward; Webster; White
Greenwood, James 104-105, 108
   on contractions 302
   on strong verbs 104-105, 106, 122

Hart, John 83
have:
   causative 142, 143, 144, 152, 155, 158, 160
   existential 152, 160, 164
   have a V 154
   +infinitive+object 161, 164
   with non-mutative intransitive verbs 138
   +object+infinitive 153-154, 161
   +object+past participle 136, 141-152, 153, 154-156, 156-158, 160, 161, 165
   +past participle 139-140, 149, 158-159, 163
   passive of experience 155, 158, 160
   passive, indirect 146, 155, 160
   with transitive verbs 138

Helsinki Corpus 14, 81, 84, 85, 109, 119, 163
material used for analysis 90-98, 109, 140, 143, 148, 150, 164, 165, 172-175, 185-190, 192, 201
and normative grammarians 108-109
period divisions of, 87, 189, 199-201
Hiberno English 224
conclusive perfect in, 136, 149, 161, 165
pronominal usage in, 232
Hunter, John:
and William Clift 287, 298, 300, 303-304, 305, 306, 307
hypercorrection 225, 226, 235, 300

innovativeness: *see* modernity
insecurity, linguistic 197, 224
irregular verbs: *see* strong verbs

Johnson, Dr Samuel 14, 66, 105-107, 108, 125, 245, 252, 271, 301
on Addison's language 257, 266, 267, 275, 276
Dictionary 110, 301
on mutative verbs 128
on periphrastic *do* 247, 252, 253, 274
on politeness 270, 278
on strong verbs 106-107, 122, 125
usage of periphrastic *do* 274
Jones, Hugh 42
Jonson, Ben:
on gender 182-183, 184
language criticised by Dryden 180
on neuter possessive 180-181, 182

Kirkby, John 109

on strong verbs 103-104, 105, 108, 126
on pronominal usage 237
Kökeritz, Helge, and the standard language 26

Lancaster-Oslo/Bergen Corpus 187-189, 192
language planning 2, 10, 103
Latin influence:
on British English 184, 204
on Scots 57
on pronominal usage 238
legal English 195-196, 200, 203, 275
literacy:
effect on standardization 116, 129
and language change 74
literate modes of speech 72, 197, 199
characteristics of, 72
Locke, John, cited by normative grammarians 243, 244, 279
London:
culture 41, 42
fashionable society 55
nonregional colloquial variety used in, 204
politeness 60, 270
London speech, as standard 83, 200, 201, 204, 224
lower-class 294-295
polite 51
Lowth, Bishop Robert 14, 44, 60, 66, 103, 106, 107, 243, 244, 245, 246, 247, 272, 291
citing evidence from contemporary authors 107, 131, 261, 276, 278
on neuter possessive 181
on periphrastic *do* 251, 253
on relative pronominals 259-260, 264, 292
on strong verbs 107-108, 122, 125

Machyn, Henry 23-24
Miège, Guy:
  on gender 184
Milton, John 106, 107, 140, 150
  cited by normative grammarians 243, 244, 245, 246, 271, 273
modernity 11, 245, 246, 247, 248, 249, 251, 252, 256, 257, 258, 265-266, 271, 273, 276
modesty device 230, 231, 234, 238
Montagu, Lady Mary Wortley 280
  and pronominal usage 219, 224, 229, 234, 236
  usage of *do* 274
More, Hanna 222, 236
Murray, Lindley 275, 307
mutative verbs 128, 138, 158, 159, 160

nonregional colloquial variety 204
nonstandard varieties 65, 115, 116, 161
  aspectual distinction in, 128
  conservativeness 120
  morphological simplification 126
  prescriptivism and effect on, 123
  strong verb pattern in, 117, 120, 124
  normative grammatical tradition 82
  see also grammarians, normative; prestige
normative rules and present-day English grammar 218
norms:
  attitudes to 2, 3
  consensus 20, 25
  local 3, 25
  non-localised 19
  regional 2, 3, 82
  of the standard 5, 21, 27, 204, 223, 233, 258, 267, 287
  standardized 21
  superimposed 20
  supra-local 2, 3, 6, 19, 26
  variable 20
  vernacular 26
  see also grammarians, normative; prestige
number 178, 179
  in pronominals 226, 259

oral modes of speech 13, 72, 197, 198, 199
  characteristics of, 72-73, 161, 162

passive:
  indirect 141, 144-146, 148, 149
  of experience 141, 144, 146-149, 154, 164
  see also get
pedantry 33, 38, 41
perfect:
  be 158-159, 161
  conclusive 136-138, 141, 142, 149-152, 155, 157, 158, 161-162, 164, 165
  have/be alternation 159, 160
  split 136, 160
  standardization of, 160-162
  see also have
perfect periphrasis, origin of, 139
periphrastic *do* 12, 13, 201, 247, 248, 249-258, 265, 266, 274, 275, 276, 288-289, 302
  see also Scotticisms
periphrastic possessive 180
  of it 171, 175, 179, 185, 192, 199, 200, 203, 204, 208-209
  of the same 178-179, 189-190, 195, 197, 198, 203, 208-209
personal pronominals 217, 230, 231, 232, 233, 234, 235, 236, 237, 238
possessives 171-206

his 172-173, 176, 189, 190, 191, 192, 194, 195, 196, 197, 198, 200, 203, 206, 207, 208-209
it 173-175, 176, 179, 189, 196, 198, 199, 200, 208-209
its 175-176, 189-190, 191, 192, 196, 197, 198, 199, 200, 203, 204, 205, 206, 208-209
nominal 175-176
the 175, 176-177
reflexive use of, 191-192, 196, 197
semantic roles of, 192-194, 198
see also grammarians, descriptive; grammarians, normative; periphrastic possessive; pronominal adverbs
Quaker use of *thee* 225
reflexives 174, 180, 191, 231, 235
relatives 171, 181, 185, 205, 206, 217, 248, 258-267, 267-269, 276, 277, 292-295, 308, 309
see also grammarians, normative
second person 171, 205, 206, 225
self pronominals, non-reflexive 220, 221, 222, 224, 229, 230, 231, 232, 233, 235, 237, 238
subject/object pronominals 217-218, 219, 220, 221, 222, 223, 224, 225, 226, 227, 228, 229
personification and gender 184, 196, 202
phonological change 22
Pickbourn, James 165
polite accent 55
polite society 74, 118, 120, 270, 272
Polite, Truly:
language 70, 72, 73, 74
characteristics of, 71-72, 73, 270
contrasted with nonstandard speech 70
speech norms 75

see also literate modes of speech; oral modes of speech
polite writing 39, 60, 270
politeness:
in conversation 34, 74
at court 36
ideals of, 8, 31, 37, 42, 67, 73, 270
and language 10, 32, 44, 51, 73, 118, 230, 231-232, 245, 258, 261, 264, 267, 270-271
and language change 74
literary 35
and pedantry 38, 39
prestige of, 43
social 8, 33, 73-74
see also the gentleman; Polite, Truly
Poole, Joshua:
on personal pronominals 181
on neuter possessive 182
Pope, Alexander 107, 243, 244, 246, 253, 259-260, 273, 278, 279, 297
possessive: *see* periphrastic possessive; personal pronominals
prescriptive grammarians: *see* grammarians, normative
prescriptivism: *see* standardization process
prestige:
linguistic 2, 201, 272, 286
norms 2, 3, 233, 259, 260, 264, 267
rise of, 1
change in, 63, 72, 74
patterns 5, 10, 247, 248, 263
social 5, 8, 201
elites 1, 7, 8
trendsetters 10-11
variety 7
Priestley, Joseph 125, 291
on neuter possessive 181
pronominal adverbs 173, 175, 177-178, 184-185, 189, 195, 196, 197, 198, 203

pronominals: *see* demonstrative pronominals; personal pronominals
pronunciation:
　Early Modern 23, 24
　history of standard English, 27
　norms in, 6
　standard 201
　variant 6
　see also received pronunication
propriety: *see* correctness, grammatical
proscriptivism 252
punctuation: *see* Clift, William
purism 9, 222, 226
purists 144, 223, 226, 233, 278
Puttenham, George 83

received pronunication (RP) 21, 22, 82
refinement 66, 71, 118
regional varieties 6, 65, 174, 178, 200, 285, 286, 287, 295, 308
　see also Clift, William; social classes
regionalisms, elimination of, 118
regulation: *see* standardization process
relative pronominals: *see* personal pronominals
Richardson, Edward:
　on neuter possessive 207
RP: *see* received pronunciation

Scotticisms 56, 57-60
　double modal 54
　finite verb forms 56, 60
　Latin influence 57
　legal terms 57
　one, impersonal 60
　periphrastic *do* 54
　strong verb forms 59
　shall/will 60
Scots:
　as a dialect 56
　educated standard 56

mixed dialect, rise of, 53
form of speech 56
rural 53
standard 3, 13, 51-60, 53, 54
　relative pronominals in, 265
Scottish Enlightenment 52, 54
Scottish influence on American usage 10
Scottish upper classes 55
selection: *see* standardization process
self: *see* personal pronominals, *self* pronominals, non-reflexive
Shaftesbury (Anthony Ashley Cooper) 32, 35, 43, 248, 251, 252, 258, 273, 279
　first use of "standard" 43
　and normative grammarians 252
　usage of periphrastic *do* 249, 250, 254, 256, 257, 266, 274, 275
　usage of relative pronominals 261, 262, 263-264, 265, 266, 267, 276, 277
Shakespeare:
　cited by normative grammarians 107, 243, 244, 246, 260, 271, 273
　Dryden's adaptations 219
　usage of causative *have* 143
　usage of conclusive perfect 150
　usage of neuter possessive 176, 192
　usage of strong verb forms 125
Sheridan, Betsy 218
　usage of pronominals 219-220, 224, 229, 233, 234, 235, 236
Sheridan, Richard 66, 67, 71
　cited by normative grammarians 243
Sheridan, Thomas 31, 55
social classes 8, 10, 51
　as represented in stage plays:
　　country squires 64, 67
　　courtiers 67, 69
　　highest 63, 68, 69
　　language fops 64, 67

linguistic characteristics 63, 65-67, 68
  archaisms 65, 66
  interjections 66, 72
  malapropisms 67
  proverbs 66
  regional dialect 65
  slang 66
  vulgarisms 66
lowest 63, 64, 65, 69, 285
new cultural elite 63
see also Polite, Truly
see also Clift, William; the gentleman
social networks 201
speech-based prose: see colloquial language
spelling: see Clift, William
standard, the:
  exposure to, 286
  movement towards, 288, 292, 305-307
standard:
  double 233, 304, 309
  Early Modern English 174
  national 3, 272
  written 285, 286, 287
standard English 27
  gender 184
  influence on Scottish writing 60
  neuter possessive 198, 200
  vs. nonstandard 13, 224, 227, 232-233, 271-272
  pronominal system 217
  see also nonstandard varieties; pronominals; strong verbs; weak verbs
standard language 2, 5, 20, 43, 271
  characteristics of, 81
standardization 4, 27, 74, 81, 84
  and development of statives and perfects 160-162
  functions of, 13, 25, 26

ideology 4, 5, 6, 8, 9, 10, 12, 21, 22, 103-104
  and normative grammarians 108-109, 246
  perception of, 82
  policies 199
  and politeness 8, 43
  term 1, 2, 81
standardization process 2, 4, 19-20, 23, 25, 82, 115, 116, 162, 200, 201, 203-204, 218, 265, 272
  acceptance 2
  codification 2, 3, 4, 5, 10, 14, 20, 82, 101, 116, 226, 243, 258, 265, 273
  elaboration 2, 3, 82
  innovation 162
  prescription 6, 8, 13, 14, 31, 44, 74, 122-123, 234, 243, 245, 271-273
  regularization 201, 226
  regulation 82, 83, 115, 198, 160-162, 243, 249
    see also strong verbs
  selection 1, 2, 6, 7, 10, 12, 13, 82, 83
    see also grammarians, normative; norms
Steele, Sir Richard 41, 248, 258, 269, 278, 279
  cited by normative grammarians 244, 273
  as editor 267, 277
  on relative pronominals 258-259, 292
  usage of periphrastic *do* 249, 250, 254, 255, 256, 257, 266, 274, 275
  usage of relative pronominals 261, 262, 263, 265, 266, 267, 276, 277
stigmatization 6, 222, 226
stigmatized social varieties 200
strong verbs:

case histories:
    bear 91-92, 104, 105, 107
    begin 92, 104, 107, 122
    break 92-93, 100, 105, 107, 126
    eat 100, 124
    get 93-94, 99, 100, 104, 105, 107
    give 93, 94, 100
    help 94-95, 105, 107
    run 95, 121, 122, 123
    speak 95-96, 100, 105
    take 96, 100, 104
    write 97, 100, 104, 105, 107
    see also Cooper; Kirkby; Wallis
and cultivated speech 118, 306
in nonstandard English 117, 120
origins and early history 85-86, 116
past tense schema 121-124, 127, 130
productive pattern 121, 123, 124
regulation of, 83, 88, 90, 92, 94, 96, 108
restructuring 87-90, 117
    inter-class transfer 89, 121
    intraparadigmatic leveling 88-99
    loss of participle suffix 89, 100
    preterite-to-past participle shift 89, 99, 103, 106, 107, 108
    strong verbs becoming weak 89, 100, 108, 116, 117, 120, 128
    see also Scotticisms
strong verb forms, alternating with weak verb forms 117, 123
    as social markers 119, 120-121, 123
    stored in mental lexicon 119-120, 124
    psychological reality of, 124, 127
    variation in, 98
stylistic change 72, 84
stylistic variation 14, 118, 195-197, 199, 203, 248, 249, 250, 251, 262, 263, 265, 266, 267, 295
subjectification 156, 158, 160-161

supraregional dialect 83
Swift, Jonathan 248, 251, 278
    cited by normative grammarians 243, 244, 246, 259, 270, 271
    on contractions 302, 309
    and prescriptivism 31, 44, 103, 279
    usage of periphrastic *do* 249, 250, 254, 255, 256, 257, 266, 274, 275
    usage of relative pronominals 261, 262, 263, 265, 266, 276, 277

Thrale, Mrs Hester Lynch:
    and pronominal usage 219-220, 234, 235
Turner, Thomas:
    and pronominal usage 220-221, 224, 227-228, 229, 230, 231, 234, 235, 236, 237

urban society 118, 120, 201
    see also the gentleman; London; politeness
Ussher, George Neville 253, 260

variants:
    dialectal 286, 288, 289, 296
        see also Clift, William
    elimination of, 12, 83, 118, 126, 160-162
    functional 126-127, 161
    and standardization 4-5, 6, 10, 11
variation:
    decrease in, 84, 178
    functional distinction in, 126-127
    in gender of nouns 183-184
    orderly 21
    in pronominal usage 233
    regional
        in pronominal usage 207, 224

social 118, 248
stable 20, 197
suppression of: *see* standardization process
in verb forms 116, 117, 118
see also personal pronominals, possessives; personal pronominals, relatives; strong verbs
varieties 4-5
see also nonstandard varieties
verbs: *see be*; *get*; *have*; periphrastic *do*; strong verbs; weak verbs
vernaculars 21, 22, 74, 233

Wallis, John 83, 101, 103, 104-105, 106, 108, 110
and standardization 103
on irregular plurals 110
on neuter possessive 181, 182
on strong verbs 98, 100, 102, 104, 108, 181
Walpole, Sir Horace 218, 231
and pronominal usage 219, 221-222, 223, 224, 230, 231, 235, 236
usage of periphrastic *do* 274
Ward, William 243, 244, 245
citing contemporary authors 273
on periphrastic *do* 253
on relative pronominals 292
weak verbs 116-121
co-occurring with strong verbs 117, 123
productive pattern 118, 121, 130
weak verb forms 126, 127-128, 129, 130
as social markers 119-120
Webster, Noah 275, 291
Wesley, John:
pronominal usage 220-221, 235, 236
Whiston, William 247-248, 258, 279
usage of periphrastic *do* 249, 250, 251, 254, 255, 256, 257, 274, 275
usage of relative pronominals 261, 262, 263, 264-265, 276, 277
White, James 243, 246, 247
on periphrastic *do* 275
Whithers, Philip 31, 119, 291
on strong verbs 126
women's language 219-220
compared to that of men 220-223
writing:
educated Scottish 60
styles of, 118, 182, 197, 258
written language:
as the norm 3-4, 5, 6, 14, 109, 119, 204
and standardization 13-14
written standard 14, 200, 201, 203-204, 233, 246
Wyld, H.C., and the standard language 22